MARRIAGE and DEATH

NOTICES

FROM
RALEIGH REGISTER AND NORTH CAROLINA
STATE GAZETTE
1799-1825

Compiled by

Carrie L. Broughton

CLEARFIELD COMPANY

Excerpted and Reprinted from the
Biennial Report of the State Library of North Carolina
Raleigh, 1942-1944

Reprinted
Genealogical Publishing Co., Inc.
Baltimore, 1962
Baltimore, 1966
Baltimore, 1975

Library of Congress Catalogue Card Number 66-26935
International Standard Book Number 0-8063-0052-3

Reprinted for
Clearfield Company, Inc. by
Genealogical Publishing Co., Inc.
Baltimore, Maryland
1989, 1995

Publisher's Preface

This valuable record of North Carolina marriages and deaths covers the entire state for the period 1799 through 1825. Over 5000 entries are contained herein with approximately two-thirds of the volume devoted to marriages and the balance to deaths. All were extracted from the weekly newspaper, THE REGISTER AND NORTH CAROLINA STATE GAZETTE, founded October 22, 1799 as the RALEIGH REGISTER and NORTH CAROLINA WEEKLY ADVERTISER.

The records are alphabetically arranged under each year. Entries under the marriages are for both bride and groom.

This reissue of our 1962 reprint is excerpted and reprinted from the BIENNIAL REPORT OF THE STATE LIBRARY OF NORTH CAROLINA, 1942-1944.

GENEALOGICAL PUBLISHING COMPANY

4

MARRIAGES

1799

Alston, Fanny to J. W. Hamlin of Halifax county, Oct. 23, Halifax. R. R. Oct. 29, 1799

Brower, Miles Lydia of New York to Henry Wills of Edenton, Nov. 1, New York. R. R. Dec. 3, 1799

Collins, Hardy to Neely Perry, Wake county, Oct. 13, Raleigh. R. R. Oct. 22, 1799

Fowler, Betsey to Rev. Roger Hancock, Oct., Wake county. R. R. Oct. 22, 1799

Hamlin, J. W. of Halifax county to Fanny Alston, Oct. 23, Halifax. R. R. Oct. 29, 1799

Hancock, Rev. Roger to Betsey Fowler, Oct., Wake county. R. R. Oct. 22, 1806

Jones, Jane to John Vail, Dec. 6, Newbern. R. R. Dec. 17, 1806

Neale, Peggy to Major G. Painter, Oct. 17, Burlington. R. R. Nov. 12, 1799

Painter, Major G. to Peggy Neale, Oct. 17, Burlington. R. R. Nov. 12, 1799

Pasteur, Dr. James of Raleigh to Miss Shepard of Glasgow county, Nov. 14. R. R. Dec. 3, 1799

Perry, Nelly to Hardy Collins, Wake county, Oct. 13, Raleigh. R. R. Oct. 22, 1799

Shepard, Miss of Glasgow county to Dr. James Pasteur of Raleigh, Nov. 14. R. R. Dec. 3, 1799

Vail, John to Jane Jones, Dec. 6, Newbern. R. R. Dec. 17, 1799

Wills, Henry of Edenton to Miles Lydia Brower of New York, Nov. 1, New York. R. R. Dec. 3, 1799

1800

Bryan, Sidney C. of Newbern to Charles W. Crawford of Beaufort county, Apr., Beaufort county. R. R. Apr. 22, 1800

Crawford, Charles M. of Beaufort county to Sidney C. Bryan of Newbern, Apr., Beaufort county. R. R. Apr. 22, 1800

Daily, Ann G. to John Snead, Mar. 26, Newbern. R. R. Apr. 8, 1800

Davis, Nancy to Josiah Dillard, Feb., Fayetteville. R. R. Feb. 18, 1800

Dillard, Josiah to Nancy Davis, Feb., Fayetteville. R. R. Feb. 18, 1800

Everett, Cynthia of Johnston county to Samuel Walton of Wake county, Nov. R. R. Dec. 2, 1800

Hall, Allman to Nancy Howard, Feb., Wilmington. R. R. Feb. 11, 1800

Hinton, Gracy to Henry Seawell of Raleigh, Apr. 3, Wake county. R. R. Apr. 8, 1800

Howard, Nancy to Allman Hall, Feb., Wilmington. R. R. Feb. 11, 1800

Hunt, Betsey to Ofborn Hunter of Johnston county, Nov. 27, Franklin county. R. R. Dec. 2, 1800

Hunter, Ofborn of Johnston county to Betsey Hunt, Nov. 27, Franklin county. R. R. Dec. 2, 1800

James, Polly to Capt. George Sears, Feb. 23, Newbern. R. R. Mar. 11, 1800

Jones, William of Johnston county to Elizabeth Turner of Wake county. Dec. 2. R. R. Dec. 9, 1800

Jordan, Thomas to Nancy Long, Jan. 16, Franklin county. R. R. Feb. 4, 1800

Kelly, Betsey to John Oliver, My. 1, Newbern. R. R. Je. 17, 1800

Lamb, Mary to Sally Simmons, Jly. 22, Wilmington. R. R. Aug. 5, 1800

Lindsay, Eliza of Newbern to Samuel Williams of Edenton, Apr. 2, Newbern. R. R. Apr. 22, 1800

Long, Nancy to Jordan Thomas, Jan. 16, Franklin county. R. R. Feb. 4, 1800

Love, Neil to Esther Vann, Mar., Fayetteville. R. R. Mar. 25, 1800

Mabry, Polly to John Young of Wake county, Mar. 3, Raleigh. R. R. Mar. 4, 1800

M'Lemore, Robert to Barbara Williams, Jan. 16, Franklin county. R. R. Feb. 4, 1800

Oliver, John to Betsey Kelly, My. 1, Newbern. R. R. Je. 17, 1800

Scurlock, Joseph of Chatham county to Mrs. Martha J. Sheppard of Greene county, Jly. 13, Greene county. R. R. Aug. 5, 1800

Scurlock, William to Apphia Taylor, Dec., Pittsborough. R. R. Dec. 9, 1800

Sears, Capt. George to Polly James, Feb. 23, Newbern. R. R. Mar. 11, 1800

Seawell, Henry of Raleigh to Gracy Hinton, Apr. 3, Wake county. R. R. Apr. 8, 1800

Sharp, Elizabeth of Hillsborough to Jacob Wilfing of Raleigh, Sept., Hillsborough. R. R. Sept. 16, 1800

Shepard, Mrs. Martha J. of Greene county to Joseph Scurlock of Chatham county, Jly. 13, Greene county. R. R. Aug. 5, 1800

Simmons, Sally to Mark Lamb, Jly. 22, Wilmington. R. R. Aug. 5, 1800

Snead, John to Ann G. Daily, Mar. 26, Newbern. R. R. Apr. 8, 1800

Taylor, Apphia to William Scurlock, Dec., Pittsborough. R. R. Dec. 9, 1800

Thomas, Jordan to Nancy Long, Jan. 16, Franklin county. R. R. Feb. 4, 1800

Turner, Elizabeth of Wake county to William Jones of Johnston county, Dec. 2. R. R. Dec. 9, 1800

Vann, Esther to Neil Love, Mar., Fayetteville. R. R. Mar. 25, 1800

Walton, Samuel of Wake county to Cynthia Everett of Johnston county. Nov. R. R. Dec. 2, 1800

Wilfong, Jacob of Raleigh to Elizabeth Sharp of Hillsborough, Sept., Hillsborough. R. R. Sept. 16, 1800

Wilkins, Samuel of Edenton to Eliza Lindsay of Newbern, Apr. 2, Newbern. R. R. Apr. 22, 1800

Young, John to Polly Mabry of Wake county, Mar. 3, Raleigh. R. R. Mar. 4, 1800

1801

Armstrong, Sally to James Coman, Jan. 15, Raleigh. R. R. Jan. 20, 1801

Avery, Jonathan to Polly Cook, Apr. 19, Wilmington. R. R. Apr. 28, 1801

Binford, Susan of Northampton county to Daniel Mason of Halifax county, Nov. 10. R. R. Nov. 17, 1801

Bland, Polly to Thomas Olive, Apr. 12, Raleigh. R. R. Apr. 14, 1801

Boylan, William of Raleigh to Betsey M'Culloch of Halifax, Nov. 4, Halifax county. R. R. Nov. 10, 1801

Bragg, John of Craven county to Mrs. Mary Taylor of Newbern, Sept. 1, Newbern. R. R. Sept. 22, 1801

Bryan, John Arthur to Eliza Smith, Nov. 26, Johnston county. R. R. Dec. 8, 1801

Caswell, Dollon of Newbern to Lemuel Hatch of Jones county, My. 21, Craven county. R. R. Je. 2, 1801

Caswell, Sally R. of Raleigh to Grove Wright of Greenville, My. 14. R. R. Je. 9, 1801

Coman, James to Sally Armstrong, Jan. 15, Raleigh. R. R. Jan. 20, 1801

Cook, Polly to Jonathan Avery, Apr. 19, Wilmington. R. R. Apr. 28, 1801

Craig, Alexander to Jane Strayhorn, Je. 11, Orange county. R. R. Je. 30, 1801

Daniel, William of Raleigh to Kitty Hicks, Feb. 5, Wake county. R. R. Feb. 10, 1801

Dickson, Capt. William of Ashe county to Peggy McDowell, Je. 4, Burke county. R. R. Jly. 7, 1801

Eaton, John R. of Granville county to Miss Somerville, Sept. 15, Granville county. R. R. Sept. 22, 1801

Grove, William B. of Fayetteville to Sally Shepherd of Orange county, Aug. 11. R. R. Aug. 18, 1801

Hatch, Lemuel of Jones county to Mrs. Dollon Caswell of Newbern, My. 21, Craven county. R. R. Je. 2, 1801

Henderson, Archibald of Salisbury to Sally Alexander of Mecklenburg county, Aug. R. R. Aug. 18, 1801

Hicks, Kitty to William Daniel of Raleigh, Feb. 5, Wake county. R. R. Feb. 10, 1801

Jennings, Mrs. Ann to Thomas Jennings, Oct. 29, Wilmington. R. R. Nov. 10, 1801

Jennings, Thomas to Mrs. Ann Jennings, Oct. 29, Wilmington. R. R. Nov. 10, 1801

Jones, Hardy to Peggy Meairs, Feb. 26, Raleigh. R. R. Mar. 3, 1801

Lowthrop, Jane to John S. Pasteur, Apr., Newbern. R. R. Apr. 21, 1801

M'Culloch, Betsey of Halifax to William Boylan of Raleigh, Nov. 4, Halifax county. R. R. Nov. 10, 1801

Macon, Miss of Warren county to William Martin of Granville county, Nov. Warren county. R. R. Nov. 17, 1801

Martin, William of Granville county to Miss Macon of Warren county, Nov. Warren county. R. R. Nov. 17, 1801

Mason, Daniel of Halifax county to Susan Binford of Northampton county, Nov. 10. R. R. Nov. 17, 1801

Massenburg, Dr. Gargiel of Raleigh to Nancy Brier of Franklin county, Dec. 24, Franklin county. R. R. Dec. 29, 1801

Meairs, Peggy to Hardy Jones, Feb. 26, Raleigh. R. R. Mar. 3, 1801

Murphey, A. D. of Hillsborough to Jane Scott of Orange county, Nov. 12, Orange county. R. R. Nov. 17, 1801

Nichols, John to Polly Thompson, Oct. 25, Wilmington. R. R. Nov. 3, 1801

Nixon, Polly to Alexander Torrans, Mar. 12, Newbern. R. R. Mar. 24, 1801

Osborne, Mr. of Salisbury to Harriet Walker of Wilmington, Dec. 18, Wilmington. R. R. Jan. 20, 1801

Pasteur, John S. to Jane Lowthrop, Apr., Newbern. R. R. Apr. 21, 1801
Polk, Col. William of Raleigh to Sally Hawkins, Jan. 1, Warren county.
    R. R. Jan. 6, 1801
Scott, Jane of Orange county to A. D. Murphey of Hillsborough. Nov. 12,
    Orange county. R. R. Nov. 17, 1801
Shepherd, Sally of Orange county to William B. Grove of Fayetteville, Aug.
    11. R. R. Aug. 18, 1801
Smith, Eliza to John Arthur Bryan, Nov. 26, Johnston county. R. R. Dec.
    8, 1801
Somerville, Miss to John R. Eaton of Granville county, Sept. 15, Granville
    county. R. R. Sept. 22, 1801
Strayhorn, Jane to Alexander Craig, Je. 11, Orange county. R. R. Je. 30,
    1801
Taylor, Mrs. Mary of Newbern to John Bragg of Craven county, Sept. 1,
    Newbern. R. R. Sept. 22, 1801
Thomas, Olive to Polly Bland, Apr. 12, Raleigh. R. R. Apr. 14, 1801
Thompson, Polly to John Nichols, Oct. 25, Wilmington. R. R. Nov. 3,
    1801
Torrans, Alexander of Newbern to Polly Nixon, Mar. 12, Newbern. R. R.
    Mar. 24, 1801
Walker, Harriet of Wilmington to Mr. Osborne of Salisbury, Dec. 18,
    Wilmington. R. R. Jan. 20, 1801
Wright, Grove of Greenville to Sally R. Caswell of Raleigh, My. 14. R. R.
    Je. 9, 1801

1802

Alston, John of Halifax county to Margaret Thomas of Nash county, Oct.
    R. R. Oct. 25, 1802
Bond, Southy of Raleigh to Nancy Kennon of Pitt county, Oct., Pitt county.
    R. R. Oct. 18, 1802
Brown, Polly to Moses Jarvis, Apr. 22, Newbern. R. R. My. 11, 1802
Burgwin, Carolina of Wilmington to George C. Clitherall of Charleston,
    My. 4. R. R. My. 18, 1802
Christophers, C. to Betsey Lane, Feb. 14, Raleigh. R. R. Feb. 16, 1802
Clarke, Jas. to Arebella Toole, Jan. 4, Tarborough. R. R. Jan. 12, 1802
Clitherall, George C. of Charleston to Caroline Burgwin of Wilmington,
    My. 4. R. R. My. 18, 1802
Cooke, Susannah to Hanson Kelly, Feb. 4, Wilmington. R. R. Feb. 16,
    1802
Creighton, Wm. to Ellen Eastwood of Savannah, Ga., Jly. 25, Wilmington.
    R. R. Aug. 2, 1802
Davis, Mrs. Elizabeth to Richard Overton, Aug. 1, Rockingham county.
    R. R. Aug. 30, 1802
Davis, Thomas H. of Wilmington to Sarah Eagles of Brunswick county,
    Oct. 28, Wilmington. R. R. Nov. 1, 1802
Dekeyfer, Caroline to John Winslow, My. 24, Fayetteville. R. R. My. 25,
    1802
Dickson, Dr. Wm. of Tennessee to Polly Gray of Franklin county, Aug. 19,
    Nashville, Tenn. R. R. Oct. 18, 1802
Dolton, John to Eliza W. Gentry, Jan. 12, Rockingham county. R. R. Jan.
    26, 1802

8

Duke, Betsey of Warren county to Dr. Thomas Hunt of Granville county, Oct., Warren county. R. R. Oct. 4, 1802

Eagles, Richard to Margaret Jones, Dec. 21, Wilmington. R. R. Dec. 27, 1802

Eagles, Sarah of Brunswick county to Thomas H. Davis of Wilmington, Oct. 28, Wilmington. R. R. Nov. 1, 1802

Eastwood, Ellen to Wm. Creighton of Savannah, Ga., Jly. 25, Wilmington. R. R. Aug. 2, 1802

Galloway, Mrs. James to Joseph Gentry, Jan. 5, Rockingham county. R. R. Jan. 26, 1802

Geer, Gilbert to Sarah Kemp, Dec. 21, Wilmington. R. R. Dec. 27, 1802

Gentry, Eliza W. to John Dolton, Jan. 12, Rockingham county. R. R. Jan. 26, 1802

Gentry, Joseph to Mrs. James Galloway, Jan. 5, Rockingham county. R. R. Jan. 26, 1802

Gilmore, Sally of Cumberland county to Simon Stephens, Nov., Wake county. R. R. Nov. 22, 1802

Gray, Polly of Franklin county to Dr. Wm. Dickson of Tennessee, Aug. 19, Nashville, Tenn. R. R. Oct. 18, 1802

Gregory, William of Camden county to Martha Long, Jly. 6, Halifax. R. R. Jly. 26, 1802

Hays, Esther of Guilford county to Arthur Scott of Baltimore, Feb. 26, Guilford county. R. R. Mar. 16, 1802

Hunt, Dr. Thomas of Granville county to Betsey Duke of Warren county, Oct., Warren county. R. R. Oct. 4, 1802

Hurley, Mrs. Elizabeth to Paris J. Tillinghast, Jly. 15, Fayetteville. R. R. Aug. 2, 1802

Jarvis, Moses to Polly Brown, Apr. 22, Newbern. R. R. My. 11, 1802

Kelly, Hanson to Susannah Cooke, Feb. 4, Wilmington. R. R. Feb. 16, 1802

Kemp, Sarah to Gilbert Geer, Dec. 21, Wilmington. R. R. Dec. 27, 1802

Kenan, Catharine to John Macoll, Aug. 15, Wilmington. R. R. Aug. 23, 1802

Kennon, Nancy of Pitt county to Southy Bond of Raleigh, Oct., Pitt county. R. R. Oct. 18, 1802

Lacy, William to Sally B. Overton, Je. 24, Rockingham county. R. R. Jly. 5, 1802

Lane, Betsey to C. Christophers, Feb. 14, Raleigh. R. R. Feb. 16, 1802

Long, George W. of Halifax to Sarah Lewis of Granville county, My. 13. R. R. My. 18, 1802

Long, Martha to William Gregory of Camden county, Jly. 6, Halifax. R. R. Jly. 26, 1802

M'Kenzie, Mrs. Eliza to John Willkings, Nov. 13, Wilmington. R. R. Nov. 15, 1802

Macoll, John to Catharine Kenan, Aug. 15, Wilmington. R. R. Aug. 23, 1802

Marshall, Thomas to Miss Watson, Nov., Newbern. R. R. Nov. 15, 1802

Moseley, Maria to Carlston Walker, Dec. 24, Wilmington. R. R. Jan. 5, 1802

Neal, James to Abigail Peebles, Dec. 19, Chatham county. R. R. Dec. 20, 1802

Overton, Richard to Mrs. Elizabeth Davis, Aug. 1, Rockingham county. R. R. Aug. 30, 1802

Overton, Sally B. to William Lacy, Je. 24, Rockingham county. R. R. Jly. 5, 1802

Peebles, Abigail to James Neal, Dec. 19, Chatham county. R. R. Dec. 20, 1802

Scott, Arthur of Baltimore to Esther Hays of Guilford county, Feb. 26, Guilford county. R. R. Mar. 16, 1802

Smith, Winifred to Nathan Stevens, Jan. 7, Wake county. R. R. Jan. 12, 1802

Smyth, Samuel to Sally Williams, Nov., Newbern. R. R. Nov. 15, 1802

Stephens, Simon to Sally Gilmore of Cumberland county, Nov., Wake county. R. R. Nov. 22, 1802

Stevens, Nathan to Winifred Smith, Jan. 7, Wake county. R. R. Jan. 12, 1802

Stoutenburg, Mrs. Rebecca to Jeffe Wingate, Nov. 3, Wilmington. R. R. Nov. 15, 1802

Thomas, Margaret of Nash county to John Alston of Halifax county, Oct. R. R. Oct. 25, 1802

Tillinghast, Paris J. to Mrs. Elizabeth Hurley, Jly. 15, Fayetteville. R. R. Aug. 2, 1802

Tinker, Susannah to Capt. Samuel Torrans, Oct. 21, Newbern. R. R. Nov. 1, 1802

Toole, Arabella to Jas. Clarke, Jan. 4, Tarborough. R. R. Jan. 12, 1802

Torrans, Capt. Samuel to Susannah Tinker, Oct. 21, Newbern. R. R. Nov. 1, 1802

Walker, Carlston to Maria Mosely, Dec. 24, Wilmington. R. R. Jan. 5, 1802

Watson, Miss to Thomas Marshall, Nov., Newbern. R. R. Nov. 15, 1802

Williams, Sally to Samuel Smyth, Nov., Newbern. R. R. Nov. 15, 1802

Willkings, John to Mrs. Eliza M'Kenzie, Nov. 13, Wilmington. R. R. Nov. 15, 1802

Wingate, Jeffe to Mrs. Rebecca Stoutenburg, Nov. 3, Wilmington. R. R. Nov. 15, 1802

Winslow, John to Caroline DeKeyfer, My. 24, Fayetteville. R. R. My. 25, 1802

1803

Alston, Temperance to Atherton Dawson, My. 12, Warren county. R. R. My. 16, 1803

Atkins, Lewis to Miss Bird, Oct. 18, Wake county. R. R. Oct. 24, 1803

Barge, Richard to Miss Parker of Cape Fear, Oct. 18, Fayetteville. R. R Oct. 24, 1803

Branch, John Jr. to Elizabeth Foort, Apr. 6, Halifax county. R. R. Apr. 11, 1803

Bennehan, Rebecca of Orange county to Duncan Cameron of Hillsborough, Mar., Orange county. R. R. Mr. 7, 1803

Bird, Miss to Lewis Atkins, Oct. 18, Wake county. R. R. Oct. 24, 1803

Bludworth, William of New Hanover county to Mary Larkins, My. 5. R. R. My. 16, 1803

Blythe, Mrs. Mary to Charles Carrol, Apr., Wilmington. R. R. My. 2, 1803

Boyd, Jane of Mecklenburg county, Va. to John D. Hawkins of Raleigh, My. 2, Mecklenburg county, Va. R. R. My. 16, 1803

Brownrigg, Thomas to Susanna Martin, Dec. 29; Halifax. R. R. Jan. 17, 1803

Bush, Mrs. William to Needham Whitfield of Wayne county, Jly. 10, Jones county. R. R. Aug. 8, 1803

Caldwell, Rev. Joseph to Susan Roan, Jly. 16, Fayetteville. R. R. Jly. 18, 1803

Cameron, Duncan of Hillsborough to Rebecca Bennehan of Orange county, Mar., Orange county. R. R. Mar. 7, 1803

Campbell, Peggy to Isham Edwards, Sept. 29, Person county. R. R. Oct. 17, 1803

Carroll, Charles to Mrs. Mary Blythe, Apr., Wilmington. R. R. My. 2, 1803

Cochran, Mrs. to James Turner, Sept. 10, Warrenton. R. R. Sept. 19, 1803

Cohen, Miss of Charleston, S. C. to Aaron Lazarus of Wilmington, My. 10, Charleston, S. C. R. R. Je. 6, 1803

Dawson, Atherton to Temperance Alston, My. 12, Warren county. R. R. My. 16, 1803

Edwards, Isham to Peggy Campbell, Sept. 29, Person county. R. R. Oct. 17, 1803

Foort, Elizabeth to John Branch, Jr., Apr. 6, Halifax county. R. R. Apr. 11, 1803

Fulwood, Mrs. Ann to Ezekiel Smith, Apr. 17, Brunswick county. R. R. My. 2, 1803

Gaston, William of Newbern to Susan Hay, Sept. 4, Fayetteville. R. R. Sept. 19, 1803

Geddy, Misshaw of Raleigh to William Hall of Haywood county, Jan. 6, Franklin county. R. R. Jan. 10, 1803

Gillespie, Elizabeth of Duplin county to Aaron Morgan of New Hanover county, My. R. R. My. 16, 1803

Gilmore, Stephen to Miss Teams, Jan., Cumberland county. R. R. Jan. 10, 1803

Green, Colonel Thomas A. to Hollon West, Oct. 5, Newbern. R. R. Oct. 24, 1803

Hall, Dr. Thomas to Mrs. Sitgreaves, Jan. 6, Halifax. R. R. Jan. 17, 1803

Hall, William of Haywood county to Misshaw Geddy of Raleigh, Jan. 6, Franklin county. R. R. Jan. 10, 1803

Harrison, Mr. to Sally Jones, Aug. 25, Newbern. R. R. Sept. 5, 1803

Hawkins, John D. of Raleigh to Jane Boyd of Mecklenburg county, Va., My. 2, Mecklenburg county, Va. R. R. My. 16, 1803

Hay, Susan to William Gaston of Newbern, Sept. 4, Fayetteville. R. R. Sept. 19, 1803

Henderson, Polly to John Lacey, My., Rockingham county. R. R. My. 30, 1803

Holcroft, Courtney to Colonel John Ingles, Nov. 12, Wake county. R. R. Nov. 14, 1803

Hunter, Henry of Wake county to Nancy Seawell of Franklin county, Dec. 7, Franklin county. R. R. Dec. 12, 1803

Ingles, Colonel John to Courtney Holcroft, Nov. 12, Wake county. R. R. Nov. 14, 1803

Jeffreys, Mrs. of Person county to James Thompson, Feb. 17, Wake county. R. R. Feb. 22, 1803

Jones, Edward of Warren county to Betsey Seawell, Feb. 17, Franklin county. R. R. Feb. 22, 1803

Jones, Martha B. to James Turner, My., Halifax county. R. R. My. 16, 1803

Jones, Polly to James Palmer of Hawfields, Dec. 26, Wake county. R. R. Jan. 4, 1803

Jones, Sally to Mr. Harrison, Aug. 25, Newbern. R. R. Sept. 5, 1803

Kollock, Mary of New Jersey to Frederic Nash of Newbern, Sept., Elizabethtown, N. J. R. R. Sept. 19, 1803

Lacey, John to Polly Henderson, My., Rockingham county. R. R. My. 30, 1803

Larkins, Mary to William Bludworth of New Hanover county, My. 5. R. R. My. 16, 1803

Lazarus, Aaron of Wilmington to Miss Cohen of Charleston, S. C., My. 10, Charleston, S. C. R. R. Je. 6, 1803

M'Rackan, James to Marianne Wingate, Nov. 6, Fayetteville. R. R. Nov. 14, 1803

M'Ree, Helen to Mr. Turner of Sampson county, Mar., Cumberland county. R. R. Mar. 21, 1803

Martin, Susanna to Thomas Brownrigg, Dec. 29, Halifax. R. R. Jan. 17, 1803

Moore, Jas. to Jean L. Overton, My. 19, Fayetteville. R. R. My. 30, 1803

Moore, Polly to Richard Stanford, Sept. 11, Person county. R. R. Sept. 26, 1803

Morgan, Aaron of New Hanover county to Elizabeth Gillespie of Duplin county, My. R. R. My. 16, 1803

Nash, Elizabeth S. to Robert Ogden, Je., Newbern. R. R. Je. 20, 1803

Nash, Frederic of Newbern to Mary Kollock of New Jersey, Sept., Elizabethtown, N. J. R. R. Sept. 19, 1803

Ogden, Robert to Elizabeth S. Nash, Je., Newbern. R. R. Je. 20, 1803

Overton, Jean L. to Jas. Moore, My. 19, Fayetteville. R. R. My. 30, 1803

Palmer, James of Hawfields to Polly Jones, Dec. 26, Wake county. R. R. Jan. 4, 1803

Parish, John of Raleigh to Miss Sims of Wake county, Mar. 1. R. R. Mar. 7, 1803

Parker, Miss of Cape Fear to Richard Barge, Oct. 18, Fayetteville. R. R. Oct. 24, 1803

Potts, Jeffe to Nancy Starling, Sept. 4, Fayetteville. R. R. Sept. 19, 1803

Rhodes, Patsey to Samuel Whitaker, Dec. 15, Wake county. R. R. Dec. 19, 1803

Roan, Susan to Rev. Joseph Caldwell, Jly. 16, Fayetteville. R. R. Jly. 18, 1803

Seawell, Betsey to Edward Jones of Warren county, Feb. 17, Franklin county. R. R. Feb. 22, 1803

Seawell, Nancy of Franklin county to Henry Hunter of Wake county, Dec. 7, Franklin county. R. R. Dec. 12, 1803

Sims, Miss of Wake county to John Parish of Raleigh, Mar. 1. R. R. Mar. 7, 1803

Sitgreaves, Mrs. to Dr. Thomas Hall, Jan. 6, Halifax. R. R. Jan. 17, 1803

Smith, Ezekiel to Mrs. Ann Fulwood, Apr. 17, Brunswick county. R. R.
My. 2, 1803
Stanford, Richard to Polly Moore, Sept. 11, Person county. R. R. Sept.
26, 1803
Starling, Nancy to Jeffe Potts, Sept. 4, Fayetteville. R. R. Sept. 19, 1803
Taylor, Charles of Granville county to Miss Turner of Wake county, Nov.
23. R. R. Nov. 28, 1803
Teams, Miss to Stephen Gilmore, Jan., Cumberland county. R. R. Jan. 10,
1803
Thompson, James of Person county to Mrs. Jeffrey, Feb. 17, Wake county.
R. R. Feb. 22, 1803
Turner, James to Martha B. Jones, My., Halifax county. R. R. My. 16,
1803
Turner, James to Mrs. Cochran, Sept. 10, Warrenton. R. R. Sept. 19, 1803
Turner, Miss of Wake county to Charles Taylor of Granville county, Nov.
23. R. R. Nov. 28, 1803
Turner, Mr. of Sampson county to Helen M'Ree, Mar., Cumberland county.
R. R. Mar. 21, 1803
West, Hollon to Colonel Thomas A. Green, Oct. 5, Newbern. R. R. Oct. 24,
1803
Whitaker, Samuel to Patsey Rhodes, Dec. 15, Wake county. R. R. Dec.
19, 1803
Whitfield, Needham of Wayne county to Mrs. William Bush, Jly. 10, Jones
county. R. R. Aug. 8, 1803
Wingate, Marianne to James M'Rackan, Nov. 6, Fayetteville. R. R. Nov.
14, 1803

1804

Alston, James to Mrs. J. Hawkins, Sept. 27, Warren county. R. R. Oct. 1,
1804
Alston, Polly Hardy to Joseph Hawkins, Dec. 22, Warren county. R. R.
Dec. 31, 1804
Apoen, Allen to Susan Williams, Mar. 11, Wilmington. R. R. Apr. 2, 1804
Avant, Rev. W. to Amy Rourk, Feb. 19, Wilmington. R. R. Mar. 12, 1804
Backhouse, Kitty to Samuel Chapman, Nov. 4, Craven county. R. R. Nov.
12, 1804
Bank, Miss of Virginia to Thomas Parish of Wake county, Jan., Wake
county. R. R. Feb. 6, 1804
Bingham, Robert of Chatham county to Miss S. M. Taylor, of Chapel Hill,
Feb. 8, Orange county. R. R. Mar. 19, 1804
Blake, Patsey to Wm. Flack of Raleigh, Oct. 11, Fayetteville. R. R. Oct.
15, 1804
Blin, Nancy to Berthick Gillespie, Jly. 12, Newbern. R. R. Jly. 25, 1804
Bludworth, Samuel to Frances Fryar of Sampson county, Oct. 4, Wilming-
ton. R. R. Oct. 15, 1804
Bond, Wm. to Fanny Doherty, Oct., Hillsborough. R. R. Oct. 15, 1804
Boyd, Ann Swepson to William Hawkins of Warren county, Dec. 24, Meck-
lenburg county, Va. R. R. Jan. 2, 1804
Carter, Jesse of Caswell county to Betsey Paine of Person county, Apr. 8,
Person county. R. R. My. 7, 1804
Chapman, Samuel to Kitty Backhouse, Nov. 4, Craven county. R. R. Nov.
12, 1804

Cock, Rebecca to John Paine, Oct. 11, Person county. R. R. Oct. 29, 1804

Coman, Robert to Jane Wade Prout, Feb. 6. Wadesborough. R. R. Feb. 20, 1804

Cuthrie, William to Lydia M'Alphin, Nov. 3, Newbern. R. R. Nov. 12, 1804

Davis, Molsey to Benjamin Evans, Nov. 21, Wilmington. R. R. Dec. 3, 1804

Doherty, Fanny to Wm. Bond, Oct., Hillsborough. R. R. Oct. 15, 1804

Dorsey, Robert to Ann Ward, Mar. 11, Wilmington. R. R. Apr. 2, 1804

Evans, Benjamin to Molsey Davis, Nov. 21, Wilmington. R. R. Dec. 3, 1804

Flack, WM. of Raleigh to Patsey Blake, Oct. 11, Fayetteville. R. R. Oct. 15, 1804

Flinn, Rev. Andrew of Fayetteville to Martha Henrietta Walker of New England, Sept. 4. R. R. Sept. 10, 1804

Farrar, Powell to Phoebe Utley, Aug. 16, Wake county. R. R. Aug. 20, 1804

Fleming, Arabella of Bladen county to W. Giles, My. 15, Wilmington. R. R. My. 28, 1804

Foote, John to Mary Kingsbury, Jly., Wilmington. R. R. Jly. 25, 1804

Fryar, Frances of Sampson county to Samuel Bludworth, Oct. 4, Wilmington. R. R. Oct. 15, 1804

Gales, Winifred to R. R. Johnson of Warren county, My. 4, Raleigh. R. R. My. 7, 1804

Galloway, John to Betsey Walker, Feb. 12, Wilmington. R. R. Feb. 27, 1804

George, Edward St. to Mildred Spicer, Mar., Wilmington. R. R. Mar. 5, 1804

Giles, W. to Arabella Fleming of Bladen county, My. 15, Wilmington. R. R. My. 28, 1804

Gillespie, Berthick to Nancy Blin, Jly. 12, Newbern. R. R. Jly. 25, 1804

Glenn, John to Sally Jones, Sept. 26, Franklin county. R. R. Oct. 1, 1804

Green, Hannah G. of Wayne county to Jesse Slocumb, Nov., Wilmington. R. R. Nov. 19, 1804

Greer, Jacob to Polly Steele, Sept. 18, Hawfields. R. R. Sept. 24, 1804

Griffith, Nancy to Abner Pasteur, Feb. 16, Newbern. R. R. Feb. 27, 1804

Guion, Ann to Dr. Hugh Jones, Aug. 4, Newbern. R. R. Aug. 20, 1804

Hatch, Benjamin of Jones county to Sarah Whitfield of Wayne county, Apr. 12. R. R. Apr. 23, 1804

Hawkins, Joseph to Polly Hardy Alston, Dec. 22, Warren county. R. R. Dec. 31, 1804

Hawkins, Mrs. J. to James Alston, Sept. 27, Warren county. R. R. Oct. 1, 1804

Hawkins, William of Warren county to Ann Swepson Boyd, Dec. 24, Mecklenburg county, Va. R. R. Jan. 2, 1804

Hunt, John R. of Granville county to Eliza Taylor of Granville county, Aug. 19, Chapel Hill. R. R. Sept. 24, 1804

Hunter, Louisa to James House of Franklin county, Sept. 18, Wake county. R. R. Sept. 24, 1804

House, James of Franklin county to Louisa Hunter, Sept. 18, Wake county. R. R. Sept. 24, 1804

Johnson, R. R. of Warren county to Winifred Gales, My. 4, Raleigh. R. R. My. 7, 1804

Jones, Ann Maria to Joseph Littlejohn, Apr. 27, Halifax. R. R. My. 28, 1804

Jones, Dr. Hugh to Ann Guion, Aug. 4, Newbern. R. R. Aug. 20, 1804

Jones, Sally to Hugh M'Lean, Jly, Fayetteville. R. R. Jly. 16, 1804

Jones, Sally to John Glenn, Sept. 26, Franklin county. R. R. Oct. 1, 1804

Kingsbury, Mary to John Foote, Jly., Wilmington. R. R. Jly. 25, 1804

Lane, Samuel to Dice Parish, Mar. 11, Wilmington. R. R. Apr. 2, 1804

Lanier, Polly to Heath Wortham, Oct. 17, Warren county. R. R. Oct. 29, 1804

Lenox, Miss F. to Samuel Tredwell of Edenton, Dec. 13, Aberdeen, Bertie county. R. R. Dec. 31, 1804

Lewis, Green of Edgecombe county to Martha Wiggins, Feb. 28, Martin county. R. R. Mar. 12, 1804

Little, John to Nancy Littlejohn, Dec. 15, Edenton. R. R. Dec. 31, 1804

Littlejohn, Joseph of Edenton to Ann Maria Jones, Apr. 27, Halifax. R. R. My. 28, 1804

Littlejohn, Nancy to John Little, Dec. 15, Edenton. R. R. Dec. 31, 1804

M'Alpin, Lydia to William Cuthrie, Nov. 3, Newbern. R. R. Nov. 12, 1804

M'Lean, Hugh to Sally Jones, Jly., Fayetteville. R. R. Jly. 16, 1804

Mears, Winifred to William Peck, Jan. 5, Raleigh. R. R. Jan. 9, 1804

Moore, Alfred to Rebecca Williams, Apr. 7, Brunswick county. R. R. Apr. 9, 1804

Paine, Betsey of Person county to Jesse Carter of Caswell county, Apr. 8, Person county. R. R. My. 7, 1804

Paine, Betsey of Warren county to Mr. Pooe of Pittsborough, Oct. R. R. Oct. 1, 1804

Paine, John to Rebecca Cock, Oct. 11, Person county. R. R. Oct. 29, 1804

Parish, Dice to Samuel Lane, Mar. 11, Wilmington. R. R. Apr. 2, 1804

Parish, Thomas of Wake county to Miss Banks of Virginia, Jan., Wake county. R. R. Feb. 6, 1804

Pasteur, Abner to Nancy Griffith, Feb. 16, Newbern. R. R. Feb. 27, 1804

Pearson, Jesse to Ann N. Steele, Mar., Salisbury. R. R. Mar. 5, 1804

Peck, William to Winifred Mears, Jan. 5, Raleigh. R. R. Jan. 9, 1804

Pooe, Mr. of Pittsborough to Betsey Paine of Warren county, Oct. R. R. Oct. 1, 1804

Potts, Nancy to Wm. Hugh Williams, Nov., Fayetteville. R. R. Nov. 29, 1804

Prout, Jane Wade to Robert Coman, Feb. 6, Wadesborough. R. R. Feb. 20, 1804

Rourk, Amy to Rev. W. Avant, Feb. 19, Wilmington. R. R. Mar. 12, 1804

Scott, Sarah to Samuel Swan, Mar., Wilmington. R. R. Mar. 5, 1804

Singleton, Elizabeth to John F. Smith, Mar. 22, Newbern. R. R. Apr. 9, 1804

Slocumb, Jesse to Hannah G. Green of Wayne county, Nov., Wilmington. R. R. Nov. 19, 1804

Smith, John F. to Elizabeth Singleton, Mar. 22, Newbern. R. R. Apr. 9, 1804

Smith, Miss to William Taylor, Dec. 17, Granville county. R. R. Dec. 31, 1804

Sommerville, John Jr. to Fanny Taylor, Dec. 18, Edenton. R. R. Dec. 31, 1804

Spicer, Mildred to Edward St. George, Mar., Wilmington. R. R. Mar. 5, 1804

Stanley, Susan to Capt. James Taylor, Apr., Newbern. R. R. Apr. 2, 1804

Steele, Ann N. to Jessie Pearson, Mar., Salisbury. R. R. Mar. 5, 1804

Steele, Polly to Jacob Greer, Sept. 18, Hawfield. R. R. Sept. 24, 1804

Swan, Samuel to Sarah Scott, Mar., Wilmington. R. R. Mar. 5, 1804

Taylor, Eliza of Granville county to John R. Hunt of Granville county, Aug. 19, Chapel Hill. R. R. Sept. 24, 1804

Taylor, Fanny to John Sommerville, Jr., Dec. 18, Edenton. R. R. Dec. 31, 1804

Taylor, Capt. James to Susan Stanley, Apr., Newbern. R. R. Apr. 2, 1804

Taylor, Miss S. M. of Chapel Hill to Robert Bingham of Chatham county, Feb. 8, Orange county. R. R. Mar. 19, 1804

Taylor, William to Miss Smith, Dec. 17, Granville county. R. R. Dec. 31, 1804

Templeton, John to Henrietta Trippe, Apr. 7, Newbern. R. R. Apr. 23, 1804

Tisdale, Nathaniel to Polly Wade, Aug. 2, Newbern. R. R. Aug. 13, 1804

Toomer, Eliza to Henry Young, Nov. 19, Wilmington. R. R. Dec. 3, 1804

Tredwell, Samuel of Edenton to Miss F. Lenox, Dec. 13, Aberdeen, Bertie county. R. R. Dec. 31, 1804

Trippe, Henrietta to John Templeton, Apr. 7, Newbern. R. R. Apr. 23, 1804

Utley, Phoebe to Powell Farrar, Aug. 16, Wake county. R. R. Aug. 20, 1804

Wade, Polly to Nathaniel Tisdale, Aug. 2, Newbern. R. R. Aug. 13, 1804

Walker, Betsey to John Galloway, Feb. 12, Wilmington. R. R. Feb. 27, 1804

Walker, Carleton of Wilmington to Sabina T. Legare, Mar. 20, Charleston, S. C. R. R. Apr. 2, 1804

Walker, Martha Henrietta of New England to Rev. Andrew Flinn of Fayetteville, Sept. 4. R. R. Sept. 10, 1804

Ward, Ann to Robert Dorsey, Mar. 11, Wilmington. R. R. Apr. 2, 1804

Webb, W. E. to Sarah Williamson, Feb. 14, Northampton county. R. R. Feb. 27, 1804

White, Mr. to Elizabeth Wrenferd, Mar. 22, Newbern. R. R. Apr. 9, 1804

Whitfield, Sarah of Wayne county to Benjamin Hatch of Jones county, Apr. 12. R. R. Apr. 23, 1804

Wiggins, Martha to Green Lewis of Edgecombe county, Feb. 28, Martin county. R. R. Mar. 12, 1804

Williams, Rebecca to Alfred Moore, Apr. 7, Brunswick county. R. R. Apr. 9, 1804

Williams, Susan to Allen Apoen, Mar. 11, Wilmington. R. R. Apr. 2, 1804

Williams, Wm. Hugh to Nancy Potts, Nov., Fayetteville. R. R. Nov. 29, 1804

Williamson, Sarah to W. E. Webb, Feb. 14, Northampton county. R. R. Feb. 27, 1804

Wortham, Heath to Polly Lanier, Oct. 17, Warren county. R. R. Oct. 29, 1804

Wrenferd, Elizabeth to Mr. White, Mar. 22, Newbern. R. R. Apr. 9, 1804

Young, Henry to Eliza Toomer, Nov. 19, Wilmington. R. R. Dec. 3, 1804

1805

Alford, Elias to Charity Hedgepeth, Nov. 28, Robeson county. R. R. Dec. 9, 1805

Allen, Mary to Benjamin White of Craven county, Jan. 1, Craven county. R. R. Jan. 14, 1805

Alston, Nancy to John Sutherland of Wake county, Oct. 17, Warren county. R. R. Oct. 28, 1805

Armstrong, Bell to Joel Williams, Jr., Mar. 28, Cumberland county. R. R. Apr. 1, 1805

Atkin, Mrs. Thomas to Samuel Holloman of Raleigh, Feb. 6, Raleigh. R. R. Feb. 11, 1805

Atkins, Eliza A. to Samuel Kittrel, Jr. of Granville county, Apr. 18, Raleigh. R. R. Apr. 22, 1805

Bachelor, Fanny to Lucas J. Benners, Jan. 6, Newbern. R. R. Jan. 28, 1805

Barbie, Henrietta to Thomas Moore, Jan. 28, Orange county. R. R. Feb. 11, 1805

Battle, Polly to Olen Lamon, Je. 27, Edgecombe county. R. R. Jly. 8, 1805

Benners, Lucas J. to Fanny Bachelor, Jan. 6, Newbern. R. R. Jan. 28, 1805

Bernard, Julia of Wilmington to William J. Scarborough of Savannah, Apr. 18, Wilmington. R. R. May 6, 1805

Blackmore, Mrs. Mary of Duplin county to Isaac R. Eaves of Swansboro, Je. 27, Duplin county. R. R. Jly. 8, 1805

Bloodworth, Thomas to Ann Evans, Jan., Wilmington. R. R. Jan. 21, 1805

Bond, Harriet to Richard Eppes, Nov., Halifax. R. R. Nov. 18, 1805

Bradley, Richard of Wilmington to Eliza Young of Bladen county, Mar. 26, Wilmington. R. R. Apr. 8, 1805

Bridges, Betsey to John Sanders, Feb. 13, Wake county. R. R. Feb. 18, 1805

Brooks, Patsey to Ezenus Bush, Nov. 28, Caswell county. R. R. Dec. 9, 1805

Bush, Ezenus to Patsey Brooks, Nov. 28, Caswell county. R. R. Dec. 9, 1805

Bush, Lois to Thomas Henslee, Nov. 21, Caswell county. R. R. Dec. 9, 1805

Calhorda, John to Polly M'Clammy, Aug. 1, Wilmington. R. R. Aug. 19, 1805

Caller, Charles to Susan Leonard, Nov. 6, Warrenton. R. R. Nov. 18, 1805

Childers, Osborn of Rockingham to Polly Hill of Raleigh, Feb. 21, Stokes county. R. R. Mar. 18, 1805

Christmas, Mrs. Jane to Capt. John Green, Oct. 13, Warren county. R. R. Oct. 28, 1805

Clements, Woodson to Keziah Duskins, Jan. 24, Wake county. R. R. Jan. 28, 1805

Courtis, Patsey to John Rand, Je. 20, Wake county. R. R. Je. 24, 1805

Dameron, Patience to Daniel Jackson, Nov. 28, Caswell county. R. R. Dec. 9, 1805

Davis, Green of Franklin county to Charlotte Hunter, Jan., Wake county. R. R. Jan. 21, 1805

Dickson, Joseph of Duplin county to Lucy Gillespie, Sept. 10, Duplin county. R. R. Sept. 23, 1805

Dickson, Lewis to Kitty Hill, Sept. 11, Duplin county. R. R. Sept. 23, 1805

Dodd, Jemina to Willie Sledge of Franklin, Feb. 6, Raleigh. R. R. Feb. 11, 1805

Dogherty, Nelly to David Yarborough, Sept., Hillsborough. R. R. Oct. 7, 1805

Drake, Silas to Aserath Rowland, Dec. 1, Robeson county. R. R. Dec. 9, 1805

Duke, Lanier of Warren county to John Washington of Granville county, Aug., Warren county. R. R. Aug. 26, 1805

Dunn, Henrietta of Duplin county to William Thompson of Sampson county, Sept., Duplin county. R. R. Sept. 23, 1805

Duskins, Keziah to Woodson Clements, Jan. 24, Wake county. R. R. Jan. 28, 1805

Eaves, Isaac R. of Swansboro to Mrs. Mary Blackmore of Duplin county, Je. 27, Duplin county. R. R. Jly. 8, 1805

Eppes, Richard to Harriet Bond, Nov., Halifax. R. R. Nov. 18, 1805

Evans, Ann to Thomas Bloodworth, Jan., Wilmington. R. R. Jan. 21, 1805

Finch, Elizabeth to John Walker, Oct. 17, Warren county. R. R. Oct. 28, 1805

Fox, Lark of Franklin county to Eliza Gholson of Brunswick county, Feb. 20. R. R. Mar. 11, 1805

Gallagher, Capt. to Ann Kewell, Sept., Washington. R. R. Sept. 30, 1805

Gaston, William to Miss M'Lure, Oct., Newbern. R. R. Oct. 21, 1805

Gerard, Mrs. of Tarborough to Harry Hunter of Williamston, Je. 24, Tarborough. R. R. Jly. 8, 1805

Gholson, Eliza of Brunswick county to Lark Fox of Franklin county, Feb. 20. R. R. Mar. 11, 1805

Gillespie, Lucy to Joseph Dickson of Duplin county, Sept. 10, Duplin county. R. R. Sept. 23, 1805

Glen, Thompson of Granville county to Polly Hodges of Cumberland county, Mar. 28. R. R. Apr. 1, 1805

Good, Benjamin to Fanny Oliver of Newbern, Apr. 21, Newbern. R. R. My. 6, 1805

Goodloe, John M. to Eliza Jelks, Nov. 14, Raleigh. R. R. Nov. 18, 1805

Gordon, Flora to John Nicholson, Nov. 28, Richmond county. R. R. Dec. 9, 1805

Graham, James of Richmond county to Betsey M'Neill of Cumberland county. Dec., Cumberland county. R. R. Dec. 9, 1805

Graves, Isbell to William Graves, Nov. 26, Caswell county. R. R. Dec. 9, 1805

Graves, William to Isbell Graves, Nov. 26, Caswell county. R. R. Dec. 9, 1805

Green, Capt. John to Mrs. Jane Christmas, Oct. 13, Warren county. R. R. Oct. 28, 1805

Harden, Jane to William Whiteside, Aug. 29, Orange county. R. R. Sept. 2, 1805

Hedgepeth, Charity to Elias Alford, Nov. 28, Robeson county. R. R. Dec. 9, 1805

Henslee, Thomas to Lois Bush, Nov. 21, Caswell county. R. R. Dec. 9, 1805

Herndon, Polly to Obid Powel of Chatham county, Jly. 4, Orange county. R. R. Jly. 15, 1805

Hill, Kitty to Lewis Dickson, Sept. 11, Duplin county. R. R. Sept. 23, 1805

Hill, Levina to Dr. Sterling Wheaton of Raleigh, Jan. 20, Franklin county. R. R. Jan. 28, 1805

Hill, Polly of Raleigh to Osborn Childers of Rockingham, Feb. 21, Stokes county. R. R. Mar. 18, 1805

Hilliard, Carter of Nash county to Amy Hunt, Sept. 18, Franklin county. R. R. Sept. 23, 1805

Hodges, Polly of Cumberland county to Thompson Glen of Granville county, Mar. 28. R. R. Apr. 1, 1805

Holloman, Samuel of Raleigh to Mrs. Thomas Atkin, Feb. 6, Raleigh. R. R. Feb. 11, 1805

Hunt, Amy to Carter Hilliard of Nash county, Sept. 18, Franklin county. R. R. Sept. 23, 1805

Hunter, Charlotte to Green Davis of Franklin county, Jan., Wake county. R. R. Jan. 21, 1805

Hunter, Harry of Williamston to Mrs. Gerard of Tarborough, Je. 24, Tarborough. R. R. Jly. 8, 1805

Ingram, Miss of Franklin to Charles Wortham of Warren county, Jan. 31. R. R. Feb. 11, 1805

Jackson, Daniel to Patience Dameron, Nov. 28, Caswell county. R. R. Dec. 9, 1805

Jelks, Eliza to John M. Goodloe, Nov. 14, Raleigh. R. R. Nov. 18, 1805

Jerkins, Thomas to Grissel Sears, Jan. 6, Newbern. R. R. Jan. 28, 1805

Johnson, Patience to Mr. Murphy, Oct. 17, Franklin county. R. R. Oct. 28, 1805

Joseph, Solomon Moses to Mrs. Euphen Alston Rhoads, Sept., Washington. R. R. Sept. 30, 1805

Kerr, Rev. John of Caswell county to Mrs. J. Williams of Halifax county, Va., Apr. 18. R. R. My. 6, 1805

King, John to Mrs. Rebecca Mebane, Aug. 29, Orange county. R. R. Sept. 2, 1805

Kittrel, Samuel Jr. of Granville county to Eliza A. Atkins, Apr. 18, Raleigh. R. R. Apr. 22, 1805

Lamon, Olen to Polly Battle, Je. 27, Edgecombe county. R. R. Jly. 8, 1805

Langley, Sally to Wesley Whitaker, Oct. 7, Raleigh. R. R. Nov. 11, 1805

Lenox, Fanny to Samuel Tredwell of Edenton, Jan., Bertie county. R. R. Jan. 21, 1805

Leonard, Susan to Charles Caller, Nov. 6, Warrenton. R. R. Nov. 18, 1805

Lewis, Lucy Ann of Granville county to James Seawell of Franklin county. R. R. Dec. 30, 1805

Lewis, Wm. of Person county to Miss Medlock of Caswell county, Jan. 31. R. R. Feb. 11, 1805

Lloyd, Polly to Roderic Sessums, Je. 27, Tarborough. R. R. Jly. 8, 1805

Long, Betsey to Thomas Harvey, Nov., Hertford. R. R. Nov. 25, 1805

Long, Nicholas of Fayetteville to Catherine Taylor of Raleigh, Mar. 28, Raleigh. R. R. Apr. 1, 1805

M'Clammy, Polly to John Calhorda, Aug. 1, Wilmington. R. R. Aug. 19, 1805

M'Clure, Miss to William Gaston, Oct., Newbern. R. R. Oct. 21, 1805

M'Farland, Flora of Richmond county to James M'Farland of Charleston, S. C., Nov. 28, Richmond county. R. R. Dec. 9, 1805

M'Farland, James of Charleston, S. C. to Flora M'Farland of Richmond county, Nov. 28, Richmond county. R. R. Dec. 9, 1805

M'Neill, Betsey of Cumberland county to James Graham of Richmond county, Dec., Cumberland county. R. R. Dec. 9, 1805

Marshall, Robert L. of Gates county to Mrs. Elizabeth Martin of Halifax county, Jan. 6. R. R. Jan. 21, 1805

Martin, Mrs. Elizabeth of Halifax county to Robert L. Marshall of Gates county, Jan. 6. R. R. Jan. 21, 1805

Mebane, Mrs. Rebecca to John King, Aug. 29, Orange county. R. R. Sept. 2, 1805

Medlock, Miss of Caswell county to Wm. Lewis of Person county, Jan. 31. R. R. Feb. 11, 1805

Morgan, Lemuel of Orange county to Mary Shaw, Jan. 24, Wake county. R. R. Feb. 11, 1805

Moore, Thomas to Henrietta Barbie of Orange county, Jan. 28. R. R. Feb. 1, 1805

Morton, Miss of Charlotte county, Va. to Rev. Hugh Shaw of Wake county. R. R. Feb. 18, 1805

Murphy, Mr. to Patience Johnson, Oct. 17, Franklin county. R. R. Oct. 28, 1805

Nicholson, Elizabeth to William Rigan, Oct. 17, Warrenton. R. R. Oct. 28, 1805

Nicholson, John to Flora Gordon, Nov. 28, Richmond county. R. R. Dec. 9, 1805

Norris, Polly to John Walton, Aug. 22, Wake county. R. R. Aug. 26, 1805

Norwood, Polly to Joseph Outerbridge, Sept. 26, Franklin county. R. R. Sept. 30, 1805

Oliver, Fanny of Newbern to Benjamin Good, Apr. 21, Newbern. R. R. My. 6, 1805

Outerbridge, Joseph to Polly Norwood, Sept. 26, Franklin county. R. R. Sept. 30, 1805

Powel, Obid of Chatham county to Polly Herndon, Jly. 4, Orange county. R. R. Jly. 15, 1805

Rand, John to Patsey Courtis, Je. 20, Wake county. R. R. Je. 24, 1805

Rhodes, Mrs. Euphen Alston to Solomon Moses Joseph, Sept., Washington. R. R. Sept. 30, 1805

Riggan, William to Elizabeth Nicholson, Oct. 17, Warrenton. R. R. Oct. 28, 1805

Rowland, Aserath to Silas Drake, Dec. 1, Robeson county. R. R. Dec. 9, 1805

Sanders, John to Betsey Bridges, Feb. 13, Wake county. R. R. Feb. 18, 1805

Scarborough, William Jr. of Savannah to Julia Bernard of Wilmington, Apr. 18, Wilmington. R. R. My. 6, 1805

Seawell, James of Franklin county to Lucy Ann Lewis of Granville county, Dec., Granville county. R. R. Dec. 30, 1805

Sessums, Roderic to Polly Lloyd, Je. 27, Tarborough. R. R. Jly. 8, 1805

Shaw, Rev. Hugh of Wake county to Miss Morton of Charlotte county, Va., Feb. R. R. Feb. 18, 1805

Shaw, Mary to Lemuel Morgan of Orange county, Jan. 24, Wake county. R. R. Feb. 11, 1805

Sledge, Willie of Franklin to Jemina Dodd, Feb. 6, Raleigh. R. R. Feb. 11, 1805

Spruill, Benjamin of Tyrrell county to Susannah Thomas of Raleigh, Dec. 19. R. R. Dec. 23, 1805

Sutherland, John of Wake county to Nancy Alston, Oct. 17, Warren county. R. R. Oct. 28, 1805

Swann, Maria to John D. Toomer, Dec. 9, Wilmington. R. R. Dec. 16, 1805

Taylor, Catherine of Raleigh to Nicholas Long of Fayetteville, Mar. 28, Raleigh. R. R. Apr. 1, 1805

Thomas, Susannah of Raleigh to Benjamin Spruill of Tyrrell county, Dec. 19. R. R. Dec. 23, 1805

Thompson, William of Sampson county to Henrietta Dunn of Duplin county, Sept., Duplin county. R. R. Sept. 23, 1805

Toomer, John D. to Maria Swann, Dec. 9, Wilmington. R. R. Dec. 16, 1805

Tredwell, Samuel of Edenton to Fanny Lenox, Jan., Bertie county. R. R. Jan. 21, 1805

Ure, Mrs. Mary to John Williams, Aug. 15, Wilmington. R. R. Sept. 2, 1805

Walker, John to Elizabeth Finch, Oct. 17, Warren county. R. R. Oct. 28, 1805

Walton, Edward of Orange county to Polly Willis, Jan. 31, Chatham county. R. R. Feb. 18, 1805

Walton, John to Polly Norris, Aug. 22, Wake county. R. R. Aug. 26, 1805

Washington, John of Granville county to Lanier Duke of Warren county, Aug., Warren county. R. R. Aug. 26, 1805

Whitaker, Wesley to Sally Langley, Oct. 7, Raleigh. R. R. Nov. 11, 1805

Wheaten, Dr. Sterling of Raleigh to Levina Hill, Jan. 20, Franklin county. R. R. Jan. 28, 1805

White, Beuajah of Lenoir county to Mary Allen of Craven county, Jan. 1, Craven county. R. R. Jan. 14, 1805

Whiteside, William to Jane Harden, Aug. 29, Orange county. R. R. Sept. 2, 1805

Williams, Joel, Jr. to Bell Armstrong, Mar. 28, Cumberland county. R. R. Apr. 1, 1805

Williams, John to Mrs. Wray Ure, Aug. 15, Wilmington. R. R. Sept. 2, 1805

Williams, Mrs. J. of Halifax county, Va. to Rev. John Kerr of Caswell county, Apr. 18. R. R. My. 6, 1805

Willis, Polly to Edward Walton of Orange county, Jan. 31, Chatham county. R. R. Feb. 18, 1805

Wortham, Charles of Warren county to Miss Ingram of Franklin, Jan. 31. R. R. Feb. 11, 1805

Yarborough, David to Neely Dogerty, Sept., Hillsborough. R. R. Oct. 7, 1805

Young, Eliza of Bladen county to Richard Bradley of Wilmington, Mar. 26, Wilmington. R. R. Apr. 8, 1805

1806

Alston, George to Mrs. Thomas Mutter, Jly. 28, Granville county. R. R. Aug. 11, 1806

Arnold, Sarah to Dudley House, Oct., Warren county. R. R. Oct. 6, 1806

Ashe, Col. Samuel to Elizabeth Shepherd, Oct. 9, Hillsborough. R. R. Oct. 20, 1806

Barron, Samuel G. to Eliza Gray, Dec. 21, Newbern. R. R. Jan. 6, 1806

Bates, Mrs. A. to Capt. John Coley of Massachusetts, Mar. 17, Newbern. R. R. Mar. 31, 1806

Beasly, Elizabeth to Lemuel Haughton of Chowan county, Jan. 28, Edenton. R. R. Feb. 10, 1806

Bell, Peggy of Orange county to William Duffy of Fayetteville, Aug. 21, Tarborough. R. R. Sept. 1, 1806

Bernier, de, Charlotte to Archibald Hooper of Wilmington, Je. 8, Chatham county. R. R. Je. 23, 1806

Blackledge, Nancy to Green Bryan, Jan., Newbern. R. R. Jan. 20, 1806

Blair, Wm. to Rachel Harvey, Nov. 29, Pasquotank county. R. R. Dec. 22, 1806

Britt, Julia of Northampton county to Lemuel Valentine, Jan. 9, Hertford county. R. R. Feb. 3, 1806

Branch, James of Halifax to Martha Hilliard, Sept. 16, Nash county. R. R. Oct. 6, 1806

Brickell, Jonathan to Mrs. M'keithan, Jan. 11, Raleigh. R. R. Jan. 20, 1806

Brown, Elizabeth to Ambrose Smith, Dec. 4, Edenton. R. R. Dec. 22, 1806

Bryan, Green to Nancy Blackledge, Jan., Newbern. R. R. Jan. 20, 1806

Chapman, John to Rachel Cunningham, Apr. 8, Rowan county. R. R. Apr. 28, 1806

Child, Samuel to Christian Lewis, Oct. 19, Hillsborough. R. R. Nov. 17, 1806

Clark, David of Plymouth to Louisa Norfleet of Scotland Neck, Sept. 2. R. R. Sept. 22, 1806

Coley, Capt. John of Massachusetts to Mrs. A. Bates, Mar. 17, Newbern. R. R. Mar. 31, 1806

Collins, Michael to Elizabeth Drake, Apr. 10, Nash county. R. R. My. 12, 1806

Connelly, William of Louisburg to Mrs. Thomas of Franklin county, Feb. Franklin county. R. R. Feb. 24, 1806

Cooke, Mark of Raleigh to Mrs. Knight of Franklin county, Feb. R. R. Feb. 24, 1806

Cotton, Henry to Sophia Mumford, Sept. 23, Tarborough. R. R. Oct. 6, 1806

Crawford, John of Rockingham to Jane Snead of Richmond county, Jan. 7, Rockingham. R. R. Feb. 3, 1806

Cunningham, Rachel to John Chapman, Apr. 8, Rowan county. R. R. Apr. 28, 1806

Curk, Sarah to Wm. Pritchard, Jan., Newbern. R. R. Feb. 3, 1806

Dancy, David of Northampton county to Fanny Wood, My., Warrenton.
R. R. My. 26, 1806

Dancy, Francis of Northampton county to Hannah Peters of Greenville
county, Va., Jan., Halifax. R. R. Jan. 27, 1806

Davis, Frances to Robert Winston, Jly. 31, Stokes county. R. R. Aug. 11,
1806

Drake, Elizabeth to Michael Collins, Apr. 10, Nash county. R. R. My. 12,
1806

Dudley, Christopher, Jr. to Leah Spicer of Topsail, Aug. 5, Wilmington.
R. R. Aug. 25, 1806

Duffy, William of Fayetteville to Peggy Bell of Orange county, Aug. 21,
Tarborough. R. R. Sept. 1, 1806

Duke, Green, Jr. to Rebecca Robinson, Oct. 23, Warren county. R. R.
Nov. 3, 1806

Edwards, Daniel of Surry county to Patsey Jones of Crabtree, Apr. 22,
Raleigh. R. R. Apr. 28, 1806

Eelbeck, Sarah to John Purnell, Oct. 8, Halifax county. R. R. Oct. 20,
1806

Ellis, Wm. Jr. to Sally Towns, Aug. 8, Warren county. R. R. Aug. 18,
1806

Estis, L. B. of Northampton county to Sarah Hunter of Warren county,
Dec. 24, Warren county. R. R. Jan. 6, 1806

Finch, Hamilton to Elitha Holloman, Jly. 13, Raleigh. R. R. Aug. 18,
1806

Fleming, James to Mrs. Shaw, Je. 1, Wilmington. R. R. Je. 16, 1806

Forbes, Mrs. of Newbern to Sarah Hatche of Jones county, Nov. 6. R. R.
Dec. 1, 1806

Gilchrist, Allen of Halifax to Dolly Lane of Raleigh, My. 29, Raleigh.
R. R. Je. 2, 1806

Gillaspie, Viney to James Somers, Jan. 28, Caswell county. R. R. Feb. 17,
1806

Gilmour, John M'K of Halifax to Sarah Tainter of Connecticut, Sept. 7,
Windham, Conn. R. R. Sept. 22, 1806

Goldson, Amy of Chatham county to Capt. George Williamson of Caswell
county, Mar. 1, Chatham county. R. R. Mar. 10, 1806

Gray, Eliza to Samuel G. Barron, Dec. 21, Newbern. R. R. Jan. 6, 1806

Guttery, James to Fanny Jones, Jan. 8, Newbern. R. R. Jan. 27, 1806

Harris, Chalbon of Montgomery county to Betsey Kirby of Anson county,
Jly. R. R. Jly. 21, 1806

Harvey, Rachel to Wm. Blair, Nov. 29, Pasquotank county. R. R. Dec.
22, 1806

Hatche, Sarah of Jones county to Mrs. Forbes of Newbern, Nov. 6. R. R.
Dec. 1, 1806

Haughton, Lemuel to Elizabeth Beasly of Chowan county, Jan. 28, Edenton. R. R. Feb. 10, 1806

Henry, John to Patsey Williams of Pittsylvania county, Va., Dec. 25.
R. R. Feb. 3, 1806

Hilliard, Martha to James Branch of Halifax, Sept. 16, Nash county. R. R.
Oct. 6, 1806

Hill, Charles A. to Rebecca Long, Apr., Franklin county. R. R. Apr. 14, 1806

Hill, Mrs. John to Dr. Whitmil Pugh, Mar. 11, Bertie county. R. R. Mar. 31, 1806

Holland, W. to Nancy Rhodes, Apr., Wake county. R. R. Apr. 7, 1806

Holley, John to Patsey Outlaw, Jan. 9, Bertie county. R. R. Feb. 3, 1806

Holloman, Elitha to Hamilton Finch, Jly. 13, Raleigh. R. R. Aug. 18, 1806

Hooper, Archibald of Wilmington to Charlotte De Bernier, Je. 8, Chatham county. R. R. Je. 23, 1806

House, Dudley to Sarah Arnold, Oct., Warren county. R. R. Oct. 6, 1806

Hunter, Sarah of Warren county to L. B. Estis of Northampton county, Dec. 24, Warren county. R. R. Jan. 6, 1806

Jeffreys, Osborn, Jr. to Jane Miller, Mar., Person county. R. R. Mar. 24, 1806

Jones, Famey to James Guttery, Jan. 8, Newbern. R. R. Jan. 27, 1806

Jones, Henry of Wake county to Sally Smith, Sept. 4, Johnston county. R. R. Sept. 15, 1806

Jones, Patsey of Crabtree to Daniel Edwards of Surry county, Apr. 22, Raleigh. R. R. Apr. 28, 1806

Jordan, Mrs. Anna of Bertie county to Richard Poindexter, Aug. 7. R. R. Aug. 18, 1806

Kimbell, Polly of Warren county to George Murphey of Granville county, Oct. 23. R. R. Nov. 3, 1806

King, Joel of Louisburg to Martha Long, Aug. 28, Franklin county. R. R. Sept. 1, 1806

Kirby, Betsey of Anson county to Chalbon Harris of Montgomery county, Jly. R. R. Jly. 21, 1806

Knight, Mrs. of Franklin county to Mark Cooke of Raleigh, Feb. R. R. Feb. 24, 1806

Lane, Dolly of Raleigh to Allen Gilchrist of Halifax, My. 29, Raleigh. R. R. Je. 2, 1806

Langley, James W. of Norfolk to Harriet Slade of Edenton, Jan. 6, Edenton. R. R. Jan. 27, 1806

Lewis, Christian to Samuel Child, Oct. 19, Hillsborough. R. R. Nov. 17, 1806

Lofton, Catharine of Lenoir county to Mark Morgan Yeargan, Mar. 2, Chapel Hill. R. R. Mar. 10, 1806

Long, Martha to Joel King of Louisburg, Aug. 28, Franklin county. R. R. Sept. 1, 1806

Long, Rebecca to Charles A. Hill, Apr., Franklin county. R. R. Apr. 14, 1806

M'Keithen, Mrs. to Jonathan Brickell, Jan. 11, Raleigh. R. R. Jan. 20, 1806

M'Lean, Hugh to Elizabeth Ochiltree, Sept. 25, Cumberland county. R. R. Oct. 20, 1806

M'Lin, Nancy of Newbern to Joseph Pearson of Salisbury, Jan., Newbern. R. R. Jan. 20, 1806

Macay, Alexander to Faribee Williams, Jly. 24, Fayetteville. R. R. Aug. 4, 1806

Manning, Wm. to Ann Taylor of Pasquotank county, Jan., Edenton. R. R. Jan. 20, 1806

Martin, Susannah to Joseph Williams of Surry county, Jly., Granville county. R. R. Jly. 21, 1806

Miller, Jane to Osborn Jeffreys, Jr., Mar., Person county. R. R. Mar. 24, 1806

Miller, Susan to Christian Tarr, Aug., Salisbury. R. R. Aug. 11, 1806

Morris, Charles to Mildred Nichols, My. 22, Sound, Wilmington. R. R. Je. 9, 1806

Mumford, Sophia to Henry Cotton, Sept. 23, Tarborough. R. R. Oct. 6, 1806

Murphey, George of Granville county to Polly Kimbell of Warren county, Oct. 23. R. R. Nov. 3, 1806

Mutter, Mrs. Thomas to George Alston, Jly. 28, Granville county. R. R. Aug. 11, 1806

Newby, Larkin to Celia Pearce, Dec. 17, Fayetteville. R. R. Dec. 29, 1806

Nichols, Mildred to Charles Morris, My. 22, Sound, Wilmington. R. R. Je. 9, 1806

Norfleet, Isaac to Mary Scull, Jan. 15, Hertford county. R. R. Feb. 3, 1806

Norfleet, Louisa of Scotland Neck to David Clark of Plymouth, Sept. 2. R. R. Sept. 22, 1806

Norris, Elizabeth to Allen Rhodes, Nov. 9, Wake county. R. R. Nov. 17, 1806

Ochiltree, Elizabeth to Hugh M'Lean, Sept. 25, Cumberland county. R. R. Oct. 20, 1806

Opiz, John to Elizabeth Snider, Sept. 11, Forsyth county. R. R. Sept. 22, 1806

Outlaw, Patsey to John Holley, Jan. 9, Bertie county. R. R. Feb. 3, 1806

Pearce, Celia to Larkin Newby, Dec. 17, Fayetteville. R. R. Dec. 29, 1806

Pearson, Joseph of Salisbury to Nancy M'Lin of Newbern, Jan., Newbern. R. R. Jan. 20, 1806

Pegues, William of South Carolina to Eliza Ward of Pittsborough, Jan. 28, Pittsborough. R. R. Feb. 17, 1806

Peters, Hannah of Greenville county, Va. to Francis Dancy of Northampton county, Jan., Halifax. R. R. Jan. 27, 1806

Poindexter, Richard to Mrs. Anna Jordan of Bertie county, Aug. 7. R. R. Aug. 18, 1806

Pritchard, Wm. to Sarah Curk, Jan., Newbern. R. R. Feb. 3, 1806

Pugh, Dr. Whitmel to Mrs. John Hill, Mar. 11, Bertie county. R. R. Mar. 31, 1806

Purnell, John to Sarah Eelbeck, Oct. 8, Halifax county. R. R. Oct. 20, 1806

Rivers, Hannah of Franklin county to Major John Scott of Virginia, Jan. 16, Virginia. R. R. Feb. 3, 1806

Robinson, Rebecca to Green Duke, Jr., Oct. 23, Warren county. R. R. Nov. 3, 1806

Rhodes, Allen to Elizabeth Norris, Nov. 9, Wake county. R. R. Nov. 17, 1806

Rhodes, Jacintha to John Whitaker, Jr., Aug. 7, Wake county. R. R. Aug. 18, 1806

Rhodes, Nancy to W. Holland, Apr., Wake county. R. R. Apr. 7, 1806

Scull, Mary to Isaac Norfleet, Jan. 15, Hertford county. R. R. Feb. 3, 1806

Scott, Major Johnson of Virginia to Hannah Rivers of Franklin county, Jan. 16, Virginia. R. R. Feb. 3, 1806

Shaw, Mrs. to James Fleming, Je. 1, Wilmington. R. R. Je. 16, 1806

Shepherd, Elizabeth to Col. Samuel Ashe, Oct. 9, Hillsborough. R. R. Oct. 20, 1806

Singleton, Richard to Betsey Tinker, Je. 1, Newbern. R. R. Je. 9, 1806

Slade, Harriet of Edenton to James W. Langley of Norfolk, Jan. 6, Edenton. R. R. Jan. 27, 1806

Smith, Ambrose to Elizabeth Brown, Dec. 4, Edenton. R. R. Dec. 22, 1806

Smith, Charity to Alexander Williams of Cumberland county, Sept. 16, Fayetteville. R. R. Oct. 6, 1806

Smith, Sally to Henry Jones of Wake county, Sept. 4, Johnston county. R. R. Sept. 15, 1806

Snead, Jane of Richmond county to John Crawford of Rockingham, Jan. 7, Rockingham. R. R. Feb. 3, 1806

Snider, Elizabeth to John Opiz, Sept. 11, Forsyth county. R. R. Sept. 22, 1806

Somers, James to Viney Gillaspie, Jan. 28, Caswell county. R. R. Feb. 17, 1806

Somerville, James of Raleigh to Catherine Vekes, Apr., Warrenton. R. R. Apr. 7, 1806

Spicer, Leah of Topsail to Christopher Dudley, Jr., Aug. 5, Wilmington. R. R. Aug. 25, 1806

Swan, John Jr. to Margaret F. Waddle, My. 20, Wilmington. R. R. Je. 9, 1806

Tainter, Sarah of Connecticut to John M'K Gilmour of Halifax, Sept. 7, Windham, Conn. R. R. Sept. 22, 1806

Tarr, Christian to Susan Miller, Aug., Salisbury. R. R. Aug. 11, 1806

Taylor, Ann of Pasquotank county to Wm. Manning, Jan., Edenton. R. R. Jan. 20, 1806

Thomas, Mrs. of Franklin county to William Connelly of Louisburg, Feb., Franklin county. R. R. Feb. 24, 1806

Tinker, Betsey to Richard Singleton, Je. 1, Newbern. R. R. Je. 9, 1806

Towns, Sally to Wm. Ellis, Jr., Aug. 8, Warren county. R. R. Aug. 18, 1806

Waddle, Margaret F. to John Swan, Jr., My. 20, Wilmington. R. R. Je. 9, 1806

Ward, Eliza of Pittsborough to William Pegues of South Carolina, Jan. 28, Pittsborough. R. R. Feb. 17, 1806

Wheaton, Dr. Calvin to Mrs. Daniel Wheaton, Jly. 15, Nashville. R. R. Aug. 4, 1806

Wheaton, Mrs. Daniel to Dr. Calvin Wheaton, Jly. 15, Nashville. R. R. Aug. 4, 1806

Whitaker, John Jr. to Jacintha Rhodes, Aug. 7, Wake county. R. R. Aug. 18, 1806

Williams, Alexander to Charity Smith of Cumberland county, Sept. 16, Fayetteville. R. R. Oct. 6, 1806

Williams, Faribee to Alexander Macay, Jly. 24, Fayetteville. R. R. Aug. 4, 1806

Williams, Joseph of Surry county to Susannah Martin, Jly., Granville county. R. R. Jly. 21, 1806 .

Williams, Patsey of Pittsylvania county, Va. to John Henry, Dec. 25. R. R. Feb. 3, 1806

Williamson, Capt. George of Caswell county to Amy Goldson of Chatham county, Mar. 1, Chatham county. R. R. Mar. 10, 1806

Winston, Robert to Frances Davis, Jly. 31, Stokes county. R. R. Aug. 11, 1806

Wood, Fanny to David Dancy of Northampton county, My., Warrenton. R. R. My. 26, 1806

Valentine, Lemuel to Julia Britt of Northampton county, Jan. 9, Hertford county. R. R. Feb. 3, 1806

Vekes, Catharine to James Somervel of Raleigh, Apr., Warrenton. R. R. Apr. 7, 1806

Yeargen, Mark Morgan to Catharine Lofton of Lenoir county, Mar. 2, Chapel Hill. R. R. Mar. 10, 1806

1807

Adams, Ann of Pittsylvania county, Va. to Nathan Chaffin of Surry county, Je. 25, Pittsylvania county, Va. R. R. Jly. 23, 1807

Adams, Mrs. to James Mumford, Aug., Fayetteville. R. R. Aug. 6, 1807

Alves, Anne to Richard Henderson, Feb. 19, Orange county. R. R. Feb. 23, 1807

Amis, John D. to Eliz. Bynum, Dec. 3, Northampton county. R. R. Dec. 10, 1807

Anthony, Eliz. to James Gordon, Dec. 8, Scotland Neck. R. R. Dec. 17, 1807

Archdell, Francis to Samuel Vines, Apr. 23, Washington. R. R. My. 7, 1807

Armistead, Maria to Wm. Goodwin, Feb., Scotland Neck. R. R. Feb. 23, 1807

Arnold, Sally to Joseph Green of Newbern, Feb., Craven county. R. R. Feb. 11, 1807

Arrington, Mary J. of Nash county to Capt. James M. Nicholson, Dec. 11. R. R. Jan. 12, 1807

Ashe, Major Samuel to Jane Moore, Jly. 14, Pleasant Hall, New Hanover county. R. R. Jly. 30, 1807

Barrow, Pherebee to Robert Justice, Dec., Scotland Neck. R. R. Dec. 10, 1807

Baskerville, Betsey of Mecklenburg county, Va. to Robert H. Jones of Warrenton, Apr. 9, Mecklenburg county, Va. R. R. Apr. 16, 1807

Beck, Rachel of Duplin county to Colin Shaw, Aug. 27, Fayetteville. R. R. Sept. 2, 1807

Benbury, Polly to Joseph Creecy, Oct. 4, Edenton. R. R. Oct. 15, 1807

Bennet, Mary to Jesse Guy, Jan., Duplin county. R. R. Feb. 2, 1807

Bill, Capt. Avery A. to Ann M. Wayne, My. 19, Wilmington. R. R. Je. 4, 1807

Blount, Benjamin to Mrs. Eliz. Evart, Je. 14, Washington. R. R. Je. 25, 1807

Blount, Dr. Frederick to Mrs. R. Bryan, Oct. 1, Newbern. R. R. Oct. 15, 1807

Bonner, Mrs. Henry to Capt. Wm. Vines, Jan., Washington. R. R. Jan. 5, 1807

Bradley, Sarah of Raleigh to Dr. George Thomas of Southampton, Va., Feb., Halifax county. R. R. Mar. 2, 1807

Bryan, Mrs. R. to Frederick Blount, Oct. 1, Newbern. R. R. Oct. 15, 1807

Burch, Rev. James of Virginia to Eleanor P. Smith, Jly. 31, Raleigh. R. R. Aug. 6, 1807

Burgwin, Geo. W. of Wilmington to Maria Nash of Newbern, Apr. 7, Newbern. R. R. Apr. 16, 1807

Bynum, Eliz. to John D. Amis, Dec. 3, Northampton county. R. R. Dec. 10, 1807

Campbell, Mrs. to Marcus George, Apr. 23, Warrenton. R. R. Apr. 30, 1807

Castex, Dr. German to Mrs. Avis O'Leary, Feb., Newbern. R. R. Feb. 23, 1807

Caswell, Richard of Raleigh to Sally Lytle of Rutherford county, Nov. 27, Nashville. R. R. Jan. 19, 1807

Chaffin, Nathan of Surry county to Ann Adams of Pittsylvania county, Va., Je. 25, Pittsylvania county, Va. R. R. Jly. 23, 1807

Christmas, Alice to Thomas Power, Sept. 3, Warren county. R. R. Sept. 10, 1807

Colston, Fanny of Edenton to Thomas Liles of Chowan county, Feb. 19, Edenton. R. R. Mar. 9, 1807

Cook, Mrs. to Weeks Parker, Nov., Tarborough. R. R. Nov. 26, 1807

Creecy, Joseph to Polly Benbury, Oct. 4, Edenton. R. R. Oct. 15, 1807

Cummings, Mary of Wilmington to Benjamin S. King of Raleigh, Nov., Wilmington. R. R. Nov. 26, 1807

Daly, Sidney to Frederick Jones, Je., Newbern. R. R. Je. 25, 1807

Dickins, Lucretia to Thomas I. Moore of Person county, Dec., Granville county. R. R. Dec. 24, 1807

Dickson, Betsey of Duplin county to Edward Ward of Onslow county, Mar. 28, Duplin county. R. R. Apr. 6, 1807

Doggitt, Betsey of Rutherford county to James Elliott of Lincoln county, Feb. 26. R. R. Mar. 30, 1807

Donaldson, Henry A. to Elizabeth M'Donald, Feb. 19, Edenton. R. R. Mar. 9, 1807

Downing, John to Miss Outlaw, Dec. 18, Bertie county. R. R. Jan. 5, 1807

Duguid, Mrs. Mary to Salma Hall, Dec. 8, Newbern. R. R. Jan. 19, 1807

Dunn, James of Duplin county to Ann Hurst of Lenoir county, Dec. 23, Lenoir county. R. R. Jan. 12, 1807

Elliott, James of Lincoln county to Betsey Doggitt of Rutherford county, Feb. 26. R. R. Mar. 30, 1807

Ennis, Eliza to John Goff, Feb. 8, Duplin county. R. R. Mar. 2, 1807

Evart, Mrs. Eliz. to Benjamin Blount, Je. 14, Washington. R. R. Je. 25, 1807

Falkener, W. A. K. of Warrenton to Betsey Johnson, Sept. 24, Warrenton. R. R. Oct. 1, 1807

Fitzgerald, James of Surry county to Polly Lester, Aug. 23, Rockford, Surry county. R. R. Sept. 17, 1807

George, Marcus to Mrs. Campbell, Apr. 23, Warrenton. R. R. Apr. 30, 1807

Goff, John to Eliza Ennis, Feb. 8, Duplin county. R. R. Mar. 2, 1807

Goodwin, Wm. to Maria Armistead, Feb., Scotland Neck. R. R. Feb. 23, 1807

Gordon, Alexander to Susan Johnston, of Caswell county, Oct. 15. R. R. Nov. 5, 1807

Gordon, James to Eliz. Anthony, Dec. 8, Scotland Neck. R. R. Dec. 17, 1807

Grimes, James to Polly Singletary, Dec. 21, Washington. R. R. Jan. 5, 1807

Gunn, Griffin of Caswell county to Dorothy Minns Mitchell, My. 28, Petersburg, Va. R. R. Je. 11, 1807

Guy, Jesse to Mary Bennet, Jan., Duplin county. R. R. Feb. 2, 1807

Hall, Salmon to Mrs. Mary Duguid, Dec. 8, Newbern. R. R. Jan. 19, 1807

Halling, Francinia Greenway to James Usher, Apr. 28, Wilmington. R. R. My. 14, 1807

Harrison, Thomas to Mildred Johnston, Nov., Caswell county. R. R. Dec. 10, 1807

Hawkins, Benjamin of Warren county to Sally Person of Granville county, Sept. 2, Granville county. R. R. Sept. 10, 1807

Henderson, Richard to Anne Alves, Feb. 19, Orange county. R. R. Feb. 23, 1807

Henderson, Samuel Sr. of Caswell county to Pricilla Nichols of Person county, Mar. 12. R. R. Apr. 6, 1807

Hill, James J. to Patsey Jeffers, Jan., Franklin county. R. R. Jan. 12, 1807

Hilliard, John of Nash county to Betsey Tunstall, Dec. 24, Franklin county. R. R. Jan. 5, 1807

Hinton, Capt. Henry of Wake county to Mary Sanders, Apr. 30, Johnston county. R. R. My. 7, 1807

Hunter, Capt. William to Sarah M'Donald, My. 11, Wilmington. R. R. My. 21, 1807

Hurst, Ann of Lenoir county to James Dunn of Duplin county, Dec. 23, Lenoir county. R. R. Jan. 12, 1807

Huske, John to Joanna T. Tillinghast of Rhode Island, Mar. 15, Fayetteville. R. R. Mar. 30, 1807

Huste, Anne to Dr. James Webb, Feb. 12, Hillsborough. R. R. Feb. 23, 1807

Jackson, Mrs. Mary to John O'Quinn, Oct., Wilmington. R. R. Oct. 22, 1807

Jeffers, Patsey to James J. Hill, Franklin county. R. R. Jan. 12, 1807

Jennings, Mrs. George to Capt. John Nelson, Apr. 16, Wilmington. R. R. Apr. 30, 1807

Jessup, George H. to Elizabeth Turner, Aug., Washington, Beaufort county. R. R. Aug. 6, 1807

Johnson, Betsey to W. A. K. Falkener of Warrenton, Sept. 24, Warrenton. R. R. Oct. 1, 1807

Johnson, Miss to John Wright, Feb., Rowan county. R. R. Feb. 23, 1807

Johnston, Chas. of Chowan county to Nancy Taylor of Franklin county, Aug., Franklin county. R. R. Aug. 20, 1807

Johnston, Mildred to Thomas Harrison, Nov., Caswell county. R. R. Dec. 10, 1807

Johnston, Susan to Alexander Gordon of Caswell county, Oct. 15. R. R. Nov. 5, 1807

Johnston, Wm. E. to Mrs. Willis, Jly. 30, Warren county. R. R. Aug. 6, 1807

Jones, Abigail of Warren county to Eli Whitaker of Halifax county, Mar. 11, Warren county. R. R. Mar. 23, 1807

Jones, Frederick to Sidney Daly, Je., Newbern. R. R. Je 25, 1807

Jones, Robert H. of Warrenton to Betsey Baskerville of Mecklenburg county, Va., Apr. 9, Mecklenburg county. R. R. Apr. 16, 1807

Jordan,. Nancy to David Terry, Nov. 12, Warren county. R. R. Nov. 19, 1807

Justice, Robert to Pherebee Barrow, Dec., Scotland Neck. R. R. Dec. 10, 1807

King, Benjamin S. of Raleigh to Mary Cummings of Wilmington, Nov., Wilmington. R. R. Dec. 3, 1807

King, Nathaniel to Ann Kirkland, My., Orange county. R. R. Je. 4, 1807

Kirkland, Ann to Nathaniel King, My., Orange county. R. R. Je. 4, 1807

Kirkwood, Mary to Joshua Potts, Dec. 24, Wilmington. R. R. Jan. 19, 1807

Leonard, Margaret to Samuel Pearce, Dec. 25, Fayetteville. R. R. Jan. 12, 1807

Lester, Polly to James Fitzgerald of Surry county, Aug. 23, Rockford, Surry county. R. R. Sept. 17, 1807

Liles, Thomas of Chowan county to Fanny Colston of Edenton, Feb. 19, Edenton. R. R. Mar. 9, 1807

Long, John of Orange county to Sibly Ramsey of Fayetteville, My. 6, Fayetteville. R. R. My. 14, 1807

Lytle, Sally of Rutherford county to Richard Caswell of Raleigh, Nov. 27, Nashville. R. R. Jan. 19, 1807

M'Donald, Elizabeth to Henry A. Donaldson, Feb. 19, Edenton. R. R. Mar. 9, 1807

M'Donald, Sarah to Capt. William Hunter, My. 11, Wilmington. R. R. My. 21, 1807

M'Kay, John to Zula Williams, Oct. 9, Fayetteville. R. R. Oct. 22, 1807

M'Millan, Ann of Bladen county to John Nicholson of Wilmington, Nov. 5. R. R. Nov. 19, 1807

Macon, Polly to James Moss, Jly. 9, Warrenton. R. R. Jly. 16, 1807

Mallett, Caroline to Carleton Walker, Je. 11, Wilmington. R. R. Je. 25, 1807

Mallett, Eliza of Fayetteville to Dr. Scott of Wilmington, Feb. 9, Fayetteville. R. R. Feb. 23, 1807

Mitchell, Dorothy Minns to Griffin Gunn, My. 28, Petersburg, Va. R. R. Je. 11, 1807

Moore, Jane to Major Samuel Ashe, Jly. 14, Pleasant Hall, New Hanover county. R. R. Jly. 30, 1807

Moore, Thomas I. of Person county to Lucretia Dickins, Dec., Granville county. R. R. Dec. 24, 1807

Moss, James to Polly Macon, Jly. 9, Warrenton. R. R. Jly. 16, 1807

Mumford, James to Mrs. Adams, Aug., Fayetteville. R. R. Aug. 6, 1807

Nash, Maria of Newbern to Geo. W. Burgwin of Wilmington, Apr. 7, Newbern. R. R. Apr. 16, 1807

Nelson,. Capt. John to Mrs. George Jennings, Apr. 16, Wilmington. R. R. Apr. 30, 1807

Newby, Henrietta to Robert Raiford, Nov. 12, Fayetteville. R. R. Nov. 26, 1807

Nichols, Priscilla of Person county to Samuel Henderson, Sr. of Caswell county, Mar. 12. R. R. Apr. 6, 1807

Nicholson, Capt. James M. of Halifax county to Mary J. Arrington of Nash county, Dec. 11. R. R. Jan. 12, 1807

Nicholson, John of Wilmington to Ann M'Millan of Bladen county, Nov. 5. R. R. Nov. 19, 1807

Norwood, William to Rebecca Thomas, Sept. 9, Granville county. R. R. Sept. 24, 1807

O'Farrel, Barnabas to Anne Jameson Williams, Dec. 3, Hillsborough. R. R. Dec. 10, 1807

O'Leary, Mrs. Avis to Dr. German Castex, Feb., Newbern. R. R. Feb. 23, 1807

O'Quin, John to Mrs. Mary Jackson, Oct., Wilmington. R. R. Oct. 22, 1807

Outlaw, Miss to John Downing, Dec. 10, Bertie county. R. R. Jan. 5, 1807

Parker, Weeks to Mrs. Cooke, Nov., Tarborough. R. R. Nov. 26, 1807

Pearce, Samuel to Margaret Leonard, Dec. 25, Fayetteville. R. R. Jan. 12, 1807

Perkinson, Martha to Thomas Reynolds, Jan. 3, Warrenton. R. R. Jan. 12, 1807

Person, Sally of Granville county to Benjamin Hawkins of Warren county, Sept. 2, Granville county. R. R. Sept. 10, 1807

Peters, Miss of Wake county to John Sanders of Johnston county, My., Wake county. R. R. Je. 4, 1807

Porie, Eliza M. to Daniel Redmond, Je. 30, Tarborough. R. R. Jly. 23, 1807

Potts, Joshua to Mary Kirkwood, Dec. 24, Wilmington. R. R. Jan. 19, 1807

Power, Thomas to Alice Christmas, Sept. 3, Warren county. R. R. Sept. 10, 1807

Purdie, Polly to Edward Reiley, Je. 14, Edenton. R. R. Je. 25, 1807

Raiford, Robert to Henrietta Newby, Nov. 12, Fayetteville. R. R. Nov. 26, 1807

Ramsey, Sibly of Fayetteville to John Long of Orange county, My. 6, Fayetteville. R. R. My. 14, 1807

Redmond, Daniel to Eliza M. Porie, Je. 30, Tarborough. R. R. Jly. 23, 1807

Reed, Elizabeth of Catawba Springs to Robertson Williamson, Nov. 27, Lincoln county. R. R. Jan. 5, 1807

Reiley, Edward to Polly Purdie, Je. 14, Edenton. R. R. Je. 25, 1807

Reynolds, Thomas to Martha Perkinson, Jan. 3, Warrenton. R. R. Jan. 12, 1807

Rogers, Derrell to Mrs. Camp, Mar., Wake county. R. R. Mar. 10, 1807

Sanders, John of Johnston county to Miss Peters of Wake county, My., Wake county. R. R. Je. 4, 1807

Sanders, Mary to Capt. Henry Hinton of Wake county, Apr. 30, Johnston county. R. R. My. 7, 1807

Scott, Dr. of Wilmington to Eliza Mallett of Fayetteville, Feb. 9, Fayetteville. R. R. Feb. 23, 1807

Seaberry, Raleigh to Kitty Swinson, Jan., Duplin county. R. R. Feb. 2, 1807

Seawell, Patsey of Moore county to H. Williams of Cumberland county, Nov. R. R. Nov. 19, 1807

Shaw, Colin to Rachel Beck of Duplin county, Aug. 27, Fayetteville. R. R. Sept. 2, 1807

Singletary, Polly to James Grimes, Dec. 21, Washington. R. R. Jan. 5, 1807

Smith, Eleanor P. to Rev. James Burch of Virginia, Jly. 31, Raleigh. R. R. Aug. 6, 1807

Standin, Henderson to Fanny Blount, Apr. 5, Edenton. R. R. Apr. 16, 1807

Stanly, Lydia D. to Wm. Ward, Nov. 24, Newbern. R. R. Dec. 17, 1807

Swinson, Kitty to Raleigh Seaberry, Jan., Duplin county. R. R. Feb. 2, 1807

Taylor, Nancy of Franklin county to Chas. Johnston of Chowan county, Aug., Franklin county. R. R. Aug. 20, 1807

Terry, David to Nancy Jordan, Nov. 12, Warren county. R. R. Nov. 19, 1807

Thomas, Dr. George of Southampton, Va. to Sarah Bradley of Raleigh, Feb., Halifax county. R. R. Mar. 2, 1807

Thomas, Rebecca to William Norwood, Sept. 9, Granville county. R. R. Sept. 24, 1807

Thomas, William to Nancy Wynne, Feb., Franklin county. R. R. Feb. 23, 1807

Tunstall, Betsey to John Hilliard of Nash county, Dec. 24, Franklin county. R. R. Jan. 5, 1807

Turner, Elizabeth to George H. Jessup, Aug., Washington, Beaufort county. R. R. Aug. 6, 1807

Usher, James to Francinia Greenway Halling, Apr. 28, Wilmington. R. R. My. 14, 1807

Vines, Samuel to Francis Archdell, Apr. 23, Washington. R. R. My. 7, 1807

Vines, Capt. Wm. to Mrs. Henry Bonner, Jan., Washington. R. R. Jan. 5, 1807

Walker, Carleton to Caroline Mallet, Je. 11, Wilmington. R. R. Je. 25, 1807

Ward, Edward of Onslow county to Betsey Dickson of Duplin county, Mar. 28, Duplin county. R. R. Apr. 6, 1807

Ward, Wm. to Lydia D. Stanly, Nov. 24, Newbern. R. R. Dec. 17, 1807

Wayne, Ann M. to Capt. Avery A. Bill, My. 19, Wilmington. R. R. Je. 4, 1807

Webb, Dr. James to Anne Huste, Feb. 12, Hillsborough. R. R. Feb. 23, 1807

Wilkinson, Mrs. Jaheshaba to Thomas Whedbee, My. 28, Edenton. R. R. Je. 11, 1807

Williams, Anne Jamesson to Barnabas O'Farrel, Dec. 3, Hillsborough. R. R. Dec. 10, 1807

Williams, H. of Cumberland county to Patsey Seawell of Moore county, Nov. R. R. Nov. 19, 1807

Williams, Zula to John M'Kay, Oct. 9, Fayetteville. R. R. Oct. 22, 1807

Williamson, Robertson to Elizabeth Reed of Catawba Springs, Nov. 27, Lincoln county. R. R. Jan. 5, 1807

Willis, Mrs. to Wm. E. Johnston, Jly. 30, Warren county. R. R. Aug. 6, 1807

Whedbee, Thomas to Mrs. Jaheshaba Wilkinson, My. 28, Edenton. R. R. Je. 11, 1807

Whitaker, Eli of Halifax county to Abigail Jones of Warren county, Mar. 11, Warren county. R. R. Mar. 23, 1807

Wright, John to Miss Johnson, Feb., Rowan county. R. R. Feb. 23, 1807

Wright, William of Duplin county to Raphel Whitfield, Dec. 23, Lenoir county. R. R. Jan. 5, 1807

Wynne, Nancy to William Thomas, Feb., Franklin county. R. R. Feb. 23, 1807

1808

Alston, Samuel of Wake county to Sarah A. D. Williams of Martin county, Nov. 11, Martin county. R. R. Dec. 8, 1808

Arnold, Sally to Joseph Green of Newbern, Feb., Craven county. R. R. Feb. 11, 1808

Atkins, Zilly to Daniel Thomas, Feb. 24, Caswell county. R. R. Mar. 10, 1808

Bagley, George to Nancy Williamson, My. 12, Caswell county. R. R. Je. 2, 1808

Bethol, Mrs. to Rev. George Roberts of Person county, Aug. 4, Rockingham. R. R. Aug. 18, 1808

Blount, Joseph of Bertie county to Fanny Connor of Pasquotank county, Jan., Pasquotank county. R. R. Jan. 28, 1808

Boyd, James to Lucy Lyne of Granville county, Jly., Warren county. R. R. Jly. 28, 1808

Branch, Thomas of Southampton to Emily Bynum, Oct. 18, Northampton county. R. R. Oct. 27, 1808

Brown, Henry to Lucia Messick, Oct. 7, Surry county. R. R. Oct. 20, 1808

Bryan, Maria to J. Justice, Dec. 31, Newbern. R. R. Jan. 14, 1808

Burwell, S. of Mecklenburg county, Va. to Miss Marshall of Granville county, Oct. R. R. Oct. 13, 1808

Bynum, Emily to Thomas Branch of Southampton, Oct. 18, Northampton county. R. R. Oct. 27, 1808

Camp, Mrs. to Durrel Rogers, Mar., Wake county. R. R. Mar. 10, 1808

Cooper, Sally to Richard Davis, Oct., Wake county. R. R. Oct. 27, 1808

Cowan, Joseph of Danville, Va. to Susan Hart of Caswell county, Je. 2. R. R. Je. 9, 1808

Davis, Hyder Aly of South Carolina to Eliza Jones, My. 26, Northampton county. R. R. Je. 2, 1808

Davis, Richard to Sally Cooper, Oct., Wake county. R. R. Oct. 27, 1808

Donoho, Polly of Caswell county, to John C. Eliot of Rutherford county, Feb. 24. R. R. Mar. 10, 1808

Eakin, John to Sally Walker of Rutherford county, Aug. 18, Rutherfordton. R. R. Sept. 15, 1808

Easton, Miss E. H. S. to John Kennedy of Beaufort county, Feb. 25, Milton, Pitt county. R. R. Mar. 3, 1808

Elliot, John C. of Rutherford county to Polly Donoho of Caswell county, Feb. 24. R. R. Mar. 10, 1808

Fabre, Mrs. Eliza to Samuel Simpson, Aug. 15, Newbern. R. R. Aug. 25, 1808

Gardner, Abigail to Capt. Benj. Simmons, Mar. 17, Jones county. R. R. Apr. 7, 1808

Green, Joseph of Newbern to Sally Arnold, Feb., Craven county. R. R. Feb. 11, 1808

Hamilton, Col. John to Nancy Scott, Apr., Pasquotank county. R. R. Apr. 7, 1808

Hart, Susan of Caswell county to Joseph Cowan of Danville, Va., Je. 2. R. R. Je. 9, 1808

Harvey, Eliza to James C. Stanly, Dec., Newbern. R. R. Dec. 29, 1808

Harvey, Eliza of Washington, Beaufort county to Edmund MacNair, Dec. 21, Washington. R. R. Dec. 29, 1808

Hatch, Mrs. Lemuel of Jones county to John S. West of Craven county, Sept. 11, Newbern. R. R. Sept. 29, 1808

Hatcher, Elizabeth to Allen Hightower, Feb. 24, Caswell county. R. R. Mar. 10, 1808

Haywood, Harriot of this State to Dr. D. Moore of Nashville, Tenn., Aug., Tenn. R. R. Aug. 4, 1808

Hightower, Allen to Elizabeth Hatcher, Feb. 24, Caswell county. R. R. Mar. 10, 1808

Hinton, Jos. B. to Rosa R. Simpkins, My. 19, Newbern. R. R. Je. 2, 1808

Jones, Eliza to Hyder Aly Davis of South Carolina, My. 26, Northampton county. R. R. Je. 2, 1808

Judkins, Nathaniel of Halifax to Sally Pasteur, Nov. 20. R. R. Dec. 29, 1808

Justice, J. to Maria Bryan, Dec. 31, Newbern. R. R. Jan. 14, 1808

Keais, Barbara to Slade Pearce, Oct. 5, Washington, Beaufort county. R. R. Oct. 20, 1808

Kennedy, John of Beaufort county to Miss E. H. S. Easton, Feb. 25, Milton, Pitt county. R. R. Mar. 3, 1808

Lewis, David of Newbern to S. Tignor, Feb., Craven county. R. R. Feb. 11, 1808

Little, Catharine to Edward Wilkinson, Nov. 22, Robeson county. R. R. Dec. 8, 1808

Lyne, Lucy of Granville county to James Boyd, Jly., Warren county. R. R. Jly. 28, 1808

M'Culloch, Major Samuel to Sarah W. Moore, My. 12, Halifax. R. R. My. 19, 1808

Machen, T. W. to Mary Rowe, My. 10, Newbern. R. R. My. 19, 1808

M'Lin, Miss E. to Rich'd Pearson of Rowan county, Mar. 3, Newbern. R. R. Mar. 24, 1808

M'Nair, Edmund of Tarboro to Eliza Harvey of Washington, Beaufort county, Dec. 21, Washington. R. R. Dec. 29, 1808

M'Queen, Ann to Richard Street of Moore county, Je., Chatham county. R. R. Je. 30, 1808

Maney, Eliza to William H. Murfree, Jan. 6, Murfreesborough. R. R. Jan. 14, 1808

Marshall, Miss of Granville county to S. Burwell of Mecklenburg county, Va., Oct. R. R. Oct. 13, 1808

Mason, D. of Halifax county to Dorothea Smith of Northampton county, Apr. 12. R. R. My. 5, 1808

Messick, Lucia to Henry Brown, Oct. 7, Surry county. R. R. Oct. 20, 1808

Moore, Dr. D. of Nashville to Harriot Haywood of this State, Aug., Tenn. R. R. Aug. 4, 1808

Moore, Sarah W. to Major Samuel M'Culloch, My. 12, Halifax. R. R. My. 19, 1808

Morris, Sally to Samuel Pearson, Jan. 12, Raleigh. R. R. Jan. 14, 1808

Murfree, William H. to Eliza Maney, Jan. 6, Murfreesborough. R. R. Jan. 14, 1808

Myatt, Cyrene to John Whitaker, Jr., Apr. 21, Wake county. R. R. Apr. 28, 1808

Paddison, Hannah to John Stewart, Mar. 8, Raleigh. R. R. Mar. 10, 1808

Parker, Theopilus to Mary Toole, Nov. 23, Tarborough. R. R. Jan. 14, 1808

Pasteur, Sally to Nathaniel Judkins of Halifax, Nov. 20. R. R. Dec. 29, 1808

Pearce, Slade to Barbara Keais, Oct. 5, Washington, Beaufort county. R. R. Oct. 20, 1808

Pearson, Rich'd of Rowan county to Miss E. M'Lin, Mar. 3, Newbern. R. R. Mar. 24, 1808

Rice, Marcey of Caswell county to Samuel Watt of Rockingham county, Jan. 28, Caswell county. R. R. Feb. 18, 1808

Roberts, Rev. George of Person county to Mrs. Bethol, Aug. 4, Rockingham. R. R. Aug. 18, 1808

Rowe, Mary to T. W. Machen, My. 10, Newbern. R. R. My. 19, 1808

Scott, Nancy to Col. John Hamilton, Apr., Pasquotank county. R. R. Apr. 7, 1808

Simpkins, Rosa R. to Jos. B. Hinton, My. 19, Newbern. R. R. Je. 2, 1808

Simpson, Samuel to Mrs. Eliza Fabre, Aug. 15, Newbern. R. R. Aug. 25, 1808

Singleton, Ann to J. Tullock, Mar. 3, Caswell county. R. R. Mar. 17, 1808

Slade, Nancy to John Stamps, Jan. 14, Caswell county. R. R. Jan. 21, 1808

Smith, Dorothea of Northampton county to D. Mason of Halifax, Apr. 12. R. R. My. 5, 1808

Stamps, John to Nancy Slade, Jan. 14, Caswell county. R. R. Jan. 21, 1808

Stanley, James C. to Eliza Harvey, Dec., Newbern. R. R. Dec. 29, 1808

Stewart, John to Hannah Paddison, Mar. 8, Raleigh. R. R. Mar. 10, 1808

Street, Richard of Moore county to Ann M'Queen, Je., Chatham county. R. R. Je. 30, 1808

Simmons, Capt. Benj. to Abigail Gardner, Mar. 17, Jones county. R. R. Apr. 7, 1808

Taylor, Ann L. to Henry Young, Aug., Granville county. R. R. Aug. 4, 1808

Thomas, Daniel to Zilly Atkins, Feb. 24, Caswell county. R. R. Mar. 10, 1808

Tignor, S. to David Lewis of Newbern, Feb., Craven county. R. R. Feb. 11, 1808

Toole, Mary to Theopilus Parker, Nov. 23, Tarborough. R. R. Jan. 14, 1808

1809

Alexander, Polly to James Pain, Sept. 20, Warren county. R. R. Oct. 12, 1809

Allen, Barton to Ellen White, Oct. 15, Newbern. R. R. Oct. 26, 1809

Alston, Sally of Franklin county to Robert Harwell of Halifax county, Dec. 7, Franklin county. R. R. Dec. 14, 1809

Backhouse, Allen of Swansboro to Ruthy Wilson of Newbern, Aug. 5, Newbern. R. R. Aug. 17, 1809

Baker, Flora to Duncan Buie, My. 9, Cumberland county. R. R. My. 25, 1809

Barker, Burley to Zilpah Barton, Apr. 27, Caswell county. R. R. My. 18, 1809

Barton, Zilpah to Burley Barker, Apr. 27, Caswell county. R. R. My. 18, 1809

Bell, John to Betsy Dunn, Oct., Wake county. R. R. Oct. 12, 1809

Bettner, Eliza to Thomas M'Lin, Feb. 16, Newbern. R. R. Mar. 9, 1809

Blake, Betsey to Samuel Steel, Mar. 21, Fayetteville. R. R. Mar. 30, 1809

Bond, Nathaniel to Penelope Dickinson, Oct. 15, Edenton. R. R. Oct. 26, 1809

Boone, Daniel of Johnston county to Louisa Boykin of Southampton, Va., Mar. 9, Southampton, Va. R. R. Mar. 23, 1809

Boykin, Louisa of Southampton, Va. to Daniel Boone of Johnston county, Mar. 9, Southampton, Va. R. R. Mar. 23, 1809

Branson, Jane to W. Tyson of Moore county, Jan. 26, Fayetteville. R. R. Feb. 9, 1809

Brown, John B. of Bladen county to Rebecca Bernard, Nov. 23. R. R. Dec. 7, 1809

Bryan, Betsey to Stephen B. Forbes, My. 13, Newbern. R. R. My. 25, 1809

Buchannan, Alex to Jane M. Turner, Jan. 26, Cumberland county. R. R. Feb. 9, 1809

Buck, Richard of Connecticut to Mary Cannon of Newbern, Jly. 29, Newbern. R. R. Aug. 10, 1809

Buie, Duncan to Flora Baker, My. 9, Cumberland county. R. R. My. 25, 1809

Burges, Elizabeth of Camden county to Jethro D. Goodman of Pasquotank county, Oct. 31, Camden county. R. R. Nov. 9, 1809

Burrow, Henry of Randolph county to Sarah Wilson of Fayetteville, Je. 29. R. R. Jly. 13, 1809

Burt, Capt. John to Delilia Lane, Feb. 15, Wake county. R. R. Feb. 23, 1809

Buxton, Frances to Henry M. Cook, Mar., Newbern. R. R. Mar. 30, 1809

Caldwell, Dr. Joseph to Mrs. William Hooper, Aug. 17, Chapel Hill. R. R. Aug. 24, 1809

Cameron, Archibald to Christian M'Keathen, My. 18, Cumberland county. R. R. My. 25, 1809

Campbell, Frances of Orange county to Willie Dilliard of Wake county, Apr. 27, Orange county. R. R. My. 4, 1809

Campbell, Hugh of Fayetteville to Henrietta Anne Mallett, Feb. 14, Wilmington. R. R. Mar. 2, 1809

Campbell, James to Winifred Turner, Apr. 13, Cumberland county. R. R. Apr. 20, 1809

Cannon, Mary of Newbern to Richard Buck of Connecticut, Jly. 29, Newbern. R. R. Aug. 10, 1809

Carney, Mahetabel H. of Newbern to James W. Thompson of Virginia,
Dec. 11. R. R. Dec. 28, 1809

Cash, Mary to Thomas C. Ellerbe of Cheraw, Nov., Wadesborough. R. R.
Dec. 7, 1809

Clinton, Moosely of Fayetteville to Alfred Rowland of Lumberton, My. 21.
R. R. Je. 1, 1809

Cook, Henry M. to Frances Buxton, Mar., Newbern. R. R. Mar. 30, 1809

Cotten, Lemuel to Mrs. Lemuel Standin, Nov. 23, Chowan county. R. R.
Dec. 7, 1809

Creekman, Patsey to John Mayo, Aug. 5, Newbern. R. R. Aug. 17, 1809

Croom, Col. William to Eliza Whitfield, Apr. 20, Lenoir county. R. R.
Apr. 27, 1809

Custis, Dr. Peter of Virginia to Mary N. Pasteur, Apr. 20, Newbern. R. R.
Apr. 27, 1809

Daniel, James of Charlotte, Va. to Mrs. Nancy Macklin of Granville county.
R. R. Sept. 21, 1809

Davis, Betsey to Sterling Pitchford, Sept. 7, Warren county. R. R. Sept.
14, 1809

Davis, Temple to Mark C. Duke, Apr. 27, Warren county. R. R. My. 4,
1809

Denton, Sarah to Duncan Gillespie, Aug. 17, Fayetteville. R. R. Sept. 7,
1809

Dickinson, John to Eliza Mair, Sept. 16, Edenton. R. R. Sept. 21, 1809

Dickinson, Penelope to Nathaniel Bond, Oct. 15, Edenton. R. R. Oct. 26,
1809

Dilliard, Willie of Wake county to Frances Campbell of Orange county,
Apr. 27, Orange county. R. R. My. 4, 1809

Dorsey, Rev. to Mary Outlaw, Oct. 31, Bertie county. R. R. Nov. 9, 1809

Dow, Mary of Fayetteville to Charlie Moore of Lumberton, Dec. 27. R. R.
Jan. 12, 1809

Dowdy, Sally of Chatham county to William Gregory of Moore county,
Mar. R. R. Mar. 23, 1809

Dudley, Ann of Onslow county to Wm. Hill of Duplin county, Mar. 6,
Onslow county. R. R. Mar. 23, 1809

Duke, Mark C. to Temple Davis, Apr. 27, Warren county. R. R. My. 4,
1809

Dunn, Betsy to John Bell, Oct., Wake county. R. R. Oct. 12, 1809

Dyal, Margaret to Thomas Williams, Je. 1, Craven county. R. R. Je. 8,
1809

Ellerbe, Thomas C. of Cheraw to Mary Cash, Nov., Wadesborough. R. R.
Dec. 7, 1809

Eppes, Hon. John W. of Virginia to Martha Jones, Apr. 15, Halifax. R. R.
Apr. 20, 1809

Ernul, Kitty to Daniel Shackelford of Newbern, Dec. 7, Craven county.
R. R. Dec. 21, 1809

Etheridge, C. to Hulda Ferebee, Oct. 31, Currituck county. R. R. Nov. 9,
1809

Ferebee, Hulda to C. Etheridge, Oct. 31, Currituck county. R. R. Nov. 9,
1809

Ferrand, Wm. of Swansborough to Nancy Jones, Apr. 24. R. R. My. 11, 1809
Forbes, Stephen B. to Betsey Bryan, My. 13, Newbern. R. R. My. 25, 1809
Foy, Elizabeth to Edward Mumford, Oct. 12, Craven county. R. R. Oct. 26, 1809
Franklin, John to Elizabeth Handcock, Jan. 24, Craven county. R. R. Feb. 9, 1809
Freeman, Elizabeth to Henry Peterson, Sept. 5, Granville county. R. R. Sept. 21, 1809
Galbreath, Grisella of Cumberland county to John Galbreath of Tennessee, Apr. 6, Cumberland county. R. R. Apr. 20, 1809
Galbreath, John of Tennessee to Grisella Galbreath of Cumberland county, Apr. 6, Cumberland county. R. R. Apr. 20, 1809
Gales, Sarah Weston to Waltham W. Seaton, Mar. 30, Raleigh. R. R. Apr. 6, 1809
Gardner, Ann to Anthony Hatch, Jan. 7, Jones county. R. R. Mar. 2, 1809
Gillespie, Duncan to Sarah Denton, Aug. 17, Fayetteville. R. R. Sept. 7, 1809
Gillespie, Jane of Duplin county to Isaac Wright of Bladen county, Jan. 5. R. R. Mar. 16, 1809
Gilmore, Nancy of Cumberland county to Acrell Myatt of Wake county, Apr. 11, Cumberland county. R. R. My. 4, 1809
Goodman, Jethro D. of Pasquotank county to Elizabeth Burges of Camden county, Oct. 31, Camden county. R. R. Nov. 9, 1809
Goodwin, Samuel to Rebecca Jelks, Jly. 25, Raleigh. R. R. Jly. 27, 1809
Gregory, William of Moore county to Sally Dowdy of Chatham county, Mar. R. R. Mar. 23, 1809
Guion, Margaret of Newbern to Dr. Andrew Scott of Wilmington, Dec. 5. R. R. Dec. 21, 1809
Hails, Susannah R. of Columbia, S. C. to John Murphy of this State, Nov. 14. R. R. Dec. 7, 1809
Handcock, Elizabeth to John Franklin, Jan. 24, Craven county. R. R. Feb. 9, 1809
Hannis, Sally to Thomas Watson, My. 4, Newbern. R. R. My. 11, 1809 .
Harrington, James of Richmond county to Eleanor Wilson, Dec. 28, Marlborough District, S. C. R. R. Jan. 19, 1809
Harris, Edward of Newbern to Sarah Kollock of Elizabethtown, N. J., Je. 5 R. R. Jly. 27, 1809
Harris, Thompson to Miss Stoublefield, My.. Rockingham county. R. R. My. 18, 1809
Harwell, Robert of Halifax county to Sally Alston of Franklin county, Dec. 7, Franklin county. R. R. Dec. 14, 1809
Hatch, Anthony to Ann Gardner, Jan. 7, Jones county. R. R. Mar. 2, 1809
Hatch, Durant, Jr. of Jones county to Mary Russell West of Newbern. Je. 15, Newbern. R. R. Je. 22, 1809
Hatch, Edward of Craven county to Betsey West of Newbern. Feb. 5. R. R. Feb. 9, 1809
Haughton, John of Chowan county to Mary Hooker of Tyrrell county, Je. R. R. Je. 8, 1809
Hawkins, Delia to Stephen Haywood of Raleigh, Aug. 1, Warren county. R. R. Aug. 3, 1809

Haynes, Elizabeth to Jas. P. McKee, Mar. 28, Bladen county. R. R. Apr. 27, 1809

Haywood, Stephen of Raleigh to Delia Hawkins, Aug. 1, Warren county. R. R. Aug. 3, 1809

Hazard, Lot of Warrenton to Esther Pain of Warren county, Dec. 30. R. R. Jan. 5, 1809

Hill, Amelia to Thos. Hutchings, Aug. 10, Newbern. R. R. Aug. 17, 1809

Hill, Margaret to Evan Jones, Nov. 9, Wilmington. R. R. Nov. 23, 1809

Hill, Wm. of Duplin county to Ann Dudley of Onslow county, Mar. 6, Onslow county. R. R. Mar. 23, 1809

Hines, Alexander to Elizabeth Vick, Feb. 14, Nash county. R. R. Feb. 23, 1809

Holmes, James of Sampson county to Sarah Northam, Mar. 15, Sampson county. R. R. Mar. 30, 1809

Hooker, Mary of Tyrrell county to John Haughton of Chowan county, Je. R. R. Je. 8, 1809

Hooper, Mrs. William to Dr. Joseph Caldwell, Aug. 17, Chapel Hill. R. R. Aug. 24, 1809

Howard, Henry B. to Miss Nutt, Jly. 13, New Hanover county. R. R. Jly. 27, 1809

Hutchings, Thos. to Amelia Hill, Aug. 10, Newbern. R. R. Aug. 17, 1809

James, Mary to Daniel L. Kenan, Mar. 13, Duplin county. R. R. Mar. 30, 1809

Jelks, Rebecca to Samuel Goodwin, Jly. 25, Raleigh. R. R. Jly. 27, 1809

Jocelyn, Samuel R. to Mary Ann Simpson of Sampson county, Jly. 4, Wilmington. R. R. Jly. 13, 1809

Johnson, Miss to W. Watson, Jly. 1, Halifax. R. R. Jly. 6, 1809

Jones, Mrs. Allen to Wm. Wright of Southampton, Va., Northampton county, My. R. R. Je. 1, 1809

Jones, Evan to Margaret Hill, Nov. 9, Wilmington. R. R. Nov. 23, 1809

Jones, Martha to Hon. John W. Eppes of Virginia, Apr. 15, Halifax. R. R. Apr. 20, 1809

Jones, Nancy to Wm. Ferrand of Swansborough, Apr. 24. R. R. My. 11, 1809

Keais, Capt. Henry to Julia Videll, Apr., Washington. R. R. Apr. 27, 1809

Kenan, Daniel L. to Mary James, Mar. 13, Duplin county. R. R. Mar. 30, 1809

Kennan, Elizabeth to Rev. David L. White of Bladen county, Jly. 6, Putnam county, Ga. R. R. Aug. 10, 1809

Kollock, Sarah of Elizabethtown, N. J. to Edward Harris of Newbern, Je. 5, Elizabethtown, N. J. R. R. Jly. 27, 1809

Lamon, Margaret of Fayetteville to Samuel Storm of Lumberton, Apr. 11, Fayetteville. R. R. Apr. 20, 1809

Latham, Agnes to Dempsey H. Williams, Apr., Newbern. R. R. Apr. 20, 1809

Lea, John to Delia Poe, Dec. 29, Chatham county. R. R. Jan. 19, 1809

Long, Mrs. G. W. of Halifax to Maj. Robert Park of Warren county, Oct. 5. R. R. Oct. 12, 1809

M'Allister, Alexander of Cumberland county to Anne Wright, Je. 1, Duplin county. R. R. Je. 15, 1809

MARRIAGE NOTICES

M'Coll, Duncan to Barbara M'Leod, Jly. 27, Fayetteville. R. R. Aug. 3, 1809

M'Keathen, Christian to Archibald Cameron, My. 18, Cumberland county. R. R. My. 25, 1809

M'Kee, Jas. P. to Elizabeth Haynes, Mar. 28, Bladen county. R. R. Apr. 27, 1809

M'Kinne, Elizabeth to Nicholson Washington of Waynesboro, Aug. 1, Wayne county. R. R. Aug. 17, 1809

M'Leod, Barbara to Duncan M'Coll, Jly. 27, Fayetteville. R. R. Aug. 3, 1809

M'Lin Thomas to Eliza Bettner, Feb. 16, Newbern. R. R. Mar. 9, 1809

M'Neill, J. to Sarah M'Neill, Nov. 7, Robeson county. R. R. Nov. 16, 1809

M'Neill, Sarah to J. M'Neill, Nov. 7, Robeson county. R. R. Nov. 16, 1809

McPherson, Catharine of Cumberland county to John M'Rae of Augusta, Ga., Je. 1. R. R. Je. 8, 1809

M'Rae, John of Augusta, Ga. to Catherine M'Pherson of Cumberland county, Je. 1. R. R. Je. 8, 1809

Mabson, Samuel C. to Elizabeth Moore, My. 18, Cedar Grove on the Sound. R. R. Je. 1, 1809

Mackay, Mary of Currituck county to Abner N. Vail of Chowan county, Nov. 23, Currituck county. R. R. Dec. 7, 1809

Macklin, Mrs. Nancy of Granville county to James Daniel of Charlotte, Va. R. R. Sept. 21, 1809

Mair, Eliza to John Dickinson, Sept. 16, Edenton. R. R. Sept. 21, 1809

Mallett, Henrietta Ann to Hugh Campbell of Fayetteville, Feb. 14, Wilmington. R. R. Mar. 2, 1809

Mayo, John to Patsey Creekman, Aug. 5, Newbern. R. R. Aug. 17, 1809

Moore, Charles of Lumberton to Mary Dow of Fayetteville, Dec. 27. R. R. Jan. 12, 1809

Moore, Elizabeth to Samuel C. Mabson, My. 18, Cedar Grove on the Sound. R. R. Je. 1, 1809

Mumford, Edward to Elizabeth Foy, Oct. 12, Craven county. R. R. Oct. 26, 1809

Mumford, Elizabeth to Maj. James Owen of Bladen county, My. 16, Fayetteville. R. R. My. 25, 1809

Murphy, John of this State to Susannah R. Hails of Columbia, S. C., Nov. 14. R. R. Dec. 7, 1809

Myatt, Acrell of Wake county to Nancy Gilmore of Cumberland county. Apr. 11, Cumberland county. R. R. My. 4, 1809

North, Seth to Mrs. Picket, My. 13, Newbern. R. R. My. 25, 1809

Northam, Sarah to James Holmes of Sampson county, Mar. 15, Sampson county. R. R. Mar. 30, 1809

Nutt, Miss to Henry B. Howard, Jly. 13, New Hanover county. R. R. Jly. 27, 1809

Outlaw, Mary to Rev. Dorsey, Oct. 31, Bertie county. R. R. Nov. 9, 1809

Owen, Maj. James of Bladen county to Elizabeth Mumford, My. 16, Fayetteville. R. R. My. 25, 1809

Pain, Esther of Warren county to Lot Hazard of Warrenton, Dec. 30. R. R. Jan. 5, 1809

Pain, James to Polly Alexander, Sept. 20, Warren county. R. R. Oct. 12, 1809

40

Park, Maj. Robert of Warren county to Mrs. G. W. Long of Halifax, Oct. 5.
R. R. Oct. 12, 1809

Parker, William to Cresy Vann, Feb. 16, Fayetteville. R. R. Mar. 2, 1809

Parks, Elizabeth of Newbern to William Spellings of Washington, Jly. 11,
Newbern. R. R. Jly. 20, 1809

Pasteur, Mary N. to Dr. Peter Custis of Virginia, Apr. 20, Newbern. R. R.
Apr. 27, 1809

Peale, John to Mrs. Lany Smith, Jly. 23, Fayetteville. R. R. Aug. 3, 1809

Pearce, Eliza to Dr. Benjamin Robinson, Feb. 16, Fayetteville. R. R. Mar.
2, 1809

Peterson, Henry to Elizabeth Freeman, Sept. 5, Granville county. R. R.
Sept. 21, 1809

Picket, Mrs. to Seth North, My. 13, Newbern. R. R. My. 25, 1809

Pitchford, Sterling to Betsey Davis, Sept. 7, Warren county. R. R. Sept.
14, 1809

Poe, Delia to John Lea, Dec. 29, Chatham county. R. R. Jan. 19, 1809

Reichel, Sophia D. to Rev. Charles F. Seidel, Je. 5, Stokes county. R. R.
Je. 15, 1809

Riddle, Sarah to David Smith of Fayetteville, Oct. 19, Chatham county.
R. R. Nov. 9, 1809

Robinson, Dr. Benjamin to Eliza Pearce, Feb. 16, Fayetteville. R. R. Mar.
2, 1809

Rowland, Alfred of Lumberton to Moosely Clinton of Fayetteville, My. 21.
R. R. Je. 1, 1809

Ryan, Mrs. Cornelius to Capt. Daniel Young, Jly. 18, Bertie county. R. R.
Jly. 26, 1809

Sampson, Mary Ann of Sampson county to Samuel R. Jocelyn, Jly. 4,
Wilmington. R. R. Jly. 6, 1809

Scott, Dr. Andrew of Wilmington to Margaret Guion of Newbern, Dec. 5.
R. R. Dec. 21, 1809

Scull, Jane to N. Williams of Wilmington, Nov. 24. R. R. Dec. 7, 1809

Seaton, Waltham W. to Sara Weston Gales, Mar. 30, Raleigh. R. R.
Apr. 6, 1809

Seidel, Rev. Charles F. to Sophia D. Reichel, Je. 5, Stokes county. R. R.
Je. 15, 1809

Shackelford, Daniel of Newbern to Kitty Ernul, Dec. 7, Craven county.
R. R. Dec. 21, 1809

Skinner, Elizabeth of Perquimons county to Wm. Wilson of Pasquotank
county, Sept. 12, Perquimons county. R. R. Sept. 21, 1809

Smiley, Nathaniel to Margaret Smith, Nov. 23, Richmond county. R. R.
Dec. 14, 1809

Smith, David of Fayetteville to Sarah Riddle, Oct. 19, Chatham county.
R. R. Nov. 9, 1809

Smith, David of Pitt county to Miss Smith of Greenville, My. 7. R. R.
Je. 1, 1809

Smith, Miss of Greenville to David Smith of Pitt county, My. 7. R. R.
Je. 1, 1809

Smith, Mrs. Lany to John Peale, Jly. 23, Fayetteville. R. R. Aug. 3, 1809

Smith, Margaret to Nathaniel Smiley, Nov. 23, Richmond county. R. R.
Dec. 14, 1809

Spellings, William of Washington to Elizabeth Parks of Newbern, Jly. 11, Newbern. R. R. Jly. 20, 1809

Spier, Julia to Hugh Telfair, Apr., Washington. R. R. Apr. 27, 1809

Standin, Mrs. Lemuel to Lemuel Cotten, Nov. 23, Chowan county. R. R. Dec. 7, 1809

Steel, Samuel to Betsey Blake, Mar. 21, Fayetteville. R. R. Mar. 30, 1809

Storm, Samuel of Lumberton to Margaret Lamon of Fayetteville, Apr. 11, Fayetteville. R. R. Apr. 20, 1809

Stoublefield, Miss to Thompson Harris, My., Rockingham county. R. R. My. 18, 1809

Stuart, Robert to Mary R. Thompson of Fayetteville, Jan. 4, Tarborough. R. R. Jan. 19, 1809

Syler, Ann of Moore county to Cornelius Tyson of Chatham county, Jan. 5, Moore county. R. R. Jan. 19, 1809

Telfair, Hugh to Julia Spier, Apr., Washington. R. R. Apr. 27, 1809

Thompson, James W. of Virginia to Mahetabel H. Carney of Newbern, Dec. 11. R. R. Dec. 28, 1809

Thompson, Mary R. of Fayetteville to Robert Stuart, Jan. 4, Tarborough. R. R. Jan. 19, 1809

Turner, Jane M. to Alex Buchannan, Jan. 26, Cumberland county. R. R. Feb. 9, 1809

Turner, Winifred to James Campbell, Apr. 13, Cumberland county. R. R. Aug. 20, 1809

Tyson, Cornelius of Chatham county to Ann Syler of Moore county, Jan. 5, Moore county. R. R. Jan. 19, 1809

Tyson, W. of Moore county to Jane Branson, Jan 26, Fayetteville. R. R. Feb. 9, 1809

Vail, Abner N. of Chowan county to Mary Mackay of Currituck county, Nov. 23, Currituck county. R. R. Dec. 7, 1809

Vann, Cresy to William Parker, Feb. 16, Fayetteville. R. R. Mar. 2, 1809

Vick, Elizabeth to Alexander Hines, Feb. 14, Nash county. R. R. Feb. 23, 1809

Videll, Julia to Capt. Henry Keais, Apr., Washington. R. R. Apr. 27, 1809

Washington, Nicholson of Waynesboro to Elizabeth M'Kinne, Aug. 1, Wayne county. R. R. Aug. 17, 1809

Watson, Thomas to Sally Hannis, My. 4, Newbern. R. R. My. 11, 1809

Watson, W. to Miss Johnson, Jly. 1, Halifax. R. R. Jly. 6, 1809

West, Betsy of Newbern to Edward Hatch of Craven county, Feb. 5. R. R. Feb. 9, 1809

West, Mary Russell of Newbern to Durant Hatch, Jr. of Jones county, Je. 15, Newbern. R. R. Je. 22, 1809

White, Rev. David L. of Bladen county to Elizabeth Kennon, Jly. 6, Putnam county, Ga. R. R. Aug. 10, 1809

White, Ellen to Burton Allen, Oct. 15, Newbern. R. R. Oct. 26, 1809

Whitfield, Eliza to Col. William Croom, Apr. 20, Lenoir county. R. R. Apr. 27, 1809

Williams, Dempsy H. to Agnes Latham, Apr., Newbern. R. R. Apr. 20, 1809

Williams, N. of Wilmington to Jane Scull, Nov. 24. R. R. Dec. 7, 1809

Williams, Thomas to Margaret Dyal, Je. 1, Craven county. R. R. Je. 8, 1809

Wilson, Eleanor to James Harrington of Richmond county, Dec. 28, Marlborough District, S. C.   R. R. Jan. 19, 1809

Wilson, Ruthy of Newbern to Allen Backhouse of Swansboro, Aug. 5, Newbern.   R. R. Aug. 17, 1809

Wilson, Sarah of Fayetteville to Henry Burrow of Randolph county, Je. 29.   R. R. Jly. 13, 1809

Wilson, Wm. of Pasquotank county to Elizabeth Skinner of Perquimons county, Sept. 12, Perquimons county.   R. R. Sept. 21, 1809

Wright, Anne to Alexander M'Allister of Cumberland county, Je. 1, Duplin county.   R. R. Je. 15, 1809

Wright, Isaac of Bladen county to Jane Gillespie of Duplin county, Jan. 5.   R. R. Mar. 16, 1809

Wright, Wm. of Southampton, Va. to Mrs. Allen Jones of Northampton county, My.   R. R. Je. 1, 1809

1810

Alston, Eliza of Warren county to Wm. Williams of Halifax county, My. 1.   R. R. My. 10, 1810

Alston, Maria to William Carney, Jly., Warren county.   R. R. Jly. 26, 1810

Andres, William, Jr. to Abby Creek, Aug. 30, Orange county.   R. R. Sept. 13, 1810

Arnold, Rev. Bridges A. to Rachael Cradwick, Nov. 7, Beaufort, Carteret county.   R. R. Nov. 22, 1810

Askew, Peggy to George Outlaw, Jr., Feb., Bertie county.   R. R. Feb. 8, 1810

Austin, Oliver to Sarah Cox, Apr. 9, Beaufort, Carteret county.   R. R. Apr. 19, 1810

Baker, Dr. John B. to Mary Gregory, My. 15, Gates county.   R. R. My. 24, 1810

Baker, John to Christian M'Donald, Jly. 19, Cumberland county.   R. R. Aug. 2, 1810

Balch, Ann K. of Bedford county, Tenn., to Zeno Cambell of Cabarrus county, Jly. 26.   R. R. Aug. 23, 1810

Barbee, Josiah to Clary Beasley, Apr. 23, Wake county.   R. R. My. 3, 1810

Beasley, Clary to Josiah Barbee, Apr. 23, Wake county.   R. R. My. 3, 1810

Bent, James R. of Edenton to Sally Hathaway of Chowan county, Je. 17, Edenton.   R. R. Je. 28, 1810

Bent, Mary to Nathan K. Strong, Apr. 22, Granville county.   R. R. My. 3, 1810

Beze, Jane to Peter Perry, My. 12, Fayetteville.   R. R. My. 24, 1810

Biddle, Rev. Mr. to Polly Simpson, Feb. 8, Craven county.   R. R. Feb. 15, 1810

Bland, Henry to Mary Ray, Feb. 25, Raleigh.   R. R. Mar. 1, 1810

Blount, Patsey of Chowan county to M'Cottor of Edenton, Sept. 11, Edenton.   R. R. Sept. 13, 1810

Blount, Thomas H. of Washington, Beaufort county to Eleanor Margaret Brown of Charles county, Md., Nov. 13, Washington, D. C.   R. R. Nov. 22, 1810

Boddie, Rebecca of Nash county to James Peters of Wake county, Mar. 22.   R. R. Apr. 5, 1810

Boon, Nancy to Wm. Lumsden, Feb. 15, Fayetteville.   R. R. Mar. 1, 1810

Boykin, William to Mrs. Harris, Dec. 10, Scotland Neck. R. R. Jan. 4, 1810

Bradley, Martha of Bladen county to Thomas Morgan of Fayetteville, Feb. R. R. Feb. 22, 1810

Bragg, John to Catharine Hall of Newbern, Je. 24, Portsmouth. R. R. Jly. 12, 1810

Branch, Mrs. of Nash county to Nathaniel Hunt of Franklin, Apr. R. R. Apr. 5, 1810

Branch, Patience W. of Halifax county to Rev. Daniel Southall of Gates Court House, Sept. 2, Halifax county. R. R. Sept. 13, 1810

Bright, Elizabeth to Edward Hodges, Je. 26, Currituck county. R. R. Jly. 12, 1810

Brodie John of Warren county to Martha Williams, Dec. 25, Franklin county. R. R. Jan. 4, 1810

Brown, Eleanor Margaret of Charles county, Md. to Thomas H. Blount of Washington, Beaufort county, Nov. 13, Washington, D. C. R. R. Nov. 22, 1810

Brown, Lucy J. to James Marshall of Wilmington, Aug. 9, Bladen county. R. R. Sept. 13, 1810

Brown, Robert W. of Wilmington to Atha Wingate of Fayetteville, Mar. 25. R. R. Apr. 5, 1810

Burch, Thomas D. of Raleigh to Mary H. Davis of Fayetteville, Mar. 8, Fayetteville. R. R. Mar. 22, 1810

Butler, Joseph of Bladen county to Mrs. Elizabeth Thames of Cumberland county, Feb. 1. R. R. Feb. 15, 1810

Cambell, Zeno of Cabarrus county to Ann K. Balch of Bedford county, Tenn., Jly. 20. R. R. Aug. 23, 1810

Cannon, Robert of Raleigh to Nancy Hill of Franklin, My. 2. R. R. My. 10, 1810

Caraway, Gideon to Louraine Sparrow of Craven county, Je. 17, Smith's creek. R. R. Jly. 12, 1810

Carney, William to Maria Alston, Jly., Warren county. R. R. Jly. 26, 1810

Carter, Rebecca of Chatham county to Col. Nicholas Long of Person county, Nov. 4, Chatham county. R. R. Nov. 22, 1810

Clardy, John to Margaret Moss, Apr., Granville county. R. R. My. 3, 1810

Clifton, Sarah of Southampton, Va. to William H. Hardie of Halifax county, My. 22. R. R. Je. 7, 1810

Collier, Mrs. Charles of Orange county to Lee Johnston of Wake county, Jly. 5, Orange county. R. R. Aug. 2, 1810

Cooke, Thomas of Newbern to Esther Wallace, Apr. 8, Beaufort. R. R. Apr. 19, 1810

Cox, Sarah to Oliver Austin, Apr. 9, Beaufort. R. R. Apr. 19, 1810

Cradwick, Rachael to Rev. Bridges A. Arnold, Nov. 7, Beaufort, Carteret county. R. R. Nov. 22, 1810

Creek, Abby to William Andres, Jr., Aug. 30, Orange county. R. R. Sept. 13, 1810

Cressy, Sarah Ann of Newbern to Dr. Lewis G. Haywood, Apr. 16, Spring Hill. R. R. My. 17, 1810

Croom, Jesse to Polly Hurdy, Feb. 25, Wayne county. R. R. Mar. 8, 1810

Cushing, Isaac T. to Elizabeth Langsdale, Jan. 11, Fayetteville. R. R. Jan. 18, 1810

Davis, Martha to Thomas Reaves of Orange county, Dec. 24, Wake county. R. R. Feb. 15, 1810

Davis, Mary H. of Fayetteville to Thomas D. Burch of Raleigh, Mar. 8, Fayetteville. R. R. Mar. 22, 1810

Davis, Thomas Junius of New Hanover county to Elizabeth M. Waters of Chatham county, Sept. 5, Chatham county. R. R. Sept. 27, 1810

Dick, Eliza of Fayetteville to James Neate of Wilmington, Jly. 19, Fayetteville. R. R. Aug. 2, 1810

Edwards, Sarah to Pleasant Hall, Oct. 28, Halifax. R. R. Nov. 15, 1810

Erby, Elizabeth of Prince George, Va. to Harwood Jones of Northampton county, Sept. 20, Northampton county. R. R. Sept. 27, 1810

Fields, Jas. to Mary Mullen, Sept., Newbern. R. R. Sept. 13, 1810

Foort, Ricks to Patsey Whitaker, Nov., Halifax county. R. R. Nov. 22, 1810

Foxhall, William to Nancy Jackson, Apr. 3, Edgecombe county. R. R. Apr. 12, 1810

Geke, Mary to Wm. Wilkings, My. 10, Wilmington. R. R. My. 31, 1810

Gessar, Mary A. to J. S. Springs, Apr. 8, Wilmington. R. R. Apr. 19, 1810

Giles, John of Jones county to Hannah Williams, Feb. 9, Duplin county. R. R. Mar. 1, 1810

Gillespie, B. C. of Newbern to Mrs. Hargett of Jones county, Oct. R. R. Nov. 1, 1810

Gilmore, Stephen, Jr. of Cumberland county to Mary N. Miller, Mar. 20, Bladen county. R. R. Mar. 29, 1810

Gilmour, William of Halifax to Polly W. Parsons of Prince George, Va., Mar. 15. R. R. Mar. 29, 1810

Greer, Theresa Maria of Rockfish to Wm. I. Love of Wilmington, Je. 21. R. R. Jly. 5, 1810

Gregory, Mary to Dr. John B. Baker, My. 15, Gates county. R. R. My. 24, 1810

Hall, Catharine to John Bragg of Newbern, Je. 24, Portsmouth. R. R. Jly. 12, 1810

Hall, Emma of Petersburg, Va. to Gideon Johnson of Warren county, Jly. 5. R. R. Jly. 12, 1810

Hall, Pleasant to Sarah Edwards, Oct. 28, Halifax. R. R. Nov. 15, 1810

Handen, Mary to Dr. M'Dowell, Nov. 4, Bladen county. R. R. Dec. 6, 1810

Hanks, William to Patsey Moore of Surry county, Oct. 11. R. R. Nov. 15, 1810

Hardie, William H. of Halifax county to Sarah Clifton of Southampton, Va., My. 22. R. R. Je. 7, 1810

Hargett, Mrs. of Jones county to B. C. Gillespie of Newbern, Oct. R. R. Nov. 1, 1810

Harris, Mrs. to William Boykin, Dec. 10, Scotland Neck. R. R. Jan. 4, 1810

Harwell, Marcus A. of Halifax to Elizabeth Moore, My. 17. R. R. My. 24, 1810

Hathaway, Sally of Chowan county to James R. Bent of Edenton, Je. 17, Edenton. R. R. Je. 28, 1810

Hawkins, Thomas to Mrs. Moss, Sept. 26, Warren county. R. R. Oct. 11, 1810

Haywood, John to Miss Huckabee, Jly. 25, Franklin county. R. R. Aug. 9, 1810

Haywood, Dr. Lewis G. to Sarah Ann Cressy of Newbern, Apr. 16, Spring-Hill. R. R. My. 17, 1810

Hill, Nancy of Franklin to Robert Cannon of Raleigh, My. 2. R. R. My. 10, 1810

Hill, Sarah to Lewis H. Toomer, Nov. 22, Wilmington. R. R. Dec. 6, 1810

Hodges, Edward to Elizabeth Bright, Je. 26, Currituck county. R. R. Jly. 12, 1810

Hogan, John of Halifax county to E. Hoskins of Chowan county, Apr. 20. R. R. My. 3, 1810

Holliday, Robert of Fayetteville to Catherine M'Queen of Chatham county, Sept. 18, Chatham county. R. R. Sept. 27, 1810

Horniblow, Mary to Dr. James Norcom, Jly. 22, Edenton. R. R. Aug. 2, 1810

Hoskins, E. of Chowan county to John Hogan of Halifax county, Apr. 20. R. R. My. 3, 1810

Hoskins, William to Mrs. Peggy Norfleet, Mar. 6, Edenton. R. R. Mar. 22, 1810

Huckabee, Miss to John Haywood, Jly. 25, Franklin county. R. R. Aug. 9, 1810

Hunt, Nathaniel of Franklin to Mrs. Branch of Nash county, Apr. R. R. Apr. 5, 1810

Hurdy, Polly to Jesse Croom, Feb. 25, Wayne county. R. R. Mar. 8, 1810

Hyman, Samuel of Williamston to Nancy Bryan of Bertie county, Feb. R. R. Feb. 8, 1810

Jackson, Nancy to William Foxhall, Apr. 3, Edgecombe county. R. R. Apr. 12, 1810

Jasper, William to Esther Shepard, Apr. 9, Beaufort. R. R. Apr. 19, 1810

Jennings, John of Anson county to Nancy Stairet of Fayetteville, Dec. 18. R. R. Jan. 11, 1810

Johnson, Gideon of Warren county to Emma Hall of Petersburg, Va., Jly. 5. R. R. Jly. 12, 1810

Johnston, Elizabeth to John Martin, Feb. 15, Fayetteville. R. R. Mar. 1, 1810

Johnston, Lee of Wake county to Mrs. Charles Collier of Orange county, Jly. 5, Orange county. R. R. Aug. 2, 1810

Johnston, Mrs. William to James Turner, Jly. 21, Warren county. R. R. Jly. 26, 1810

Jones, Atlas to Rebecca Street, Je. 7, Moore county. R. R. Je. 14, 1810

Jones, Capt. Cadwaller to Rebecca Long, Nov. 6, Halifax. R. R. Nov. 15, 1810

Jones, Elizabeth to Jos. Perry, Mar. 1, Halifax county. R. R. Mar. 8, 1810

Jones, Francis to Sarah Stewart, Je. 12, Edenton. R. R. Jly. 21, 1810

Jones, Harwood of Northampton county to Elizabeth Erby of Prince George, Va., Sept. 20, Northampton county. R. R. Sept. 27, 1810

Jones, Penelope of Johnston county to Willie Jones of Wake county, Dec. 28. R. R. Jan. 4, 1810

Jones, Richard B. of Philadelphia to Frances A. Leach of Newbern, Sept. 9. R. R. Sept. 27, 1810

Jones, Sally of Carteret county to Solomon B. Shanawolf, Sept. 1. R. R.
Sept. 13, 1810

Jones, Willie of Wake county to Penelope Jones of Johnston county, Dec.
28. R. R. Jan. 4, 1810

King, Mary Ann to Hugh M'Lean, Dec. 8, Fayetteville. R. R. Dec. 20, 1810

Kirkland, Ann to Thomas C. Ruffin, Jan., Hillsboro. R. R. Jan. 11, 1810

Langsdale, Elizabeth to Isaac T. Cushing, Jan. 11, Fayetteville. R. R.
Jan. 18, 1810

Lea, Nancy of Chatham county to Thomas Smith of Mecklenburg county,
Aug. 9, Chatham county. R. R. Aug. 16, 1810

Leach, Frances A. of Newbern to Richard B. Jones of Philadelphia, Sept.
9. R. R. Sept. 27, 1810

Leecraft, Nancy to Daniel Perry, Apr. 9, Beaufort. R. R. Apr. 19, 1810

Lewis, Dr. Mills of Virginia to Polly Wiggins of Edgecombe county, Jly. 10.
R. R. Aug. 23, 1810

Lisle, Anne of Gloucester county, Va. to George M'Williams, Apr. 5, Tarborough. R. R. Apr. 19, 1810

Long, Col. Nicholas of Person county to Rebecca Carter of Chatham
county, Nov. 4, Chatham county. R. R. Nov. 22, 1810

Long, Rebecca to Capt. Cadwaller Jones, Nov. 6, Halifax. R. R. Nov. 15,
1810

Love, Wm. I. of Wilmington to Theresa Maria Greer of Rockfish, Je. 21.
R. R. Jly. 5, 1810

Lumsden, Wm. to Nancy Boon, Feb. 15, Fayetteville. R. R. Mar. 1, 1810

M'Cottor, John of Edenton to Patsey Blount of Chowan county, Sept. 11,
Edenton. R. R. Sept. 13, 1810

M'Donald, Christian to John Baker, Jly. 19, Cumberland county. R. R.
Aug. 2, 1810

M'Dowell, Dr. to Mary Handen, Nov. 4, Bladen county. R. R. Dec. 6, 1810

M'Lean, Hugh to Mary Ann King, Dec. 8, Fayetteville. R. R. Dec. 20,
1810

M'Lean, Hugh to Peggy Peabody, Sept. 25, Cumberland county. R. R.
Oct. 11, 1810

Macmain, Margaret to James Seydan, Apr. 14, Newbern. R. R. Apr. 19,
1810

M'Queen, Catharine of Chatham county to Robert Holliday of Fayetteville,
Sept. 18, Chatham county. R. R. Sept. 27, 1810

M'Williams, George to Anne Lisle of Gloucester county, Va., Apr. 5, Tarborough. R. R. Apr. 19, 1810

Marshall, James of Wilmington to Lucy J. Brown, Aug. 9, Bladen county.
R. R. Sept. 13, 1810

Martin, John to Elizabeth Johnston, Feb. 15, Fayetteville. R. R. Mar. 1,
1810

Miller, Mary N. to Stephen Gilmore, Jr. of Cumberland county, Mar. 20,
Bladen county. R. R. Mar. 29, 1810

Mitchell, Elizabeth to Bazel S. Orme, Apr. 14, Newbern. R. R. Apr. 19,
1810

Moore, Elizabeth to Marcus A. Harwell of Halifax, My. 17. R. R. My. 24,
1810

Moore, Patsy of Surry county to William Hanks, Oct. 11. R. R. Nov. 15, 1810

Morgan, Thomas of Fayetteville to Martha Bradley of Bladen county, Feb. R. R. Feb. 22, 1810

Moss, Margaret to John Clardy, Apr., Granville county. R. R. My. 3, 1810

Moss, Mrs. to Thomas Hawkins, Sept. 26, Warren county. R. R. Oct. 11, 1810

Mulle, Mary to Jas. Fields, Sept., Newbern. R. R. Sept. 13, 1810

Neate, James of Wilmington to Eliza Dick of Fayetteville, Jly. 19, Fayetteville. R. R. Aug. 2, 1810

Norcom, Dr. James to Mary Horniblow, Jly. 22, Edenton. R. R. Aug. 2, 1810

Norfleet, James to Mary O'Malley, Jly. 14, Edenton. R. R. Jly. 26, 1810

Norfleet, Peggy to William Hoskins, Mar. 6, Edenton. R. R. Mar. 22, 1810

Nott, Jas. K. to Mary Williamson, Je. 21, Caswell county. R. R. Je. 28, 1810

O'Malley, Mary to James Norfleet, Jly. 14, Edenton. R. R. Jly. 26, 1810

Orme, Bazel S. to Elizabeth Mitchell, Apr. 14, Newbern. R. R. Apr. 19, 1810

Outlaw, George, Jr. to Peggy Askew, Feb., Bertie county. R. R. Feb. 8, 1810

Parsons, Polly W. of Prince George, Va. to William Gilmour of Halifax, Mar. 15. R. R. Mar. 29, 1810

Peabody, Peggy to Hugh M'Lean, Sept. 25, Cumberland county. R. R. Oct. 11, 1810

Pearson, Col. J. A. of Rowan county to Mrs. B. M. Willson, Sept. 6. R. R. Sept. 27, 1810

Peck, William of Raleigh to Martha Williams of Virginia, Jan., Orange county. R. R. Jan. 11, 1810

Perry, Daniel to Nancy Leecraft, Apr. 9, Beaufort county. R. R. Apr. 19, 1810

Perry, Jos. to Elizabeth Jones, Mar. 1, Halifax county. R. R. Mar. 8, 1810

Perry, Peter to Jane Beze, My. 12, Fayetteville. R. R. My. 24, 1810

Peters, James of Wake county to Rebecca Boddie of Nash county, Mar. 22. R. R. Apr. 5, 1810

Pugh, Ann of Martin county to Wm. Williams, My. 22, Williamston. R. R. My. 31, 1810

Ray, Mary to Henry Bland, Feb. 25, Raleigh. R. R. Mar. 1, 1810

Reeves, Thomas of Orange county to Martha Davis, Dec. 24, Wake county. R. R. Feb. 15, 1810

Reed, Rebecca to Joseph Sutton of Chowan county, Jly. 31, Perquimans county. R. R. Aug. 16, 1810

Rogers, Rachael E. to John Vanhook, Dec. 9, Person county. R. R. Dec. 20, 1810

Ruffin, Thomas C. to Ann Kirkland, Jan., Hillsboro. R. R. Jan. 11, 1810

Sackett, Richard to Mrs. Samuel Fisher, Feb., Newbern. R. R. Feb. 8, 1810

Sanders, Margaret of Brunswick to Robert A. Taylor of Lewisburg, Feb. 14, Brunswick county, Va. R. R. Feb. 22, 1810

Sawyer, Lemuel to Mary Snowden, Aug. 11, Camden county. R. R. Aug. 23, 1810

Seydan, James to Margaret Macmain, Apr. 14, Newbern. R. R. Apr. 19, 1810

Shanawolf, Solomon B. of Newbern to Sally Jones of Carteret county, Sept. 1, R. R. Sept. 13, 1810

Shelton, Martha to William Wooten, Dec. 19, Halifax county. R. R. Jan. 4, 1810

Shelton, Polly S. of Iredell county to Rev. William W. Sheppard of Surry county, Jan. 1. R. R. Sept. 8, 1810

Shepard, Esther to William Jasper, Apr. 9, Beaufort. R. R. Apr. 19, 1810

Shepperd, Rev. Wm. W. of Surry county to Polly S. Shelton of Iredell county, Jan. 1. R. R. Feb. 8, 1810

Simpson, Polly to Rev. Mr. Biddle, Feb. 8, Craven county. R. R. Feb. 15, 1810

Smith, Thomas of Mecklenburg county to Nancy Lea of Chatham county, Aug. 9, Chatham county. R. R. Aug. 16, 1810

Snowden, Mary to Lemuel Sawyer, Aug. 11, Camden county. R. R. Aug. 23, 1810

Southall, Rev. Daniel of Gates Court-House to Patience W. Branch of Halifax county, Sept. 2, Halifax county. R. R. Sept. 13, 1810

Sparrow, Louraine to Gideon Caraway of Craven county, Je. 17, Smith's creek. R. R. Jly. 12, 1810

Springs, J. S. to Mary A. Gessar, Apr. 8, Wilmington. R. R. Apr. 19, 1810

Stairet, Nancy of Fayetteville to John Jennings of Anson county, Dec. 18. R. R. Jan. 11, 1810

Stewart, Sarah to Francis Jones, Je. 12, Edenton. R. R. Jly. 21, 1810

Street, Rebecca to Atlas Jones, Je. 7, Moore county. R. R. Je. 14, 1810

Strong, Nathan K. to Mary Bent, Apr. 22, Granville county. R. R. My. 3, 1810

Sutton, Joseph of Chowan county to Rebecca Reed, Jly. 31, Perquimans county. R. R. Aug. 16, 1810

Taylor, Robert A. of Lewisburg to Margaret Sanders of Brunswick, Feb. 14, Brunswick county, Va. R. R. Feb. 22, 1814

Thames, Mrs. Elizabeth of Cumberland county to Joseph Butler of Bladen county, Feb. 1. R. R. Feb. 15, 1810

Toomer, Lewis H. to Sarah Hill, Nov. 22, Wilmington. R. R. Dec. 6, 1810

Turner, James to Mrs. William Johnston, Jly. 21, Warren county. R. R. Jly. 26, 1810

Vanhook, John to Rachael E. Rogers, Dec. 9, Person county. R. R. Dec. 20, 1810

Wallace, Esther to Thomas Cooke of Newbern, Apr. 8, Beaufort. R. R. Aug. 19, 1810

Waters, Elizabeth M. of Chatham county to Thomas Junius Davis of New Hanover county, Sept. 5, Chatham county. R. R. Sept. 27, 1810

Watts, Rev. John to Elizabeth Kennedy, Dec. 1, Williamston. R. R. Feb. 8, 1810

Whitaker, Patsey to Ricks Foort, Nov., Halifax county. R. R. Nov. 22, 1810

Wiggins, Polly of Edgecombe county to Dr. Mills Lewis of Virginia, Jly. 10. R. R. Aug. 23, 1810

Wilkings, Wm. to Mary Geke, My. 10, Wilmington. R. R. My. 31, 1810

Williams, Hannah to John Giles of Jones county, Feb. 9, Duplin county. R. R. Mar. 1, 1810

Williams, Martha to John Brodie of Warren county, Dec. 25, Franklin county. R. R. Jan. 4, 1810

Williams, Martha of Virginia to William Peck of Raleigh, Jan., Orange county. R. R. Jan. 11, 1810

Williams, Rebecca L. of Surry county to John H. Wimbush of Halifax county, Sept. 16, Surry county. R. R. Oct. 11, 1810

Williams, Wm. to Ann Pugh of Martin county, My. 22, Williamston. R. R. My. 31, 1810

Williams, Wm. of Halifax county to Eliza Alston of Warren county, My. 1. R. R. My. 10, 1810

Williamson, Mary to Jas. K. Nott, Je. 21, Caswell county. R. R. Je. 28, 1810

Wilson, Mrs. B. M. to Col. J. A. Pearson of Rowan county, Sept. 6. R. R. Sept. 7, 1810

Wimbush, John H. of Halifax county, Va., to Rebecca L. Williams of Surry county, Sept. 16, Surry county. R. R. Oct. 11, 1810

Wingate, Atha of Fayetteville to Robert W. Brown of Wilmington, Mar. 25. R. R. Apr. 5, 1810

Wooten, William to Martha Shelton, Dec. 19, Halifax county. R. R. Jan. 4, 1810

Young, Capt. Daniel to Mrs. Cornelius Ryan, Jly. 18, Bertie county. R. R. Jly. 26, 1810

1811

Allen, Mary G. to Rev. Pleasant Thurman, Edenton, My. 22. R. R. Je. 7, 1811

Alston, Col. Joseph of Halifax county to Mrs. Martha Hill of Franklin county, Apr., Franklin county. R. R. Apr. 26, 1811

Alston, Martha to Col. Joseph Hawkins, Apr. 5, Warren county. R. R. Apr. 28, 1811

Anderson, Alex'r to Mary Howard, Nov. 22, Wilmington. R. R. Dec. 13, 1811

Ashe, Samuel P. of Halifax to Jane H. Puckett, Jly. 6, Henderson, Ky. R. R. Jly. 26, 1811

Auld, Miss to Dr. James Bogle, My., Fayetteville. R. R. My. 24, 1811

Bateman, Capt. Daniel to Louis Spruill, Sept. 26, Tyrrell county. R. R. Oct. 18, 1811

Balinger, Temple to Alee Howell, Jly. 25, Guilford county. R. R. Aug. 9, 1811

Barge, Sally to Colin McIver, My. 1, Fayetteville. R. R. My. 17, 1811

Barnes, Mary to James Clybourn, Dec. 8, Robeson county. R. R. Dec. 20, 1811

Barringer, Daniel L. of Cabarrus county to Ann White, Jly. 18, Raleigh. R. R. Jly. 19, 1811

Beasley, Ann to Alexander Smith, Sept. 12, Granville county. R. R. Sept. 27, 1811

Beck, Coziah Ann of Duplin county to David Ochilter of Fayetteville, Jan. 1, Duplin county. R. R. Jan. 17, 1811

Becton, Frederick E. of Lenoir county to Sarah Everett of Wayne county, Oct., Wayne county. R. R. Oct. 25, 1811

Berry, Rev. Richard T. of Beaufort county to Mahetabel Rew of Gar Bacon, Jan., Gar Bacon. R. R. Jan. 17, 1811

Biggs, Elizabeth to Thomas Ellison, My. 8, Craven county. R. R. My. 24, 1811

Birchett, Eleanor to George Clark Somervell, Mar. 28, Mecklenburg county, Va. R. R. Apr. 5, 1911

Blount, Mar. Ann of Washington to W. W. Rodman of New York, Je. 6, Washington. R. R. Je. 21, 1811

Bogle, Dr. James to Miss Auld, My., Fayetteville. R. R. My. 24, 1811

Bond, Rebecca to Henry Elliot, Jan. 21, Chowan county. R. R. Feb. 14, 1811

Bowen, Rev. Thomas to Mrs. Rebecca Garrett, Apr. 21, Beaufort county. R. R. My. 10, 1811

Boyd, Mary to Dr. Joseph W. Hadkins of Warren county, Sept. 10, Mecklenburg county, Va. R. R. Oct. 18, 1811

Bradford, Mary to Col. Eli. B. Whitaker, Je., Halifax county. R. R. Je. 14, 1811

Brickell, Benjamin of Franklin county to Nancy Davis of Nash county, Sept., Nash county. R. R. Sept. 27, 1811

Briggs, Samuel G. of Wake county to Patsey Hill of Raleigh, Jan. 22, Raleigh. R. R. Jan. 24, 1811

Brower, David to Jane Kirkman, Dec. 22, Randolph county. R. R. Dec. 20, 1811

Brown, Mary to Alexandre C. Miller, Jly. 7, Bladen county. R. R. Jly. 19, 1811

Bunting, Anne of Turkey Creek to N. Hardy of Wilmington, Dec. 30. R. R. Feb. 14, 1811

Burch, Eliza to John M'Caleb of Wilmington, Nov. 22, Smithville. R. R. Dec. 13, 1811

Burlingham, Mary of Franklin county to Simon A. Bryan of Bertie county, Jan. 17, Franklin county. R. R. Jan. 24, 1811

Burns, Elizabeth of Chatham county to Isaiah Durham of Orange county, Feb. 3, Chatham county. R. R. Feb. 14, 1811

Burton, A. M. of Charlotte to Elizabeth Fullenwilder of Lincoln county, Je., Lincolnton. R. R. Je. 28, 1811

Bustin, Sarah of Halifax county to Simon Turner of Wake county, Nov. 3, Halifax county. R. R. Nov. 29, 1811

Brownrigg, Polly of Edgecombe county to Samuel Vines of Greene county, Jly. 21, Edgecombe county. R. R. Aug. 16, 1811

Bryan, Lewis C. to Mrs. Mary Croom, Aug. 5, Lenoir county. R. R. Sept. 6, 1811

Bryan, Mrs. Mary K. to E. Vernon, Je. 2, Wilmington. R. R. Je. 7, 1811

Bryan, Simon A. of Bertie county to Mary Burlingham of Franklin county, Jan. 17, Franklin county. R. R. Jan. 24, 1811

Campbell, Miss to William B. Miller of Wilmington, Mar. 10, Topsail sound. R. R. Mar. 28, 1811

Carney, Mrs. Jane of Newbern to William Vines, Apr., Washington. R. R. Apr. 19, 1811

Carney, Gen. Stephen W. of Halifax county to Ann Northcutt of Norfolk county, Va., Jan. 6. R. R. Jan. 24, 1811

Carr, Elizabeth to Adam Tooley, Sept., Greene county. R. R. Oct. 4, 1811

Carstarphen, Jas. to Mary Powell, Mar. 22, Halifax county. R. R. May 3, 1811

Caswell, Eliza to William Hill, Je. 27, Newbern. R. R. Jly. 5, 1811

Christmas, Polly to Richard Power, Oct. 30, Warren county. R. R. Nov. 22, 1811

Clark, Rachel B. of Richmond county to William L. MacNeill of Fayetteville, Jan. 1, Rockingham. R. R. Jan. 17, 1811

Clingman, Jacob to Jane Poindexter, Aug. 13, Surry county. R. R. Aug. 30, 1811

Clybourn, James to Mary Barnes, Dec. 8, Robeson county. R. R. Dec. 20, 1811

Cobb, Penelope of Jones county to Joshua Croom, Dec. 31, Kinston. R. R. Jan. 17, 1811

Cocke, Miss to Halcott Tyrrell of Warren county, Nov. 2, Warren county. R. R. Nov. 8, 1811

Cocke, Nancy to Jno. Owen, Jly. 31, Warren county. R. R. Aug. 9, 1811

Cole, Mrs. Elizabeth of Newbern to William Vine of Beaufort county, Apr. 10. R. R. Apr. 26, 1811

Conway, William to Mary Shute, Apr. 14, Newbern. R. R. Apr. 26, 1811

Coots, Jas. to Mary Findley, Jly. 30, Guilford county. R. R. Aug. 9, 1811

Cotten, Whitmel to Polly Foreman, Oct. 24, Halifax county. R. R. Nov. 15, 1811

Cowan, John to Isabella Hartman, Nov. 7, Wilmington. R. R. Nov. 29, 1811

Creecy, Agnes to William Righton of Chowan county, Sept. 5, Edenton. R. R. Sept. 27, 1811

Creecy, Joseph to Nancy Creecy, Mar. 5, Perquimons county. R. R. Mar. 21, 1811

Creecy, Nancy to Joseph Creecy, Mar. 5, Perquimons county. R. R. Mar. 21, 1811

Croom, Joshua to Penelope Cobb of Jones county, Dec. 31, Kinston. R. R. Jan. 17, 1811

Croom, Mrs. Mary to Lewis C. Bryan, Aug. 5, Lenoir county. R. R. Sept. 6, 1811

Cutlar, Mary Jane of Wilmington to Edward Mills of Brunswick county, Jly. 11. R. R. Jly. 26, 1811

Dabney, Celia of Gloucester county, Va. to John Wyatt of Raleigh, Jan., Gloucester county, Va. R. R. Jan. 17, 1811

Daniel, Chesley of South Carolina formerly of Raleigh to Eliza Pugh Weightman of Alexandria, My. 9, Raleigh. R. R. My. 10, 1811

Davidson, Andrew T. to Jane Martin, Feb. 28, Charlotte. R. R. Mar. 28, 1811

Davis, Baxter to Elizabeth Strain, Dec. 5, Orange county. R. R. Dec. 13, 1811

Davis, Nancy of Nash county to Benjamin Brickell of Franklin county, Sept., Nash county. R. R. Sept. 27, 1811

Davis, Wm. of Mecklenburg, Va. to Susan Bullock, Aug., Granville county. R. R. Sept. 6, 1811

Dillard, Edward to Minerva Ruffin of Rockingham, My. 16, Petersburg. R. R. My. 24, 1811

Du Pre, Daniel of Raleigh to Christiana Bentley Saunders of Powhatan county, Va., Oct. 15. R. R. Nov. 8, 1811

Durham, Isaiah of Orange county to Elizabeth Burns of Chatham county, Feb. 3, Chatham county. R. R. Feb. 14, 1811

Eaton, Harriot of Warren county to Capt. Grandison Field of Mecklenburg, Va., Mar. 27. R. R. Apr. 12, 1811

Eaton, Nancy to Hugh Henderson, Sept. 5, Halifax. R. R. Sept. 20, 1811

Edgy, Elizabeth to Nathaniel Weeks, Sept. 7, Newbern. R. R. Sept. 20, 1811

Elliot, Henry to Rebecca Bond, Jan. 31, Chowan county. R. R. Feb. 14, 1811

Ellis, Mrs. Arete to Col. Joseph Nelson, My. 11, Newbern. R. R. My. 24, 1811

Ellison, Alderson to Lucretia Palmer, Je. 9, Beaufort county. R. R. Jly 5, 1811

Ellison, Thomas to Elizabeth Biggs, My. 8, Craven county. R. R. My. 24, 1811

Ely, Horace of Plymouth to Mary Jane D. G. Roulhac, Je. 2, Martin county. R. R. Je. 21, 1811

Everitt, Sarah of Wayne county to Frederick E. Becton of Lenoir county, Oct., Wayne county. R. R. Oct. 25, 1811

Falcon, Martha B. of Warren county to Dr. Walker of Belfield, Va., Jan. 16, Warren county. R. R. Jan. 24, 1811

Fenner, Ann of Franklin county to Thomas Henderson of Raleigh, My. 29, Franklin county. R. R. My. 31, 1811

Ferguson, Nancy to Lawrence O'Brien, Dec. 29, Tarborough. R. R. Jan. 17, 1811

Field, Capt. Grandison of Mecklenburg, Va. to Harriot Eaton of Warren county, Mar. 27. R. R. Apr. 12, 1811

Findley, Mary to Jas. Coots, Jly. 30, Guilford county. R. R. Aug. 9, 1811

Fishee, Mary to Capt. Thomas Fuet of Newbern, Jly. 6, Philadelphia. R. R. Aug. 9, 1811

Foreman, Polly to Whitmel Cotten, Oct. 24, Halifax county. R. R. Nov. 15, 1811

Forster, Alexius M. of Wilmington to Elizabeth A. Rogers, Mar. 24, Brunswick county. R. R. Apr. 12, 1811

Freear, Richard of Northampton county to Evelina B. Wynne, Sept. 4, Franklin county. R. R. Sept. 20, 1811

Fuet, Capt. Thomas of Newbern to Mary Fisher, Jly. 6, Philadelphia. R. R. Aug. 9, 1811

Fullenwider, Elizabeth of Lincoln county to A. M. Burton of Charlotte, Je., Lincolnton. R. R. Je. 28, 1811

Gallaher, Crawford to Isbel Johnston, Sept. 10, Iredell county. R. R. Oct. 11, 1811

Gallant, Daniel of Mecklenburg county to Nancy S. C. Hunter of Huntersville, Sept. 5, Lincoln county. R. R. Sept. 27, 1811

Garrett, Mrs. Rebecca to Rev. Thomas Bowen, Apr. 21, Beaufort county. R. R. My. 10, 1811

Gee, Sarah to William B. Lockhart, Feb. 26, Northampton county. R. R. Mar. 7, 1811

Gibson, Elisha to Nancy Gibson, Aug. 18, Richmond county. R. R. Aug. 30, 1811

Gibson, Nancy to Elisha Gibson, Aug. 18, Richmond county. R. R. Aug. 30, 1811

Glasgow, Jesse to Milly Hasket, Oct. 24, Randolph county. R. R. Nov. 27, 1811

Good, Polly to Wm. Moore of Newbern, My. 30. R. R. Je. 14, 1811

Gordon, John of Gates county to Mary Wootten of Halifax county, Oct., Halifax county. R. R. Oct. 25, 1811

Grant, Jas. of Wake county to Elizabeth Whitaker, Jan. 15, Halifax county. R. R. Jan. 24, 1811

Green, Miss to Dennis O'Brien, Je. 27, Warren county. R. R. Jly. 5, 1811

Green, John S. to Eliza Latham, Je. 20, Craven county. R. R. Jly 5, 1811

Green, Mary to Thomas Wright, Dec. 20, Wilmington. R. R. Jan. 3, 1811

Green, Nancy of Warren county to John Long of Rowan county, Apr. 15, Warren county. R. R. My. 31, 1811

Griffith, William to Clariss Hughes, My. 5, Wilmington. R. R. My. 17, 1811

Guion, John W. of Raleigh to Mary Wade of Newbern, Dec. 8, Newbern. R. R. Dec. 20, 1811

Guy, Nancy A. to Dr. Robert H. Helme, Jan. 6, Johnston county. R. R. Jan. 17, 1811

Hall, Susannah of Brunswick county to John Howard of Wilmington, Nov. 10. R. R. Nov. 29, 1811

Hardy, N. of Wilmington to Anne Bunting of Turkey Creek, Dec. 30. R. R. Feb. 14, 1811

Hartman, Isabella to John Cowan, Nov. 7, Wilmington. R. R. Nov. 29, 1811

Haskett, Milly to Jesse Glasgow, Oct. 24, Randolph county. R. R. Nov. 29, 1811

Hatch, Haskall to Ann Runnele, Mar. 11, Jones county. R. R. My. 3, 1811

Hawkins, Col. Joseph to Martha Alston, Apr. 5, Warren county. R. R. Apr. 26, 1811

Hawkins, Dr. Joseph W. of Warren county to Mary Boyd, Sept. 10, Mecklenburg county, Va. R. R. Oct. 18, 1811

Helms, Dr. Robert H. to Nancy A. Guy, Jan. 6, Johnston county. R. R. Jan. 17, 1811

Henderson, Hugh to Nancy Eaton, Sept. 5, Halifax. R. R. Sept. 20, 1811

Henderson, Thomas of Raleigh to Ann Fenner of Franklin county, My. 29, Franklin county. R. R. My. 31, 1811

Hill, Mrs. Martha of Franklin county to Col. Joseph Alston of Halifax county, Apr., Franklin county. R. R. Apr. 26, 1811

Hill, Patsey of Raleigh to Samuel G. Briggs of Wake county, Jan. 22, Raleigh. R. R. Jan. 24, 1811

Hill, William to Eliza Caswell, Je. 27, Newbern. R. R. Jly. 5, 1811

Hinton, Polly Willis to Ransom Hinton, Dec. 27, Wake county. R. R. Jan. 3, 1811

Hinton, Ransom to Polly Willis Hinton, Dec. 27, Wake county. R. R. Jan. 3, 1811

Hoskins, Baker to Margaret Skinner, Oct. 8, Perquimons county. R. R. Oct. 25, 1811

Houze, Isaac of Franklin county to Sarah W. Ward, Warren county, Jan. R. R. Jan. 10, 1811

Howard, John of Wilmington to Susannah Hall of Brunswick county, Nov. 10. R. R. Nov. 29, 1811

Howard, Mary to Alex'r Anderson, Nov. 22, Wilmington. R. R. Dec. 13, 1811

Howell, Alee to Temple Balinger, Jly. 25, Guilford county. R. R. Aug. 9, 1811

Hughes, Clarissa to Willim Griffith, My. 5, Wilmington. R. R. My. 17, 1811

Hunter, Nancy S. C. of Huntersville to Daniel Gallant of Mecklenburg county, Sept. 5, Lincoln county. R. R. Sept. 27, 1811

Huson, Betsey to J. Robb, Feb. 27, Charlotte. R. R. Mar. 14, 1811

Johnston, Isbel to Crawford Gallaher, Sept. 10, Iredell county. R. R. Oct. 11, 1811

Jones, Edward to Elizabeth H. Rainey, Oct. 10, Caswell county. R. R. Oct. 25, 1811

Jordan, Mary to Amos Madden, Jly. 25, Newbern. R. R. Aug. 9, 1811

Kenan, Hannah of Wilmington to Reuben Loring of Boston, My. 12. R. R. My. 24, 1811

Kettrell, Martha to Allen Rainey, Jan. 22, Granville county. R. R. Jan. 31, 1811

Kirkman, Jane to David Brower, Dec. 22, Randolph county. R. R. Dec. 27, 1811

Latham, Eliza to John S. Green, Je. 20, Craven county. R. R. Jly. 5, 1811

Leary, Elder Wm. to Mrs. Phoebe Messer, Jan. 3, Currituck county. R. R. Jan. 24, 1811

Liles, Th's to Rebecca Baddams, My. 16, Chowan county. R. R. My. 31, 1811

Lindsay, Susan of Guilford county to Joseph Wood of Randolph county, Je. 13, Guilford county. R. R. Je. 28, 1811

Liscomb, Eliza to Thomas Vaughan, Oct. 31, Halifax county. R. R. Nov. 15, 1811

Lockhart, William B. to Sarah Gee, Feb. 26, Northampton county. R. R. Mar. 7, 1811

Long, John of Rowan county to Nancy Green of Warren county, Apr. 15, Warren county. R. R. My. 31, 1811

Loring, Reuben of Boston to Hannah Kenan of Wilmington, My. 12. R. R. My. 24, 1811

Love, William to Elizabeth Macay, Mar. 21, Salisbury. R. R. Apr. 5, 1811

Lowrie, Hon. Samuel to Mary Gordon Norfleet, Jly., Bertie county. R. R. Jly. 5, 1811

M'Caleb, John of Wilmington to Eliza Burch, Nov. 22, Smithville. R. R. Dec. 13, 1811

M'Donald, Fanny to Dr. Benjamin Norcom, Jan. 10, Edenton. R. R. Jan. 24, 1811

M'Iver, Colin to Sally Barge, My. 1, Fayetteville. R. R. My. 10, 1811

M'Kee, Jas. of Raleigh to Priscilla Macon, Oct., Franklin county. R. R. Nov. 8, 1811

M'Neill, William L. of Fayetteville to Rachel B. Clark of Richmond county, Jan. 1, Rockingham. R. R. Jan. 17, 1811

M'Rea, Roderick of Cumberland county to Christian Murchison, My. 9, Moore county. R. R. My. 17, 1811

Macay, Elizabeth to William Love, Mar. 21, Salisbury. R. R. Apr. 5, 1811

Macon, Priscilla to Jas. M'Kee of Raleigh, Oct., Franklin county. R. R. Nov. 8, 1811

Madden, Amos to Mary Jordan, Jly. 25, Newbern. R. R. Aug. 9, 1811

Marshal, Thomas to Mary Watson, Jan. 6, Newbern. R. R. Jan. 17, 1811

Martin, Jane to Andrew T. Davidson, Feb. 28, Charlotte. R. R. Mar. 28, 1811

Mason, Benjamin to Julia Wallace, Jan. 17, Craven county. R. R. Jan. 31, 1811

Meares, William B. to Susan Pendleton, Nov. 25, Wilmington, R. R. Dec. 13, 1811

Messer, Mrs. Phoebe to Elder Wm. Leary, Jan. 13, Currituck county. R. R. Jan. 24, 1811

Miller, Alexandre C. to Mary Brown, Jly. 7, Bladen county. R. R. Jly. 19, 1811

Miller, William B. of Wilmington to Miss Campbell, Mar. 10, Topsail. R. R. Mar. 28, 1811

Mills, Edward of Brunswick county to Mary Jane Cutlar of Wilmington, Jly. 11. R. R. Jly. 26, 1811

Minter, Richard to Nancy Ragland, Jan. 24, Chatham county. R. R. Jan. 31, 1811

Mitchell, J. to Rebecca Wilcox, Sept. 19, Fayetteville. R. R. Sept. 27, 1811

Mitchell, James to Rebecca Wilcox, Sept. 16, Fayetteville. R. R. Oct. 11, 1811

Moody, Eppes to Matilda Bowlings, Aug. 6, Franklin. R. R. Aug. 16, 1811

Moore, Wm. to Polly Good of Newbern, My. 30. R. R. Je. 14, 1811

Murchison, Christian to Roderick M'Rea of Cumberland county, My. 9, Moore county. R. R. My. 17, 1811

Neale, Penelope of Craven county to Valentine Wallace of Carteret county, Dec. 22, Craven county. R. R. Jan. 10, 1811

Nelson, David to Mary Strain, Sept. 26, Orange county. R. R. Oct. 11, 1811

Nelson, Col. Joseph to Mrs. Arete Ellis, My. 11, Newbern. R. R. My. 24, 1811

Noe, Samuel to Elizabeth Warren, Jly. 14, Orange county. R. R. Aug. 9, 1811

Norcom, Dr. Benjamin to Fanny M'Donald, Jan. 10, Edenton. R. R. Jan. 24, 1811

Norfleet, Mary Gordon to Hon. Samuel Lowrie, Jly., Bertie county. R. R. Jly. 5, 1811

Northcutt, Ann of Norfolk county, Va. to Gen. Stephen W. Carney of Halifax county, Va., Jan. 6. R. R. Jan. 24, 1811

O'Brien, Dennis to Miss Green, Je. 27, Warren county. R. R. Jly. 5, 1811

O'Brien, Lawrence to Nancy Ferguson, Dec. 29, Tarborough. R. R. Jan. 17, 1811

Ochilter, David of Fayetteville to Coziah Ann Beck of Duplin county, Jan. 1, Duplin county. R. R. Jan. 17, 1811

O'Kelly, John to Mason Pate, My. 4, Orange county. R. R. My. 17, 1811

Orme, James to Mary Vance, Dec. 24, Wilmington. R. R. Jan. 3, 1811

Owen, Jno. to Nancy Cocke, Jly. 31, Warren county. R. R. Aug. 9, 1811

Palmer, Lucretia to Alderson Ellison, Je. 9, Beaufort county. R. R. Jly. 5, 1811

Pate, Mason to John O'Kelly, My. 4, Orange county. R. R. My. 17, 1811

Pendleton, Susan to William Meares, Nov. 25, Wilmington. R. R. Dec. 13, 1811

Poindexter, Jane to Jacob Clingman, Aug. 13, Surry county. R. R. Aug. 30, 1811

Pope, John to Nancy H. Speight, My. 9, Greene county. R. R. My. 31, 1811

Powell, Mary to Jas. Carstarphen, Mar. 22, Halifax county. R. R. My. 3, 1811

Power, Richard to Polly Christmas, Oct. 30, Warren county. R. R. Nov. 22, 1811

Pride, Frederick L. J. to Amaryllis J. Sitgreaves, Jly., Halifax. R. R. Jly. 5, 1811

Puckett, Jane H. to Samuel P. Ashe, Jly. 6, Henderson, Ky. R. R. Jly. 26, 1811

Ragland, Nancy to Richard Minter, Jan. 24, Chatham county. R. R. Jan. 31, 1811

Rainey, Allen to Martha Kettrell, Jan. 22, Granville county. R. R. Jan. 31, 1811

Rainey, Elizabeth H. to Edward D. Jones, Oct. 10, Caswell county. R. R. Oct. 25, 1811

Randatt, Mrs. Rachel to John Sanders, Oct. 24, Randolph county. R. R. Nov. 29, 1811

Rawlings, Matilda to Eppes Moody, Aug. 6, Franklin. R. R. Aug. 16, 1811

Righton, William to Agnes Creecy of Chowan county, Sept. 5, Edenton. R. R. Sept. 27, 1811

Robb, J. to Betsy Huson, Feb. 27, Charlotte. R. R. Mar. 14, 1811

Rodman, W. W. of New York to Mary Ann Blount of Washington, Je. 6, Washington. R. R. Je. 21, 1811

Rogers, Elizabeth A. to Alexus M. Forster of Wilmington, Mar. 24, Brunswick county. R. R. Apr. 12, 1811

Roulhac, Mary Jane D. G. to Horace Ely of Plymouth, Je. 2, Martin county. R. R. Je. 21, 1811

Ruffin, Minerva of Rockingham to Edward Dillard, My. 16, Petersburg. R. R. My. 24, 1811

Runnels, Ann to Haskell Hatch, Mar. 11, Jones county. R. R. My. 3, 1811

Salmons, Paulina to John Smith, Mar., Stokes county. R. R. Mar. 14, 1811

Saunders, Christiana Bentley of Powhatan county, Va. to Daniel Du Pre Daniel of Raleigh, Oct. 15. R. R. Nov. 8, 1811

Saunders, John to Mrs. Rachel Randatt, Oct. 24, Randolph county. R. R. Nov. 29, 1811

Shute, Harry to Hannah Stevenson, Jly. 18, Craven county. R. R. Aug. 9, 1811

Shute, Mary to William Conway, Apr. 14, Newbern. R. R. Apr. 26, 1811

Sitgreaves, Amaryllis J. to Frederick L. J. Pride, Jly., Halifax. R. R. Jly. 5, 1811

Skinner, Margaret to Baker Hoskins, Oct. 8, Perquimons county. R. R. Oct. 25, 1811

Smith, Alexander to Ann Beasley, Sept. 12, Granville county. R. R. Sept. 27, 1811

Smith, John to Paulina Salmons, Mar., Stokes county. R. R. Mar. 14, 1811

Somervell, George Clark to Eleanor Birchett, Mar. 28, Mecklenburg county, Va. R. R. Apr. 5, 1811

Speight, Nancy to John Pope, My. 9, Greene county. R. R. My. 31, 1811

Spruill, Lois to Capt. Daniel Bateman, Sept. 26, Tyrrell county. R. R. Oct. 18, 1811

Stevenson, Hannah to Harry Shute, Jly. 18, Craven county. R. R. Aug. 9, 1811

Strain, Elizabeth to Baxter Davis, Dec. 5, Orange county. R. R. Dec. 13, 1811

Strain, Mary to David Nelson, Sept. 26, Orange county. R. R. Oct. 11, 1811

Streets, Hannah to Samuel Webb, Jan. 22, Duplin county. R. R. Feb. 14, 1811

Thurman, Rev. Pleasant to Mary G. Allen of Edenton, My. 22. R. R. Je. 7, 1811

Tooley, Adam to Elizabeth Carr, Sept., Greene county. R. R. Oct. 4, 1811

Travis, Mr. to Miss Forster, My., Wilmington. R. R. My. 17, 1811

Turner, Simon of Wake county to Sarah Bustin of Halifax county, Nov. 3, Halifax county. R. R. Nov. 29, 1811

Tyrrell, Halcott of Warren county to Miss Cocke, Nov. 2, Warren county. R. R. Nov. 8, 1811

Vance, Mary to James Orme, Dec. 24, Wilmington. R. R. Jan. 3, 1811

Vaughan, Thomas to Eliza Liscomb, Oct. 31, Halifax county. R. R. Nov. 15, 1811

Vernon, E. to Mrs. Mary K. Bryan, Je. 2, Wilmington. R. R. Je. 7, 1811

Vine, William of Beaufort county to Mrs. Elizabeth Cole of Newbern, Apr. 10. R. R. Apr. 26, 1811

Vines, Samuel of Greene counnty to Polly Brownrigg of Edgecombe county, Jly. 21, Edgecombe county. R. R. Aug. 16, 1811

Vines, William to Mrs. Jane Carney of Newbern, Apr., Washington. R. R. Apr. 19, 1811

Wade, Mary of Newbern to John W. Guion of Raleigh, Dec. 8, Newbern. R. R. Dec. 20, 1811

Walker, Dr. of Belfield, Va. to Martha B. Falcon of Warren county, Jan. 16, Warren county. R. R. Jan. 24, 1811

Wallace, Julia to Benjamin Mason, Jan. 17, Craven county. R. R. Jan. 31, 1811

Wallace, Valentine of Carteret county to Penelope Neale of Craven county, Dec. 22, Craven county. R. R. Jan. 10, 1811

Ward, Sarah W. of Warren county to Isaac Houze of Franklin county, Jan., Warren county. R. R. Jan. 10, 1811

Warren, Elizabeth to Samuel Noe, Jly. 14, Orange county. R. R. Aug. 9, 1811
Watson, Mary to Thomas Marshal, Jan. 6, Newbern. R. R. Jan. 17, 1811
Webb, Samuel to Hannah Streets, Jan. 22, Duplin county. R. R. Feb. 14, 1811
Weeks, Nathaniel to Elizabeth Edgy, Sept. 7, Newbern. R. R. Sept. 20, 1811
Weightman, Eliza Pugh of Alexandria to Daniel Chesley of South Carolina
    (Formerly of Raleigh), My. 9, Raleigh. R. R. My. 10, 1811
Whitaker, Col. Eli B. to Mary Bradford, Je., Halifax county. R. R. Je. 14,
    1811
Whitaker, Elizabeth to Ja's Grant of Wake county, Jan. 15, Halifax county.
    R. R. Jan. 24, 1811
White, Ann to Daniel L. Barringer of Cabarrus county, Jly. 18, Raleigh.
    R. R. Jly. 19, 1811
Wilcox, Rebecca to P. Mitchell, Sept. 19, Fayetteville. R. R. Sept. 27, 1811
Wood, Joseph of Randolph county to Susan Lindsay of Guilford county, Je.
    13, Guilford county. R. R. Je. 28, 1811
Wootten, Mary of Halifax county to John Gordon of Gates county, Oct., Hali-
    fax county. R. R. Oct. 25, 1811
Wright, Thomas to Mary Green, Dec. 20, Wilmington. R. R. Jan. 3, 1811
Wyatt, John of Raleigh to Celia Dabney of Gloucester county, Va., Jan.,
    Gloucester county. Va. R. R. Jan. 17, 1811
Wynne, Evelina B. to Richard Freear of Northampton county, Sept. 4,
    Franklin county. R. R. Sept. 20, 1811

1812

Adams, Charles L. to Elizabeth Everitt, Aug. 26, Wilmington. R. R. Sept. 11,
    1812
Allen, Maj. Daniel B. to Lucretia Faulcon, Sept. 16, Warren county. R. R.
    Sept. 25, 1812
Alston, Matilda to William Williams, Je., Warren county. R. R. Je. 19, 1812
Alston, Sarah of Warren county to Seth Jones of Wake county, Apr. 8, War-
    ren county. R. R. Apr. 10, 1812
Armstead, Richard of Plymouth to Eliza Smith of Newbern, Dec. 19. R. R.
    Jan. 10, 1812
Austin, Major of Virginia to Elizabeth Burges of Halifax county, Jan. R. R.
    Jan. 24, 1812
Barge, Capt. Francis to Hannah Harris, Jan. 9, Newbern. R. R. Jan. 24, 1812
Blackledge, Mary to Jeremiah Brown, Oct. 15, Newbern. R. R. Oct. 30, 1812
Blackwell, Samuel to Margaret Rea, Nov. 10, Murfreesborough. R. R. Nov.
    27, 1812
Blalock, Eliza to Samuel Rimmer, Nov. 19, Person county. R. R. Dec. 4, 1812
Blount, Elizabeth to John Cheshire, Jan., Edenton. R. R. Jan. 8, 1812
Bouge, Josiah to Elizabeth Miers, Sept. 9, Chowan county. R. R. Oct. 16, 1812
Bozman, Mary of Bertie county to Henry Niel of Edenton, Mar. 29. R. R.
    Apr. 17, 1812
Brown, Jeremiah to Mary Blackledge, Oct. 15, New Bern. R. R. Oct. 30, 1812
Brown, Maj. Thomas to Miss Purdie, Apr. 30, Bladen county. R. R. My. 8,
    1812
Bryan, Nancy to William Hampton, Mar. 10, Wilkes county. R. R. Mar. 27,
    1812
Bryan, Sarah to Asa Jones, Dec. 26, Newbern. R. R. Jan. 10, 1812

Buie, William to Margaret MacIver, Sept. 8, Moore county. R. R. Sept. 25, 1812

Bunting, Penelope to Thomas Kenan Morresse, Oct., Sampson county. R. R. Oct. 9, 1812

Burch, John to Eliza Cooper, Feb. 20, Person county. R. R. Mar. 6, 1812

Burges, Elizabeth of Halifax county to Major Austin of Virginia, Jan. R. R. Jan. 24, 1812

Burton, Patsey to Thomas Moore, Feb. 6, Guilford county. R. R. Feb. 21, 1812

Casso, Mary to Alexander Lucas, Jan. 14, Raleigh. R. R. Jan. 24, 1812

Chambers, Edward of Luenburg, Va. to Mrs. Halcott Towns, Warren county, Jly. R. R. Jly. 10, 1812

Charles, John to Rebecca Hargrave, Jan. 23, Guilford county. R. R. Feb. 7, 1812

Cheshire, John to Elizabeth Blount, Jan., Edenton. R. R. Jan. 8, 1812

Collier, Catharine to James Herndon, Jan. 27, Orange county. R. R. Feb. 7, 1812

Cooper, Eliza to John Burch, Feb. 20, Person county. R. R. Mar. 6, 1812

Cowper, Mary to Bridger Montgomery, Feb. 18, Murfreesborough. R. R. Mar. 6, 1812

Cunningham, Alexander of Person county to Miss Wilson of Pittsylvania county, Va., Feb., Pittsylvania county, Va. R. R. Feb. 28, 1812

Dancy, Martha M. to Dr. Henry W. Rhodes, Jly. 14, Northampton county. R. R. Jly. 31, 1812

Daves, Thomas to Harriot Hatch, Mar. 11, Craven county. R. R. Apr. 3, 1812

Dickinson, William of Washington to Mrs. Nancy Lemon of Franklin county, Jan. 1. R. R. Jan. 10, 1812

Dismukes, Rachel to William Hamlet, Sept. 30, Chatham county. R. R. Oct. 9, 1812

Dubrutz, Eliza of Fayetteville to John A. Ramsey of Chatham county, Jly. 23, Fayetteville. R. R. Jly. 31, 1812

Eccles, Fanny to John Pearce, My. 13, Fayetteville. R. R. My. 15, 1812

Evans, Ephraim to Betsey Lee, Dec. 17, Johnston county. R. R. Feb. 7, 1812

Everitt, Elizabeth to Charles L. Adams, Aug. 26, Wilmington. R. R. Sept. 11, 1812

Faulcon, Lucretia to Maj. Daniel B. Allen, Sept. 16, Warren county. R. R. Sept. 25, 1812

Foy, Major Enoch to Phoebe Sanderson, Je. 4, Jones county. R. R. Je. 26, 1812

Frederick, Jane to George Tipler of Wilmington, Feb. 13, Duplin county. R. R. Apr. 3, 1812

Freeman, Maria to John Snow of Warrenton, Oct., Warren county. R. R. Oct. 16, 1812

Gardner, Thomas to Miss Wallace, Apr. 12, Wilmington. R. R. Apr. 17, 1812

Goodloe, John of Tennessee to Polly Macon of Warren county, Je. 17. R. R. Je. 19, 1812

Gorham, Penelope to Robert Green of Wayne county, Apr., Pitt county. R. R. Apr. 3, 1812

Green, Robert of Wayne county to Penelope Gorham, Apr., Pitt county. R. R. Apr. 3, 1812

Hamlet, William to Rachel Dismukes, Sept. 30, Chatham county. R. R. Oct. 9, 1812

Hampton, William to Nancy Bryan, Mar. 10, Wilkes county. R. R. Mar. 27, 1812

Hanks, Lydia of Grayson county, Va. to Edw. Moor of Surry county, My., Grayson county, Va. R. R. My. 29, 1812

Hargrave, Rebecca to John Charles, Jan. 23, Guilford county. R. R. Feb. 7, 1812

Harris, Hannah to Capt. Francis Barge, Jan. 9, Newbern. R. R. Jan. 24, 1812

Hatch, Harriot to Thomas Daves, Mar. 11, Craven county. R. R. Apr. 3, 1812

Hawes, Dr. E. to Sarah Woods, My. 10, Newbern. R. R. Je. 5, 1812

Hay, David of Fayetteville to Susannah Sheppard of Orange county, Oct. 3. R. R. Oct. 12, 1812

Henderson, Dr. James M. to Mrs. Margaret M. Jones, Mar. 19, Wilmington. R. R. Apr. 3, 1812

Herndon, James to Catharine Collier, Jan. 27, Orange county. R. R. Feb. 7, 1812

Hill, Frederick J. of Wilmington to Ann J. Watters of Pittsborough, Chatham county, Apr. 2, Forceput. R. R. Apr. 17, 1812

Hoskins, Dolly of King & Queen county, Va. to Robert Ruffin of this State, Dec. 14. R. R. Jan. 3, 1812

Jarrett, Mrs. Esther to John Mitchell of South Carolina, Jly. 8, Charlotte. R. R. Jly. 31, 1812

Jeffreys, Elizabeth M. of Caswell county to Thomas M'Gehee of Person county, Dec. 9. R. R. Dec. 25, 1812

Jennings, George to Anne Joyce, Feb. 27, Rockingham county. R. R. Mar. 20, 1812

Jocelyn, Samuel R. to Mrs. Jane Langdon, Jan. 19, Wilmington. R. R. Jan. 31, 1812

Johnston, Stephen to Peggy Teague, My. 7, Chatham county. R. R. My. 22, 1812

Jones, Asa to Sarah Bryan, Dec. 26, Newbern. R. R. Jan. 10, 1812

Jones, Elizabeth to Peter Peterson, Mar. 26, Newbern. R. R. Apr. 3, 1812

Jones, Mrs. Margaret M. to Dr. James M. Henderson, Mar. 19, Wilmington. R. R. Apr. 3, 1812

Jones, Penelope to Richard Smith of Raleigh, Feb. 25, Wake county. R. R. Feb. 28, 1812

Jones, Seth of Wake county to Sarah Alston of Warren county, Apr. 8, Warren county. R. R. Apr. 10, 1812

Joyce, Anne to George Jennings, Feb. 27, Rockingham county. R. R. Mar. 20, 1812

Kirkland, Betsey of Hillsboro to George McNeill of Fayetteville, Sept., Hillsboro. R. R. Sept. 25, 1812

Lane, Martha to John Williams of Cumberland county, Apr. 15, Wake county. R. R. Apr. 24, 1812

Langdon, Mrs. Jane to Samuel R. Jocelyn, Jan. 19, Wilmington. R. R. Jan. 31, 1812

Latham, Sarah of Fayetteville to J. M. Levi of Wilmington, Feb. 23, Fayetteville. R. R. Feb. 28, 1812

Leary, Chas. of Chowan county to Margaret Skinner of Perquimons county, Dec. 17, Perquimons county. R. R. Jan. 10, 1812

Lee, Betsey to Ephraim Evans, Dec. 17, Johnston county. R. R. Feb. 7, 1812

Lemon, Mrs. Nancy of Franklin county to William Dickinson of Washington, Jan. 1. R. R. Jan. 10, 1812

Levi, J. M. of Wilmington to Sarah Latham of Fayetteville, Feb. 23, Fayetteville. R. R. Feb. 28, 1812

Lucas, Alexander to Mary Casso, Jan. 14, Raleigh. R. R. Jan. 24, 1812

Macon, Polly of Warren county to John Goodloe of Tennessee, Je. 17. R. R. Je. 19, 1812

McCullers, Wm. of Wake county to Sarah Sanders of Johnston county, Dec. 22. R. R. Dec. 25, 1812

M'Daniel, Margaret Ann of Washington to William M'Pheeters of Raleigh, Mar. 10, Washington. R. R. Mar. 27, 1812

M'Dermot, Daniel of Chowan county to Margaret Parish of Edenton, Sept. 5. R. R. Sept. 18, 1812

M'Gehee, Thomas of Person county to Elizabeth M. Jeffreys of Caswell county, Dec. 9. R. R. Dec. 25, 1812

M'Intyre, John to Eleanor Morrison, Feb. 10, Fayetteville. R. R. Mar. 6, 1812

M'Iver, Margaret to William Buie, Sept. 8, Moore county. R. R. Sept. 25, 1812

M'Kellar, Maj. Peter to Henrietta M'Neill, Apr. 21, Cumberland county. R. R. My. 22, 1812

M'Millan, Margaret B. to James M'Ree, Mar. 27, Elizabethtown, Bladen county. R. R. Mar. 3, 1812

M'Neill, George of Fayetteville to Betsey Kirkland of Hillsboro, Sept., Hillsboro. R. R. Sept. 25, 1812

M'Neill, Henrietta to Major Peter M'Kellar, Apr. 21, Cumberland county. R. R. My. 22, 1812

M'Pheeters, William of Raleigh to Margaret Ann M'Daniel of Washington, Mar. 10, Washington. R. R. Mar. 27, 1812

M'Ree, James to Margaret B. McMillan, Mar. 27, Elizabethtown, Bladen county. R. R. Apr. 3, 1812

Malone, Pomfret to Nancy Wells, Sept. 24, Person county. R. R. Oct. 2, 1812

Mason, William of Brunswick county to Judith Weaver of Northampton county, Jan. R. R. Jan. 24, 1812

Mendenhall, Richard of Jamestown to Mary Pegg, Feb. 17, Guilford county. R. R. Feb. 21, 1812

Miers, Elizabeth to Josiah Bouge, Sept. 9, Chowan county. R. R. Oct. 16, 1812

Miller, David M. to Margaret Telfair, Apr. 6, Wilmington. R. R. Apr. 17, 1812

Mitchell, John of South Carolina to Mrs. Esther Jarrett, Jly. 8, Charlotte. R. R. Jly. 31, 1812

Molton, T. to Sarah Ward, Oct., Duplin county. R. R. Oct. 9, 1812

Montgomery, Bridger to Mary Cowper, Feb. 18, Murfreesborough. R. R. Mar. 6, 1812

Moor, Edw. of Surry county to Lydia Hanks, My., Grayson county, Va. R. R. My. 29, 1812

Moore, Thomas to Patsey Burton, Feb. 6, Guilford county. R. R. Feb. 21, 1812

Morresse, Thomas Kenan to Penelope Bunting, Oct., Sampson county. R. R. Oct. 9, 1812

Morrison, Eleanor to John MacIntyre, Feb. 10, Fayetteville. R. R. Mar. 6, 1812

Niel, Henry of Edenton to Mary Bozman of Bertie county, Mar. 29. R. R. Apr. 17, 1812

Parish, Margaret of Edenton to Daniel M'Dermot of Chowan county, Sept. 5. R. R. Sept. 18, 1812

Pearce, John to Fanny Eccles, My. 13, Fayetteville. R. R. My. 15, 1812

Peggy, Mary to Richard Mendenhall of Jamestown, Feb. 17, Guilford county. R. R. Feb. 21, 1812

Peterson, Peter to Elizabeth Jones, Mar. 26, Newbern. R. R. Apr. 3, 1812

Polk, Thomas C. to Mary Elizabeth Trotter, Oct. 20, Salisbury. R. R. Oct. 30, 1812

Purdie, Miss to Maj. Thomas Brown, Apr. 30, Bladen county. R. R. My. 8, 1812

Ramsey, John A. of Chatham county to Eliza Dubrutz of Fayetteville, Jly. 23, Fayetteville. R. R. Jly. 31, 1812

Rea, Margaret to Samuel Blackwell, Nov. 10, Murfreesborough. R. R. Nov. 27, 1812

Rhodes, Dr. Henry W. to Martha M. Dancy, Jly. 14, Northampton county. R. R. Jly. 31, 1812

Rhodes, Sarah to George Ryan, Jr., My. 24, Bertie county. R. R. Je. 5, 1812

Rimmer, Samuel to Eliza Blalock, Nov. 19, Person county. R. R. Dec. 4, 1812

Ruffin, Robert of this State to Dolly Hoskins, of King & Queen county, Va., Dec. 14. R. R. Jan. 3, 1812

Ryan, George, Jr. to Sarah Rhodes, My. 24, Bertie county. R. R. Je. 5, 1812

Sanders, Allen to Leah Toms, My. 26, Perquimons county. R. R. Je. 19, 1812

Sanders, Sarah of Johnston county to Wm. M'Cullers of Wake county, Dec. 22. R. R. Dec. 25, 1812

Sheals, Ann of Plymouth to Thomas Simons of Tarborough, Dec. 18. R. R. Jan. 24, 1812

Sheppard, Susannah of Orange county to David Hay of Fayetteville, Oct. 3. R. R. Oct. 23, 1812

Simons, Thomas of Tarborough to Ann Sheals of Plymouth, Dec. 18. R. R. Jan. 24, 1812

Skinner, Margaret of Perquimons county to William Spence of Pasquotank county, Jan. 15, Edenton. R. R. Feb. 7, 1812

Skinner, Margaret of Perquimons county to Chas. Leary of Chowan county, Dec. 17, Perquimons county. R. R. Jan. 10, 1812

Small, George to Sarah Young, Oct. 11, Edenton. R. R. Oct. 23, 1812

Smith, Eliza of Newbern to Richard Armstead of Plymouth, Dec. 19. R. R. Jan. 10, 1812

Smith, Richard of Raleigh to Penelope Jones, Feb. 25, Wake county. R. R. Feb. 28, 1812

Snow. John of Warrenton to Maria Freeman, Oct., Warren county. R. R. Oct. 16, 1812

Spence, William of Pasquotank county to Margaret Skinner of Perquimons county, Jan. 15, Edenton. R. R. Feb. 7, 1812

Teague, Peggy to Stephen Johnston, My. 7, Chatham county. R. R. My. 22. 1812

Tipler, George of Wilmington to Jane Frederick, Feb. 13, Duplin county. R. R. Apr. 3, 1812

Toms, Leah to Allen Sanders, My. 26, Perquimons county. R. R. Je. 19, 1812

Towns, Mrs. Halcott of Warren county to Edward Chambers of Luenburg. Va., Jly. R. R. Jly. 10, 1812

Trotter, Mary Elizabeth to Thomas C. Polk, Oct. 20, Salisbury. R. R. Oct. 30, 1812

Wallace, Miss to Thomas Gardner, Apr. 12, Wilmington. R. R. Apr. 17, 1812

Ward, Sarah to T. Molton, Oct., Duplin county. R. R. Oct. 9, 1812

Watters, Ann J. of Pittsborough to Frederick J. Hill of Wilmington, Apr. 2, Forceput. R. R. Apr. 17, 1812

Weaver, Judith of Northampton county to William Mason of Brunswick county, Jan. R. R. Jan. 24, 1812

Wells, Nancy to Pomfret Malone, Sept. 24, Person county. R. R. Oct. 2, 1812

Williams, John of Cumberland county to Martha Lane, Apr. 15, Wake county. R. R. Apr. 24, 1812

Williams, Wm. to Matilda Alston, Je., Warren county. R. R. Je. 19, 1812

Wilson, Miss of Pittsylvania county, Va. to Alexander Cunningham of Person county, Feb., Pittsylvania county, Va. R. R. Feb. 28, 1812

Woods, Sarah to Dr. E. Hawes, My. 10, Newbern. R. R. Je. 5, 1812

Young, Sarah to George Small; Oct. 11, Edenton. R. R. Oct. 23, 1812

1814

Alston, Emily of Halifax county to James Fitts of Warrenton, My. 30, Halifax county. R. R. Jly. 8, 1814

Anthony, Joseph F. to Ann Marshall, Jan. 30, Beaufort, Carteret county. R. R. Feb. 18, 1814

Baker, Hance of Norfolk to Mrs. Martha Knowis, My. 18, Raleigh. R. R. My. 27, 1814

Baker, Simons J. of Martin county to Mrs. Harry Hunter, Dec. 22, Raleigh. R. R. Dec. 23, 1914

Barnes, Samuel Thomas of Scotland Neck to Martha Keys of Washington, Beaufort county, Feb. R. R. Feb. 11, 1814

Black, Nancy to Daniel Graham, Feb. 8, Cumberland county. R. R. Feb. 18, 1814

Bowring, Charles to Miss Snodwen, Apr. 5, Camden county. R. R. Apr. 22, 1814

Brooks, Sally to James H. Rogers, Nov. 20, Chatham county. R. R. Dec. 9, 1814

Burges, Dr. A. S. H. to Polly Gilmour, My. 18, Raleigh. R. R. My. 20, 1814

Burton, Col. F. N. W. of Granville county to Miss Murfree of Murfreesborough, Mar. R. R. Mar. 11, 1814

Carrington, Mrs. Ann to Abner Neale, Mar., Washington, Beaufort county. R. R. Mar. 11, 1814

Casso, Margaret to Lieut. Miles, U. S. Infantry, Je. 9, Raleigh. R. R. Je. 10, 1814

Christmas, Frances Moore to Lewis Wilhite of Guilford county, Dec. 19, Orange county. R. R. Jan. 14, 1814

Cook, Mary to James Kirkpatrick, Feb. 24, Cumberland county. R. R. Mar. 11, 1814

Cox, Fred I. to Hollon Patrick, Feb. 8, Craven county. R. R. Mar. 4, 1814

Dilliard, Betsey to Albert Utley, Mar., Wake county. R. R. Mar. 25, 1814

Dunlap, David R. to Charlotte Jennings, Feb. 2, Wadesboro. R. R. Feb. 18, 1814

Empie, Rev. Mr. to Mrs. Wright, Mar. 24, Wilmington. R. R. Apr. 22, 1814

Evans, Jonathan to Elizabeth Smith, Feb. 22, Cumberland county. R. R. Mar. 11, 1814

Faison, William of Sampson county to Susan Moseley of Lenoir county, Feb. R. R. Feb. 18, 1814

Farrar, Jane to Alsey Sanders, Apr. 10, Wake county. R. R. Apr. 22, 1814

Field, Patsy to Miles M'Daniel, Sept. 22, Randolph county. R. R. Oct. 14, 1814

Fitts, James of Warrenton to Emily Alston of Halifax county, My. 30, Halifax county. R. R. Jly. 8, 1814

Foy, Frances of Craven county to William S. Hill of Jones county, Jly. 4. R. R. Aug. 5, 1814

Fulford, K. to David Hellen, Feb. 21, Beaufort, Carteret county. R. R. Mar. 4, 1814

Gilmour, Polly to Dr. A. S. H. Burges, My. 18, Raleigh. R. R. My. 20, 1814

Graham, Daniel to Nancy Black, Feb. 8, Cumberland county. R. R. Feb. 18, 1814

Graham, Eliza of Murfreesborough to Isaac Tull, Lenoir county, Feb. 1. R. R. Feb. 11, 1814

Graves, John W. of Caswell county to Patsey Hinton of Wake county, Oct. 26. R. R. Oct. 28, 1814

Grice, Harriet of Beaufort to Joseph B. Stickney of Washington, Feb. 3. R. R. Mar. 4, 1814

Guion, Elizabeth to Francis Hawkes, Dec., Newbern. R. R. Dec. 30, 1814

Hawks, Francis to Elizabeth Guion, Dec., Newbern. R. R. Dec. 30, 1814

Hawkins, Lucy of Warren county to Lewis Henry of Fayetteville, Dec., Warren county. R. R. Dec. 30, 1814

Hellen, David to K. Fulford, Feb. 21, Beaufort, Carteret county. R. R. Mar. 4, 1814

Henderson, Fanny to Dr. Taylor, of Oxford, My. 22. R. R. Je. 24, 1814

Henry, Lewis of Fayetteville to Lucy Hawkins of Warren county, Dec., Warren county. R. R. Dec. 30, 1814

Hill, William S. of Jones county to Frances Foy of Craven county, Jly. 4. R. R. Aug. 5, 1814

Hinton, Patsey of Wake county to John W. Graves of Caswell county, Oct. 26. R. R. Oct. 28, 1814

Holloman, Betsey of Northampton county to Willis Newsom of Wake county, Dec. 23, Northampton county. R. R. Jan. 14, 1814

Horney, Amy to John Love, Jly. 21, Stokes county. R. R. Aug. 5, 1814

Hunter, Mrs. Harry to Simons J. Baker of Martin county, Dec. 22, Raleigh. R. R. Dec. 23, 1814

Jennings, Charlotte to David R. Dunlap, Feb. 2, Wadesboro. R. R. Feb. 18, 1814

Jones, John D. to Ann Nixon, My. 19, Wilmington. R. R. My. 27, 1814

Jones, Wm. D. to Mary Johnston, My., Warren county. R. R. Je. 3, 1814

Johnston, Mary to Wm. D. Jones, My., Warren county. R. R. Je. 3, 1814

Keys, Martha of Washington, Beaufort county to Samuel Thomas Barnes of Scotland Neck, Feb. R. R. Feb. 11, 1814

Kirkpatrick, James to Mary Cook, Feb. 24, Cumberland county. R. R. Mar. 11, 1814

Knowis, Mrs. Martha to Hance Baker of Norfolk, My. 18, Raleigh. R. R. My. 27, 1814

Lane, Joseph of Raleigh to Martha Moye of Pitt county, Nov. 23, Pitt county. R. R. Dec. 2, 1814

Leigh, William to Mary M'Daniel, Sept. 28, Caswell county. R. R. Oct. 21, 1814

Love, John to Amy Horner, Jly. 21, Stokes county. R. R. Aug. 5, 1814

Lucas, Benjamin to Susan H. Rivers, Apr. 4, Franklin county. R. R. Apr. 29, 1814

M'Connell, Col. Walter of Guilford county to Patsey Peoples of Rockingham, Feb. 10. R. R. Feb. 25, 1814

Macnamca, Robert of Columbia to Eliza Ann Steele, Je. 28, Rowan county. R. R. Jly. 15, 1814

M'Daniel, Mary to William Leigh, Sept. 28, Caswell county. R. R. Oct. 21, 1814

M'Daniel, Miles to Patsey Field, Sept. 22, Randolph county. R. R. Oct. 14, 1814

Marshall, Ann to Joseph F. Anthony, Jan. 30, Beaufort, Carteret county. R. R. Feb. 18, 1814

Martin, John to Susan Rabateau, Apr. 4, Raleigh, R. R. Apr. 15, 1814

Miles, Lieut. U. S. Infantry to Margaret Casso, Je. 9, Raleigh. R. R. Je. 10, 1814

Moseley, Susan of Lenoir county to William Faison of Sampson county, Feb. R. R. Feb. 18, 1814

Moye, Martha of Pitt county to Joseph Lane of Raleigh, Nov. 23, Pitt county. R. R. Dec. 2, 1814

Murfree, Miss of Murfreesborough to Col. F. N. W. Burton of Granville, Mar. R. R. Mar. 11, 1814

Myatt, Czarina of Wake county to Malcom Shaw of Cumberland county, Oct. 14. R. R. Oct. 28, 1814

Neale, Abner to Mrs. Ann Carrington, Mar., Washington, Beaufort county. R. R. Mar. 11, 1814

Newsom, Willis of Wake county to Betsy Holloman of Northampton county, Dec. 23, Northampton county. R. R. Jan. 14, 1814

Nixon, Ann to John D. Jones, My. 19, Wilmington. R. R. My. 27, 1814

Parker, Thomas to Milly Watkins, Dec. 30, Person county. R. R. Jan. 14, 1814

Patrick, Hollon to Fred I. Cox, Feb. 8, Craven county. R. R. Mar. 4, 1814

Peoples, Patsey of Rockingham to Col. Walter M'Connell of Guilford county, Feb. 10. R. R. Feb. 25, 1814

Rabateau, Susan to John Martin, Apr. 4, Raleigh. R. R. Apr. 15, 1814

Richardson, Cynthia to Courtney Upchurch, Apr. 21, Chatham county. R. R. Apr. 29, 1814

Rivers, Susan H. to Benjamin Lucas, Apr. 4, Franklin county. R. R. Apr. 29, 1814

Rogers, James H. to Sally Brooks, Nov. 20, Chatham county. R. R. Dec. 9, 1814

Sanders, Alsey to Jane Farrar, Apr. 10, Wake county. R. R. Apr. 22, 1814

Shaw, Malcom of Cumberland county to Czarina Myatt of Wake county, Oct. 14. R. R. Oct. 28, 1814

Slade, Eliza C. to Madison Yancey, Aug. 2, Raleigh. R. R. Aug. 8, 1814

Smith, Elizabeth to Jonathan Evans, Feb. 22, Cumberland county. R. R. Mar. 11, 1814

Snodwen, Miss to Charles Bowring. Apr. 5, Camden county. R. R. Apr. 22, 1814

Steele, Eliza Ann to Robert Macnamca of Columbia, Je. 28, Rowan county. R. R. Jly. 15, 1814

Stickney, Joseph B. of Washington to Harriet Grice of Beaufort county, Feb. 3. R. R. Mar. 4, 1814

Taylor, Dr. of Oxford to Fanny Henderson, My. 22, Williamsborough. R. R. Je. 24, 1814

Tull, Isaac of Lenoir county to Eliza Graham of Murfreesborough, Feb. 1. R. R. Feb. 11, 1814

Upchurch, Courtney to Cynthia Richardson, Apr. 21, Chatham county. R. R. Apr. 29, 1814

Utley, Albert to Betsey Dilliard, Mar., Wake county. R. R. Mar. 25, 1814

Walker, James W. to Eliza Young, My. 26, Wilmington. R. R. Je. 3, 1814

Watkins, Milly to Thomas Parker, Dec. 30, Person county. R. R. Jan. 14, 1814

Wright, Mrs. to Rev. Mr. Empie. Mar. 24, Wilmington. R. R. Apr. 22, 1814

Yancey, Madison to Eliza C. Slade, Aug. 2, Raleigh. R. R. Aug. 8, 1814

Young, Eliza to James W. Walker, My. 26, Wilmington. R. R. Je. 3, 1814

1815

Adam, Eliza to John A. Cameron, Jan., Fayetteville. R. R. Jan. 13, 1815

Adkins, Mary to William Anderson, Jly. 13, Wilmington. R. R. Jly. 21, 1815

Alston, Margaret to Capt. R. G. Cotten, My. 18, Chatham county. R. R. My. 26, 1815

Allen, Col. Vine of Newbern to Ann G. Green of Wayne county, Feb. 15. R. R. Mar. 3, 1815

Alves, James to Maria David, Jan. 26, Fayetteville. R. R. Feb. 10, 1815

Anderson, John to Miss E. W. Gloster, Jan. 17, Warrenton. R. R. Jan. 27, 1814

Anderson, William to Mary Adkins, Jly. 13, Wilmington. R. R. Jly. 21, 1815

Andrews, Nelson to Mary Sugg, Aug. 1, Wake county. R. R. Aug. 4, 1815

Avery, Col. Isaac T. to Harriet E. Erwin of Burke county, Je. 25. R. R. Aug. 4, 1815

Bacon, Joseph to Sally Wayne, Feb. 2, Raleigh. R. R. Feb. 3, 1815

Baker, Fanny to Mr. Savre, My. 10, Raleigh. R. R. My. 12, 1815

Baldwin, Larkin L. to Hetty Lamb, Nov. 27, Guilford county. R. R. Dec. 8, 1815

Banks, Frances to James Hinton, My. 23, Wake county. R. R. My. 26, 1815

Baskerville, Charles to Miss Willis of Warrenton, Nov. 21, Warren county. R. R. Nov. 24, 1815

Bell, Thomas to Rebecca Chapman, Jan., Chatham county. R. R. Jan. 27, 1815

Bernard, Emily to Talcott Burr of Wilmington, Feb. 14. R. R. Feb. 24, 1815

Berry, Eliza Sarah to John Crawford, Mar. 18, Wilmington. R. R. Mar 31, 1815

Blackledge, Wm. Jr. to Mary Hatch, Apr. 26, Craven county. R. R. My. 12, 1815

Blount, Polly H. to John Myers of Washington, Oct. 12, Beaufort county. R. R. Oct. 20, 1815

Bryant, Wm. of Johnston county to Mrs. Hardy Sanders, Feb., Wake county. R. R. Mar. 3, 1815

Burr, Talcott to Emily Bernard of Wilmington, Feb. 14. R. R. Feb. 24, 1815

Cain, Mary of Orange county to Solomon Southerland of Wake county, Jan. 12. R. R. Jan. 27, 1815

Cameron, John A. to Eliza Adam, Jan., Fayetteville. R. R. Jan. 13, 1815

Chapman, Rebecca to Thomas Bell, Jan., Chatham county. R. R. Jan. 27, 1815

Clark, Julia to James Townes, Dec., Fayetteville. R. R. Dec. 22, 1815

Connor, Eliza Eppes of Mecklenburg county to John D. Graham of Lincoln county, Je. 13. R. R. Jly. 7, 1815

Cotten, Capt. R. G. to Margaret Alston, My. 18, Chatham county. R. R. My. 26, 1815

Crane, James to Susan Houselander, Feb. 24, Burlington. R. R. Mar. 10, 1815

Crawford, John to Sarah Eliza Berry, Mar. 18, Wilmington. R. R. Mar. 31, 1815

Davidson, Wm. of Petersburg to Rhoda T. Ragsdale, Oct. 11, Granville county. R. R. Oct. 20, 1815

Davis, John of Mecklenburg, Va. to Martha Johnson, Dec. 18, Warren county. R. R. Dec. 29, 1815

Davis, Kincher to Frances Pleasants, Aug. 1, Raleigh. R. R. Aug. 4, 1815

Davis, Maria to James Alves, Jan. 26, Fayetteville. R. R. Feb. 10, 1815

Davis, Dr. Stephen of Warrenton to Sarah Johnson of Warren county, Feb. R. R. Mar. 3, 1815

Dismukes, Elizabeth E. of Chatham county to Stephen Moore of Person county, Chatham county, Nov. 22. R. R. Dec. 8, 1815

Dudley, Edward of Wilmington to Eliza H. Haywood, Nov. 21, Raleigh. R. R. Nov. 24, 1815

Erwin, Harriet E. to Col. Isaac T. Avery of Burke county, Je. 26. R. R. Aug. 4, 1815

Erwin, John P. of Tenn. to Frances L. Williams of Surry county, Jly. 13. R. R. Aug. 4, 1815

Falconer, Dr. Thomas of Raleigh to Nancy O'Bryan, Dec. 15, Wake county. R. R. Dec. 22, 1815

Fort, Nancy to Parker Rand, Jly., Wake county. R. R. Jly. 7, 1815

Foushee, Daniel to Hannah Petty, Jan. 22, Chatham county. R. R. Feb. 3, 1815

Foushee, Daniel to Elizabeth Ward, Nov. 20, Chatham county. R. R. Dec. 1815

Foushee, William to Ann Thompson, Jan. 22, Chatham county. R. R. Feb. 3, 1815

Fowler, Patsey to Harrison Terrell, Mar. 9, Wake county. R. R. Mar. 24, 1815

Freeman, Miss to Joel H. Lane of Raleigh, Jan., Warrenton. R. R. Jan. 13, 1815

Graham, John of Lincoln county to Mrs. M'Lauchlan of Mecklenburg county, Je. 13, Lincoln county. R. R. Je. 30, 1815

Graham, John D. of Lincoln county to Eliza Eppes Connor of Mecklenburg county, Je. 13. R. R. Jly. 7, 1815

Graham, Mary of Duplin county to John Tull of Lenoir county, Nov. 28. R. R. Dec. 22, 1815

Graves, Nancy to Capt. Wm. Graves, My. 25, Caswell county. R. R. Je. 2, 1815

Graves, Capt. Wm. to Nancy Graves, My. 25, Caswell county. R. R. Je. 2, 1815

Gloster, Miss E. D. to John Anderson, Jan. 17, Warrenton. R. R. Jan. 27, 1815

Gooding, Jacob to Susan Stanly, Jan. 19, Newbern. R. R. Feb. 3, 1815

Green, Ann G. of Wayne county to Col. Vine Allen of Newbern, Feb. 15. R. R. Mar. 3, 1815

MARRIAGE NOTICES 67

Green, Major James to Ann Cochran, Je. 26, Wilmington. R. R. Jly 7, 1815

Gregory, William to Polly M. Sloan, Mar. 10, Duplin county. R. R. Apr. 28, 1815

Hall, Wm. of South Washington to Jane Kenan, Jan. 31, Duplin county. R. R. Feb. 10, 1815

Hardy, Agness of Perquimons county to Williamson Wynn of Chowan county, Jly. 10. R. R. Jly. 21, 1815

Hatch, Mary to Wm. Blackledge, Jr., Apr. 26, Craven county. R. R. My. 12, 1815

Haywood, Eliza H. to Edward Dudley, Nov. 21, Raleigh. R. R. Nov. 24, 1815

Headen, Isaac to Tempy Headen, Je. 1, Chatham county. R. R. Je. 23, 1815

Headen, Tempy to Isaac Headen, Je. 1, Chatham county. R. R. Je. 23, 1815

Hill, Wm. of New Hanover county to Eliza K. Marshall, Apr. 12, Raleigh. R. R. Apr. 14, 1815

Hinton, James to Frances Banks, My. 23, Wake county. R. R. My. 26, 1815

Hinton, John H. of Raleigh to Miss Puckett, Aug., Chapel Hill. R. R. Aug. 18, 1815

Hooper, Wm. of Chapel Hill to Frances Jones of Chatham county, Jan., Chatham county. R. R. Jan. 13, 1815

Houselander, Catharine to John Janson, Feb. 24, Burlington. R. R. Mar. 10, 1815

Houselander, Mary to James Terwiliger, Feb. 24, Burlington. R. R. Mar. 10, 1815

Houselander, Nicholas to Polly Norris, Feb. 24, Burlington. R. R. Mar. 10, 1815

Houselander, Susan to James Crane, Feb. 24, Burlington. R. R. Mar 10, 1815

Inge, Francis of Granville county to Rebecca C. Williams, Dec., Warren county. R. R. Dec. 22, 1815

Iredell, James to Fanny Tredwell, Je. 6, Edenton. R. R. Je. 23, 1815

Janson, John to Mrs. Catharine Houselander, Feb. 24, Burlington. R. R. Mar. 10, 1815

Johnson, Martha to John Davis of Mecklenburg Va., Dec. 18, Warren county. R. R. Dec. 29, 1815

Johnson, Sarah of Warren county to Dr. Stephen Davis of Warrenton, Feb. R. R. Mar. 3, 1815

Jones, Frances of Chatham county to Wm. Hooper of Chapel Hill, Jan., Chatham county. R. R. Jan. 13, 1815

Kenan, Jane to Wm. Hall of South Washington, Jan. 31, Duplin county. R. R. Feb. 10, 1815

Kirkman, Rebecca to Alfred Lane, Oct. 29, Randolph county. R. R. Nov. 10, 1815

Lamb, Hetty to Larkin L. Baldwin, Nov. 27, Guilford county. R. R. Dec. 8, 1815

Lane, Joel H. of Raleigh to Miss Freeman, Jan., Warrenton. R. R. Jan. 13, 1815

Lane, Alfred to Rebecca Kirkman, Oct. 29, Randolph county. R. R. Nov. 10, 1815

Lea, Susan of Caswell county to James Succoch of Greensborough, My. 4. R. R. My. 19, 1815

Leigh, John Roscoe of Tarborough to Elizabeth Nixon, Dec. 26, New Hanover county. R. R. Jan. 27, 1815

Leonard, Rebecca of Brunswick county to Frederick Sullivan, Feb. 7. R. R. Feb. 24, 1815

Lindsay, Miss to John Slade of Greensboro, Nov. 14, Guilford county. R. R. Nov. 24, 1815

Lyon, Robert of Caswell county to Peggy Stephens of Halifax county, Va., Jan. R. R. Jan. 20, 1815

M'Coll, Gilbert to Margaret Stewart, Oct. 17, Cumberland county. R. R. Oct. 27, 1815

M'Laughlan, Mrs. of Mecklenburg county to John Graham of Lincoln county, Je. 13, Lincoln county. R. R. Je. 30, 1815

Macon, Priscilla to Carter Nunnery, Warren county, Apr. 27, Warrenton. R. R. My. 5, 1815

Marshall, Eliza K. to Wm. Hill of New Hanover county, Apr. 12, Raleigh. R. R. Apr. 14, 1815

Moore, Stephen of Person county to Miss Elizabeth E. Dismukes of Chatham county, Nov. 22. R. R. Dec. 8, 1815

Myers, John of Washington to Polly H. Blount, Oct. 12, Beaufort county. R. R. Oct. 20, 1815

Nelson, Fred B. of Newbern to Winifred Owens, My. 5, Beaufort county. R. R. My. 12, 1815

Newsom, Willis of Wake county to Betsey Holloman of Northampton county, Dec. 23, Northampton county. R. R. Jan. 14, 1815

Nixon, Elizabeth to John Roscoe Leigh, Dec. 26, New Hanover county. R. R. Jan. 27, 1815

Norris, Polly to Nicholas Houselander, Feb. 24, Burlington. R. R. Mar. 10, 1815

Nunnery, Carter to Priscilla Macon, Warren county, Apr. 27, Warrenton. R. R. My. 5, 1815

O'Bryan, Nancy to Dr. Thomas Falconer, Dec. 16, Wake county. R. R. Dec. 22, 1815

Ochiltree, David to Lucy Ann Winslow, Apr. 27, Fayetteville. R. R. My. 19, 1815

Owens, Winifred to Fred B. Nelson of Newbern, My. 5, Beaufort county. R. R. My. 12, 1815

Partin, Drury of Wake county to Tempy Winn of Va., Mar. R. R. Apr. 14, 1815

Peace, Nancy to John W. Young, Jly. 19, Raleigh. R. R. Jly. 21, 1815

Petty, Hannah to Daniel Foushee, Jan. 22, Chatham county. R. R. Feb. 3, 1815

Perry, Samuel to Matilda West, Feb., Chatham county. R. R. Feb. 10, 1815

Perry, Samuel to Eliza B. Williams, Je. 8, Warren county. R. R. Je. 16, 1815

Pleasants, Frances to Kichen Davis, Aug. 1, Raleigh. R. R. Aug. 4, 1815

Puckett, Miss to John H. Hinton of Raleigh, Aug. R. R. Aug. 18, 1815

Ragsdale, Rhoda T. to Wm. Davidson of Petersburg, Oct. 11, Granville county. R. R. Oct. 20, 1815

Rand, Parker to Nancy Fort, Jly., Wake county. R. R. Jly. 7, 1815

Royals, Thomas to Eleanor Walker, Aug. 10, Orange county. R. R. Aug. 18, 1815

Sanders, Mrs. Hardy to Wm. Bryant of Johnston county, Feb., Wake county. R. R. Mar. 3, 1815

Savre, Mr. to Fanny Baker, My. 10, Raleigh. R. R. My. 12, 1815

Shaw, Mary to Elijah Weems, Nov., Raleigh. R. R. Nov. 17, 1815

Slade, John of Greensboro to Miss Lindsey, Nov. 14, Guilford county. R. R. Nov. 24, 1815

Sloan, Polly M. to William Gregory, Mar. 10, Duplin county. R. R. Apr. 28, 1815

Smith, Rebecca of Northampton county to Robert Williams of Raleigh, Feb. R. R. Feb. 24, 1815

Sneed, Junius of Raleigh to Julia Taylor, Je. 30, Raleigh. R. R. Jly. 7, 1815

Stanly, Susan to Jacob Gooding, Jan. 19, Newbern. R. R. Feb. 3, 1815

Stephens, Peggy of Halifax county, Va. to Robert Lyon of Caswell county, Jan. R. R. Jan. 20, 1815

Stewart, Margaret to Gilbert M'Coll, Oct. 17, Cumberland county. R. R. Oct. 27, 1815

Southerland, Solomon A. of Wake county to Mary Cain of Orange county, Jan. 12. R. R. Jan. 27, 1815

Succock, James of Greensborough to Susan Lea of Caswell county, My. 4. R. R. My. 19, 1815

Sugg, Mary to Nelson Andrews, Aug. 1, Wake county. R. R. Aug. 4, 1815

Sullivan, Frederick to Rebecca Leonard of Brunswick county, Feb. 7. R. R. Feb. 24, 1815

Taylor, Julia to Junius Sneed of Raleigh, Je. 30, Raleigh. R. R. Jly. 7, 1815

Terrell, Harrison to Patsey Fowler, Mar. 9, Wake county. R. R. Mar. 24, 1815

Terwiliger, James to Mary Houselander, Feb. 24, Burlington. R. R. Mar. 10, 1815

Thompson, Ann to William Foushee, Jan. 22, Chatham county. R. R. Feb. 3, 1815

Townes, James to Julia Clark, Dec., Fayetteville. R. R. Dec. 22, 1815

Tredwell, Fanny to James Iredell, Je. 6, Edenton. R. R. Je. 23, 1815

Tull, John of Lenoir county to Mary Graham of Duplin county. Nov. 28. R. R. Dec. 22, 1815

Walker, Eleanor to Thomas Royals, Aug. 10, Orange county. R. R. Aug. 18, 1815

Ward, Elizabeth to Daniel Foushee, Nov. 20, Chatham county. R. R. Dec. 8, 1815

Wayne, Sally to Joseph Bacon, Feb. 2, Raleigh. R. R. Feb. 3, 1815

Weems, Elijah to Mary Shaw, Nov., Raleigh. R. R. Nov. 17, 1815

West, Matilda to Samuel Perry, Feb., Chatham county. R. R. Feb. 10, 1815

Wilhite, Lewis of Guilford county to Frances Moore Christmas, Dec. 19, Orange county. R. R. Jan. 14, 1815

Williams, Eliza B. to Samuel Perry, Je. 8, Warren county. R. R. Je. 16, 1815

Williams, Frances L. of Surry county to John P. Erwin of Tenn., Jly. 13. R. R. Aug. 4, 1815

Williams, Rebecca C. to Francis Inge of Granville county, Dec., Warren county. R. R. Dec. 22, 1815

Williams, Robert of Raleigh to Rebecca Smith of Northampton county, Feb. R. R. Feb. 24, 1815

Willis, Miss of Warrenton to Charles Baskerville of Warrenton, Nov. 21, Warren county. R. R. Nov. 24, 1815

Winn, Tempy of Va. to Drury Partin of Wake county, Mar. R. R. Apr. 14, 1815

Winslow, Lucy Ann to David Ochiltree, Apr. 27, Fayetteville. R. R. My. 19, 1815

Wynn, Williamson of Chowan county to Agness Hardy of Perquimons county, Jly. 10. R. R. Jly. 21, 1815

Young, John W. to Nancy Peace, Jly. 19, Raleigh. R. R. Jly. 14, 1815

1818

Alston, Col. Lemuel J. of Alabama territory to Mrs. Joseph J. Williams, Jr. of Halifax county, Feb. 3, Halifax county. R. R. Feb. 13, 1818

Anderson, John to Julia Taylor of this State, My. 7, Washington, D. C. R. R. My. 22, 1818

Austin, Hannan to Charles Stuart of Fayetteville, Feb. 25, Tarborough. R. R. Mar. 20, 1818

Baker, James to May C. Broadfoot, Mar. 12, Fayetteville. R. R. Mar. 27, 1818

Baker, John C. of Brunswick county to Harriet Saunders, Apr. 23, Wake county. R. R. Apr. 24, 1818

Bass, Maclin to Sarah Judkins, Nov., Halifax county. R. R. Nov. 20, 1818

Bird, Empson to Mary Jordan, Mar. 5, Orange county. R. R. Mar. 27, 1818

Bowell, Eliza Ann to Archibald Ochiltree, My. 14, Fayetteville. R. R. My. 29, 1818

Boyd, Mary to Stephen D. Rice, Feb. 5, Rockingham. R. R. Feb. 27, 1818

Boykins, Rebecca to John Edwards, Aug. 19, Wake county. R. R. Aug. 21, 1818

Broadfast, Mary C. to James Baker, Mar. 12, Fayetteville. R. R. Mar. 27, 1818

Brown, Betsey to Rev. Daniel Smith, My. 12, Robeson county. R. R. My. 29, 1818

Brownrigg, Thomas to Mrs. James Hathaway, Apr. 11, Edenton. R. R. Apr. 17, 1818

Bunch, Micajah to Sarah Standin of Chowan county, Je. R. R. Je. 19, 1818

Bynum, John W. of Chatham county to Eliza Daniel, Nov. 10, Wake county. R. R. Nov. 13, 1818

Cameron, John A. to Mrs. Halliday, Oct. 19, Fayetteville. R. R. Dec. 4, 1818

Cameron, Dr. T. N. to Jane A. Wilder, Oct. 26, Petersburg, Va. R. R. Dec. 4, 1818

Cannon, Col. N. of Tennessee to Raphael U. Welborn, Nov., Wilkes county. R. R. Nov. 13, 1818

Carloss, William of South Carolina to Sarah M'Leran. Apr. 16, Fayetteville. R. R. My. 1, 1818

Carthy, Catherine to Peter Custis, Jan. 15. Newbern. R. R. Jan. 30, 1818

Cobb, John of Lenoir county to Miss Grist. Je., Washington. R. R. Je. 19, 1818

Cobb, John to Ann Grist of Beaufort county, My. 25. R. R. My. 29, 1818

Cocke, Sally to Alexander Winstead, Aug. 8, Person county. R. R. Aug. 28, 1818

Cole, Jas. C. to Mary C. Snead, Aug. 25, Newbern. R. R. Sept. 11, 1818

Cooke, Mrs. Margaret to Bennet Partin, Aug. 27, Chapel Hill. R. R. Sept. 4, 1818

Cooper, Wm. W. to Frances A. Spaight, Oct. 15, Murfreesboro. R. R. Oct. 16, 1818

Custus, Peter to Catharine Carthey, Jan. 15, Newbern. R. R. Jan. 30, 1818

Crittenden, Margaret of Halifax county to Dr. Anthony A. Wyche of Virginia, Nov. 12, Halifax county. R. R. Nov. 20, 1818

Croom, Willie J. of Lenoir county to Elizabeth Holliday of Greene county, Dec. 16. R. R. Jan. 2, 1818

Daniel, Eliza to John W. Bynum, Chatham county, Nov. 10, Wake county. R. R. Nov. 13, 1818

Daniel, Woodson of Granville county to Betsey Mitchell of Lewisburg, Feb. 23. R. R. Feb. 27, 1818

Davis, Anna to Joseph Summerl, Jly. 2, Fayetteville. R. R. Jly. 17, 1818

Donoho, Col. Archimedes to Mary Williamson, Dec., Person county. R. R. Dec. 18, 1818

Edwards, John to Rebecca Boykin, Aug. 19, Wake county. R. R. Aug. 21, 1818

Everett, Dr. S. B. to Amelia Parker, My. 10, Brunswick county. R. R. My. 29, 1818

Exum, John to Olza Johnson of Granville county, Dec., Edgecombe county. R. A. Jan. 2, 1818

Fonville, Elizabeth to Valentine Richardson, Aug. 23, Craven county. R. R. Sept. 11, 1818

Foster, Dr. Isaac to Margaret Long of Murfreesborough, Aug. 2, Hertford county. R. R. Aug. 21, 1818

Frazer, John A. to Frances A. Jones, Jan. 8, Craven county. R. R. Jan. 23, 1818

Freeman, George W. to Mrs. Ann Yates Gholson, Oct. 25, Franklin county. R. R. Dec. 4, 1818

Gales, Carolina Matilda to Major Thomas L. West of Bertie county, Mar. 18. R. R. Mar. 27, 1818

Gholson. Mrs. Ann Yates to George W. Freeman, Oct. 25, Franklin county. R. R. Dec. 4, 1818

Grist, Ann of Beaufort county to John Cobb, My. 25. R. R. My. 29, 1818

Gilmour, Stephen of Cumberland county to Amy Pearson of Wake county, My. 27. R. R. My. 29, 1818

Grist, Miss to John Cobb of Lenoir county, Je., Washington. R. R. Je. 19, 1818

Halliday, Mrs. to John A. Cameron, Oct. 19, Fayetteville. R. R. Dec. 4, 1818

Halsey, Mary Jane to Samuel Langdon, My. 13, Wilmington. R. R. My. 29, 1818

Hathaway, Mrs. James to Thomas Brownrigg, Apr. 11, Edenton. R. R. Apr. 17, 1818

Haughton. Edward to Abs Walton, Mar., Gates county. R. R. Mar. 13, 1818

Harris, Julia Ann to Capt. John T. Lane, Aug. 16, Craven county. R. R. Sept. 11. 1818

Heidleburg. Margaret to Gray Westbrook, Mar. 25, Greene county. R. R. Apr. 17. 1818

Hill, Albert G. to Mrs. Maria Lash, Apr. 8, Fayetteville. R. R. Apr. 24, 1818

Hill, Louisa to George Spruil of Edgecombe county, Dec., Halifax county. R. R. Dec. 18, 1818

Holliday, Elizabeth of Greene county to Willie J. Croom of Lenoir county, Dec. 16. R. R. Jan. 2, 1818

Hunter, Mary to Capt. Thomas G. Scott of Raleigh, Jly. 22, Raleigh. R. R. Jly. 24, 1818

Jeffreys, Lucy of Franklin county to Wm. Terrell of Wake county, Sept. 29. R. R. Oct. 9, 1818

Jocelyn, Mrs. M. A. of Sampson county to Dr. S. Williams, My. 12, Wilmington. R. R. My. 29, 1818

Johnson, Olza of Granville county to John Exum, Dec., Edgecombe county. R. R. Jan. 2, 1818

Jones, Francis A. to John A. Frazer, Jan. 8, Craven county. R. R. Jan. 23, 1818

Jordan, Mary to Empson Bird, Mar. 5, Orange county. R. R. Mar. 27, 1818

Judkins, Sarah to Maclin Bass, Nov., Halifax county. R. R. Nov. 20, 1818

Kollock, Rev. Shepard K. of Guilford county to Sarah R. Littlejohn, Feb. 19, Oxford. R. R. Feb. 20, 1818

Lane, Capt. John T. to Julia Ann Harris, Aug. 16, Craven county. R. R. Sept. 11, 1818

Langdon, Samuel to Mary Jane Halsey, My. 13, Wilmington. R. R. My. 29, 1818

Lash, Mrs. Maria to Albert G. Hill, Apr. 8, Fayetteville. R. R. Apr. 24, 1818

Littlejohn, Sarah R. to Rev. Shepard K. Kollock of Guilford county, Feb. 19, Oxford. R. R. Feb. 20, 1818

Lloyd, Richard to Louisiana B. Mascoll, Nov. 18, Wilmington. R. R. Dec. 4, 1818

Long, Margaret of Murfreesborough to Dr. Isaac Foster, Aug. 2, Hertford county. R. R. Aug. 21, 1818

Long, Mary A. of Halifax county to Dr. William Polk of Raleigh, Je. 1. R. R. Je. 12, 1818

M'Leran, Sarah to William Carloss of South Carolina, Apr. 16, Fayetteville. R. R. My. 1, 1818

Mascoll, Louisiana B. to Richard Lloyd, Nov. 18, Wilmington. R. R. Dec. 4, 1818

Mitchell, Betsey of Lewisburg to Daniel Woodson of Granville county, Feb. 23. R. R. Feb. 27, 1818

Myatt, Peninah to Jno. B. White, Jan. 22, Wake county. R. R. Jan. 30, 1818

Ochiltree, Archibald to Eliza Ann Bowell, My. 14, Fayetteville. R. R. My. 29, 1818

Outlaw, George of Bertie county to Mrs. Harrison Smith, Washington county, Jan. 29, Washington county. R. R. Feb. 6, 1818

Parker, Amelia to Dr. S. B. Everett, My. 10, Brunswick county. R. R. My. 29. 1818

Partin, Bennet to Mrs. Margaret Cooke, Aug. 27, Chapel Hill. R. R. Sept. 4, 1818

Pasteur, Elizabeth to John I. Pasteur, Mar. 21, Farmville, Craven county. R. R. My. 1, 1818

Pasteur, John I. to Elizabeth Pasteur, Mar. 21, Farmville, Craven county. R. R. My. 1, 1818

Pearson, Amy of Wake county to Stephen Gilmour of Cumberland county, My. 27. R. R. My. 29, 1818

Picot, Peter O. of Plymouth to Martha Potter of Granville county, Je., Chapel Hill. R. R. Je. 19, 1818

Polk, Dr. William of Raleigh to Mary A. Long of Halifax county, Je. 1. R. R. Je. 12, 1818

Potter, Martha of Granville county to Peter O. Picot of Plymouth, Je., Chapel Hill. R. R. Je. 19, 1818

Powell, Phebe to Warren Wallace, Mar. 26, Pitt county. R. R. Apr. 17, 1818

Pugh, Mary to John Smallwood, Apr. 23, Bertie county. R. R. My. 8, 1818

Reed, John H. of Massachusetts to Raphel Rountree of Pitt county, Feb. 25. R. R. Mar. 20, 1818

Rice, Stephen D. to Mary Boyd, Feb. 5, Rockingham county. R. R. Feb. 27, 1818

Richardson, Valentine to Elizabeth Fonville, Aug. 23, Craven county. R. R. Sept. 11, 1818

Rountree, Rachel of Pitt county to John H. Reed of Massachusetts, Feb. 26. R. R. Mar. 20, 1818

Sanders, Theophilus to Angelina Whitaker, Mar. 10, Raleigh. R. R. Mar. 13, 1818

Saunders, Harriet to John C. Baker of Brunswick county, Apr. 23, Wake county. R. R. Apr. 24, 1818

Scott, Capt. Thomas G. of Raleigh to Mary Hunter, Jly. 22, Raleigh. R. R. Jly. 24, 1818

Shaw, Robert to Lucy Watson, Mar. 8, Halifax. R. R. Mar. 20, 1818

Smallwood, John to Mary Pugh, Apr. 23, Bertie county. R. R. My. 8, 1818

Smith, Rev. Daniel to Betsey Brown, My. 12, Robeson county. R. R. My. 29, 1818

Smith, Mrs. Harrison of Washington county to George Outlaw of Bertie county, Jan. 29, Washington county. R. R. Feb. 6, 1818

Snead, Mary C. to Jas. C. Cole, Aug. 25, Newbern. R. R. Sept. 11, 1818

Snell, Caleb to Susan Tilman, Nov. 29, Craven county. R. R. Dec. 18, 1818

Spaight, Frances A. to Wm. W. Cooper, Oct. 15, Murfreesboro. R. R. Oct. 16, 1818

Spivey, Repsey to Col. Charles Wynne, Jr., Apr. 20, Granville county. R. R. My. 29, 1818

Spruil, George of Edgecombe county to Louisa Hill, Dec., Halifax county. R. R. Dec. 18, 1818

Summerl, Joseph to Ann Davis, Jly. 2, Fayetteville. R. R. Jly. 17, 1818

Standin, Sarah to Macajah Bunch of Chowan county, Je. R. R. Je. 17, 1818

Stuart, Charles of Fayetteville to Hannan Austin, Feb. 25, Tarborough. R. R. Mar. 20, 1818

Taylor, Julia of this State to John Anderson, My. 7, Washington, D. C. R. R. My. 22, 1818

Terrell, Wm. of Wake county to Lucy Jeffreys of Franklin county, Sept. 29. R. R. Oct. 9, 1818

Tilman, Susan to Caleb Snell, Nov. 29, Craven county. R. R. Dec. 18, 1818

Turner, Henry B. to Mary S. Turner, Apr. 28, Wake county. R. R. Apr. 3, 1818

Turner, Mary S. to Henry B. Turner, Apr. 28, Wake county. R. R. Apr. 3, 1818

Wallace, Warren to Phebe Powell, Mar. 26, Pitt county. R. R. Apr. 17, 1818

Walton, Abs to Edward Haughton, Mar., Gates county. R. R. Mar. 13, 1818

Watson, Lucy to Robert Shaw, Mar. 8, Halifax. R. R. Mar. 20, 1818

Welborn, Raphael S. to Col. N. Cannon of Tennessee, Nov., Wilkes county. R. R. Nov. 13, 1818

West, Major Thomas L. of Bertie county to Carolina Matilda Gales, Mar. 18. R. R. Mar. 27, 1818

Westbrook, Gray to Margaret Heidleburg, Mar. 25, Greene county. R. R. Apr. 17, 1818

Whitaker, Angelina to Theophilus Sanders, Mar. 10, Raleigh. R. R. Mar. 13, 1818

White, Jno. B. to Peninah Myatt, Jan. 22, Wake county. R. R. Jan. 30, 1818

Wilder, Jane A. to Dr. T. N. Cameron, Oct. 26, Petersburg. R. R. Dec. 4, 1818

Williams, Mrs. Joseph J., Jr. of Halifax county to Col. Lemuel J. Alston of Alabama territory, Feb. 3, Halifax county. R. R. Feb. 13, 1818

Williams, Dr. S. to Mrs. M. A. Jocelyn of Sampson county, My. 12, Wilmington. R. R. My. 29, 1818

Williamson, Mary to Col. Archimedes Donoho, Dec., Person county. R. R. Dec. 18, 1818

Winstead, Alexander to Sally Cocke, Aug. 8, Person county. R. R. Aug. 28, 1818

Wooster, John to Lucy A. Wright, My. 10, Wilmington. R. R. My. 29, 1818

Wright, Lucy A. to John Wooster, My. 10, Wilmington. R. R. My. 29, 1818

Wyche, Anthony C. of Virginia to Margaret Crittenden of Halifax county, Nov. 12, Halifax county. R. R. Nov. 20, 1818

Wynne, Col. Charles, Jr. to Repsey Spivey, Apr. 20, Granville county. R. R. My. 29, 1818

1819

Albright, George of Guilford county to Sarah Albright of Orange county, Sept. 21. R. R. Oct. 29, 1819

Albright, Sarah of Orange county to George Albright of Guilford county, Sept. 21. R. R. Oct. 29, 1819

Alston, Caroline to Dr. Solomon B. Williams, Feb. 24, Warren county. R. R. Mar. 12, 1819

Atkins, James M. of Raleigh to Mary J. Walker, Sept. 21, Brunswick county, Va. R. R. Oct. 1, 1819

Badger, George E. of Hillsborough to Rebecca Turner, Dec. 24, Warren county. R. R. Jan. 1, 1819

Bailey, Elizabeth to David Hodge of Columbia county, Nov., Georgia. R. R. Dec. 3, 1819

Barnett, Susan to John Hinton of Raleigh, Oct. 12, Wake county. R. R. Oct. 15, 1819

Baynor, Jane to Newton Wilcox, Mar. 25, Washington. R. R. Apr. 2, 1819

Benners, Lucas to Evelina R. Tomlinson, Aug. 17, Craven county. R. R. Aug. 20, 1819

Blackledge, Wm. of Newbern to Mrs. Bryan Whitfield, Mar., Wayne county. R. R. Mar. 12, 1819

Blandchard, Rachael to William Fonville, Jan. 7, Orange county. R. R. Jan. 15, 1819

Boswell, James to Polly Meroney, Oct. 21, Caswell county. R. R. Nov. 5, 1819

Bowers, Susanna H. to James C. Sloan of Mecklenburg county, Dec. 24, Rowan county. R. R. Jan. 8, 1819

Boylan, James J. to Jane Lane, Mar. 15, Raleigh. R. R. Mar. 19, 1819

Branson, Hannah to John McIver, Nov. 23, Fayetteville. R. R. Dec. 3, 1819

Brantley, John to Nancy Petty, Aug. 19, Chatham county. R. R. Aug. 27, 1819

Brown, Mary W. of Petersburg, Va. to Henry Maney, Mar. 4, Hertford county. R. R. Mar. 19, 1819

Bullock, Frances to Macon Green, Jan., Warren county. R. R. Jan. 22, 1819

Bunn, Drusilla to Redman Bunn, Aug. 6, Nash county. R. R. Sept. 3, 1819

Bunn, Redman to Drusilla Bunn, Aug. 6, Nash county. R. R. Sept. 3, 1819

Burt, Jas. to Mary Lockhart, Sept. 15, Wake county. R. R. Sept. 17, 1819

Buxton, Jarvis to Ann Potts, Mar. 24, Beaufort county. R. R. Apr. 2, 1819

Cain, Charity to Willie P. Mangum, Sept. 30, Orange county. R. R. Oct. 15, 1819

Cameron, Hugh to Catharine M. Dugald, Jan. 21, Cumberland county. R. R. Feb. 5, 1819

Casso, Eliza to Joseph Harvey, Feb. 16, Raleigh. R. R. Feb. 12, 1819

Clark, Hezekiah S. to Abigail Mendenhall, Sept. 21, Guilford county. R. R. Oct. 29, 1819

Cook, Miss to Solomon Terrell, Je., Wake county. R. R. Je. 4, 1819

Cove, Harriet of Bertie county to Samuel Haughton of Chowan county, Jly. 22. R. R. Aug. 6, 1819

Crawford, Julia H. to John Hill of Stokes county, Feb. 9, Rockingham county. R. R. Mar. 5, 1819

Davis, Nicholas to Amanda Lewis of Virginia, Apr. 3, Oxford. R. R. Apr. 9, 1819

Dearing, Capt. James H. of Alabama to Julia Ann Searcy, Je. 10, Mt. Pleasant. R. R. Je. 25, 1819

Dudley, Jane to Dr. Alford Guthery of South Washington, Dec. 22. R. R. Jan. 1, 1819

Dugald, Catherine M. to Hugh Cameron, Jan. 21, Cumberland county. R. R. Feb. 5, 1819

Edwards, Mrs. Martha to Rev. Henry Warren, Jly., Wake county. R. R. Jly. 23, 1819

Felton, General Boon of Hertford county to Betsey White, Mar. 4, Raleigh. R. R. Mar. 5, 1819

Fenner, Matilda M. to Dr. Lewis Coor of Pender county, Feb. 23, Raleigh. R. R. Feb. 26, 1819

Findley, Sarah to Oliver L. Kelly, Jan. 17, Newbern. R. R. Feb. 5, 1819

Fonvielle, Hannah to George Garrison, Jr., Nov. 18, Orange county. R. R. Nov. 26, 1819

Fonvielle, William to Rachael Blandchard, Jan. 7, Orange county. R. R. Jan. 15, 1819

Freeman, Wm. D. to Harriet T. Green, Jan. 26, Franklin county. R. R. Feb. 5, 1819

Garland, Mrs. Rebecca W. to Dr. John R. Lucas of Mecklenburg county, Va., Je. 27, Bertie county. R. R. Jly. 2, 1819

Garrison, George, Jr. to Hannah Fonvielle, Nov. 18, Orange county. R. R. Nov. 26, 1819

Gilmour, Claudia J. of Raleigh to Haywood Johnson of Warren, Nov., Petersburg, Va. R. R. Dec. 3, 1819

Gordon, Mr. to Mrs. Edward Jones, Nov. 11, Shocco Springs, Warren county. R. R. Nov. 12, 1819

Graffenried, de. Dr. John to Ann Alston, Oct. 14, Chatham county. R. R. Oct. 22, 1819

Green, Harriet T. to Wm. D. Freeman, Jan. 26, Franklin county. R. R. Feb. 5, 1819

Green, Macon to Frances Bullock, Jan., Warren county. R. R. Jan. 22, 1819

Green, William of Wilmington to Sarah Sneed, Dec., Williamsborough. R. R. Jan. 1, 1819

Grimes, Mrs. Frances to Isaac Powell, Jly. 6, Johnston county. R. R. Jly. 16, 1819

Guthery, Dr. Alfred of South Washington to Jane Dudley, Dec. 22, Wilmington. R. R. Jan. 1, 1819

Harvey, Joseph to Eliza Casso, Feb. 16, Raleigh. R. R. Feb. 12, 1819

Haughton, Samuel of Chowan county to Harriet Cove of Bertie county, Jly. 22. R. R. Aug. 6, 1819

Hill, John of Stokes county to Julia H. Crawford, Feb. 9, Rockingham county. R. R. Mar. 5, 1819

Hill, Mary to Capt. Robert Minzies, Oct. 5, Rockingham county. R. R. Oct. 8, 1819

Hines, Richard of Washington to Susan Wilkins of Edgecombe county, Dec. 10, Edgecombe county. R. R. Jan. 1, 1819

Hinton, John of Raleigh to Susan Barnett, Oct. 12, Wake county. R. R. Oct. 15, 1819

Hodge, David to Elizabeth Bailey of Columbia county, Nov., Georgia. R. R. Dec. 3, 1819

James, Hinton of New Hanover to Mary Ann Watson, Jan. 21, Hillsboro. R. R. Feb. 5, 1819

Johnson, Haywood of Warren county to Claudia J. Gilmour of Raleigh, Nov., Petersburgh, Va. R. R. Dec. 3, 1819

Jones, Gen. Calvin of Raleigh to Temperance Jones, Apr. 15, Franklin county. R. R. Apr. 23, 1819

Jones, Mrs. Edward to Mr. Gordon, Nov. 11, Shocco Springs, Warren county. R. R. Nov. 12, 1819

Jones, Mary Elizabeth to John M. Roberts, Jan. 13, Newbern. R. R. Jan. 29, 1819

Jones, Temperance to Gen. Calvin Jones of Raleigh, Apr. 15, Franklin county. R. R. Apr. 23, 1819

Kelly, Oliver L. to Sarah Findley, Jan. 17, Newbern. R. R. Feb. 5, 1819

Kincannon, Polly to John Wright, Surry county, Feb. 17. R. R. Mar. 12, 1819

Lane, Durant to Mary Whitfield, Jan. 17, Newbern. R. R. Feb. 5, 1819

Lane, Jane to James J. Boylan, Mar. 15, Raleigh. R. R. Mar. 19, 1819

Lewis, Amanda of Virginia to Nichola Davis, Apr. 3, Oxford. R. R. Apr. 9, 1819

Lovick, Elizabeth to Capt. John S. Smith, Dec. 15, Craven county. R. R. Jan. 1, 1819

Lucas, Dr. John R. of Mecklenburg county, Va. to Mrs. Rebecca W. Garland, Je. 27, Bertie county. R. R. Jly. 2, 1819

Mason, James to Sarah Trevathan, Aug. 3, Wilmington. R. R. Aug. 13, 1819

M'Cabe, Catherine to Capt. Benj. Rogers of Wake county, Jly. 8, Orange county. R. R. Jly. 16, 1819

M'Clelland, Mary to Dr. Ruffin of Raleigh, Je. 10, Salisbury. R. R. Jly. 2, 1819

M'Iver, John to Hannah Branson, Nov. 23, Fayetteville. R. R. Dec. 3, 1819

M'Kethan, Alexander to Maria Slade, Apr. 7, Raleigh. R. R. Apr. 9, 1819

Maney, Henry to Mary W. Brown of Petersburg, Mar. 4, Hertford county. R. R. Mar. 19, 1819

Mangum, Willie P. to Charity Cain, Sept. 30, Orange county. R. R. Oct. 15, 1819

Mendenhall, Abigail to Hezekiah S. Clark, Sept. 21, Guilford county. R. R. Oct. 29, 1819

Meroney, Polly to James Boswell, Oct. 21, Caswell county. R. R. Nov. 5, 1819

Minzies, Capt. Robert to Mary Hill, Oct. 5, Rockingham county. R. R. Oct. 8, 1819

Mitchell, Rev. Elisha of this State to Maria North, Dec., Connecticut. R. R. Dec. 31, 1819

Mitchell, James W. to Catherine Schaw, Jan. 14, Wilmington. R. R. Jan. 22, 1819

Mitchell, Randolph of Orange county to Margaret Tyrrell, Oct. 7, Caswell county. R. R. Oct. 29, 1819

Morrison, Jas. of Cabarrus county to Peggy Simons of Mecklenburg county, Feb. 25. R. R. Mar. 12, 1819

Nall, Mary of Moore county to Jacob Tyson, Jan. 20, Moore county. R. R. Feb. 5, 1819

Outlaw, Dr. Joseph to Hannah Stone, Aug. 15, Bertie county. R. R. Oct. 1, 1819

Pender, Dr. Lewis Coor to Matilda M. Fenner, Feb. 23, Raleigh. R. R. Feb. 26, 1819

Petty, John to Patsey Smith, Oct. 9, Pittsborough. R. R. Nov. 19, 1819

Petty, Nancy to John Brantley, Aug. 19, Chatham county. R. R. Aug. 27, 1819

Polhill, John G. of Augusta, Ga. to Harriet A. Taylor of Hillsborough, Sept. 30, Hillsborough. R. R. Oct. 15, 1819

Potts, Ann to Jarvis Buxton, Mar. 24, Beaufort county. R. R. Apr. 2, 1819

Potts, Mary to John Weisiger, My. 5, Fayetteville. R. R. My. 28, 1819

Powell, Isaac to Mrs. Frances Grimes, Jly. 6, Johnston county. R. R. Jly. 16, 1819

Raboteau, Mary to John C. Stedman, Sept. 22, Raleigh. R. R. Sept. 24, 1819

Roberts, John M. to Mary Elizabeth Jones, Jan. 13, Newbern. R. R. Jan. 29, 1819

Rogers, Capt. Benj. of Wake county to Catherine M'Cabe, Jly. 8, Orange county. R. R. Jly. 16, 1819

Ruffin, Dr. of Raleigh to Mary M'Clelland, Je. 10, Salisbury. R. R. Jly. 2, 1819

Schaw, Catherine to James W. Mitchell, Jan. 14, Wilmington. R. R. Jan. 22, 1819

Shaw, Nelly of Orange county to William Street of Caswell county, Dec. 23. R. R. Jan. 15, 1819

Simons, Peggy of Mecklenburg county to Jas. Morrison of Cabarrus county, Feb. 25. R. R. Mar. 12, 1819

Slade, Maria to Alexander M'Kethan, Apr. 7, Raleigh. R. R. Apr. 9, 1819

Sloan, James C. of Mecklenburg county to Susanna H. Bowers, Dec. 24, Rowan county. R. R. Jan. 8, 1819

Smith, Benjamin B. of Raleigh to Laura Worthington, Feb. 11, Wake county. R. R. Feb. 12, 1819

Smith, David of Wilmington to Sophia Williams, My., Chatham county. R. R. My. 7, 1819

Smith, Capt. John S. to Elizabeth Lovick, Dec. 15, Craven county. R. R. Jan. 1, 1819

Smith, Patsey to John Petty, Oct. 9, Pittsborough. R. R. Nov. 19, 1819

Sneed, Sarah to William Green of Wilmington, Dec., Williamsborough. R. R. Jan. 1, 1819

Spruill, Mrs. Charles to Richard Wood, Jan. 19, Tyrrell county. R. R. Feb. 5, 1819

Stedman, John C. to Mary Raboteau, Sept. 22, Raleigh. R. R. Sept. 24, 1819

Stone, Hannah to Dr. Joseph Outlaw, Aug. 15, Bertie county. R. R. Oct. 1, 1819

Street, William of Caswell county to Nelly Shaw of Orange county, Dec. 23. R. R. Jan. 15, 1819

Swinson, Theophilus to Mrs. Andrew Thally, Duplin county. R. R. Nov. 26, 1819

Taylor, Harriet A. of Hillsborough to John C. Polhill of Augusta, Ga., Sept. 30, Hillsborough. R. R. Oct. 15, 1819

Terrell, Solomon to Miss Cook, Je., Wake county. R. R. Je. 4, 1819

Thally, Mrs. Andrew to Theophilus Swinson, Oct. 20, Duplin county. R. R. Nov. 26, 1819

Tomlinson, Evelina R. to Lucas Benners, Aug. 17, Craven county. R. R. Aug. 20, 1819

Trevathan, Sarah to James Mason, Aug. 3, Wilmington. R. R. Aug. 13, 1819

Turner, Rebecca to George E. Badger of Hillsborough, Dec. 24, Warren county. R. R. Jan. 1, 1819

Tyrrell, Margaret to Randolph Mitchell of Orange county, Oct. 7, Caswell county. R. R. Oct. 29, 1819

Tyson, Jacob to Mary Nall of Moore county, Jan. 20, Moore county. R. R. Feb. 5, 1819

Walker, Mary J. to James M. Atkins of Raleigh, Sept. 21, Brunswick county. R. R. Oct. 1, 1819

Walton, Mrs. William to John Whitaker, Sr., Sept. 30, Wake county. R. R. Oct. 1, 1819

Warren, Rev. Henry to Mrs. Martha Edwards, Jly., Wake county. R. R. Jly. 23, 1819

Watson, Mary Ann to James Hinton of New Hanover county, Jan. 21, Hillsboro. R. R. Feb. 5, 1819

Weisiger, John to Mary Potts, My. 5, Fayetteville. R. R. My. 28, 1819

Whitaker, John, Sr. to Mrs. William Walton, Sept. 30, Wake county. R. R. Oct. 1, 1819

White, Betsey to General Boon Felton of Hertford county, Mar. 4, Raleigh. R. R. Mar. 5, 1819

Whitfield, Mrs. Bryan to Wm. Blackledge of Newbern, Mar., Wayne county. R. R. Mar. 12, 1819

Whitfield, Mary to Durant Lane, Jan. 17, Newbern. R. R. Feb. 5, 1819

Wilcox, Newton to Jane Baynor, Mar. 25, Washington. R. R. Mar. 2, 1819

Wilkins, Susan of Edgecombe county to Richard Hines of Washington, Dec. 10, Edgecombe county. R. R. Jan. 1, 1819

Williams, Dr. Solomon B. to Caroline Alston, Feb. 24, Warren county. R. R. Mar. 12, 1819

Williams, Sophia to David Smith of Wilmington, My., Chatham county. R. R. My. 7, 1819

Wood, Richard to Mrs. Charles Spruill, Jan. 19, Tyrrell county. R. R. Feb. 5, 1819

Worthington, Laura to Benjamin B. Smith of Raleigh, Feb. 11, Wake county. R. R. Feb. 12, 1819

Wright, John to Polly Kincannon of Surry county, Feb. 17. R. R. Mar. 12, 1819

1820

Alston, William of Alabama to Mary Haywood, Je. 22, Halifax county. R. R. Jly. 7, 1820

Anderson, Margaret to Major John W. Wright, Apr. 23, Fayetteville. R. R. Apr. 28, 1820

Avery, Margaret S. to John Murphey, Mar. 8, Burke county. R. R. Mar. 31, 1820

Ballard, Benjamin B. to Elizabeth Riddick, Oct. 12, Gates county. R. R. Dec. 29, 1820

Benbo, Thomas to Anna Mendenhall, Feb. 10, Guilford county. R. R. Mar. 3, 1820

Blake, Dr. James of Washington, D. C. to Margaret Davidson of Charlotte, Sept. 14, Charlotte. R. R. Oct. 6, 1820

Baker, Frederick to Elizabeth Kilpatrick, Mar. 23, Lenoir county. R. R. Apr. 14, 1820

Blacksmith, Wm. Daniel to Elizabeth Richardson, Jly. 6, Wake county. R. R. Jly. 7, 1820

Brock, Capt. Caleb to Mary F. Jones, Je. 22, Rowan county. R. R. Jly. 14, 1820

Brownrigg, Sarah of Chowan county to Capt. W. Sparkman of Bertie county, Jan. 6. R. R. Jan. 21, 1820

Bryan, Mr. of Sacred Harmony to Holly Moore, Feb., Raleigh. R. R. Feb. 18, 1820

Burnett, Nancy to Edwin Snipes, Nov. 9, Chatham county. R. R. Nov. 17, 1820

Candy, Susan to Bartholomew Crab, Mar. 14, Wayne county. R. R. Mar. 31, 1820

Chalmers, Mary to Benj. W. Williams of Moore county, Oct. 19, Fayetteville. R. R. Oct. 27, 1820

Clarke, Sarah to Franklin Turner of Wadesborough, Oct. 24, Fayetteville. R. R. Oct. 27, 1820

Clay, James to Elizabeth Lockhart, My. 26, Wake county. R. R. Je. 2, 1820

Clinch, Col. Duncan L. of U. S. Army to Miss B. M'Intosh, Nov. 8. R. R. Jan. 7, 1820

Clitherall, Eliza of Smithville to Junius A. Moore of Wilmington, My. 22. R. R. Je. 9, 1820

Coffin, Elizabeth to Nioma Hiatt, Feb., Guilford county. R. R. Mar. 3, 1820

Connor, Henry W. M. of Lincoln county to Catherine Davidson, Je. 29, Iredell county. R. R. Jly. 14, 1820

Cowan, Col. John to Jane Amelia Dick, Jan. 20, Wilmington. R. R. Jane. 28, 1820

Cox, Caroline Ann of Edenton to Joseph Eagles of Wilmington, Feb. 8, Edenton. R. R. Feb. 18, 1820

Cox, Thomas to Olivia Norfleet, Feb. 15, Scotland Neck. R. R. Mar. 3, 1820

Crab, Bartholomew to Susan Candy, Mar. 14, Wayne county. R. R. Mar. 31, 1820

Crawford, Jane to Willis Sellers, Jly. 27, Orange county. R. R. Aug. 11, 1820

Dalrymple, Mary to John M'Iver, Jan. 13, Moore county. R. R. Feb. 4, 1820

Davidson, Catherine to Henry W. M. Connor of Lincoln county, Je. 29, Iredell county. R. R. Jly. 14, 1820

Davidson, Margaret of Charlotte to Dr. James Blake of Washington, D. C., Sept. 14, Charlotte. R. R. Oct. 6, 1820

Dick, Jane Amelia to Col. John Cowan, Jan. 20, Wilmington. R. R. Jan. 28, 1820

Donald, Major Robert to Mrs. Nancy Latta of Orange county, Nov. 16, Guilford county. R. R. Dec. 8, 1820

Eagles, Joseph of Wilmington to Caroline Ann Cox of Edenton, Feb. 8, Edenton. R. R. Feb. 18, 1820

Eaton, Rebecca to John H. Fenner, Je. 1, Halifax county. R. R. Je. 16, 1820

Elliott, Catharine to Jesse B. Shepherd, Sept. 28, Cumberland county. R. R. Oct. 6, 1820

Emmit, Capt. William C. of Murfreesborough, Tenn. to Rebecca C. Stokes of Wilkes county, Je. 22. R. R. Jly. 14, 1820

Farrish, Fanny of Chatham county to James M. M'Laurin of Fayetteville, Jan. 6, Chatham county. R. R. Jan. 21, 1820

Fenner, John H. to Rebecca Eaton, Je. 1, Halifax county. R. R. Je. 16, 1820

Floyd, Mary to Dilworth Sledge, Jan., Raleigh. R. R. Feb. 4, 1820

Fontaine, Miss E. L. of Henry county, Va. to Edmond Winston of Rockingham county, Aug. 16. R. R. Sept. 1, 1820

Forney, Lavinia to John Fullenwider, Mar. 1, Lincoln county. R. R. Apr. 7, 1820

Fraser, John of Hertford county to Miss Granberry of Bertie county, My. R. R. My. 19, 1820

Fullenwider, John, Jr. to Lavinia Forney, Mar. 1, Lincoln county. R. R. Apr. 7, 1820

Granberry, Miss of Bertie county to John Fraser of Hertford county, My. R. R. My. 19, 1820

Graves, Henrietta to Hon. Thomas Settle of Rockingham, Sept. 21, Caswell county. R. R. Oct. 6, 1820

Guion, John W. to Mary Tillman, Jly. 23, Newbern. R. R. Aug. 11, 1820

Hankins, John to Catherine Roberts, My. 10, Edenton. R. R. My. 26, 1820

Harris, Eliza to John Watson, Oct. 5, Chatham county. R. R. Oct. 27, 1820

Harris, Sampson to Isabella Lister, Feb. 9, Guilford county. R. R. Mar. 3, 1820

Harrison, Robert of Raleigh to Miss Tucker, Feb., Franklin county. R. R. Feb. 25, 1820

Hassam, J. H. to Margaret Nicholls, Dec. 14, Raleigh. R. R. Dec. 15, 1820

Haughton, Mala to Mary M'Laughlin, My. 11, Washington county. R. R. My. 26, 1820

Haywood, Mary to William Alston of Alabama, Je. 22, Halifax county. R. R. Jly. 7, 1820

Henderson, Elizabeth to Hamilton Jones, Jly. 10, Chapel Hill. R. R. Jly. 21, 1820

Henderson, Dr. William of Waynesboro to Mary Ann Slade, Jan. 27, Martin county. R. R. Feb. 4, 1820

Henley, Rebecca to James Hodgin, Apr. 6, Randolph county. R. R. Apr. 21, 1820

Hiatt, Nioma to Elizabeth Coffin, Feb., Guilford county. R. R. Mar. 3, 1820

Hicks, Thomas to Mary C. Sawyer, Nov. 2, Orange county. R. R. Nov. 17, 1820

Hill, John A. of Wilmington to Miss E. D. D. Nicoll of Connecticut, Nov.
R. R. Nov. 24, 1820

Hillyard, Martha H. P. to L. G. Watson of Greensborough, Oct. 31, Granville county. R. R. Nov. 17, 1820

Hinton, Charles L. of Wake county to Ann Perry of Franklin county, Dec. 27.
R. R. Dec. 29, 1820

Hodgin, James to Rebecca Henley, Apr. 6, Randolph county. R. R. Apr.
21, 1820

Hoit, Rebecca to William Unthank, Feb. 9, Guilford county. R. R. Mar. 3,
1820

Horniblow, Eliza to Dr. Frederick Hoskins, My. 10, Edenton. R. R. My. 26,
1820

Hoskins, Dr. Frederick of Plymouth to Eliza Horniblow, My. 10, Edenton.
R. R. My. 26, 1820

Hudgens, Dr. Pleasant of Salisbury to Mary Winslow of New Orleans, Dec.
20, New Orleans. R. R. Feb. 11, 1820

Jones, Hamilton to Elizabeth Henderson, Jly. 10, Chapel Hill. R. R. Jly. 21,
1820

Jones, Mary F. to Capt. Caleb Brock, Je. 22, Rowan county. R. R. Jly 14, 1820

Jordan, Wm. Hill to Maria Miller, Sept. 5, Bertie county. R. R. Sept. 22, 1820

Kilpatrick, Elizabeth to Frederick Baker, Mar. 23, Lenoir county. R. R.
Apr. 7, 1820

Knox, Mary to John T. Scott of Alabama and this State, Dec. 5, Sneedsborough. R. R. Dec. 22, 1820

Latta, Mrs. Nancy of Orange county to Major Robert Donald, Nov. 16. R. R.
Dec. 8, 1820

Lister, Isabella to Sampson Harris, Feb. 9, Guilford county. R. R. Mar. 3,
1820

Lockhart, Elizabeth to James Clay, My. 26, Wake county. R. R. Je. 2, 1820

M'Alester, Louisa to Capt. James Ward of the U. S. Army, Feb. 19, Wilmington. R. R. Mar. 3, 1820

M'Intosh, Miss B. to Col. Duncan L. Clinch, Nov. 8. R. R. Jan. 7, 1820

M'Iver, John to Mary Dalrymple, Jan. 13, Moore county. R. R. Feb. 4, 1820

M'Laughlin, Mary to Mala Haughton, My. 11, Washington county. R. R.
My. 26, 1820

M'Laurin, James M. of Fayetteville to Fanny Farrish of Chatham county,
Jan. 6, Chatham county. R. R. Jan. 21, 1820

M'Lean, Neil to Margaret Murphy, Feb. 3, Robeson county. R. R. Feb. 25,
1820

M'Leod, Donald Roy to Elinor Murphey, Sept. 14, Fayetteville. R. R. Sept.
22, 1820

Manning, John of Raleigh to Julia Sledge, My. 17, Franklin county. R. R.
My. 26, 1820

Marshall, James of Anson county to Eliza M. Richardson of Bladen county,
Sept. 6, Bladen county. R. R. Oct. 13, 1820

Mendenhall, Anna to Thomas Benbo, Feb. 10, Guilford county. R. R. Mar. 3,
1820

Mendenhall, Moses H. of Guilford county to Mary Ann Stockton of Stokes
county, Feb. 9, Stokes county. R. R. Mar. 3, 1820

Miller, Maria to Wm. Hill Jordan, Sept. 5, Bertie county. R. R. Sept. 22, 1820

Moore, Eliza of Albemarle county, Va. to Henry C. Moore of Orange county, Oct. 19. R. R. Nov. 17, 1820

Moore, Henry C. of Orange county to Eliza Moore of Albemarle county, Va., Oct. 19. R. R. Nov. 17, 1820

Moore, Holly to Mr. Bryan of Sacred Harmony, Feb., Raleigh. R. R. Feb. 18, 1820

Moore, Mary E. A. to Abner Stith, Je. 14, Northampton county. R. R. Je. 22, 1820

Moore, Junius A. of Wilmington to Eliza Clitherall of Smithville, My. 22. R. R. Je. 9, 1820

Moss, Sarah to Richard Roberts. Dec. 20, Mecklenburg county, Va. R. R. Feb. 4, 1820

Murchison, John to Isabella Ray, Feb. 3, Fayetteville. R. R. Feb. 25, 1820

Murphey, Cornelia to John P. Carter of Salisbury, Jan. 4, Orange county. R. R. Jan. 26, 1820

Murphey, Eleanor to Roy Donald M'Leod, Sept. 14, Fayetteville. R. R. Sept. 22, 1820

Murphey, John to Margaret S. Avery, Mar. 8, Burke county. R. R. Mar. 31, 1820

Murphy, Margaret to Neil M'Lean, Feb. 3, Robeson county. R. R. Feb. 25, 1820

Nall, Winifred to Mrs. Aaron Tyson, Jan. 12, Moore county. R. R. Feb. 4, 1820

Nicoll, Miss E. A. D. of Connecticut to John A. Hill of Wilmington, Nov. R. R. Nov. 24, 1820

Nicholls, Margaret to J. H. Hassam, Dec. 14, Raleigh. R. R. Dec. 15, 1820

Nixon, Nancy to Thomas Winslow, Apr. 5, Randolph county. R. R. Apr. 21, 1820

Norfleet, Olivia to Thomas Cox, Feb. 15, Scotland Neck. R. R. Mar. 3, 1820

Perry, Ann of Franklin county to Charles L. Hinton of Wake county, Dec. 27. R. R. Dec. 29, 1820

Ponton, Mungo T. to Martha Turner, Je. 1, Halifax county. R. R. Je. 16, 1820

Ray, Isabella to John Murchison, Feb. 3, Fayetteville. R. R. Feb. 25, 1820

Richardson, Elizabeth to Wm. D. Blacksmith, Jly. 6, Wake county. R. R. Jly. 7, 1820

Richardson, Eliza N. of Bladen county to James Marshall of Anson county, Sept. 6, Bladen county. R. R. Oct. 13, 1820

Riddick, Elizabeth to Benjamin B. Ballard, Oct. 12, Gates county. R. R. Dec. 29, 1820

Roberts, Catharine to John Hankins, My. 10, Edenton. R. R. My. 26, 1820

Roberts, Richard of Raleigh to Sarah Moss, Dec. 20, Mecklenburg county, Va. R. R. Feb. 4, 1820

Sawyer, Mary C. to Thomas Hicks, Nov. 2, Orange county. R. R. Nov. 17, 1820

Scott, John to Caroline L. Miner of Newbern, Jly. 5, Hillsborough. R. R. Jly. 21, 1820

Scott, John T. of Alabama and this State to Mary Knox, Dec. 5, Sneedsborough. R. R. Dec. 22, 1820

Sellers, Willis to Jane Crawford, Jly. 27, Orange county. R. R. Aug. 11, 1820

Settle, Hon. Thomas of Rockingham to Henrietta Graves, Sept. 21, Caswell county. R. R. Oct. 6, 1820

Shepherd, Jesse B. to Catherine Elliott, Sept. 28, Cumberland county. R. R. Oct. 6, 1820

MARRIAGE NOTICES

Skinner, Edmund to Emily Wood, Je. 18, Hertford. R. R. Aug. 4, 1820

Slade, Mary Ann to Dr. William Henderson of Waynesboro, Jan. 27, Martin county. R. R. Feb. 4, 1820

Sledge, Dilworth to Mary Floyd, Jan., Raleigh. R. R. Feb. 4, 1820

Sledge, Julia to John Manning of Raleigh, My. 17, Franklin county. R. R. My. 26, 1820

Sledge, Lucinda to Ruffin Tucker of Raleigh, Sept. 13, Franklin county. R. R. Sept. 22, 1820

Snipes, Edwin to Nancy Burnett, Nov. 9, Chatham county. R. R. Nov. 17, 1820

Sparkman, Capt. W. of Bertie county to Sarah Brownrigg of Chowan county, Jan. 6. R. R. Jan. 21, 1820

Stockton, Mary Ann of Stokes county to Moses H. Mendenhall of Guilford county, Feb. 9, Stokes county. R. R. Mar. 3, 1820

Stokes, Rebecca C. of Wilkes county to Capt. William Emmit of Murfreesborough, Tenn., Je. 22. R. R. Jly 14, 1820

Tillman, Mary to John W. Guion, Jly. 23, Newbern. R. R. Aug. 11, 1820

Turner, Franklin of Wadesborough to Sarah Clarke, Oct. 24, Fayetteville. R. R. Oct. 27, 1820

Turner, Martha to Mungo T. Ponton, Je. 1, Halifax county. R. R. Je. 16, 1820

Tucker, Ruffin of Raleigh to Lucinda Sledge, Sept. 13, Franklin county. R. R. Sept. 22, 1820

Tucker, Miss to Robert Harrison of Raleigh, Feb., Franklin county. R. R. Feb. 25, 1820

Tyson, Mrs. Aaron to Winifred Nall, Jan. 12, Moore county. R. R. Feb. 4, 1820

Unthank, William to Rebecca Hoit, Feb. 9, Guilford county. R. R. Mar. 3, 1820

Ward, Capt. James of U. S. Army to Louisa M'Alester, Feb. 9, Wilmington. R. R. Mar. 3, 1820

Watson, John to Eliza Harris, Oct. 5, Chatham county. R. R. Oct. 27, 1820

Watson, L. G. of Greensborough to Martha H. P. Hillyard, Oct. 31, Granville county. R. R. Nov. 17, 1820

Welch, Major William of Haywood county to Polly Kimbrough of Surry county, Apr. 27. R. R. My. 26, 1820

White, Mrs. John D. to Henry Wills of Edenton, Apr. 9, Petersburg. R. R. My. 19, 1820

Williams, Benj. W. of Moore county to Mary Chalmers, Oct. 19, Fayetteville. R. R. Oct. 27, 1820

Wills, Henry of Edenton to Mrs. John D. White, Apr. 9, Petersburg, Va. R. R. My. 19, 1820

Winslow, Mary of New Orleans to Dr. Pleasant Hudgens, Dec. 20, New Orleans. R. R. Feb. 11, 1820

Winslow, Thomas to Nancy Nixon, Apr. 5, Randolph county. R. R. Apr. 21, 1820

Winston, Edmond of Rockingham county to Miss E. L. Fontaine of Henry county, Va., Aug. 16. R. R. Sept. 1, 1820

Wood, Emily to Edmund Skinner, Je. 18, Hertford. R. R. Aug. 4, 1820

Wright, Major John W. to Margaret Anderson, Apr. 23, Fayetteville. R. R. Apr. 28, 1820

1821

Alexander, Eliza of Cabarrus county to James A. Means of Concord, Feb. 20, Cabarrus county. R. R. Mar. 16, 1821

Ashford, Wm. to Polly Blackman, Oct. 18, Sampson county. R. R. Nov. 16, 1821

Bailey, John L. to Miss P. E. Brownrigg, Je. 26, Edenton. R. R. Jly. 13, 1821

Barnes, Peter to Matilda Sexton, Apr. 26, Wake county. R. R. My. 4, 1821

Bell, Col. Brickhouse to Mrs. M. Downs, Mar. 11, Camden county. R. R. Mar. 23, 1821

Berry, James A. to Catharine Ann Hill, Apr. 19, Wilmington. R. R. My. 4, 1821

Berry, Richard to Sarah Slade, Mar. 1, Newbern. R. R. Mar. 16, 1821

Billings, Rev. Dr. Thomas to Mrs. John Skinner of Chowan county, Feb. 4, Montpelier. R. R. Feb. 16, 1821

Bingham, Lemuel to Jane M. Miller, Dec. 5, Salisbury. R. R. Dec. 21, 1821

Blackman, Polly to Wm. Ashford, Oct. 18, Sampson county. R. R. Nov. 16, 1821

Blackwell, Ann Evilina to Eli Smallwood of Newbern, Oct. 31, New York. R. R. Nov. 16, 1821

Blount, Eliza A. H. to Dr. John T. Dabney of Montgomery county, Apr., Tennessee. R. R. My. 24, 1821

Brandon, David C. to Mary M'Adin, Apr. 14, Caswell county. R. R. My. 4, 1821

Brickell, Lavinia to Jas. C. Jones, Sept. 6, Windsor. R. R. Sept. 21, 1821

Broadfoot, Margaret to Jas. H. Hooper, Nov. 14, Fayetteville. R. R. Nov. 23, 1821

Brooks, Eliza Ann to Capt. Thomas N. Gautier of Wilmington, Jly., Bladen county. R. R. Jly. 13, 1821

Brooks, Joseph to Hannah Harper, Dec. 14, Chatham county. R. R. Jan. 5, 1821

Brown, Eliza Ann to Capt. Thomas Gautier of Wilmington, Jly., Bladen county. R. R. Jly. 13, 1821

Brown, Joseph to Hannah Harper, Dec. 14, Chatham county. R. R. Jan. 5, 1821

Brownrigg, Miss P. E. to John L. Bailey, Je. 26, Edenton. R. R. Jly 13, 1821

Bryan, Mary Ann Elizabeth B. to Dr. Jesse Isler, Dec. 26, Granville county. R. R. Jan. 5, 1821

Campbell, Col. James of Leaksville to Sophia W. Spencer of Charlotte county, Va., My. 23. R. R. Je. 8, 1821

Carter, John P. of Salisbury to Cornelia Murphey, Jan. 4, Orange county. R. R. Jan. 26, 1821

Cash, Col. Bogan of Wadesboro to Elizabeth Ellerby of South Carolina, Oct. 18. R. R. Nov. 16, 1821

Catron, John to Matilda Childers, Jan. 25, Nashville. R. R. Feb. 23, 1821

Charrier, Jane C. to John Slade of Edenton, Je. 19, Pembroke, Chowan county. R. R. Jly. 6, 1821

Chauncey, Col. Samuel to Mary Congleton, Apr. 15, Beaufort county. R. R. My. 4, 1821

Childers, Matilda to John Catron, Jan. 25, Nashville. R. R. Feb. 23, 1821

Clifton, John L. to Ann King, Oct. 18, Sampson county. R. R. Nov. 16, 1821

Cochran, Joshua W. to Caroline A. Davis, Oct. 29, Fayetteville. R. R. Nov. 16, 1821

Congleton, Mary to Col. Samuel Chauncey, Apr. 15, Beaufort county. R. R. My. 4, 1821

Croom, Hardy B. to Frances Smith, Je. 19, Newbern. R. R. Jly. 6, 1821

Crouse, Thomas to Eliza Lash of Raleigh, Je., Stokes county. R. R. Je. 29, 1821

Cummins, Frances to Samuel Pullen, Jan. 9, Raleigh. R. R. Jan. 12, 1821

Dabney, Dr. John T. to Eliza A. H. Blount of Montgomery county, Apr., Tennessee. R. R. My. 24, 1821

Davie, Frederick W. to Octavia T. Dessaussure, My. 1, Catawba county. R. R. My. 25, 1821

Davis, Caroline A. to Joshua W. Cochran, Oct. 29, Fayetteville. R. R. Nov. 16, 1821

Davis, Eliza to John Walker of Wilmington, Jly. 12, Fayetteville. R. R. Jly. 27, 1821

Davis, Harriet of Guilford county to John Scott of Greensborough. Feb. 1. R. R. Feb. 16, 1821

Deford, William M. to Rosa Smith, Feb., Halifax. R. R. Feb. 2, 1821

Dessaussure, Octavia T. to Frederick W. Davie, My. 1, Catawba county. R. R. My. 25, 1821

Dick, John M. of Guilford county to Parthenia Williamson, Sept. 4, Person county. R. R. Sept. 14, 1821

Dilliard, Mary Ann to Dr. James Reeks of Haywood, Chatham county, Dec. 30, Raleigh. R. R. Feb. 2, 1821

Dixon, Miss C. to Frederick Foy of Onslow county, Mar. 1, Greene county. R. R. Mar. 23, 1821

Dobbin, John M. to Margaret M'Queen of Chatham county, Mar. 1, Fayetteville. R. R. Mar. 16, 1821

Downs, Mrs. M. to Bell Brickhouse, Mar. 11, Camden county. R. R. Mar. 23, 1821

Eccles, John D. of Fayetteville to Elizabeth P. Jones, Dec. 24, Chatham county. R. R. Jan. 5, 1821

Ellerby, Elizabeth of South Carolina to Col. Bogan Cash of Wadesboro, Oct. 18. R. R. Nov. 16, 1821

Erwin, Margaret to James McDowell, Feb. 22, Lincoln county. R. R. Apr. 13, 1821

Farrar, John of Mecklenburg county, Va. to Mary Minter, Jan. 8, Chatham county. R. R. Feb. 9, 1821

Fitzharris, Laurence to Catherine E. Purviance, Feb. 18, Fayetteville. R. R. Mar. 2, 1821

Fowler, Mary to Moses Jarvis, Mar. 24, Craven county. R. R. Apr. 13, 1821

Foy, Frederick of Onslow county to Miss C. Dixon, Mar. 1, Greene county. R. R. Mar. 23, 1821

Freeman, Frederick of Newbern to Elizabeth Nichols, Dec. 26, Raleigh. R. R. Dec. 28, 1821

Fuller, Zylphia to Thomas Marshall of Carteret county, Jan. 25, Beaufort. R. R. Feb. 23, 1821

Garland, Dr. John T. of Milton to Isabella Christiana Glenn of Halifax county, Va., My. 16. R. R. Je. 1, 1821

Gautier, Capt. Thomas N. to Eliza Ann Brown of Wilmington, Jly., Bladen county. R. R. Jly. 13, 1821

Glenn, Isabella Christiana of Halifax county, Va. to Dr. John T. Garland of Milton, My. 16. R. R. Je. 1, 1821

Gregory, Marinda to Thomas H. Hill of Craven county, Feb. 7, Onslow county. R. R. Feb. 23, 1821

Hand, Ann to Hinton James, Feb. 22, New Hanover county. R. R. Mar. 2, 1821

Harper, Hannah to Joseph Brooks, Dec. 14, Chatham county. R. R. Jan. 5, 1821

Hatch, Lemuel to Ann Simmons, Feb. 20, Jones county. R. R. Feb. 23, 1821

Hatch, Richard B. of Jones county to Clarissa Rhodes of Wayne county, Dec. 26, Onslow county. R. R. Jan. 12, 1821

Hawkins, Emily to Maj. James Nutall, Feb. 28, Granville county. R. R. Mar. 30, 1821

Haywood, Margaret to Louis D. Henry, Dec. 27, Fayetteville. R. R. Jan. 5, 1821

Henry, Louis D. to Margaret Haywood, Dec. 27, Fayetteville. R. R. Jan. 5, 1821

High, Rebecca K. to Jones H. Murray of Louisburg, Nov. 15, Wake county. R. R. Nov. 23, 1821

Hill, Catharine Ann to James A. Berry, Apr. 19, Wilmington. R. R. My. 4, 1821

Hill, Thomas H. of Craven county to Marinda Gregory, Feb. 7, Onslow county. R. R. Feb. 23, 1821

Hogan, Mary to Kimbrough Jones of Wake county, My. 10, Randolph county. R. R. My. 18, 1821

Holmes, Penelope of Sampson county to Major Edmund B. Whitfield, Jan. 23, Wayne county. R. R. Feb. 23, 1821

Hooper, Jas. H. to Margaret Broadfoot, Nov. 14, Fayetteville. R. R. Nov. 23, 1821

Hunter, Sarah J. to Robert Macauley, Nov. 8, Springhill. R. R. Nov. 16, 1821

Isler, Dr. Jesse of Lenoir county to Mary Ann Eliza Bryan, Dec. 26, Granville county. R. R. Jan. 5, 1821

James, Hinton to Ann Hand, Feb. 22, New Hanover county. R. R. Mar. 2, 1821

Jarvis, Matilda to P. L. Wicks of Savannah, Ga., Mar. 1, Newbern. R. R. Mar. 16, 1821

Jarvis, Moses to Mary Fowler, Mar. 24, Craven county. R. R. Apr. 13, 1821

Johnson, Margaret to Green Perry of Franklin, Oct., Warren county. R. R. Oct. 26, 1821

Johnson, Sally to Thos. White of Warrenton, Apr. 9, Warren county. R. R. Apr. 27, 1821

Johnston, Col. Charles W. of Warren county to Mary Jane Robinson of Virginia, Nov. 24. R. R. Dec. 28, 1821

Jones, Amelia to John Pulliam, Nov., Wake county. R. R. Dec. 28, 1821

Jones, Elizabeth P. to John D. Eccles of Fayetteville, Dec. 24, Chatham county. R. R. Jan. 5, 1821

Jones, Jas. C. to Lavinia Brickell, Sept. 6, Windsor. R. R. Sept. 21, 1821

Jones, Kimbrough of Wake county to Mary P. Hogan, My. 10, Randolph county. R. R. My. 18, 1821

King, Ann to John L. Clifton, Oct. 18, Sampson county. R. R. Nov. 16, 1821

Law, Hervey of Fayetteville to Maria Savage, Mar. 4, Wilmington. R. R. Mar. 23, 1821

Lash, Eliza of Raleigh to Thomas Crouse, Je., Stokes county. R. R. Je. 29, 1821

Little, Lucy to Edward Terry of Mecklenburg county, Va., Apr. 11, Warren county. R. R. Apr. 27, 1821

Lloyd, Jas. R. of Tarboro to Ann Slade, Oct., Martin county. R. R. Oct. 26, 1821

Long, Maria to John S. Shepard of Newbern, Nov. 27, Halifax county. R. R. Dec. 21, 1821

Lowe, Exum H. to Elizabeth Sessums, Nov., Tarborough. R. R. Nov. 23, 1821

Lyon, Mr. of Caswell county to Mary Olive, My. 19, Wake county. R. R. Je. 22, 1821

M'Adin, Mary to David C. Brandon, Apr. 14, Caswell county. R. R. My. 4, 1821

M'Cauley, Robert to Sarah J. Hunter, Nov. 8, Springhill. R. R. Nov. 16, 1821

M'Dowell, James to Margaret Erwin, Feb. 22, Lincoln county. R. R. Apr. 13, 1821

M'Queen, Margaret of Chatham county to John M. Dobbin, Mar. 1, Fayetteville. R. R. Mar. 16, 1821

Marshall, Thomas of Carteret county to Zylphia Fuller, Jan. 25, Beaufort. R. R. Feb. 23, 1821

Means, James A. of Concord to Eliza Alexander of Cabarrus county, Feb. 20, Cabarrus county. R. R. Mar. 16, 1821

Miles, Thos. to Scheherezade Price, Apr. 11, Wake county. R. R. Apr. 27, 1821

Miller, Jane M. to Lemuel Bingham, Dec. 5, Salisbury. R. R. Dec. 21, 1821

Minter, Mary to John Farrar of Mecklenburg, Va., Jan. 8, Chatham county. R. R. Feb. 9, 1821

Moore, Mary E. E. to Abner Stith, Je. 14, Northampton county. R. R. Je. 22, 1821

Murray, James H. of Louisburg to Rebécca K. High, Nov. 15, Wake county. R. R. Nov. 23, 1821

Murphey, Cornelia to John P. Carter of Salisbury, Jan. 4, Orange county. R. R. Jan. 26, 1821

Nichols, Elizabeth to Frederick Freeman, Dec. 26, Raleigh. R. R. Dec. 28, 1821

Norfleet, Felicia to Dr. Geo. W. Vaughan, Nov. 18, Halifax. R. R. Nov. 23, 1821

Nutall, Maj. James to Emily Hawkins, Feb. 28, Granville county. R. R. Mar. 30, 1821

Olive, Mary to Mr. Lyon of Caswell county, My. 19, Wake county. R. R. Je. 22, 1821

Perry, Green of Franklin to Margaret Johnson, Oct., Warren county.
R. R. Oct. 26, 1821

Price, Scheherezade to Thos. Miles, Apr. 11, Wake county. R. R. Apr. 27, 1821

Pullen, Samuel to Frances Cummins, Jan. 9, Raleigh. R. R. Jan. 12, 1821

Pulliam, John of Granville county to Amelia Jones, Nov., Wake county.
R. R. Dec. 28, 1821

Purviance, Catherine E. to Laurence Fitzharris, Feb. 18, Fayetteville.
R. R. Mar. 2, 1821

Ramsey, Joseph of Raleigh to Elizabeth Stedman, Nov. 1, Pittsborough.
R. R. Nov. 9, 1821

Reeks, Dr. James of Haywood, Chatham county to Mary Ann Dilliard, Dec.
30, Raleigh. R. R. Feb. 2, 1821

Rhodes, Clarissa of Wayne county to Richard B. Hatch of Jones county,
Dec. 26, Onslow county. R. R. Jan. 12, 1821

Robinson, Mary Jane of Virginia to Col. Charles W. Johnston, Nov. 24.
R. R. Dec. 28, 1821

Rogers, Dr. John to Margaret L. Shepherd, Sept. 27, Hillsborough. R. R.
Oct. 12, 1821

Root, J. A. of Wilmington to Jerusha Savage, Mar. 4, Wilmington. R. R.
Mar. 23, 1821

Savage, Jerusha to J. A. Root of Wilmington, Mar. 4, Wilmington. R. R.
Mar. 23, 1821

Savage, Maria to Hervey Law of Fayetteville, Mar. 4, Wilmington. R. R.
Mar. 23, 1821

Sawyer, Lemuel from this State to Camilla Wurtz, Dec. 24, Washington,
D. C. R. R. Jan. 12, 1821

Scarborough, Judith to Samuel Staw, Jly. 4, Currituck county. R. R. Aug.
10, 1821

Scott, John of Greensborough to Harriet Davis of Guilford county, Feb. 1.
R. R. Feb. 16, 1821

Sessums, Elizabeth to Exum H. Lowe, Nov., Tarborough. R. R. Nov. 23, 1821

Sexton, Matilda to Peter Barnes, Apr. 26, Wake county. R. R. My. 4, 1821

Shaw, Samuel to Judith Scarborough, Jly. 4, Currituck county. R. R.
Aug. 10, 1821

Shephard, John S. of Newbern to Maria Long, Nov. 27, Halifax county.
R. R. Dec. 21, 1821

Shepperd, Margaret L. to John Rogers, Sept. 27, Hillsborough. R. R.
Oct. 12, 1821

Simmons, Ann to Lemuel Hatch, Feb. 20, Jones county. R. R. Feb. 23, 1821

Skinner, Mrs. Anne of Chowan county to Rev. Dr. Thomas Billings, Feb.
4. R. R. Feb. 16, 1821

Slade, Ann to Jos. R. Lloyd, Oct., Martin county. R. R. Oct. 26, 1821

Slade, John of Edenton to Jane C. Charrier, Je. 19, Chowan county. R. R.
Jly. 6, 1821

Slade, Sarah to Richard T. Berry, Mar. 1, Newbern. R. R. Mar. 16, 1821

Smallwood, Eli of Newbern to Ann Evilina Blackwell, Oct. 31, New York.
R. R. Nov. 16, 1821

Smith, Frances to Hardy B. Croom, Je. 19, Newbern. R. R. Jly. 6, 1821

Smith, Rosa to William M. Deford, Feb., Halifax. R. R. Feb. 2, 1821

Spencer, Sophia W. of Charlotte county, Va. to Col. James Campbell of
Leaksville, My. 23. R. R. Je. 8, 1821

Stanfield, Joseph to Parthenia Vanhook, Apr. 5, Person county. R. R.
Apr. 27, 1821

Staw, Samuel to Judith Scarborough, Jly. 4, Currituck county. R. R. Aug.
10, 1821

Stedman, Elizabeth to Joseph Ramsey of Raleigh, Nov. 1, Pittsborough.
R. R. Nov. 9, 1821

Stith, Abner to Mary E. A. Moore, Je. 14, Northampton county. R. R.
Je. 22, 1821

Terry, Edward of Mecklenburg county, Va. to Lucy Little, Apr. 11, Warren
county. R. R. Apr. 27, 1821

Tucker, Mary B. to Thomas B. Whitaker, Aug. 21, Wake county. R. R.
Aug. 24, 1821

Vanhook, Parthenia to Joseph Stanfield, Apr. 5, Person county. R. R.
Apr. 27, 1821

Vaughan, Dr. Geo. W. to Felicia L. Norfleet, Nov. 18, Halifax. R. R. Nov.
23, 1821

Walker, John of Wilmington to Eliza Davis, Jly. 12, Fayetteville. R. R.
Jly. 27, 1821

Whitaker, Thomas B. to Mary B. Tucker, Aug. 21, Wake county. R. R.
Aug. 24, 1821

White, Thos. of Warrenton to Sally Johnson, Apr. 9, Warren county.
R. R. Apr. 27, 1821

Whitfield, Major Edmund B. to Penelope Holmes of Sampson county,
Jan. 23, Wayne county. R. R. Feb. 23, 1821

Wicks, P. L. of Savannah, Ga. to Matilda Jarvis, Mar. 1, Newbern. R. R.
Mar. 16, 1821

Williamson, Parthenia to John M. Dick of Guilford county, Sept. 4, Person
county. R. R. Sept. 14, 1821

Wilson, Alexander of Raleigh to Mary Willis of Ireland, Jly. 9, Baltimore.
R. R. Jly. 27, 1821

Willis, Mary of Ireland to Alexander Wilson, of Raleigh, Jly. 9, Baltimore.
R. R. Jly. 27, 1821

Wurtz, Camilla to Lemuel Sawyer from this State, Dec. 24, Washington,
D. C. R. R. Jan. 12, 1821

1822

Allen, Chasteen of Amelia county, Va. to Jane Turner of Warren county,
Nov. 27, Warren county. R. R. Dec. 6, 1822

Alston, Gideon, Jr. of Warren county to Eliza Branch of Franklin county,
Oct., Franklin county. R. R. Oct. 11, 1822

Alston, John of Chatham county to Adeline Williams, Dec. 12, Franklin
county. R. R. Dec. 20, 1822

Anderson, Walker of Hillsborough to Phebe R. Hawks, Jly. 29, Newbern.
R. R. Aug. 9, 1822

Archer, Dr. R. A. to Julian Proudfit, Dec. 16, Nash county. R. R. Dec. 27,
1822

Armstrong, Thos. D. to Juicy Tate, Sept. 26, Orange county. R. R. Oct.
18, 1822

Atkinson, Col. Tho's to Betsy P. Samuel, Aug. 15, Caswell county. R. R. Aug. 30, 1822

Avery, Mary Caroline of Smithville to John M. Van Cleef of Wilmington, Sept. 12. R. R. Sept. 20, 1822

Avery, Mrs. of Johnston county to Branch Walthall, Oct. 22, Wake county. R. R. Oct. 25, 1822

Battle, Jas. S. of Edgecombe county to Sallie Westray, Dec. 3, Nash county. R. R. Dec. 27, 1822

Beard, John L. of Salisbury to Milly Cress of Concord, Je. 20, Concord. R. R. Jly. 4, 1822

Beatty, William G. of Bladen county to Eliza Pearson of Rowan county, Feb. 16. R. R. Mar. 1, 1822

Blackwell, Charles of Louisburg to Martha Robinson of Granville county, Oct. 23, Granville county. R. R. Nov. 8, 1822

Blake, Miles of Fayetteville to Mary Parish, Nov. 26, Bladen county. R. R. Dec. 6, 1822

Blount, Caroline to Benj. Runyon, My. 28, Beaufort county. R. R. Je. 7, 1822

Bond, Israel to Mary Walton, My. 26, Wake county. R. R. My. 31, 1822

Bonner, Joseph of Washington, Beaufort county to Sally Ann Crawford of Beaufort county, My. 30. R. R. Je. 14, 1822

Branch, Eliza of Franklin county to Gideon Alston, Jr. of Warren county, Oct., Franklin county. R. R. Oct. 11, 1822

Brewer, Nancy to James Russel, My. 30, Hillsborough. R. R. Je. 14, 1822

Bryan, John H. to Mary Shepard, Dec. 20, Newbern. R. R. Jan. 4, 1822

Buie, John R. of Fayetteville to Margaret M'Farland, Feb. 14, Richmond county. R. R. Mar. 8, 1822

Bulloch, Ann M. of Warren county to Archibald Henderson of Warren county, Oct. 1, Warren county. R. R. Oct. 18, 1822

Bullock, Fanny to John Hunt, Nov. 6, Granville county. R. R. Nov. 15, 1822

Busby, James to Eliza Sturdivant, My. 30, Wake county. R. R. Je. 7, 1822

Bush, Dr. L. B. of Wayne county to Mary C. Wright, Sept. 3, Duplin county. R. R. Sept. 13, 1822

Byrd, Edward to Mrs. Jesse Cherry, Feb. 7, Martin county. R. R. Feb. 22, 1822

Cabe, Margaret to John W. Caldwell, Oct. 1, Guilford county. R. R. Oct. 11, 1822

Caldwell, John W. to Margaret Cabe, Oct. 1, Guilford county. R. R. Oct. 11, 1822

Calhorda, John P. to Zilphia Martin, Je. 18, Wilmington. R. R. Je. 21, 1822

Camp, Benjamin B. to Mary Rea, Mar. 13, Murfreesboro. R. R. Mar. 22, 1822

Campbell, Col. John W. of Madison to Ann W. Clark, Mar. 26, Milledgville, Ga. R. R. Apr. 5, 1822

Chambers, Mrs. Anna to George Miller, Je. 13, Rowan county. R. R. Je. 28, 1822

Cherry, Mrs. Jesse to Edward Byrd, Feb. 7, Martin county. R. R. Feb. 22, 1822

Cherry, Sam'l H. to Charlotte Coor of Wayne county, Dec. 15, Waynesboro. R. R. Dec. 27, 1822

Clark, Ann W. to Col. John W. Campbell of Madison, Mar. 26, Milledgeville, Ga. R. R. Apr. 5, 1822

Cleef, Van John M. of Wilmington to Mary Caroline Avery of Smithville, Sept. 12. R. R. Sept. 20, 1822

Cobbs, Martha M. to Wm. H. Phillips of Hillsborough, Aug. 6, Raleigh. R. R. Aug. 9, 1822

Coffin, Joseph Jr. to Sarah Stuart, Nov. 10, Guilford county. R. R. Nov. 22, 1822

Coman, Maria to Jas. R. Love of Haywood county, Nov. 26, Raleigh. R. R. Nov. 27, 1822

Conyers, Dr. Wm. D. of Georgia to Elizabeth Perry of Franklin county, Nov. 6. R. R. Dec. 6, 1822

Coor, Charlotte of Wayne county to Sam'l H. Cherry, Dec. 15, Waynesboro. R. R. Dec. 27, 1822

Craton, Isaac of Rutherfordton to Elizabeth Miller, Feb. 31, Rutherford county. R. R. Mar. 15, 1822

Crawford, Sally Ann of Beaufort county to Joseph Bonner of Washington, Beaufort county, My. 30. R. R. Je. 14, 1822

Cress, Milly of Concord to John L. Beard, Je. 20, Concord. R. R. Jly. 4, 1822

Davis, Dr. Goodorum of Fayetteville to Sarah R. Harvey of Bladen county, My. 21, Cumberland county. R. R. Je. 7, 1822

Dickens, Grizey P. to Samuel H. Smith, Oct. 10, Person county. R. R. Nov. 8, 1822

Dickson, Mary to Mark Wilson of Milton, Jan. 17, Gosport. R. R. Jan. 25, 1822

Eaton, Eliza to Rob't. Freear, Nov. 4, Granville county. R. R. Nov. 15, 1822

Ellis, Mary R. to Dr. John McCauley, Oct. 2, Orange county. R. R. Oct. 18, 1822

Freear, Rob't to Eliza Eaton, Nov. 4, Granville county. R. R. Nov. 15, 1822

Freeman, Dr. David C. to Emily W. Telfair, Jly. 3, Washington. R. R. Jly. 12, 1822

Freeman, Martha M. to Robt. G. Greene of Wayne county, Mar. 14, Franklin county. R. R. Mar. 29, 1822

Frihck, James to Emily Hunter, Jly. 31, Johnston county. R. R. Aug. 2, 1822

Glenn, Mary P. to Benjamin M. Perry, Nov. 1, Franklin county. R. R. Nov. 8, 1822

Glisson, Daniel, Jr. to Nancy Herring, Oct. 8, Duplin county. R. R. Nov. 22, 1822

Graves, Gen. Barzillai of Caswell county to Mrs. Mary Royall of Halifax county, Oct. 23, Halifax county. R. R. Nov. 8, 1822

Greene, Robt. G. of Wayne county to Martha M. Freeman, Mar. 14, Franklin county. R. R. Mar. 29, 1822

Greenlee, Samuel of Burke county to Minerva K. Sackett of Rutherfordton, Je. 4, Rutherfordton . R. R. Je. 28, 1822

Guthrie, Elizabeth to John Rorke, Oct. 12, Wake county. R. R. Oct. 18, 1822

Hall, William P. of Caswell county to Mrs. Nancy Johnston, Mar. 16, Scotland Neck. R. R. Apr. 26, 1822

Hanner, Alexander of Guilford county to Mrs. Alfred Lane, Nov. 26, Randolph county. R. R. Dec. 6, 1822

Harris, John W. to Mrs. Leathe Reid, Dec. 5, Wake county. R. R. Dec. 27, 1822

Harvey, Sarah R. of Bladen county to Dr. Goodorum Davis of Fayetteville, My. 21, Cumberland county. R. R. Je. 7, 1822

Hatch, Gen. Durant to Mrs. John S. West, Je., Newbern. R. R. Je. 21, 1822

Hatch, Maria to Francis W. Nelson, Jan. 3, Jones county. R. R. Jan. 18, 1822

Hawks, Phebe R. to Walker Anderson of Hillsborough, Jly. 29, Newbern. R. R. Aug. 9, 1822

Henderson, Archibald E. of Granville county to Ann M. Bullock of Warren county, Oct. 1, Warren county. R. R. Oct. 18, 1822

Henshaw, Jesse to Milley Price, Jan. 17, Randolph county. R. R. Feb. 8, 1822

Henshaw, Sara to Peter Lawrence, Jan. 12, Randolph county. R. R. Feb. 8, 1822

Herring, Nancy to Daniel Glisson, Jr., Oct. 8, Duplin county. R. R. Nov. 22, 1822

Hester, Col. Joseph of Granville county to Mary H. Whitehead, Mar. 21, Wake county. R. R. Mar. 29, 1822

Hewlett, Nancy to Thomas W. Scott, Sept., Madison county, Alabama. R. R. Sept. 6, 1822

Hicks, Edward of Brunswick county, Va. to Elizabeth Stone, Oct. 3, Wake county. R. R. Oct. 18, 1822

Higbie, Mrs. Thisbie to Rev. Willis Reeves, Jan. 10, Wake Forest. R. R. Jan. 18, 1822

Hill, Susan to William D. Moseley, My. 23, New Hanover county. R. R. My. 31, 1822

Hinton, Noall of Bertie county to Chloe A. Slade, Mar. 7, Martin county. R. R. Mar. 15, 1822

Hogg, Gavin of Bertie county to Ann B. Johnson of Connecticut, My., Raleigh. R. R. My. 24, 1822

Holder, Miss S. of Milton to Martin P. Huntington, My. 2, Milton. R. R. My. 24, 1822

Horn, William to Amy King, Nov. 12, Orange county. R. R. Nov. 22, 1822

Howard, John of Granville county to Mrs. Susanna Overby of Mecklenburg county, Va., Aug. 1. R. R. Aug. 16, 1822

Hunt, John to Fanny Bullock, Nov. 6, Granville county. R. R. Nov. 15, 1822

Hunter, Emily to James Frihck, Jly. 31, Johnston county. R. R. Aug. 2, 1822

Huntington, Martin P. to Miss S. Holder of Milton, My. 2, Milton. R. R. My. 24, 1822

Jenkins, James to Ann M'Leran, Je. 13, Fayetteville. R. R. Je. 28, 1822

Johnson, Ann B. of Connecticut to Gavin Hogg of Bertie county, My., Raleigh. R. R. My. 24, 1822

Johnson, Mary to Egbert Shepherd of Orange county, Feb., Warren county. R. R. Mar. 1, 1822

Johnston, Mrs. Nancy to William P. Hall of Caswell county, Mar. 16, Scotland Neck. R. R. Apr. 26, 1822

Jones, Gen. W. W. of Wilmington to Eliza Littlejohn, My. 7, Oxford. R. R. My. 17, 1822

King, Amy to William Horn, Nov. 12, Orange county. R. R. Nov. 22, 1822

Laird, William P. to Mary Ann Selby, Jly. 26, Raleigh. R. R. Aug. 2, 1822

Lane, Mrs. Alfred to Alexander Hanner of Guilford county, Nov. 26, Randolph county. R. R. Dec. 6, 1822

Lawrence, Peter to Sarah Henshaw, Jan. 12, Randolph county. R. R. Feb. 8, 1822

Lawrence, Peter P. to Mrs. Martha McCotter, Oct. 19, Edenton. R. R. Nov. 1, 1822

Littlejohn, Eliza to Gen. W. W. Jones, My. 7, Oxford. R. R. My. 17, 1822

Long, Edward to Mary Royster, Feb. 14, Raleigh. R. R. Feb. 22, 1822

Love, Jas. R. of Haywood county to Maria Coman, Nov. 26, Raleigh. R. R. Nov. 29, 1822

Lowther, Wm. to Ann Sawyer, Mar. 21, Edenton. R. R. Apr. 5, 1822

McCauley, Dr. John to Mary R. Ellis, Oct. 2, Orange county. R. R. Oct. 18, 1822

McCotter, Mrs. Martha to Peter P. Lawrence, Oct. 19, Edenton. R. R. Nov. 1, 1822

McCullers, Rebecca to Stephen Stephenson, Jan. 29, Wake county. R. R. Feb. 1, 1822

McFarland, Margaret to John R. Buie of Fayetteville, Feb. 14, Richmond county. R. R. Mar. 8, 1822

McKenzie, Ann to Joseph L. Morris, Jan. 31, Richmond county. R. R. Mar. 8, 1822

McLeran, Ann to James Jenkins, Je. 13, Fayetteville. R. R. Je. 28, 1822

Martin, Zilphia to John P. Calhorda, Je. 18, Wilmington. R. R. Je. 21, 1822

Miller, Elizabeth to Isaac Craton of Rutherfordton, Feb. 31, Rutherford county. R. R. Mar. 15, 1822

Miller, George to Mrs. Anna Chambers, Je. 13, Rowan county. R. R. Je. 28, 1822

Moore, Mrs. Ann to Joseph Scurlock, Feb. 28, Chatham county. R. R. Mar. 22, 1822

Moore, Elizabeth to Francis Waddell, Je., Brunswick county. R. R. Je. 14, 1822

Morris, Joseph L. to Ann M'Kenzie, Jan. 31, Richmond county. R. R. Mar. 8, 1822

Moseley, William D. to Susan Hill, My. 23, New Hanover county. R. R. My. 31, 1822

Murray, James to Sarah Royster, My. 23, Raleigh. R. R. My. 31, 1822

Nash, Enoch of Indiantown to Elizabeth Sawyer, Je. 13, Camden county. R. R. Jly. 4, 1822

Nelson, Francis W. of Newbern to Maria Hatch, Jan. 3, Jones county. R. R. Jan. 18, 1822

Overby, Mrs. Susanna of Mecklenburg county, Va. to John Howard of Granville county, Aug. 1. R. R. Aug. 16, 1822

Parrish, Mary to Miles Blake of Fayetteville, Nov. 26, Bladen county. R. R. Dec. 6, 1822

Pearson, Eliza of Rowan county to William G. Beatty of Bladen county, Feb. 16. R. R. Mar. 1, 1822

Perry, Benjamin M. to Mary P. Glenn, Nov. 1, Franklin county. R. R. Nov. 8, 1822

Perry, Elizabeth of Franklin county to Dr. Wm. D. Conyers of Georgia, Nov. 6. R. R. Dec. 6, 1822

Phifer, Ann to Col. John N. Phifer, Je. 11, Cabarrus county. R. R. Je. 28, 1822

Phifer, Col. John N. to Ann Phifer, Je. 11, Cabarrus county. R. R. Je. 28, 1822

Phillips, Wm. H. of Hillsborough to Martha M. Cobbs, Aug. 6, Raleigh. R. R. Aug. 9, 1822

Price, Elijah of Stantonsburg to Temperance Thomas, Dec. 11, Edgecombe county. R. R. Jan. 18, 1822

Price, Milley to Jesse Hinshaw, Jan. 17, Randolph county. R. R. Feb. 8, 1822

Proudfit, Julian to Dr. R. A. Archer, Dec. 16, Nash county. R. R. Dec. 27, 1822

Pugh, Major F. of Franklin to Mrs. Wm. Smith of Granville county, Nov. R. R. Nov. 15, 1822

Ransom, Major Robert of Warren county to Priscilla Whitaker, Dec. 10, Halifax county. R. R. Dec. 20, 1822

Rea, Mary to Benjamin B. Camp, Mar. 13, Murfreesboro. R. R. Mar. 22, 1822

Reeves, Rev. Willis of Orange county to Mrs. Thisbie Higbie, Jan. 10, Wake Forest. R. R. Jan. 18, 1822

Reid, Mrs. Leathe to John W. Harris, Dec. 5, Wake county. R. R. Dec. 27, 1822

Rhoades, Miss to Samuel Whitaker, My., Wake county. R. R. My. 3, 1822

Roberts, Eliza of Orange county to John Willfong of Hillsborough, Oct. 10, Orange county. R. R. Oct. 25, 1822

Robinson, Martha of Granville county to Charles Blackwell of Louisburg, Oct. 23, Granville county. R. R. Nov. 8, 1822

Rorke, John to Elizabeth Guthrie, Oct. 12, Wake county. R. R. Oct. 18, 1822

Ross, Dr. Joseph W. to Sophia Springs, Feb. 21, Mecklenburg county. R. R. Mar. 15, 1822

Royall, Mrs. Mary of Halifax county to Gen. Barzillai Graves of Caswell county, Oct. 23, Halifax county. R. R. Nov. 8, 1822

Royster, Mary to Edward Long, Feb. 14, Raleigh. R. R. Feb. 22, 1822

Royster, Sarah to James Murray, My. 23, Raleigh. R. R. My. 31, 1822

Runyon, Benjamin to Caroline Blount, My. 28, Beaufort county. R. R. Je. 7, 1822

Russel, James to Nancy Brewer, My. 30, Hillsborough. R. R. Je. 14, 1822

Sackett, Minerva K. of Rutherfordton to Samuel Greenlee of Burke county, Je. 4, Rutherfordton. R. R. Je. 28, 1822

Samuel, Betsy P. to Col. Thos. Atkinson, Aug. 15, Caswell county. R. R. Aug. 30, 1822

Sanders, Archibald to Delia Sanders, Mar., Johnston county. R. R. Mar. 29, 1822

Sanders, Delia to Archibald Sanders, Mar., Johnston county. R. R. Mar. 29, 1822

Sawyer, Ann to Wm. Lowther, Mar. 21, Edenton. R. R. Apr. 5, 1822

Sawyer, Elizabeth to Enoch Nash of Indiantown, Je. 13, Camden county. R. R. Jly. 4, 1822

Scott, Thomas W. of Raleigh to Nancy Hewlett, Sept., Madison county, Ala. R. R. Sept. 6, 1822

Scurlock, Joseph to Mrs. Ann Moore, Feb. 28, Chatham county. R. R. Mar. 22, 1822

Selby, Mary Ann to William P. Laird, Jly. 26, Raleigh. R. R. Aug. 2, 1822

Shaw, John to Nancy Walker, Dec. 20, Orange county. R. R. Jan. 4, 1822

Shephard, Mary to John H. Bryan, Dec. 20, Newbern. R. R. Jan. 4, 1822

Shepherd, Egbert of Orange county to Mary Johnson, Feb., Warren county. R. R. Mar. 1, 1822

Sims, Rebecca to Capt. Samuel Wortham, Feb. 19, Orange county. R. R. Mar. 8, 1822

Slade, A. M. of Martin county to Eliza Sulton of Bertie county, Jan. 29, Bertie county. R. R. Feb. 22, 1822

Slade, Chloe A. to Noall Hinton of Bertie county, Mar. 7, Martin county. R. R. Mar. 15, 1822

Smith, Samuel H. to Grizey P. Dickens, Oct. 10, Person county. R. R. Nov. 8, 1822

Smith, Mrs. Wm. of Granville county to Major F. Pugh of Franklin, Nov. R. R. Nov. 15, 1822

Springs, Sophia to Dr. Joseph W. Ross, Feb. 21, Mecklenburg county. R. R. Mar. 15, 1822

Stephenson, Stephen to Rebecca M'Cullers, Jan. 29, Wake county. R. R. Feb. 1, 1822

Stone, Elizabeth to Edward Hicks of Brunswick county, Va., Oct. 3, Wake county. R. R. Oct. 18, 1822

Stuart, Sarah to Joseph Coffin, Jr., Nov. 10, Guilford county. R. R. Nov. 22, 1822

Sturdivant, Eliza to James Busby, My. 30, Wake county. R. R. Je. 7, 1822

Sutton, Eliza of Bertie county to A. M. Slade of Martin county, Jan. 29, Bertie county. R. R. Feb. 22, 1822

Tate, Eloisa Matilda Mary of Alabama to George Tunstall of Raleigh, Jly. 4. R. R. Aug. 16, 1822

Tate, Juicy to Thos. D. Armstrong, Sept. 26, Orange county. R. R. Oct. 18, 1822

Telfair, Emily W. to Dr. David C. Freeman, Jly. 3, Washington. R. R. Jly. 12, 1822

Thomas, Temperance to Elijah Price of Stantonsburg, Dec. 11, Edgecombe county. R. R. Jan. 18, 1822

Tunstall, George of Raleigh to Eloisa Matilda Mary Tate of Alabama, Jly. 4. R. R. Aug. 16, 1822

Turner, Jane of Warren county to Chasteen Allen of Amelia county, Va., Nov. 27, Warren county. R. R. Dec. 6, 1822

Waddell, Francis to Elizabeth Moore, Je., Brunswick county. R. R. Je. 14, 1822

Walker, Nancy to John Shaw, Dec. 20, Orange county. R. R. Jan. 4, 1822

Walthall, Branch to Mrs. Avery of Johnston county, Oct. 22, Wake county. R. R. Oct. 25, 1822

Walton, Mary to Israel Bond, My. 26, Wake county. R. R. My. 31, 1822

West, Mrs. John S. to Gen. Durant Hatch, Je., Newbern. R. R. Je. 21, 1822

Westray, Sallie to Jas. S. Battle of Edgecombe county, Dec. 3, Nash county. R. R. Dec. 27, 1822

Whitaker, David to Lucinda Whitaker, Mar. 26, Wake county. R. R. Mar. 29, 1822

Whitaker, Lucinda to David Whitaker, Mar. 26, Wake county. R. R. Mar. 29, 1822

Whitaker, Priscilla to Major Robert Ransom of Warren county, Dec. 10, Halifax county. R. R. Dec. 20, 1822

Whitaker, Samuel to Miss Rhodes, My., Wake county. R. R. My. 3, 1822

Whitehead, Mary H. to Col. Joseph Hester of Granville county, Mar. 21, Wake county. R. R. Mar. 29, 1822

Willfong, John of Hillsborough to Eliza Roberts of Orange county, Oct. 10, Orange county. R. R. Oct. 25, 1822

Williams, Adeline to John Alston of Chatham county, Dec. 12, Franklin county. R. R. Dec. 20, 1822

Wilson, Mark of Milton to Mary Dickson, Jan. 17, Gosport. R. R. Jan. 25, 1822

Wortham, Samuel to Capt. Rebecca Sims, Feb. 19, Orange county. R. R. Mar. 8, 1822

Wright, Mary C. to Dr. L. B. Bush of Wayne county, Sept. 3, Duplin county. R. R. Sept. 13, 1822

Wright, Hon. R. of Maryland to Elizabeth Harriot Robertson of Virginia, Mar. 19, Washington, D. C. R. R. Mar. 29, 1822

1823

Adkins, Lucy to Iver M'Callum, Jan. 16, Wilmington. R. R. Jan. 24, 1823

Alexander, Mrs. Ann to John Mariner, Aug. 28, Tyrrell county. R. R. Sept. 26, 1823

Alexander, Benjamin F. to Hannah Wilson, Jly. 24, Mecklenburg county. R. R. Aug. 22, 1823

Allison, James to Elizabeth Wilson, Jan. 9, Orange county. R. R. Feb. 7, 1823

Alston, Emeline E. of Chatham county to William Hamlin of Halifax county, Jan. 23. R. R. Jan. 31, 1823

Alston, Sarah N. to Marion Sanders of South Carolina, Je. 10, Halifax county. R. R. Je. 20, 1823

Armistead, Stark to Mrs. James Tunstall of Bertie county, Jly. 2, Williamsborough. R. R. Jly. 25, 1823

Armstrong, Barbary to Thomas Davis, Feb. 13, Duplin county. R. R. Feb. 21, 1823

Armstrong, Elizabeth to William Lyon, Mar. 11, Stokes county. R. R. Mar. 14, 1823

Atkins, Samuel to Mouring Harrison, Sept. 24, Wake county. R. R. Sept. 26, 1823

Baird, Margaret R. to Samuel Smith of Tennessee, Feb. 11, Buncombe county. R. R. Mar. 7, 1823

Ball, James to Anna Read, Sept. 25, Warren county. R. R. Oct. 3, 1823

Barnes, William S. to Elizabeth Sumner, Apr. 8, Gates county. R. R. My. 9, 1823

Barnet, John of Person county to Martha Pointer, Apr. 2, Halifax county, Va. R. R. Apr. 18, 1823

Barnett, Lavinia to Benj. Maitland, Oct. 31, Plymouth. R. R. Nov. 14, 1823

Barr, Margaret to Capt. John Houston, Sept. 23, Rowan county. R. R. Oct. 10, 1823

Bell, Charlotte of Pasquotank county to Edmund Blount, My. 18. R. R. Je. 6, 1823

Bell, Sarah to Charles Harrell, Sept. 23, Elizabeth City. R. R. Aug. 9, 1823

Blount, Edmund to Charlotte Bell of Pasquotank county, My. 18. R. R. Je. 6, 1823

Boice, Eliza to Dr. Robert Boyd, Je. 11, Wake county. R. R. Je. 27, 1823

Bolton, Charles to Ann Staffield, My. 15, Person county. R. R. My. 30, 1823

Bond, James to Penelope Leggett, Jan. 14, Bertie county. R. R. Feb. 7, 1823

Boyd, Dr. Robert to Eliza Boice, Je. 11, Wake county. R. R. Je. 27, 1823

Bradley, John to Nancy Pleasants, Jan., Wake county. R. R. Jan. 31, 1823

Brevard, Robert A. of Lincoln county to Sarah H. Davidson of Iredell county, Jly. 29. R. R. Aug. 22, 1823

Brittain, Gen'l. Philip to Sophia Lewis, Sept. 2, Buncombe county. R. R. Sept. 19, 1823

Bryan, Mary to Rev. Rich'd Mason, Je. 10, Newbern. R. R. Je. 20, 1823

Bullock, William to Mary Hunt, Jan. 8, Granville county. R. R. Jan. 24, 1823

Cade, Parthenia to John Mullins, Mar. 25, Fayetteville. R. R. Apr. 11, 1823

Campbell, Wm. to Eliza M'Lean, Jly. 17, Lincoln county. R. R. Aug. 22, 1823

Carter, G. Archibald to Letitia Wilson, Je. 17, Rowan county. R. R. Jly. 4, 1823

Charlton, Thomas I. to Mrs. Samuel Haughton of Chowan county, Jly. 8. R. R. Jly. 25, 1823

Clark, Stephen to Mary Roberts, My. 22, Orange county. R. R. Je. 6, 1823

Cook, Mary to David Oswall, Jr., Je. 22, Lumberton. R. R. Jly. 4, 1823

Corbett, Ann to Eli L. Larkins of Washington, Jan. 30, New Hanover county. R. R. Feb. 21, 1823

Cotten, Clarissa to Robert Keating, Mar. 30, Edenton. R. R. Apr. 11, 1823

Cowan, Robert H. of Wilmington to Sarah Stone, Oct. 2, Wake county. R. R. Oct. 3, 1823

Crawford, Mrs. Eliza to I. R. Douglass, Feb. 13, Wilmington. R. R. Feb. 21, 1823

Creecy, Joseph of Chowan county to Sophia Trotman of Gates county, Apr. 1. R. R. Apr. 18, 1823

Davidson, Sarah H. of Iredell county to Robert A. Brevard of Lincoln county, Jly. 29. R. R. Aug. 22, 1823

Davis, Eliza to Thomas P. Wortham of Warren county, Dec. 18, Mecklenburg county, Va. R. R. Dec. 26, 1823

Davis, Thomas to Barbary Armstrong, Feb. 13, Duplin county. R. R. Feb. 21, 1823

Day, Sarah Ann to Thomas Ragland of Georgia and this State, Nov. 6, Jones county. R. R. Nov. 21, 1823

Dick, James of Alamance county to Martha Galbreath, Jan. 16, Guilford county. R. R. Jan. 31, 1823

Dixon, Geo. W. to Antoinette Hunt, Jan. 9, Newbern. R. R. Jan. 24, 1823

Dodson, Elizabeth H. to Benjamin B. Dye, My. 15, Milton. R. R. My. 30, 1823

Donnell, Samuel to Priscilla Ogburn, My. 22, Guilford county. R. R. Je. 6, 1823

Douglass, I. R. to Mrs. Eliza Crawford, Feb. 13, Wilmington. R. R. Feb. 21, 1823

Dye, Benjamin B. to Elizabeth H. Dodson, My. 15, Milton. R. R. My. 30, 1823

Edwards, Weldon of Warren county to Lucy Norfleet of Halifax county, Je. 25. R. R. Jly. 4, 1823

Falcon, Isaac N. of Halifax county to Martha Whitmill Falconer of Franklin county, Oct. 15, Warren county. R. R. Nov. 7, 1823

Falconer, Martha Whitmill of Franklin county to Isaac N. Falcon of Halifax, Oct. 15, Warren county. R. R. Nov. 7, 1823

Forbes, Stephen B. to Maria Tisdale, Mar. 12, Newbern. R. R. Aug. 21, 1823

Farquhar, Abraham to Julia Lipscomb, Mar. 27, Person county. R. R. Apr. 18, 1823

Galbreth, Martha to James Dick of Alamance county, Jan. 16, Guilford county. R. R. Jan. 31, 1823

German, Capt. of Tennessee to Mary Scott, Jly. 15. R. R. Aug. 22, 1823

Gillam, William of South Carolina to Theresa Matthieu of Salisbury, Jly. 3, Salisbury. R. R. Aug. 1, 1823

Gould, Rev. Daniel to Mrs. Zilphia Torrence, Sept. 25, Statesville. R. R. Aug. 9, 1823

Green, Thomas to Nancy Willis, Aug. 7, Warrenton. R. R. Aug. 15, 1823

Hall, Nancy of Rowan county to Dr. William M'Kay of Sampson county, Sept. 25. R. R. Oct. 10, 1823

Hall, Sidney to Isaac Lamb, Feb. 9, Camden county. R. R. Feb. 21, 1823

Halsey, Joseph to Mary Wynne, Oct. 31, Tyrrell county. R. R. Nov. 14, 1823

Hamlin, William of Halifax county to Emeline E. Alston of Chatham county, Jan. 23. R. R. Jan. 31, 1823

Hardin, William H. of Raleigh to Maria Hill of New Hanover county, Jan. 15, New Hanover county. R. R. Jan. 17, 1823

Harrell, Charles to Sarah Bell, Sept. 23, Elizabeth City. R. R. Aug. 9, 1823

Harrison, Mourning to Samuel Atkins, Sept. 24, Wake county. R. R. Sept. 26, 1823

Hart, Miss A. E. to Henry Pipkin, Aug. 16, Northampton county. R. R. Aug. 22, 1823

Haughton, Mrs. Samuel to Thomas I. Charlton of Chowan county, Jly. 8. R. R. Jly. 25, 1823

Hawks, Francis L. of Newbern to Emily Kirby of Connecticut, Nov. 11. R. R. Nov. 28, 1823

Hicks, John R. to Rebecca Wood, Sept. 24, Granville county. R. R. Oct. 17, 1823

High, Delilah H. to Henry Hunter, Nov. 12, Wake county. R. R. Nov. 14, 1823

Hill, Major James K. to Sarah Ann Hurst, Feb. 11, Duplin county. R. R. Feb. 21, 1823

Hill, Maria of New Hanover county to William H. Hardin of Raleigh, Jan. 15, New Hanover county. R. R. Jan. 17, 1823

Hill, Martha to Thomas Johnson of Warren county, Jan. 28, Franklin county. R. R. Jan. 31, 1823

Hilton, Mrs. James to Sherwood Kennedy, Apr. 13, Davidson county. R. R. My. 16, 1823

Hinton, Elizabeth to Warner M. Lewis, Oct. 29, Granville county. R. R. Nov. 14, 1823

Hoke, Susannah to Robert F. Lawrence, Je. 5, Lincoln county. R. R. Jly. 11, 1823

Houston, Capt. John to Margaret Barr, Sept. 23, Rowan county. R. R. Oct. 10, 1823

Houston, Lydia to William R. Roane of Burke county, Mar. 18, Cabarrus county. R. R. April 11, 1823

Hunt, Antoinette to Geo. W. Dixon, Jan. 9, Newbern. R. R. Jan. 24, 1823

Hunt, Mary to William Bullock, Jan. 8, Granville county. R. R. Jan. 24, 1823

Hunter, Henry to Delilah H. High, Nov. 12, Wake county. R. R. Nov. 14, 1823

Hurst, Sarah Ann to Major James K. Hill, Feb. 11, Duplin county. R. R. Feb. 21, 1823

Jessups, Hezekiah of Guilford county to Polly King of Stokes county, My. 22, Stokes county. R. R. Je. 13, 1823

Johnson, Anna Hayes to Gen. Romulus M. Sanders of Milton, My. 26, Charleston, S. C. R. R. Je. 13, 1823

Johnson, Thomas of Warren county to Martha Hill, Jan. 28, Franklin county. R. R. Jan. 31, 1823

Jones, Elizabeth to Samuel Stoct, Apr. 13, Davidson county. R. R. My. 16, 1823

Keating, Robert to Clarissa Cotten, Mar. 30, Edenton. R. R. Apr. 11, 1823

Kennedy, Sherwood to Mrs. James Hilton, Apr. 13, Davidson county. R. R. My. 16, 1823

Kerr, Elizabeth to Dr. James Wilson, Aug. 26, Rowan county. R. R. Sept. 12, 1823

King, Polly of Stokes county to Hezekiah Jessups of Guilford county, My. 22, Stokes county. R. R. Je. 13, 1823

Kirby, Emily of Connecticut to Francis L. Hawks of Newbern, Nov. 11. R. R. Nov. 28, 1823

Knox, Mrs. Mary to Dr. Edmund S. Lindsay of Currituck county, Sept. 3, Pasquotank county. R. R. Sept. 19, 1823

Lamb, Isaac to Sidney Hall, Feb. 9, Camden county. R. R. Feb. 21, 1823

Larkins, Eli L. of Wilmington to Ann Corbett, Jan. 30, New Hanover county. R. R. Feb. 21, 1823

Lawrence, Alexander J. to Mrs. Maria Snow, Jly. 29, Franklin county. R. R. Aug. 1, 1823

Lawrence, Robert E. to Susannah Hoke, Je. 5, Lincoln county. R. R. Jly. 11, 1823

Leggett, Penelope to James Bond, Jan. 14, Bertie county. R. R. Feb. 7, 1823

Lewis, Sophia to Gen'l. Philip Brittain, Sept. 2, Buncombe county. R. R. Sept. 19, 1823

Lewis, Warner M. of Milton to Elizabeth Hinton, Oct. 29, Granville county. R. R. Nov. 14, 1823

Lindsay, Dr. Edmund S. of Currituck county to Mrs. Mary Knox, Sept. 3, Pasquotank county. R. R. Sept. 19, 1823

Lindsay, Jonathan to Mrs. Ann M'Donald, Apr. 24, Fayetteville. R. R. My. 16, 1823

Lipscomb, Julia to Abraham Farquhar, Mar. 27, Person county. R. R. Apr. 18, 1823

Lipscomb, William to Mrs. S. Rountree of Orange county, Mar. 27, Person county. R. R. Apr. 18, 1823

Lockman, Miss to Spencer Shelton, Jly. 15, Lincoln county. R. R. Aug. 22, 1823

Lyon, William to Elizabeth Armstrong, Mar. 11, Stokes county. R. R. Mar. 14, 1823

M'Callum, Iver to Lucy Adkins, Jan. 16, Wilmington. R. R. Jan. 24, 1823

M'Donald, Mrs. Ann to Jonathan Lindsey, Apr. 24, Fayetteville. R. R. My. 16, 1823

M'Kay, Dr. William of Sampson county to Nancy Hall of Rowan county. Sept. 25. R. R. Oct. 10, 1823

M'Lean, Eliza to Wm. Campbell, Sept. 17, Lincoln county. R. R. Aug. 22, 1823

M'Leran, Maria to F. C. Reston of Wilmington, Mar. 27, Fayetteville. R. R. Apr. 11, 1823

Maitland, Benj. to Lavinia Barnett, Oct. 31, Plymouth. R. R. Nov. 14, 1823

Mariner, John to Mrs. Ann Alexander, Aug. 28, Tyrrell county. R. R. Sept. 26, 1823

Martin, Robert to Polly Settle, Je., Rockingham Court-House. R. R. Je. 27, 1823

Mason, Rev. Rich'd to Mary Bryan, Je. 10, Newbern. R. R. Je. 20, 1823

Matthieu, Theresa of Salisbury to William Gillam of South Carolina, Jly. 3, Salisbury. R. R. Aug. 1, 1823

Morgan, Sophia to Barnet Winstead, Mar. 23, Person county. R. R. Apr. 18, 1823

Morrison, Louisa to John Phifer of Cabarrus county, Apr. 8, Mecklenburg county. R. R. My. 2, 1823

Mullins, John to Parthenia Cade, Mar. 25, Fayetteville. R. R. Apr. 11, 1823

Murphey, William D. to Betsey Whitted, Oct. 28, Chapel Hill. R. R. Nov. 7, 1823

Nelson, John W. to Mary Prentiss, Apr. 10, Newbern. R. R. My. 2, 1823

Norfleet, Lucy of Halifax county to Weldon Edwards of Warren county, Je. 25. R. R. Jly. 4, 1823

Nunnally, William H. to Nancy Price, My. 22, Caswell county. R. R. Je. 13, 1823

Ogburn, Priscilla to Samuel Donnell, My. 22, Guilford county. R. R. Je. 6, 1823

Orents, Capt. Jacob to Jane Rutledge, Sept. 17, Lincoln county. R. R. Aug. 22, 1823

Oswall, David, Jr. to Mary Cook, Je. 22, Lumberton. R. R. Jly. 4, 1823

Patton, Elizabeth of Asheville to Dr. George D. H. Phillips of South Carolina, Je. 12. R. R. Jly. 11, 1823

Pedigrew, Thos. to Celia Tate, Dec. 4, Orange county. R. R. Dec. 16, 1823

Phifer, John of Cabarrus county to Louisa Morrison, Apr. 8, Mecklenburg county. R. R. My. 2, 1823

Philips, Dr. George D. H. of South Carolina to Elizabeth Patton of Asheville, Je. 12. R. R. Jly. 11, 1823

Pipkin, Henry to Miss A. E. Hart, Aug. 16, Northampton county. R. R. Aug. 22, 1823

Pleasants, Nancy to John Bradley, Jan., Wake county. R. R. Jan. 31, 1823

Pointer, Martha to John Barnet of Person county, Apr. 2, Halifax county, Va. R. R. Apr. 18, 1823

Prentiss, Mary to John W. Nelson, Apr. 10, Newbern. R. R. My. 2, 1823

Price, Nancy to William H. Nunnally, My. 22, Caswell county. R. R. Je. 13, 1823

Ragland, Thomas of Georgia and this State to Sarah Ann Day, Nov. 6, Jones county, Ga. R. R. Nov. 21, 1823

Ratts, Polly to Jacob Wiseman, My. 15, Davidson county. R. R. Je. 6, 1823

Ravens, Mrs. John to Isaac Saterfield, Feb. 20, Person county. R. R. Apr. 18, 1823

Read, Anna to James Ball, Sept. 25, Warren county. R. R. Oct. 3, 1823

Reaves, Mary to John Wadkins, Sept. 10, Warren county. R. R. Oct. 3, 1823

Reston, F. C. of Wilmington to Maria McLeran, Mar. 27, Fayetteville. R. R. Apr. 11, 1823

Rice, Dorothy C. to Jonathan R. Waltington, Je. 12, Caswell county. R. R. Je. 27, 1823

Rigsbee, Edward of Raleigh to Martha Sims, Jly. 25, Wake county. R. R. Aug. 1, 1823

Roane, William R. of Burke county to Lydia Houston, Mar. 18, Cabarrus county. R. R. Apr. 11, 1823

Roberts, Mary to Stephen Clark, My. 22, Orange county. R. R. Je. 6, 1823

Rountree, Mrs. S. of Orange county to William Lipscomb, Mar. 27, Person county. R. R. Apr. 18, 1823

Rusher, Jacob to Christina Verble, Aug. 7, Rowan county. R. R. Aug. 22, 1823

Russel, Mary to Stephen Theach, Mar. 16, Bertie county. R. R. Apr. 4, 1823

Rutledge, Jane to Capt. Jacob Orents, Sept. 17, Lincoln county. R. R. Aug. 22, 1823

Sanders, Marion of South Carolina to Sarah N. Alston, Je. 10, Halifax county. R. R. Je. 20, 1823

Sanders, Gen. Romulus M. of Milton to Anna Hayes Johnson, My. 26, Charleston, S. C. R. R. Je. 13, 1823

Saterfield, Isaac to Mrs. John Ravens, Feb. 20, Person county. R. R. Apr. 18, 1823

Satterthwaite, Fanny to Hosea Tyson, Apr. 24, Hyde county. R. R. My. 9, 1823

Scott, Mary to Capt. German of Tennessee, Jly. 15. R. R. Aug. 22, 1823

Settle, Polly to Robert Martin, Jr., Rockingham Court House. R. R. Je. 27, 1823

Shelton, Spencer to Miss Lockman, Jly. 15, Lincoln county. R. R. Aug. 22, 1823

Simms, Winifred to Nathaniel Thompson of Raleigh, Jan. 7, Wake county. R. R. Jan. 17, 1823

Smith, Samuel of Tennessee to Margaret Baird, Feb. 11, Buncombe county. R. R. Mar. 7, 1823

Snow, Mrs. Maria to Alexander J. Lawrence, Jly. 29, Franklin county. R. R. Aug. 1, 1823

Staffield, Ann to Charles Bolton, My. 15, Person county. R. R. My. 30, 1823

Stoct, Samuel to Elizabeth Jones, Apr. 13, Davidson county. R. R. My. 16, 1823

Stone, Sarah to Robert Cowan of Wilmington, Oct. 2, Wake county. R. R. Oct. 3, 1923

Sumner, David E. of Hertford county to Margaret Taylor, My. 1, Wake county. R. R. My. 2, 1823

Sumner, Elizabeth to William S. Barnes, Apr. 8, Gates county. R. R. My. 9, 1823

Tate, Celia to Thos. Pedigrew, Dec. 4, Orange county. R. R. Dec. 12, 1823

Taylor, Elizabeth L. to Dr. Phillip H. Thomas, My. 1, Granville county. R. R. My. 16, 1823

Taylor, Margaret to David E. Sumner of Hertford county, My. 1, Wake county. R. R. My. 2, 1823

Theach, Stephen to Mary Russel, Mar. 16, Bertie county. R. R. Apr. 4, 1823

Tisdale, Maria to Stephen B. Forbes, Mar. 12, Newbern. R. R. Mar. 21, 1823

Thomas, Dr. Phillip H. of Milton to Elizabeth L. Taylor, My. 1, Granville county. R. R. My. 16, 1823

Thompson, Nathaniel of Raleigh to Winifred Simms, Jan. 7, Wake county. R. R. Jan. 17, 1823

Torrence, Mrs. Zilphia to Rev. Daniel Gould, Jly. 25, Statesville. R. R. Aug. 8, 1823

Tunstall, Mrs. James to Stark Armistead of Bertie county, Jly. 2, Williamsborough. R. R. Jly. 25, 1825

Tyson, Hosea to Fanny Satterthwaite, Apr. 24, Hyde county. R. R. My. 9, 1823

Verble, Christina to Jacob Rusher, Aug. 7, Rowan county. R. R. Aug. 22, 1823

Wadkins, John to Mary Reaves, Sept. 10, Warren county. R. R. Oct. 3, 1823

Ward, James to Mrs. Joshua Ward, My. 24, Bertie county. R. R. Je. 13, 1823

Ward, Mrs. Joshua to James Ward, My. 24, Bertie county. R. R. Je. 13, 1823

Watlington, Jonathan R. to Dorothy C. Rice, Je. 12, Caswell county. R. R. Je. 27, 1823

Whitted, Betsey to William D. Murphey, Oct. 28, Chapel Hill. R. R. Nov. 7, 1823

Willis, Nancy to Thomas Green, Aug. 7, Warrenton. R. R. Aug. 15, 1823

Wilson, Elizabeth to James Allison, Jan. 9, Orange county. R. R. Feb. 7, 1823

Wilson, Hannah to Benjamin F. Alexander, Jly. 24, Mecklenburg county. R. R. Aug. 22, 1823

Wilson, Dr. James to Elizabeth Kerr, Aug. 26, Rowan county. R. R. Sept. 12, 1823

Wilson, Letitia to Archibald G. Carter, Je. 17, Rowan county. R. R. Jly. 4, 1823

Winstead, Barnet to Sophia Morgan, Mar. 23, Person county. R. R. Apr. 18, 1823

Wiseman, Jacob to Polly Ratts, My. 15, Davidson. R. R. Je. 6, 1823

Wood, Rebecca to John R. Hicks, Sept. 24, Granville county. R. R. Oct. 17, 1823

Wortham, Thomas P. of Warren county to Eliza Davis, Dec. 18, Mecklenburg county, Va. R. R. Dec. 26, 1823

Wynne, Mary to Joseph Halsey, Oct. 31, Tyrrell county. R. R. Nov. 14, 1823

1824

Allen, Jane to Joseph Terril, Jan. 29, Orange county. R. R. Feb. 27, 1824

Allen, Reynolds to Betsey Ann Harrison, Feb. 3, Wake county. R. R. Feb. 13, 1824

Alston, Martha to Dr. Thomas E. Shell of Warrenton, Oct., Halifax county. R. R. Oct. 15, 1824

Alston, Martha J. of Warren county to John Burges of Halifax, Jly. 29. R. R. Aug. 13, 1824

Andrews, Susannah R. to William Williams of Raleigh, Nov. 25, Washington, D. C. R. R. Dec. 3, 1824

Anthony, Obed to Mary Pike, Oct. 14, Guilford county. R. R. Nov. 5, 1824

Aykroyd, James to Elizabeth Bettner, Jly. 12, Newbern. R. R. Jly. 23, 1824

Baily, John to Elizabeth Mathis, Je. 10, Lincoln county. R. R. Jly. 30, 1824

Baker, Blake of Warren county to Martha Hamlin, Oct. 13, Halifax county. R. R. Oct. 22, 1824

Baldwin, Jas. to Rosina Sessamon, Jan. 15, Davidson county. R. R. Jan. 30, 1824

Barbee, Rev. Gab. of Orange county to Ann E. Bledsoe, Nov. 2, Wake county. R. R. Dec. 10, 1824

Bettner, Elizabeth to James Aykroyd, Jly. 12, Newbern. R. R. Jly. 23, 1824

Blackburn, Capt. Robert to Polly A. Sherill, My. 13, Lincoln county. R. R. Je. 11, 1824

Blake, Isham to Margaret Crosby, Oct. 27, Fayetteville. R. R. Oct. 29, 1824

Blackledge, Louisa to Geo. Whitfield, Jan. 8, Lenoir county. R. R. Jan. 30, 1824

Blackman, Elizabeth A. to Dr. Tho's Ward of Warren county, Je. 15, Waynesboro. R. R. Jly. 23, 1824

Bledsoe, Ann E. to Rev. Gab. Barbee of Orange county, Nov. 2, Wake county. R. R. Dec. 10, 1824

Bond, Sarah A. L. to W. Russell Minor, Nov. 2, Windsor. R. R. Nov. 12, 1824

Bostick, Solomon to Hannah Dockery, My. 12, Richmond county. R. R. Je. 11, 1824

Bourdeaux, Margaret E. to Archibald Simpson, Dec. 7, Long Creek. R. R. Dec. 31, 1824

Boyce, Miss to James Boyd, Mar. 8, Wake county. R. R. Apr. 16, 1824

Boyd, James to Miss Boyce, Mar. 8, Wake county. R. R. Apr. 16, 1824

Boyd, Nancy of Pitt county to Jos. B. Hinton of Beaufort, Dec. 2, Pitt county. R. R. Dec. 31, 1824

Browning, Wm. of Franklin county to Sally Pullen, Apr. 28, Wake county. R. R. My. 14, 1824

Bryan, Nancy to Doctor Francis Durval, Feb. 5, Trenton. R. R. Feb. 20, 1824

Burges, John of Halifax to Martha J. Alston of Warren county, Jly. 29. R. R. Aug. 13, 1824

Burns, James H. to Margaret Morrison, Jan. 9, Cabarrus county. R. R. Jan. 30, 1824.

Campbell, Ann to John Waddell of Wilmington, Dec. 23, Brunswick county. R. R. Dec. 31, 1824

Carter, Weldon to Henrietta Merritt of Halifax county, Sept. 15, Scotland Neck. R. R. Oct. 8, 1824

Cassaday, James to Sophia Jennett, Jan. 15, Wilmington. R. R. Jan. 23, 1824

Chisholm, Angus of Montgomery county to Jane Harris of Iredell county, Dec. 27. R. R. Feb. 10, 1824

Clancy, James to Phebe Thompson, Sept. 16, Hillsborough. R. R. Oct. 8, 1824

Clendenin, Sarah to William Roach, Sept. 8, Orange county. R. R. Oct. 8, 1824

Cobbs, Thos. of Raleigh to Sarah Hopkins, Dec. 2, Johnston county. R. R. Dec. 10, 1824

Cole, W. L. of Richmond county to Harriet Ellerbe of Cheraw, S. C., Je. 2. R. R. Je. 18, 1824

Coleman, Sarah L. to John W. Mosely, My. 11, Warrenton. R. R. My. 21, 1824

Collier, Frederick to Lucretia M. Hunt, Feb. 19, Orange county. R. R. Mar. 19, 1824

Collins, Michael of Nash county to Mary Cottrell of Warren county, Dec. 23, Warren county. R. R. Jan. 2, 1824

Compton, Linney of Orange county to William G. DeBrular of Frederick county, Va., Sept. R. R. Sept. 3, 1824

Cook, Mary to Rev. Cyrus Johnson, Dec. 30, Cabarrus county. R. R. Jan. 30, 1824

Cottrell, Mary of Warren county to Michael Collins of Nash county, Dec. 23, Warren county. R. R. Jan. 2, 1824

Creecy, Penelope to John D. Pipkin of Gates county, Jan. 6, Chowan county. R. R. Jan. 23, 1824

Crenshaw, Samuel to Eliza Harris, Mar. 25, Wake county. R. R. Apr. 2, 1824

Croom, Isaac of Lenoir county to Sarah A. Pearson of Rowan county, Je. 10, R. R. Je. 25, 1824

Crosby, Margaret to Isham Blake, Oct. 27, Fayetteville. R. R. Oct. 29, 1824

Crutchfield, Henry to Hannah Sheridan, My. 25, Randolph county. R. R. Je. 11, 1824

Curry, Jane to Sam'l Kirkpatrick, Nov. 11, Orange county. R. R. Dec. 3, 1824

Daniel, Martitia to Jonathan Worth of Guilford county, Apr. 20, Orange county. R. R. My. 7, 1824

Davidson, Sarah F. to Thomas I. Johnson of Petersburg, Va., Sept. 9, Charlotte. R. R. Oct. 8, 1824

Davis, John of this State to Lydia Ann Morse, Oct. 7, New York. R. R. Nov. 5, 1824

Davis, Mary K. of Mecklenburg county to Albert G. Macon of Warren county, Sept. 29. R. R. Oct. 8, 1824

DeBrular, William G. of Frederick county, Va. to Linney Compton of Orange county, Sept. R. R. Sept. 3, 1824

Dockery, Hannah to Solomon Bostick, My. 12, Richmond county. R. R. Je. 11, 1824

Dockery, Maj. Alfred to Sarah L. Turner, Mar. 1, Anson county. R. R. Apr. 16, 1824

Dunn, Eliza W. to George C. Mendenhall of Guilford county, My. 28, Montgomery county. R. R. Je. 11, 1824

Durham, Hannah to Thomas Faucett, Feb. 19, Orange county. R. R. Mar. 19, 1824

Duval, Doctor Francis to Nancy Bryan, Feb. 5, Trenton. R. R. Feb. 20, 1824

Ellerbe, Harriet of Cheraw, S. C. to W. L. Cole of Richmond county, Je. 2. R. R. Je. 18, 1824

Elliott, Sarah to Alfred H. Marsh, Apr. 7, Randolph county. R. R. My. 14, 1824

Falconer, Mrs. Ann to David Jones of Granville county, Oct. 30, Raleigh. R. R. Nov. 5, 1824

Faucett, Thomas to Hannah Durham, Feb. 19, Orange county. R. R. Mar. 19, 1824

Flemming, Mitchell of Missouri to Jimmy Stevenson of Cabarrus county, Dec. 15. R. R. Feb. 13, 1824

Fletcher, George to Mary Ann Kennedy, Jan., Fayetteville. R. R. Jan. 30, 1824

Flowers, Catharine to Solomon Seaboth, Je. 10, Lincoln county. R. R. Jly. 30, 1824

Ford, Margaret to Wm. Williams, Jan. 11, Rowan county. R. R. Jan. 30, 1824

Forney, Caroline Matilda of Lincoln county to Ransom G. Hunley of South Carolina, Oct. 21, Lincoln county. R. R. Nov. 12, 1824

Foster, Hannah to Banister Parrish of Granville county, Dec. 23, Warren county. R. R. Jan. 23, 1824

Franklin, Bernard of Surry county to Rebecca Wellborn of Wilkes county. R. R. Dec. 3, 1824

Fulton, Susan A. to Matthew Locke, Feb. 3, Salisbury. R. R. Feb. 20, 1824

Geren, Kollock Abraham of Greensborough to Mrs. Sarah Tyson, Oct., Pittsborough. R. R. Oct. 22, 1824

Gibson, David to Elizabeth Little, Sept. 16, Orange county. R. R. Oct. 8, 1824

Gillet, Dr. Jasper of Wake county to Sarah Thomas, Nov., Louisburg. R. R. Nov. 12, 1824

Graham, Mary of Lincoln county to Rev. Robert H. Morrison of Fayetteville, Apr. 29, Lincoln county. R. R. My. 28, 1824

Hall, William B. of Raleigh to Sarah O. Legrand, Jan. 29, Montgomery county. R. R. Feb. 20, 1824

Hamlin, Martha to Blake Baker of Warren county, Oct. 13, Halifax county. R. R. Oct. 22, 1824

Hardiman, Wm. of Tennessee to Mary M. M. Hilliard, Je. 17, Halifax county. R. R. Jly. 2, 1824

Hargrave, Susan to Dr. Joseph H. Hilliard, Feb. 15, Davidson county. R. R. Mar. 19, 1824

Harris, Eliza to Samuel Crenshaw, Mar. 25, Wake county. R. R. Apr. 2, 1824

Harris, Jane of Iredell county to Angus Chisholm of Montgomery county, Dec. 27. R. R. Feb. 10, 1824

Harrison, Emily to James Hartsfield, Aug. 17, Franklin county. R. R. Sept. 3, 1824

Hartsfield, James to Emily Harrison, Aug. 17, Franklin county. R. R. Sept. 3, 1824

Hatfield, Elizabeth to Richard N. Oliver, Feb. 5, Newbern. R. R. Feb. 20, 1824

Hall, Nancy to John Horn, Jan. 29, Orange county. R. R. Feb. 27, 1824

Hawkins, Lucy D. to Thomas H. Kean of Granville county, Jan. 7, Franklin county. R. R. Jan. 23, 1824

Hawkins, Mrs. William to Richard Russell of Warren county, Apr. 8, Franklin county. R. R. Apr. 16, 1824

Hayes, Martha to Benj. Johnson, Dec. 22, Mecklenburg county. R. R. Feb. 13, 1824

Hilliard, Dr. Joseph H. to Susan Hargrave, Feb. 15, Davidson county. R. R. Mar. 19, 1824

Hilliard, Mary M. M. to Wm. Hardiman of Tennessee, Je. 17, Halifax county. R. R. Jly. 2, 1824

Hinton, Delany to Thomas L. Ragsdale, Jly. 10, Johnston county. R. R. Jly. 23, 1824

Hinton, Jos. B. of Beaufort to Nancy Boyd of Pitt county, Dec. 2, Pitt county. R. R. Dec. 31, 1824

Hogan, Rev. William of Philadelphia to Mrs. Henrietta M'Kay of Smithville, Aug. 19. R. R. Sept. 3, 1824

Hopkins, Maj. Archibald to Mrs. Martha Hunter, Feb. 25, Wake county. R. R. Feb. 27, 1824

Hopkins, Sarah to Thos. Cobbs of Raleigh, Dec. 2, Johnston county. R. R. Dec. 10, 1824

Horn, John to Nancy Hall, Jan. 29, Orange county. R. R. Feb. 27, 1824

Howard, Geo. W. to Caroline Stanly, Nov. 10, Newbern. R. R. Dec. 3, 1824

Howe, Mary E. C. to Dr. Alexander W. Mebane, Feb., Bertie county. R. R. Mar. 5, 1824

Huggins, Margaret to Ira West, Jan. 6, Iredell county. R. R. Jan. 30, 1824

Humley, Ransom G. of South Carolina to Caroline Matilda Forney of Lincoln county, Oct. 21, Lincoln county. R. R. Nov. 12, 1824

Humphrey, Elenor to Daniel Shackelford, My. 20, Onslow county. R. R. Je. 11, 1824

Hunt, Jane to Morgan Taylor, My. 19, Richmond county. R. R. Je. 11, 1824

Hunter, Mrs. Martha to Maj. Archibald Hopkins, Feb. 25, Wake county. R. R. Feb. 27, 1824

Jacqueline, Ann to Thomas B. Slade of this State, My., Jones county, Ga. R. R. My. 21, 1824

Jennett, Sophia to James Cassadey, Jan. 15, Wilmington. R. R. Jan. 23, 1824

Johnson, Dr. Benj. to Martha Hayes, Dec. 22, Mecklenburg county. R. R. Feb. 13, 1824

Johnson, Rev. Cyrus to Mary Cook, Dec. 30, Cabarrus county. R. R. Jan. 30, 1824

Johnson, Thomas I. of Petersburg, Va. to Sarah F. Davidson, Sept. 9, Charlotte. R. R. Oct. 8, 1824

Jones, Caroline P. to Samuel F. Patterson of Wilkesboro, My. 12, Wilkes county. R. R. Je. 4, 1824

Jones, Eliza to Dr. John Young, Mar. 11. Wake county. R. R. Mar. 19, 1824

Jones, Josiah of Chowan county to Lasthenia Smith of Bertie county, Sept. 5. R. R. Oct. 8, 1824

Jones, Mary of Halifax county to Dr. S. Wheaton of Raleigh, Nov. 25, Wake county. R. R. Dec. 3, 1824

Jones, David of Granville county to Mrs. Ann Falconer, Oct. 30, Raleigh. R. R. Nov. 5, 1824

Johnson, Dr. Wood T. of Louisburg to Josephine Outerbridge, Aug. 18, Franklin county. R. R. Aug. 20, 1824

Judkins, Thomas J. of Warren county to Rebecca W. Pegram of Franklin county, Dec. 27, Franklin county. R. R. Feb. 6, 1824

Kean, Thomas H. of Granville county to Lucy D. Hawkins, Jan. 7, Franklin county. R. R. Jan. 23, 1824

Kennedy, Mary Ann to George Fletcher, Jan., Fayetteville. R. R. Jan. 30, 1824

Kerr, Mary G. of Halifax county, Va. to Nicholas Williams of Surry county, Aug. 4, Halifax county, Va. R. R. Aug. 27, 1824

Kirkpatrick, Sam'l to Jane Curry, Nov. 11, Orange county. R. R. Dec. 3, 1824

Lance, John G. of Cheraw to Rosannah Try, Feb. 12, Wadesborough. R. R. Mar. 5, 1824

Lane, Ann to Moses Mordecai, Jan. 6, Wake county. R. R. Jan. 9, 1824

Lee, Kitty H. to Dr. George May, Oct. 12, Washington, D. C. R. R. Oct. 15, 1824

Legrand, Sarah C. to William B. Hall of Raleigh, Jan. 29, Montgomery county. R. R. Feb. 20, 1824

Lindeman, D. to Martha C. Pulliam, Jan. 28, Raleigh. R. R. Jan. 30, 1824

Little, Cynthia to Col. Eli W. Ward of Onslow county, Je. 10, Warren county. R. R. Je. 25, 1824

Little, Elizabeth to David Gibson, Sept. 16, Orange county. R. R. Oct. 8, 1824

Littlejohn, Mary E. of Oxford to Lewis P. Williamson of Northampton county, Jan. 15, Oxford. R. R. Jan. 23, 1824

Locke, Matthew to Susan A. Fulton, Feb. 3, Salisbury. R. R. Feb. 20, 1824

M'Bride, Eliza to Dr. Archibald M'Queen, Jan. 29, Moore county. R. R. Feb. 27, 1824

M'Jimsey, Mary Ann of Baltimore to James M'Lelland, Je. 20, Stateville. R. R. Jly. 30, 1824

M'Kay, Mrs. Henrietta of Smithville to Rev. William Hogan of Philadelphia, Aug. 19. R. R. Sept. 3, 1824

M'Kay, Jane of Richmond county to Tillotson O'Bryan Smith of Mississippi, Feb. 1, Rockingham. R. R. Feb. 20, 1824

M'Lelland, James to Mary Ann M'Jimsey of Baltimore, Je. 20, Statesville. R. R. Jly. 30, 1824

M'Queen, Dr. Archibald to Eliza M'Bride, Jan. 29, Moore county. R. R. Feb. 27, 1824

Macon, Albert G. of Warren county to Mary K. Davis of Mecklenburg county, Sept. 29. R. R. Oct. 8, 1824

Mangum, Priestly H. of Hillsborough to Rebecca H. Sutherland, Feb. 12, Wake county. R. R. Feb. 20, 1824

Marsh, Alfred H. to Sarah Elliott, Apr. 7, Randolph county. R. R. My. 14, 1824

Martin, Frances of Wake county to Samuel Smith of Caswell county, Feb. 12, Wake county. R. R. Feb. 27, 1824

Mathis, Elizabeth to John Baily, Je. 10, Lincoln county. R. R. Jly. 30, 1824

May, Dr. George to Kitty H. Lee, Oct. 12, Washington, D. C. R. R. Oct. 15, 1824

Mebane, Dr. Alexander W. to Mary E. C. Howe, Feb., Bertie county. R. R. Mar. 15, 1824

Mebane, Margaret to Samuel Mebane, Feb. 9, Orange county. R. R. Feb. 27, 1824

Mebane, Samuel to Margaret Mebane, Feb. 9, Orange county. R. R. Feb. 27, 1824

Mendenhall, George C. of Guilford county to Eliza W. Dunn, My. 28, Montgomery county. R. R. Je. 11, 1824

Merritt, Henrietta to Weldon Carter, Halifax county, Sept. 15, Scotland Neck. R. R. Oct. 8, 1824

Miner, W. Russell to Sarah A. L. Bond, Nov. 2, Windsor. R. R. Nov. 12, 1824

Mitchell, Elizabeth to Moses S. Pratt, Je. 6, Chapel Hill. R. R. Je. 11, 1824

Mitchell, Peter to Betsey Person, Oct. 14, Warrenton. R. R. Oct. 22, 1824

Moore, Cynthia to Franklin Stafford, Jan. 8, Mecklenburg county. R. R. Jan. 30, 1824

Mordecai, Moses to Ann Lane, Jan. 6, Wake county. R. R. Jan. 9, 1824

Morgan, Martha of Murfreesborough to James Worrell of Hertford county, Aug. 13, Murfreesborough. R. R. Sept. 3, 1824

Moore, Susan to Hugh D. Waddell of New Hanover county, Aug. 26, Orange county. R. R. Sept. 10, 1824

Morrison, Margaret to James H. Burns, Jan. 9, Cabarrus county. R. R. Jan. 30, 1824

Morrison, Rev. Robert H. of Fayetteville to Mary Graham of Lincoln county, Apr. 29, Lincoln county. R. R. My. 28, 1824

Morse, Lydia Ann to John Davis of this State, Oct. 7, New York. R. R. Nov. 5, 1824

Mosely, John W. to Sarah L. Coleman, My. 11, Warrenton. R. R. My. 21, 1824

Murdaugh, Margaret to Joseph D. White, Je. 1, Bertie county. R. R. Je. 18, 1824

Nance, E. A. to James Tomlinson of Johnston county, Mar. 25, Wake county. R. R. Mar. 26, 1824

Niel, John F. of Edenton to Elizabeth Wood of Tyrrell county, My. 28, Hertford county. R. R. Je. 18, 1824

O'Daniel, John to Elizabeth Thompson, Sept. 14, Orange county. R. R. Oct. 8, 1824

O'Daniel, Sarah to Alfred Pickard, Sept. 11, Orange county. R. R. Oct. 8, 1824

Oliver, Richard N. to Elizabeth Hatfield, Feb. 5, Newbern. R. R. Feb. 20, 1824

Outerbridge, Josephine to Dr. Wood T. Johnson of Louisburg, Aug. 18, Franklin county. R. R. Aug. 20, 1824

Parrish, Banister of Granville county to Hannah Foster, Dec. 23, Warren county. R. R. Jan. 23, 1824

Patterson, Samuel F. of Wilkesboro to Caroline P. Jones, My. 12, Wilkes county. R. R. Je. 4, 1824

Pearson, Sarah A. of Rowan county to Isaac Croom of Lenoir county, Je. 10. R. R. Je. 25, 1824

Pegram, Rebecca W. of Franklin county to Thomas J. Judkins of Warren county, Dec. 27, Franklin county. R. R. Feb. 6, 1824

Person, Betsey to Peter Mitchell, Oct. 14, Warrenton. R. R. Oct. 22, 1824

Pettaway, Mark of Halifax county to Martha Williams, My. 26, Warren county. R. R. Je. 4, 1824

Pickard, Alfred to Sarah O'Daniel, Sept. 11, Orange county. R. R. Oct. 8, 1824

Picket, Mrs. James to Thomas Berry, Sept. 14, Orange county. R. R. Oct. 8, 1824

Philips, Mrs. Caroline to Absalom B. Smith, Oct., Northampton county. R. R. Oct. 15, 1824

Pike, Mary to Obed Anthony, Oct. 14, Guilford county. R. R. Nov. 5, 1824

Pipkin, John D. of Gates county to Penelope Creecy, Jan. 6, Chowan county. R. R. Jan. 23, 1824

Pitchford, Nancy to Amos P. Sledge, Mar. 3, Warren county. R. R. Mar. 16, 1824

Pratt, Moses S. to Elizabeth Mitchell, Je. 6, Chapel Hill. R. R. Je. 11, 1824

Pullen, Sally to Wm. Browning of Franklin county, Apr. 28, Wake county. R. R. My. 14, 1824

Pulliam, Martha C. to D. Lindeman, Jan. 28, Raleigh. R. R. Jan. 30, 1824

Ragsdale, Thomas L. to Delany Hinton, Jly. 10, Johnston county. R. R. Jly. 23, 1824

Rhea, Naomi˙ Jane of this State to Dr. Frederick Stewart of Lexington, Feb. 19, Sparta, Ga. R. R. Mar. 19, 1824

Riddick, Joseph to Nancy Walton, Jan. 8, Chowan county. R. R. Jan. 23, 1824

Roach, William to Sarah Clendenin, Sept. 8, Orange county. R. R. Oct. 8, 1824

Ross, Martin, Jr. to Elizabeth Townsend, Apr. 8, Perquimons county. R. R. Apr. 30, 1824

Russell, Richard of Warren county to Mrs. William Hawkins, Apr. 8, Franklin county. R. R. Apr. 16, 1824

Rust, Mrs. Delphia to John Washington of Granville county, Oct. 19, Franklin county. R. R. Oct. 29, 1824

Sasser, Ann to Lemuel Whitfield, Jan., Wayne county. R. R. Jan. 23, 1824

Seaborth, Solomon to Catherine Flowers, Je. 10, Lincoln county. R. R. Jly. 30, 1824

Shackelford, Daniel of Newbern to Eleanor Humphrey, My. 20, Onslow county. R. R. Je. 11, 1824

Shell, Dr. Thomas E. of Warrenton to Martha Alston, Oct., Halifax county. R. R. Oct. 15, 1824

Sheridan, Hannah to Henry Crutchfield, My. 25, Randolph county. R. R. Je. 11, 1824

Sheril, Polly A. to Capt. Robert Blackburn, My. 13, Lincoln county. R. R. Je. 11, 1824

Simpson, Archibald to Margaret E. Bordeau, Dec. 7, Long Creek. R. R. Dec. 31, 1824

Slade, Thomas B. of this State to Ann Jacqueline, My., Jones county, Ga. R. R. My. 21, 1824

Sledge, Amos P. to Nancy Pitchford, Mar. 3, Warren county. R. R. Mar. 16, 1824

Small, Joseph to Elizabeth M. Bain, Feb. 5, Pittsborough. R. R. Feb. 13, 1824

Smith, Absalom B. to Mrs. Caroline B. Philips, Oct., Northampton county. R. R. Oct. 15, 1824

Smith, Elizabeth to Col. Henry C. Williams, Jly. 27, Warren county. R. R. Aug. 6, 1824

Smith, Lasthenia of Bertie county to Josiah Jones of Chowan county. Sept. 5. R. R. Oct. 8, 1824

Smith, Samuel of Caswell county to Frances Martin of Wake county, Feb. 12, Wake county. R. R. Feb. 27, 1824

Smith, Tillotson O'Bryan of Mississippi to Jane M'Kay of Richmond county, Feb. 1, Rockingham. R. R. Feb. 20, 1824

Sossaman, Rosina to Jas. Baldwin, Jan. 15, Davidson county. R. R. Jan. 30, 1824

Stafford, Franklin to Cynthia Moore, Jan. 8, Mecklenburg county. R. R. Jan. 30, 1824

Stanly, Caroline to Geo. W. Howard, Nov. 10, Newbern. R. R. Dec. 3, 1824

Stevenson, Jimmy of Cabarrus county to Mitchell Flemming of Missouri, Dec. 15. R. R. Feb. 13, 1824

Stewart, Dr. Frederick S. of Lexington to Naomi Jane Rhea of this State, Feb. 19, Sparta, Ga. R. R. Mar. 19, 1824

Stone, Sarah to John Welch, Jr. of Granville county, Oct. 14, Franklin county. R. R. Oct. 29, 1824

Sutherland, Rebecca H. to Priestly H. Mangum of Hillsborough, Feb. 12, Wake county. R. R. Feb. 20, 1824

Taylor, Morgan to Jane Hunt, My. 19, Richmond county. R. R. Je. 11, 1824

Terril, Joseph to Jane Allen, Jan. 29, Orange county. R. R. Feb. 27, 1824

Thomas, Berry to Mrs. James Picket, Sept. 14, Orange county. R. R. Oct. 8, 1824

Thomas, Sarah to Dr. Jasper Gillet of Wake county, Nov., Louisburg. R. R. Nov. 12, 1824

Thompson, Elizabeth to John O'Daniel, Sept. 14, Orange county. R. R. Oct. 8, 1824

Thompson, Phebe to James Clancy, Sept. 16, Hillsborough. R. R. Oct. 8, 1824

Tomlinson, James of Johnston county to E. A. Nance, Mar. 25, Wake county. R. R. Mar. 26, 1824

Townsend, Elizabeth to Martin Ross, Jr., Apr. 8, Perquimons county. R. R. Apr. 30, 1824

Troy, Rosannah to John G. Lance of Cheraw, S. C., Feb. 12, Wadesborough. R. R. Mar. 5, 1824

Turner, Sarah L. to Maj. Alfred Dockery, Mar. 1, Anson county. R. R. Apr. 16, 1824

Tyson, Mrs. Sarah to Kollock Abraham Geren of Greensborough, Oct., Pittsborough. R. R. Oct. 22, 1824

Waddell, Hugh D. of New Hanover county to Susan Moore, Aug. 26, Orange county. R. R. Sept. 10, 1824

Waddell, John, Jr. of Wilmington to Ann Campbell, Dec. 23, Brunswick county. R. R. Dec. 31, 1824

Walton, Nancy to Joseph Riddick, Jan. 8, Chowan county. R. R. Jan. 23, 1824

Ward, Col. Eli W. of Onslow county to Cynthia Little, Je. 10, Warren county. R. R. Je. 25, 1824

Ward, Dr. Tho's of Warren county to Elizabeth A. Blackman, Je. 15, Waynesboro. R. R. Jly. 23, 1824

Washington, John of Granville county to Mrs. Delphia Rust, Oct. 19, Franklin county. R. R. Oct. 29, 1824

Welch, John, Jr. of Granville county to Sarah Stone, Oct. 14, Franklin county. R. R. Oct. 29, 1824

Wellborn, Rebecca of Wilkes county to Bernard Franklin of Surry county, Nov. 26. R. R. Dec. 3, 1824

West, Ira to Margaret Huggins, Jan. 6, Iredell county. R. R. Jan. 30, 1824

Wheaton, Dr. S. of Raleigh to Mary Jones of Halifax county, Nov. 25, Wake county. R. R. Dec. 3, 1824

White, Joseph D. to Margaret Murdaugh, Je. 1, Bertie county. R. R. Je. 18, 1824

Whitfield, Geo. to Louisa Blackledge, Jan. 8, Lenoir county. R. R. Jan. 30, 1824

Whitfield, Lemuel to Ann Sasser, Jan., Wayne county. R. R. Jan. 23, 1824

Williams, Col. Henry C. to Elizabeth Smith, Jly. 27, Warren county. R. R. Aug. 6, 1824

Williams, Martha to Mark Pettaway of Halifax county, My. 26, Warren county. R. R. Je. 4, 1824

Williams, Nicholas of Surry county to Mary G. Kerr of Halifax county, Va., Aug. 4, Halifax county, Va. R. R. Aug. 27, 1824

Williams, Wm. to Margaret Ford, Jan. 11, Rowan county. R. R. Jan. 30, 1824

Williams, William of Raleigh to Susannah R. Andrews, Nov. 25, Washington, D. C . R. R. Dec. 3, 1824

Williamson, Lewis P. of Northampton county to Mary E. Littlejohn of Oxford, Jan. 15, Oxford. R. R. Jan. 23, 1824

Wood, Elizabeth of Tyrrell county to John F. Niel of Edenton, My. 28, Hertford county. R. R. Je. 18, 1824

Worrell, James of Hertford county to Martha Morgan of Murfreesborough, Aug. 13, Murfreesborough. R. R. Sept. 3, 1824

Worth, Jonathan of Guilford county to Martitia Daniel, Apr. 20, Orange county. R. R. My. 7, 1824

Young, Dr. John to Eliza Jones, Mar. 11, Wake county. R. R. Mar. 19, 1824

112

1825

Allan, Mary to Dr. Thomas H. Wright, Je. 9, Wilmington. R. R. Je. 21, 1825

Allen, John of Lincoln county to Polly Williams of Pendleton, S. C., Je. 23, Lincoln county. R. R. Jly. 19, 1825

Alsobrook, David of Chapel Hill to Mary Neal of Orange county, Je. 16. R. R. Je. 28, 1825

Alston, Jane to Mr. Tyson, Oct., Chatham county. R. R. Oct. 14, 1825

Anderson, Dr. Athelston of Nashville to Miss Irby, Je. 2, Mecklenburg county, Va. R. R. Jly. 15, 1825

Anderson, William to Martha Faucett, Oct. 6, Orange county. R. R. Nov. 1, 1825

Arey, Joseph to Selina C. Staiert, Apr. 26, Fayetteville. R. R. My. 10, 1825

Atkinson, James of Virginia to Patsey Faulkner of Lincoln county, Je. 23. R. R. Jly. 19, 1825

Avery, Nancy to James M. O'Neill, Apr. 5, Burke county. R. R. Apr. 26, 1825

Bacon, Joseph G. to Rebecca Carrington, Feb. 3, Hillsborough. R. R. Feb. 25, 1825

Baine, Rev. George A. to Frances Carney, Oct. 30, Newbern. R. R. Nov. 1, 1825

Baird, Israel of Buncombe county to Mary Tate, Apr. 4, Burke county. R. R. Apr. 26, 1824

Ballard, Wm. W. to Amelia Davis, My. 13, Fayetteville. R. R. My. 24, 1825

Barnett, Polly to Dempsey Holder, Sept. 24, Wilkes county. R. R. Oct. 25, 1825

Barringer, Margaret to John Boyd of Charlotte, Jan. 20, Cabarrus county. R. R. Feb. 8, 1825

Bass, John of Granville county to Abigail Solomon, Jly. 13, Granville county. R. R. Jly. 19, 1825

Bates, John to Eleanor Pickett, Jan. 26, Wadesborough. R. R. Feb. 8, 1825

Battle, William H. of Edgecombe county to Lucy M. Plummer, Je. 1, Warrenton. R. R. Je. 7, 1825

Beach, Lucinda A. to Archibald Largent, Apr. 5, Burke county. R. R. Apr. 26, 1825

Benbury, Sarah to Lemuel Halsey, Mar. 22, Chowan county. R. R. Apr. 5, 1825

Bird, Silas of Lancaster District, S. C. to Mrs. Susannah M'Cain, Jly. 9, Mecklenburg county. R. R. Jly. 19, 1825

Bivens, William to Miss Chapman, Oct. 6, Orange county. R. R. Nov. 1, 1825

Black, Isabella to Norman Campbell, Aug. 22, Cumberland county. R. R. Oct. 4, 1825

Blalock, William to Mary Wilder, Mar. 3, Wake county. R. R. Mar. 15, 1825

Blount, Thomas M. of Edenton to Elizabeth Knight of Phila., Mar. 29, Edenton. R. R. Apr. 19, 1825

Boddie, Mary of Nash county to Josiah Crudup of Wake county, My. 5, Nash county. R. R. My. 17, 1825

Booth, Julia to John Peabody, Feb., Fayetteville. R. R. Feb. 22, 1825

Borden, William Hill to Elizabeth Dixon, My. 17, Newbern. R. R. My. 31, 1825

Bowen, Ellen to Jas. Marsh, Sept., Beaufort county. R. R. Sept. 6, 1825

Bowers, Col. George of Ashe county to Nancy Bryan of Wilkes county, Feb. 10. R. R. Mar. 22, 1825

Bowman, Rev. James H. of Maury county, Tenn. to Elizabeth S. M'Corkle of Rowan county, Aug. 9, Rowan county. R. R. Sept. 2, 1825

Boyd, John of Charlotte to Margaret Barringer, Jan. 20, Cabarrus county. R. R. Feb. 8, 1825

Boyden, N. to Ruth Martin, Jan. 20, Stokes county. R. R. Feb. 22, 1825

Boylan, Mrs. Jane of Wake county to Samuel Williams of Cumberland county, My. 12, Wake county. R. R. My. 17, 1825

Bradley, Penelope to William Howentown, Je. 15, Enfield. R. R. Je. 28, 1825

Brandon, Catharine of Halifax, Va. to Jas. H. White of Milton, Je. 22, Person county. R. R. Jly. 8, 1825

Bridges, Horace D. to Louisa G. Johnson, My. 26, Chatham county. R. R. Je. 28, 1825

Brown, Eliza R. A. of Granville county, Va. to Richard F. Yarbrough, Je. 22, Wake Forest. R. R. Je. 24, 1825

Brown, Dr. Anderson of Orange county to Sarah C. D. Payne of Fredericktown, Md., My. 31, Guilford county. R. R. Je. 28, 1825

Brown, James R. to Sarah A. Craig, Feb. 9, Wilmington. R. R. Mar. 1, 1825

Bryan, Alice to John G. Kinsey, Newbern, Apr. 10. R. R. Apr. 26, 1825

Bryan, Ann S. to James H. Smith, Aug. 7, Johnston county. R. R. Aug. 12, 1825

Bryan, Nancy of Wilkes county to Col. George Bowers of Ashe county, Feb. 10. R. R. Mar. 22, 1825

Bullock, Col. William to Sarah Jones, Feb., Chowan county. R. R. Feb. 25, 1825

Burbank, Eliza Ann to Joseph Potts, Je. 9, Washington, Beaufort county. R. R. Je. 28, 1825

Burwell, Lucy A. to Dr. Charles Sturdivant of Granville county, Je. 2, Mecklenburg, Va. R. R. Je. 21, 1825

Burke, Maj. Jno. M'Neill of Person county to Sarah Ann Pledger of Wilcox county, Jan. 20. R. R. Feb. 15, 1825

Burton, Horace A. of Granville county to Margaret D. Williams of Warren county, Je. 2. R. R. Je. 21, 1825

Butler, Harriet M. to John Williams, My. 8, Elizabeth City. R. R. My. 24, 1825

Butts, Ann P. of Northampton county to Allen James of Petersburg, Va., My. 5, Northampton county. R. R. My. 31, 1825

Caldwell, Robert to Mariah Latta, Jly. 13, Guilford county. R. R. Jly. 26, 1825

Campbell, Alexander to Eleanor Whitaker, Nov. 23, Raleigh. R. R. Nov. 25, 1825

Campbell, Norman to Isabella Black, Aug. 22, Cumberland county. R. R. Oct. 4, 1825

Carney, Frances to Rev. George A. Baine, Oct. 30, Newbern. R. R. Nov. 1, 1825

Carrington, Rebecca to Joseph G. Bacon, Feb. 3, Hillsborough. R. R. Feb. 25, 1825

Carter, Nancy C. T. of Halifax county to Richard M'Cain of Petersburg, My. 17, Halifax county. R. R. My. 24, 1825

Chambers, William to Ann C. M'Connaughey, Apr. 14, Rowan county. R. R. Apr. 26, 1825

Chapman, Miss to William Bivens, Oct. 6, Orange county. R. R. Nov. 1, 1825

Cheek, Elbert of Warrenton to Susan Hayes of Warren county, Je. 1. R. R. Je. 7, 1825

Christmas, Susan to Dr. James A. Craig, Feb. 17, Orange county. R. R. Mar. 11, 1825

Churchill, Claudius B. to Lucy Holliday, Jan., Newbern. R. R. Jan. 14, 1825

Clanton, Frances M. to Maclain Sledge, Je. 6, Warren county. R. R. Je. 17, 1825

Clarke, William F. of Raleigh to Catherine B. Halander, Jly. 15, Oxford. R. R. Jly. 19, 1825

Clemmons, Angelina to Thomas Hall, My. 15, Davidson ciunty. R. R. Je. 28, 1825

Cochran, Mary to Wm. Villines, Aug. 30, Person county. R. R. Sept. 13, 1825

Cochran, Maj. William G. of Caswell county to Elizabeth Liston Travis, My. 10, Philadelphia. R. R. Je. 7, 1825

Coit, Jas. of Cheraw, S. C. to Francis S. Taber of Fayetteville, Jan. 12, Fayetteville. R. R. Jan. 28, 1825

Collins, Annis to Lewis M. Cowper, Dec. 22, Portsmouth, Va. R. R. Jan 7, 1825

Collins, Ann McD. to Spencer O'Brian, Apr. 7, Halifax county. R. R. Apr. 12, 1825

Coman, Margaret to John R. Love of Haywood county, Oct. 16, Raleigh. R. R. Feb. 18, 1825

Conner, Mrs. Elizabeth to James Kay, Jan., Newbern. R. R. Jan. 14, 1825

Cottrell, Benj'n of Warren county to Mary J. Daniel of Wake county, My. 13. R. R. My. 17, 1825

Cowper, Lewis M. of Murfreesborough to Annis Collins, Dec. 22, Portsmouth, Va. R. R. Jan. 7, 1825

Cox, Peggy to David M'Crory, Oct. 4, Orange county. R. R. Nov. 1, 1825

Craig, Dr. James A. to Susan Christmas, Feb. 17, Orange county. R. R. Mar. 11, 1825

Craig, Sarah A. to James R. Brown, Feb. 9, Wilmington. R. R. Mar. 1, 1825

Crudup, Josiah of Wake county to Mary Boddie of Nash county, My. 5, Nash county. R. R. My. 17, 1825

Curtis, Matilda to Wm. S. M'Ewen of Raleigh, Sept., Connecticut. R. R. Sept. 23, 1825

Daniel, Chesley of Raleigh to Susan G. Ford, Feb., South Carolina. R. R.
Feb. 4, 1825

Daniel, John R. J. to Martha L. Stith, Apr. 5, Halifax. R. R. Apr. 12, 1825

Daniel, Mary J. of Wake county to Benj'n Cottrell of Warren county, My.
13. R. R. My. 17, 1825

Davie, Allen I. to Rosa Powell, Jly. 21, Halifax. R. R. Aug. 2, 1825

Davies, Susan of Raleigh to Adam Hutchison, Feb. 10, Augusta. R. R.
Feb. 22, 1825

Davis, Alfred of Georgia to Elizabeth Yarbrough of Franklin county,
Sept. 14, Franklin county. R. R. Sept. 20, 1825

Davis, Amelia to Wm. W. Ballard, My. 13, Fayetteville. R. R. My. 24,
1825

Davis, Thomas to Keziah Wheeler, Oct. 6, Guilford county. R. R. Oct. 18,
1825

Davis, Wm. F. of Norfolk county, Va. to Mrs. Melissa Gold, My. 5, Currituck Court House. R. R. My. 24, 1825

Dejarnett, Elizabeth to Asa Vestal, My. 12, Huntsville. R. R. My. 31, 1825

Dicken, Mrs. Martha to James J. Pittman, Apr. 5, Halifax county. R. R.
Apr. 12, 1825

Dickerson, Jane of Virginia to James Gwynn of Wilkesboro. R. R. Mar.
22, 1825

Dinkins, Mary to Washington Morrison, Oct. 20, Mecklenburg county.
R. R. Nov. 1, 1825

Dixon, Elizabeth to William Hull Borden, My. 17, Newbern. R. R. My. 31,
1825

Donaldson, Eliza to Thomas C. Hooper, My. 25, Fayetteville. R. R. Je. 7,
1825

Drake, Harriot to Benjamin Ivy, Aug. 22, Halifax county. R. R. Oct. 4,
1825

Drake, Mathew M. to Winifred Fitz, Nov., Warren county. R. R. Nov. 8,
1825

Dukenmenier, Elizabeth to Thos. Foster of Augusta, Ga., Sept. 22, Fayetteville. R. R. Oct. 14, 1825

Dunnavant, M. W. to Eliza J. B. Stiner, Mar. 29, Halifax. R. R. Apr. 5,
1825

Earnest, David of Burke county to Eveline Jones of Wilkes county, My.
10, Wilkes county. R. R. My. 31, 1825

Earnhart, Sarah to Amos Fite, Apr. 14, Rowan county. R. R. My. 3, 1825

Elliott, Robt. to Christiana M'Lean, Apr. 7, Iredell county. R. R. Apr. 26,
1825

Eure, Elisha H. to Mrs. Elizabeth Johnson, Apr. 14, Halifax county. R. R.
Apr. 26, 1825

Faucett, Martha to William Anderson, Oct. 6, Orange county. R. R. Nov.
1, 1825

Faulkner, Patsey of Lincoln county to James Atkinson of Virginia, Je.
R. R. Jly. 19, 1825

Fisher, Anthony of Tennessee to Nancy R. Turner, Sept. 8, Caswell county.
R. R. Sept. 23, 1825

Fite, Amos to Sarah Earnhart, Apr. 14, Rowan county. R. R. My. 3, 1825

Fitz, Winifred to Mathew M. Drake, Nov., Warren county. R. R. Nov. 8,
1825

Fonvielle, Richard, Jr. of Craven county to Ann Grant of Jones county, Mar. 24, Jones county. R. R. Apr. 12, 1825

Fonville, Elizabeth to Henry R. Foy, Je. 9, New Hanover county. R. R. Je. 21, 1825

Ford, Susan G. to Chesley Daniel of Raleigh, Feb., South Carolina. R. R. Feb. 4, 1825

Foscue, Eliza to Daniel S. Saunders of Onslow county, Jan., Jones county. R. R. Jan. 28, 1825

Foster, Thos. of Augusta, Ga. to Elizabeth Dukenmenier, Sept. 22, Fayetteville. R. R. Oct. 14, 1825

Foy, Henry R. to Elizabeth Fonville, Je. 9, New Hanover county. R. R. Je. 21, 1825

Francis, Henry to Elizabeth Hawkins, Jly. 3, Bertie county. R. R. Jly. 26, 1825

Freeman, Geo. W. of Franklin county to Theresa T. Tartt of Edgecombe county, Dec. 13, Edgecombe county. R. R. Dec. 27, 1825

Freeman, Miss L. S. of Massachusetts to Weston R. Gales of Raleigh, Apr. 21, Sandwich, Mass. R. R. My. 10, 1825

Frizell, William T. to Mary Wilson, Jly. 27, Fayetteville. R. R. Aug. 9, 1825

Fulmore, James to Martha Powell, Feb., Lumberton. R. R. Feb. 22, 1825

Gales, Weston R. of Raleigh to Miss L. S. Freeman of Massachusetts, Apr. 21, Sandwich, Mass. R. R. My. 10, 1825

Gentry, Tabitha S. to P. G. Harden, Sept. 21, Rockingham county. R. R. Oct. 25, 1825

Gilmore, Margaret to Robert Sloan, Sept. 29, Mecklenburg county. R. R. Oct. 14, 1825

Gold, Mrs. Melissa to Wm. F. Davis of Norfolk county, Va., My. 5, Currituck Court House. R. R. My. 24, 1825

Goodloe, Adeline to Dabney Goodloe, Sept., Franklin county. R. R. Sept. 9, 1825

Goodloe, Dabney to Adeline Goodloe, Sept., Franklin county. R. R. Sept. 9, 1825

Goodwyn, Robert T. of Fayetteville to Caroline F. Mumford, Aug. 4, Bladen county. R. R. Aug. 9, 1825

Govan, Andrew R. to Mary P. Jones, Mar. 10, Northampton county. R. R. Mar. 18, 1825

Grant, Ann of Jones county to Richard Fonvielle, Jr. of Craven county, Mar. 24, Jones county. R. R. Apr. 12, 1825

Graves, Nancy to Capt. William Graves, My, Caswell county. R. R. My. 24, 1825

Graves, Capt. William to Nancy Graves, My., Caswell county. R. R. My. 24, 1825

Gwynn, James of Wilkesborough to Jane Dickerson of Virginia, Mar. 1. R. R. Mar. 22, 1825

Hager, Aaron to Miss L. N. Steely of Lincoln county, Je. 23. R. R. Jly. 19, 1825

Hakey, Rebecca Ann of Wilmington to Joseph Towns of Cheraw, S. C., Feb., Wilmington. R. R. Mar. 1, 1825

Halander, Catharine B. to William F. Clarke of Raleigh, Jly. 15, Oxford. R. R. Jly. 19, 1825

Hall, Thomas to Angelina Clemmons, My. 15, Davidson county. R. R. Je. 28, 1825

Halsey, Lemuel to Sarah Benbury, Mar. 22, Chowan county. R. R. Apr. 5, 1825

Harden, P. G. to Tabitha S. Gentry, Sept. 21, Rockingham county. R. R. Oct. 25, 1825

Hardy, James F. of Newberry District, S. C. to Jane Patton of Asheville, Dec. 23, Asheville. R. R. Jan. 28, 1825

Hardy, Susanna to Rev. Orwin Maye, Apr. 21, Greene county. R. R. My. 17, 1825

Harris, Arthur to Mrs. B. Harris, Aug. 24, Montgomery county. R. R. Sept. 6, 1825

Harris, Charity to James Sedgwick, Sept. 1, Guilford county. R. R. Sept. 13, 1825

Harris, Dr. James S. to Jane J. Hayes, Sept. 20, Lincoln county. R. R. Nov. 8, 1825

Hudson, Lawrence to Margaret Hendren, Aug. 4, Rowan county. R. R. Sept. 2, 1825

Hunter, Jacob to Ruth T. High, Jly. 19, Wake Forest. R. R. Jly. 26, 1825

Hutchison, Adam to Susan Davies of Raleigh, Feb. 10, Augusta. R. R. Feb. 22, 1825

Ingram, Dr. Jno. to Lydia M'Millan, Sept. 8, Moore county. R. R. Sept. 20, 1825

Irby, Miss to Dr. Athelston Anderson of Nashville, Je. 2, Mecklenburg county, Va. R. R. Jly. 15, 1825

Ivy, Benjamin to Harriot Drake, Aug. 22, Halifax county. R. R. Oct. 4, 1825

James, Allen of Petersburg, Va. to Ann P. Butts of Northampton county, My., Northampton county. R. R. My. 31, 1825

James, Sedgwick to Charity Harris, Sept. 1, Guilford county. R. R. Sept. 13, 1825

Jay, James to Mrs. Elizabeth M'Kissack, Jan., Person county. R. R. Jan. 7, 1825

Jones, Eveline of Wilkes county to David Earnest of Burke county, My. 10, Wilkes county. R. R. My. 31, 1825

Jones, Mary P. to Andrew P. Govan, Mar. 10, Northampton county. R. R. Mar. 18, 1825

Jones, Nancy of Wilkes county to Ambrose Mills of Rutherford county, Feb. 1, Rutherford county. R. R. Feb. 22, 1825

Jones, Sarah of Warren county to William Taylor of Granville county, Aug. 2. R. R. Aug. 9, 1825

Jones, Col. Tignal to Emily High, Jan. 25, Wake county. R. R. Feb. 25, 1825

Johnson, Benjamin to Mary Ann Joyner, Apr. 14, Halifax. R. R. Apr. 26, 1825

Johnson, Caroline to John M'Neill, Aug. 24, Richmond county. R. R. Sept. 2, 1825

Johnson, Mrs. Elizabeth to Elisha H. Eure, Apr. 14; Halifax county. R. R. Apr. 26, 1825

Johnson, James to Mary Ann O'Quin, Mar., Fayetteville. R. R. Mar. 11, 1825

Johnson, Louisa G. to Horace D. Bridges, My. 26, Chatham county. R. R. Je. 28, 1825

Johnson, Margaret to Wm. Patton, Sept. 27, Orange county. R. R. Nov. 8, 1825

Johnson, Thomas D. to Miss S. G. M'Aden, Feb. 24, Caswell county. R. R. Mar. 11, 1825

Johnson, William, Jr. to Eliza Pearson, My. 25, Anson county. R. R. Je. 7, 1825

Johnston, Dovey to Rev. Jas. Stafford, Aug. 23, Rowan county. R. R. Sept. 6, 1825

Johnston, Henry to Nancy Nantz, Je. 23, Mecklenburg county. R. R. Jly. 19, 1825

Johnston, Nancy to John Rankin, Je. 23, Lincoln county. R. R. Jly. 19, 1825

Joyner, Mary Ann to Benjamin Johnson, Apr. 14, Halifax. R. R. Apr. 26, 1825

Kay, James to Mrs. Elizabeth Conner, Jan., Newbern. R. R. Jan. 14, 1825

Killian, Nancy to John Hoke, Apr. 7, Burke county. R. R. My. 3, 1825

Kimbell, Mary C. of Warren county to Peyton H. Liles of Raleigh, Nov., Alabama. R. R. Jan. 14, 1825

Kinsey, John G. to Alice Bryan, Apr. 10, Newbern. R. R. Apr. 26, 1825

Knight, Elizabeth of Phila. to Thomas M. Blount of Edenton, Mar. 29, Edenton. R. R. Apr. 19, 1825

Kornegay, Miss to John Rhodes, Nov. 17, Wayne county. R. R. Nov. 29, 1825

Largent, Archibald to Lucinda A. Beach, Apr. 5, Burke county. R. R. Apr. 26, 1825

Latta, Mariah to Robert Caldwell, Jly. 13, Guilford county. R. R. Jly. 26, 1825

LeGrand, Edwin O. of Montgomery county to Martha O. M'Gehee, Feb. 9, Person county. R. R. Feb. 25, 1825

Lesurer, Elizabeth A. P. to Capt. James M. Scales, Nov. 10, Rockingham county. R. R. Dec. 9, 1825

Liles, Peyton H. of Raleigh to Mary C. Kimbell of Warren county, Nov., Alabama. R. R. Jan. 14, 1825

Love, John R. of Haywood county to Margaret Coman, Oct. 16, Raleigh. R. R. Feb. 18, 1825

Lucas, Sarah to Jonathan P. Sneed of Hillsborough, Mar. 24, Chatham county. R. R. Apr. 5, 1825

Lumsden, Eliza E. to George W. McDonald, Je. 7, Fayetteville. R. R. Je. 14, 1825

M'Aden, Miss S. G. to Thomas E. Johnson, Feb. 24, Caswell county. R. R. Mar. 11, 1825

M'Cain, Mrs. Susannah to Silas Bird of Lancaster District, S. C., Jly. 9, Mecklenburg county. R. R. Jly. 19, 1825

M'Cain, Richard of Petersburg to Nancy C. T. Carter of Halifax county, My. 17, Halifax county. R. R. My. 24, 1825

M'Connaughey, Ann C. to William Chambers, Apr. 14, Rowan county. R. R. Apr. 26, 1825

M'Corkle, Elizabeth S. of Rowan county to Rev. James H. Bowman of Maury county, Tenn., Aug. 9, Rowan county. R. R. Sept. 2, 1825

M'Crory, David to Peggy Cox, Oct. 4, Orange county. R. R. Nov. 1, 1825

M'Donald, George W. to Eliza E. Lumsden, Je. 7, Fayetteville. R. R. Je. 14, 1825

M'Ewen, Wm. S. of Raleigh to Matilda Curtis, Sept., Connecticut. R. R. Sept. 23, 1825

M'Gehee, Martha O. to Edwin O. LeGrand of Montgomery county, Feb. 9, Person county. R. R. Feb. 25, 1825

M'Iver, Mrs. Ann to Green Womack of Pittsborough, Nov., Moore county. R. R. Nov. 8, 1825

M'Kessack, Mrs. Elizabeth to James Jay, Jan., Person county. R. R. Jan. 7, 1825

M'Lean, Christiana to Robt. Elliott, Apr. 7, Iredell county. R. R. Apr. 26, 1825

M'Learen, Frances P. B. of Chatham county to Thomas Williamson of Caswell county, Je. 21. R. R. Oct. 18, 1825

M'Leron, Mrs. of Chatham county to Thos. Williamson of Caswell county, Je. 21. R. R. Sept. 13, 1825

M'Neill, John to Caroline Johnson, Aug. 24, Richmond county. R. R. Sept. 2, 1825

M'Rae, Margaret Mary to Doyle O'Harlon of Wilmington, Oct. 10, Fayetteville. R. R. Oct. 18, 1825

M'Rum, Rachel to John Rogers, Sept. 22, Mecklenburg county. R. R. Oct. 14, 1825

Marsh, Jas. to Ellen Bowen of Beaufort county, Sept. R. R. Sept. 6, 1825

Martin, Benjamin S. to Sally Rousaw, Je. 28, Wilkes county. R. R. Jly. 22, 1825

Martin, Jno. B. to Nancy Harris, Aug. 24, Montgomery county. R. R. Sept. 6, 1825

Martin, Ruth to N. Boyden, Jan. 20, Stokes county. R. R. Feb. 22, 1825

Mathews, Sarah to Major John Michael, My. 10, Lincolnton. R. R. My. 31, 1825

Mebane, Elbridge to Miss Moore, Oct. 6, Orange county. R. R. Nov. 1, 1825

Mebane, Jas., Jr. of Tennessee to Rebecca P. Mebane, Sept. 1, Orange county. R. R. Sept. 20, 1825

Mebane, Rebecca P. to Jas. Mebane, Jr. of Tennessee, Sept. 1, Orange county. R. R. Sept. 20, 1825

Merony, John A. to Mary Hendricks, Aug. 9, Rowan county. R. R. Sept. 2, 1825

Michael, Major John to Sarah Mathews, My. 10, Lincolnton. R. R. My. 31, 1825

Miller, Hardy to Penelope Smith, Je. 14, Bertie county. R. R. Je. 28, 1825

Miller, Wm. to Catherine Mowry, Aug. 14, Rowan county. R. R. Sept. 2, 1825

Mills, Ambrose of Rutherford county to Nancy Jones of Wilkes county, Feb. 1, Rutherford county. R. R. Feb. 22, 1825

Maye, Rev. Irwin to Susannah Hardy, Apr. 21, Greene county. R. R. My. 17, 1825

Montgomery, Edward to Tabitha P. Penix, Feb. 22; Caswell county. R. R. Mar. 11, 1825

Montgomery, Nancy to Bembury Walton of Gates county, Jan., Bertie county. R. R. Feb. 8, 1825

Moore, Alfred of Hertford to Kezia Nixon of Perquimons county, My. 5. R. R. My. 24, 1825

Moore, Miss to Elbridge Mebane, Oct. 6, Orange county. R. R. Nov. 1, 1825

Norris, Thos. of Guilford county to Elizabeth York of Rockingham county, Sept. 8, Rockingham county. R. R. Sept. 23, 1825

Morrison, Washington to Mary Dinkins, Oct. 20, Mecklenburg county. R. R. Nov. 1, 1825

Mowry, Catherine to Wm. Miller, Aug. 14, Rowan county. R. R. Sept. 2, 1825

Mumford, Caroline F. to Robert T. Goodwyn of Fayetteville, Aug. 4, Bladen county. R. R. Aug. 9, 1825

Nantz, Nancy to Henry Johnston, Je. 23, Mecklenburg county. R. R. Jly. 19, 1825

Neal, Mary of Orange county to David Alsobrook of Chapel Hill, Je. 16. R. R. Je. 28, 1825

Nevill, Patrick H. to Lydia Smith, Je. 17, Halifax county. R. R. Je. 28, 1825

Nixon, Kezia of Perquimons county to Alfred Moore of Hertford, My. 5. R. R. My. 24, 1825

Norfleet, Penelope to Thomas Satterfield, Feb., Chowan county. R. R. Feb. 25, 1825

Nuttall, Mary to James Patterson, My. 12, Granville county. R. R. My. 31, 1825

O'Brian, Spencer of Warrenton to Ann McD. Collins, Apr. 7, Halifax county. R. R. Apr. 12, 1825

O'Harlon, Doyle of Wilmington to Margaret Mary M'Rae, Oct. 10, Fayetteville. R. R. Oct. 18, 1825

O'Neill, James M. to Nancy Avery, Apr. 5, Burke county. R. R. Apr. 26, 1825

O'Quin, Mary Ann to James Johnson, Mar., Fayetteville. R. R. Mar. 11, 1825

Paisley, Polly M. to Rev. John Rankin, Je., Greensborough. R. R. Je. 7, 1825

Patterson, James to Mary Nuttall, My. 12, Granville county. R. R. My. 31, 1825

Patton, Jane of Asheville to James F. Hardy of Newberry District, S. C., Dec. 23, Asheville. R. R. Jan. 28, 1825

Patton, Wm. to Margaret Johnson, Sept. 27, Orange county. R. R. Nov. 8, 1825

Payne, Sarah C. D. of Fredericktown, Md. to Dr. Anderson Brown of Orange county, My. 31, Guilford county. R. R. Je. 28, 1825

Peabody, John to Julia Booth, Feb., Fayetteville. R. R. Feb. 22, 1825

Pearson, Eliza to William Johnson, Jr., My. 25, Anson county. R. R. Je. 7, 1825

Penix, Tabitha P. to Edward Montgomery, Feb. 22, Caswell county. R. R. Mar. 11, 1825

Pettijohn, Capt. John C. of Plymouth to Martha Pew of Martin county, Dec. 26, Martin county. R. R. Jan. 14, 1825

Pew, Martha of Martin county to Capt. John C. Pettijohn of Plymouth, Dec. 26, Martin county. R. R. Jan. 14, 1825

Pickett, Eleanor to John Bates, Jan. 26, Wadesborough. R. R. Feb. 8, 1825
Pittman, James J. to Mrs. Martha Dicken, Apr. 5, Halifax county. R. R. Apr. 12, 1825
Pledger, Sarah Ann of Wilcox county to Maj. Jno. M'Neill of Person county, Jan. 20. R. R. Feb. 15, 1825
Plummer, Lucy M. to William Battle of Edgecombe county, Je. 1, Warrenton. R. R. Je. 7, 1825
Potts, Joseph to Eliza Ann Burbank, Je. 9, Washington, Beaufort county. R. R. Je. 28, 1825
Powell, Martha to James Fulmore, Feb., Lumberton. R. R. Feb. 22, 1825
Powell, Rosa to Allen I. Davie, Jly. 21, Halifax. R. R. Aug. 2, 1825
Primrose, Robert to Anne Stevens, Nov. 15, Newbern. R. R. Nov. 22, 1825
Proudfit, Wm. to Eliza Walker, Oct. 20, Halifax county. R. R. Nov. 8, 1825
Ramey, Elizabeth to Zachariah Hoover, Sr., My. 19, Caswell county. R. R. My. 31, 1825
Rankin, John to Nancy Johnston, Je. 23, Lincoln county. R. R. Jly. 19, 1825
Rankin, Rev. John to Polly M. Paisley, Je., Greensborough. R. R. Je. 7, 1825
Reynolds, Joel of Hillsborough to Celia A. Moore, Je. 22. R. R. Jly. 8, 1825
Reynolds, Wesley to Matilda Welch, Apr. 7, Iredell county. R. R. Apr. 26, 1825
Rhodes, John to Miss Kornegay, Nov. 17, Wayne county. R. R. Nov. 29, 1825
Riley, Jesse of Lincoln county to Sally Worke of Mecklenburg county, Je. 23. R. R. Jly. 19, 1825
Roach, Jno. to Sally Ray, Aug. 26, Orange county. R. R. Sept. 20, 1825
Robards, Eliza L. of Granville county to Charles G. Rose of Person county, Je. 29, Granville county. R. R. Jly. 8, 1825
Roberts, William B. to Sarah Wills, Jan., Edenton. R. R. Feb. 8, 1825
Rogers, John to Rachel M'Rum, Sept. 22, Mecklenburg county. R. R. Oct. 14, 1825
Rose, Charles G. of Person county to Eliza L. Robards of Granville county, Je. 29, Granville county. R. R. Jly. 8, 1825
Ross, Evelina E. to Dr. John M. Harris, Apr. 19, Mecklenburg county. R. R. My. 3, 1825
Satterfield, Thomas to Penelope Norfleet, Feb., Chowan county. R. R. Feb. 25, 1825
Saunders, Daniel S. of Onslow county to Eliza Foscue, Jan., Jones county. R. R. Jan. 28, 1825
Scales, Capt. James M. to Elizabeth A. P. Lesurer, Nov. 10, Rockingham county. R. R. Dec. 9, 1825
Sedberry, David to Nancy Stancil, Sept. 1, Richmond county. R. R. Sept. 20, 1825
Sledge, M'Clain to Frances M'Clanton, Je. 6, Warren county. R. R. Je. 17, 1825
Sloan, Robert to Margaret Gilmore, Sept. 29, Mecklenburg county. R. R. Oct. 14, 1825

Smith, James H. to Ann S. Bryan, Aug. 7, Johnston county. R. R. Aug. 12, 1825

Smith, Lydia to Patrick H. Nevill, Je. 17, Halifax county. R. R. Je. 28, 1825

Smith, Penelope to Hardy Miller, Je. 14, Bertie county. R. R. Je. 28, 1825

Smoot, Nancy to Richard Williams, My. 12, Rowan county. R. R. Je. 28, 1825

Sneed, Jonathan P. of Hillsborough to Sarah Lucas, Mar. 24, Chatham county. R. R. Apr. 5, 1825

Solomon, Abigail to John Bass of Granville county, Jly. 13, Granville county. R. R. Jly. 22, 1825

Stafford, Rev. Jas. to Dovey Johnston, Aug. 23, Rowan county. R. R. Sept. 6, 1825

Staiert, Selina C. to Joseph Arey, Apr. 26, Fayetteville. R. R. My. 10, 1825

Steely, Miss L. N. to Aaron Hager of Lincoln county, Je. 23. R. R. Jly. 19, 1825

Stevens, Anne to Robert Primrose, Nov. 15, Newbern. R. R. Nov. 22, 1825

Stevens, Catharine A. of Raleigh to Wm. L. Hawley of Fayetteville, Sept., Roachland county, N. Y. R. R. Sept. 30, 1825

Stiner, Eliza J. B. to M. V. Dinnavant, Mar. 29, Halifax. R. R. Apr. 5, 1825

Stith, Martha L. to John R. J. Daniel, Apr. 5, Halifax county. R. R. Apr. 12, 1825

Stoddard, Mary Ann to Thomas G. Thurston of Wilmington, Aug., Albany, N. Y. R. R. Sept. 2, 1825

Sturdivant, Dr. Charles of Granville county to Lucy A. Burwell, Je. 2, Mecklenburg county, Va. R. R. Je. 21, 1825

Taber, Francis S. of Fayetteville to Jas. Coit of Cheraw, S. C., Jan. 12, Fayetteville. R. R. Jan. 28, 1825

Tartt, Theresa T. of Edgecombe county to Geo. W. Freeman of Franklin county, Dec. 13, Edgecombe county. R. R. Dec. 27, 1825

Tate, Mary to Israel Baird of Buncombe county, Apr. 4, Burke county. R. R. Apr. 26, 1825

Taylor, William of Granville county to Sarah Jones of Warren county, Aug. 2. R. R. Aug. 9, 1825

Thurston, Alice C. to George Howard, Mar. 26, Halifax. R. R. Apr. 5, 1825

Thurston, Thomas G. of Wilmington to Mary Ann Stoddard, Aug., Albany, N. Y. R. R. Sept. 2, 1825

Tomkies, John F. of Virginia to Margaret M. Hoyle of Lincoln county, Nov. 10, Lincoln county. R. R. Nov. 22, 1825

Towns, Joseph of Cheraw, S. C. to Rebecca Ann Halsey of Wilmington, Feb., Wilmington. R. R. Mar. 1, 1825

Travis, Elizabeth Liston to Maj. William G. Cochran of Caswell county, My. 10, Philadelphia. R. R. Je. 7, 1825

Turner, Nancy R. to Anthony Fisher of Tennessee, Sept. 8, Caswell county. R. R. Sept. 23, 1825

Tyson, Mr. to Miss Jane Alston, Oct., Chatham county. R. R. Oct. 14, 1825

Urquhart, James of Southampton, Va. to Antoinette Hill, Apr. 5, Halifax county. R. R. Apr. 12, 1825

Vestal, Asa to Elizabeth Dejarnett, My. 12, Huntsville. R. R. My. 31, 1825

Villines, Wm. to Mary Cochran, Aug. 30, Person county. R. R. Sept. 13, 1825
Walker, Eliza to Wm. Proudfit, Oct. 20, Halifax county. R. R. Nov. 8, 1825
Walter, Bembury of Gates county to Nancy Montgomery, Jan., Bertie county. R. R. Feb. 8, 1825
Welch, Matilda to Wesley Reynolds, Apr. 7, Iredell county. R. R. Apr. 26, 1825
Whitaker, Eleanor to Alexander Campbell, Nov. 23, Raleigh. R. R. Nov. 25, 1825
White, Jas. H. of Milton to Catharine Brandon of Halifax, Va., Je. 22, Person county. R. R. Jly. 8, 1825
Wilder, Mary to William Blalock, Mar. 3, Wake county. R. R. Mar. 15, 1825
Williams, Eliza to Malachi Haughton, Mar. 22, Edenton. R. R. Apr. 5, 1825
Williams, John to Harriet M. Butler, My. 8, Elizabeth City. R. R. My. 24, 1825
Williams, Margaret D. of Warren county to Horace A. Burton of Granville county, Je. 2. R. R. Je. 21, 1825
Williams, Polly of Pendleton, S. C. to John Allen of Lincoln county, Je. 23, Lincoln county. R. R. Jly. 19, 1825
Williams, Richard to Nancy Smoot, My. 12, Rowan county. R. R. Je. 28, 1825
Williams, Samuel of Cumberland county to Mrs. Jane Boylan of Wake county, My. 12, Wake county. R. R. My. 17, 1825
Williamson, Thomas of Caswell county to Frances P. B. Mclearen of Chatham county, Je. 21. R. R. Oct. 18, 1825
Williamson, Thos. of Caswell county to Mrs. M'Leron of Chatham county, Je. 21. R. R. Sept. 13, 1825
Wills, Sarah to William B. Roberts, Jan., Edenton. R. R. Feb. 8, 1825
Wilson, Mary to William T. Frizell, Jly. 27, Fayetteville. R. R. Aug. 9, 1825
Womack, Green of Pittsborough to Mrs. Ann McIver, Nov., Moore county. R. R. Nov. 8, 1825
Woodard, Wm. to Caroline Blount, Sept., Beaufort county. R. R. Sept. 6, 1825
Worke, Sally of Mecklenburg county to Jesse Riley of Lincoln county, Je. 23. R. R. Jly. 19, 1825
Wright, Dr. Thomas H. to Mary Allan, Je. 9, Wilmington. R. R. Je. 21, 1825
Yarbrough, Elizabeth of Franklin county to Alfred Davis of Georgia, Sept. 14, Franklin county. R. R. Sept. 20, 1825
Yarbrough, Richard F. of Fayetteville to Eliza R. A. Brown of Granville county, Va., Je. 22, Wake Forest. R. R. Je. 24, 1825
Yorke, Elizabeth of Rockingham county to Thos. Morris of Guilford county, Sept. 8, Rockingham county. R. R. Sept. 23. 1825

DEATHS

1799

Badger, Thomas of Newbern d. Oct., Washington, Beaufort county. R. R. Oct. 22, 1799

Henry, William of Craven county, d. Oct., Newbern. R. R. Oct. 22, 1799

Holmes, Samuel, Oct. 28, Raleigh. R. R. Oct. 29, 1799

Iredell, James, Oct. 20, Edenton. R. R. Oct. 29, 1799

Lawrence, Mary, Oct. 26, Edenton. R. R. Nov. 19, 1799

Page, Abner of New York, d. Oct. 16, Raleigh. R. R. Oct. 22, 1799

Pelbeck, William, Dec. 7, Edenton. R. R. Dec. 31, 1799

Polk, Mrs. William of Raleigh, d. Oct. 2, Charlotte. R. R. Oct. 22, 1799

Williams, John, Nov., Granville county. R. R. Nov. 19, 1799

Winslow, Joshua of Fayetteville, d. Oct. 20, Wilmington. R. R. Oct. 29, 1799

1800

Allen, John, Dec. 2, Washington, Beaufort county. R. R. Dec. 9, 1800

Bagge, Trangutt, Apr. 1, Salem. R. R. Apr. 22, 1800

Barker, Abner, Feb., Wake county. R. R. Feb. 18, 1800

Blount, Mrs. William, My. 27, New Bern. R. R. Je. 3, 1800

Bryan, Nathan, Dec. 7, Lenoir county. R. R. Dec. 16, 1800

Burgess, Dempsey, Jan. 13, Camden county. R. R. Feb. 4, 1800

Cutting, Dr. James S., Jan. 12, Newbern. R. R. Jan. 28, 1800

Dawson, William, Apr. 16, Wake county. R. R. May 20, 1800

Duffy, Elizabeth, Oct. 23, Hillsboro. R. R. Nov. 4, 1800

Felbank, Mrs. Elizabeth, Jan., Halifax. R. R. Jan. 28, 1800

Foy, Thos., Mar., Jones county. R. R. Mar. 25, 1800

Frilick, Joseph, Jan. 28, Newbern. R. R. Feb. 11, 1800

Gilchrist, Mrs. Martha, Sept. 7, Halifax. R. R. Sept. 23, 1800

Gregory, James, Nov. 28, Gates county. R. R. Dec. 9, 1800

Gregory, Gen., Apr., Camden county. R. R. Apr. 22, 1800

Harris, Henry, Feb. 22, Newbern. R. R. Mar. 11, 1800

Hunley, Capt. R., Mar. 11, Newbern. R. R. Mar. 25, 1800

Lockhart, Mrs., Sept., Raleigh. R. R. Sept. 23, 1800

McKinney, Richard, Jan. 27, Wayne county. R. R. Feb. 18, 1800

McNeill, Malcom, Nov., Moore county. R. R. Dec. 2, 1800

McQueen, Mrs. Alexander M., Sept., Fayetteville. R. R. Sept. 23, 1800

Maule, Major Moses of Beaufort county, Jan. 1, Washington, Beaufort county. R. R. Jan. 28, 1800

Moody, Robert, Dec. 21, Edenton. R. R. Jan. 14, 1800

Nash, Abner, Jan. 17, Newbern. R. R. Jan. 28, 1800

Neale, Abner, Dec. 2, Washington, Beaufort county. R. R. Dec. 9, 1800

Pendleton, Mrs. Elizabeth, Aug. 27, Newbern. R. R. Sept. 16, 1800

Person, Thomas of Warren county, d. Nov. 16, Franklin county. R. R. Nov. 25, 1800

White, Haywood, Apr. 3, Raleigh. R. R. Apr. 8, 1800

Witherspoon, Mrs. David, Feb. 7, Pembroke. R. R. Feb. 25, 1800

1801

Abrams, John of Boston, Oct. 20, Wilmington. R. R. Oct. 27, 1801

Adam, Robert of Fayetteville, Je. 11, Sound, Wilmington. R. R. Je. 13, 1801

DEATH NOTICES

Bennett, William, Jan. 19, Edenton. R. R. Feb. 10, 1801
Butters, Abigail, Nov., Wilmington. R. R. Nov. 24, 1801
Cobb, Tobias, Jan., Rocky Point. R. R. Jan. 6, 1801
Cochran, Col. Richard of Orange county, Dec. 25, Fayetteville. R. R. Jan. 6, 1801
Donaldson, Southwell, Sept., Tarborough. R. R. Sept. 8, 1801
Dunham, Mrs., Je. 17, Newbern. R. R. Je. 30, 1801
Hatch, Mrs. Charles, Sept. 27, Craven county. R. R. Oct. 13, 1801
Hawkins, Philemon, Sept., Warren county. R. R. Sept. 22, 1801
Jeffries, Paul, Jly. 16, Person county. R. R. Jly. 21, 1801
Johnston, Mrs. Samuel, Feb., Martin county. R. R. Feb. 10, 1801
Jones, Willie of Halifax, Je. 8, Wake county. R. R. Je. 13, 1801
Justice, Col. John, Sept., Halifax county. R. R. Sept. 8, 1801
Lanier, Thomas of Surry county, Dec. 22. R. R. Feb. 3, 1801
Lee, John of Petersburg, Oct. 13, Surry county. R. R. Oct. 27, 1801
Locke, General Matthew, Sept. 7, Rowan county. R. R. Oct. 13, 1801
Mackenzie, Malcom, Mar. 16, Wilmington. R. R. Mar. 17, 1801
M'Dowell, General Joseph, Jly. 11, Burke county. R. R. Aug. 18, 1801
Patillo, Henry, Aug., Granville county. R. R. Aug. 25, 1801
Price, Jeff, Mar. 19, Wake county. R. R. Mar. 24, 1801
Purviance, Mrs., Jan. 23, Fayetteville. R. R. Feb. 3, 1801
Ramsey, John, Sept., Chatham county. R. R. Sept. 8, 1801
Routledge, Col. Thomas, Sept., Duplin county. R. R. Sept. 22, 1801
Sanders, Mrs. John, My. 3, Johnston county. R. R. My. 12, 1801
Scurlock, Mrs. Sarah, Apr., Chatham county. R. R. Apr. 14, 1801
Smith, Mrs. Arthur, Jly., Scotland Neck. R. R. Jly. 21, 1801
Spain, David, My. 19, Wake county. R. R. My. 26, 1801
Travers, John of Fayetteville, Aug. 28, Charleston. R. R. Sept. 22, 1801
Vultieur, George, Jan. 29, Newbern. R. R. Feb. 10, 1801
Waine, Edward, Je. 11, Raleigh. R. R. Je. 13, 1801
Whitmore, Mrs. K. of Bath, Je. 19, Norfolk. R. R. Je. 30, 1801
Wilkins, Mrs. John, Nov. 20, Wilmington. R. R. Nov. 24, 1801
Wilson, Mrs. James, Apr. 6, Newbern. R. R. Apr. 21, 1801

1802

Ashe, Col. John B., Nov. 27, Halifax. R. R. Nov. 29, 1802
Atkins, Rodman, Jan. 18, Raleigh. R. R. Feb. 2, 1802
Bartlett, Mrs. Mary, Oct. 22, Wilmington. R. R. Nov. 1, 1802
Bell, Bythal, Nov., Edgecombe county. R. R. Nov. 29, 1802
Bexley, Lewis of Newbern, Je. 5. R. R. Je. 8, 1802
Burke, John, Dec. 14, Wilmington. R. R. Dec. 20, 1802
Conan, Mathew, Aug. 19, Raleigh. R. R. Aug. 23, 1802
Crawley, Mrs. John, My. 17, Wake county. R. R. My. 18, 1802
Davie, Mrs., Apr. 14, Halifax. R. R. Apr. 20, 1802
Davis, Mrs. Buckner, Mar., Warren county. R. R. Mar. 9, 1802
Foort, John, Nov., Halifax. R. R. Nov. 29, 1802
Gains, Mrs. James, My. 3, Chatham county. R. R. Je. 8, 1802
Hill, Mrs. Jane, Apr. 10, Wilmington. R. R. Apr. 20, 1802
Hill, John, Dec. 29, Bertie county. R. R. Jan. 19, 1802
Hinton, Samuel, Jan., Wake county. R. R. Jan. 26, 1802
Howard, Thomas, Sr., Apr. 4, Wilmington. R. R. Apr. 13, 1802

Jocelin, Frederic of Wilmington, My. 19, Norfolk. R. R. Je. 8, 1802
Johnston, Charles, Jly. 28, Edenton. R. R. Aug. 16, 1802
Jones, William, Jly. 24, New Hanover county. R. R. Aug. 2, 1802
Marshall, Frederick William, Feb. 11, Salem. R. R. Feb. 16, 1802
Moore, Dr., Nov., Person county. R. R. Nov. 15, 1802
Moore, Rev. John, Jr., My. 18, Wake county. R. R. My. 25, 1802
Morris, Pettigrew, Nov. 14, Bladen county. R. R. Dec. 20, 1802
Murfree, Mrs. Hardy, Mar. 19, Murfreesborough. R. R. Apr. 6, 1802
Nicholas, John, Apr. 1, New Hanover county. R. R. Apr. 13, 1802
Pearson, Samuel, My. 4, Wake county. R. R. My. 11, 1802
Peck, Dr. David, My. 25, Newbern. R. R. Je. 8, 1802
Phillips, Col. Exum, Nov., Edgecombe county. R. R. Nov. 15, 1802
Puckett, John, Jan. 21, Chapel Hill. R. R. Feb. 2, 1802
Puryear, Mr., Oct. 24, Raleigh. R. R. Oct. 25, 1802
Ransom, Mrs. James, Mar., Warren county. R. R. Mar. 9, 1802
Robinson, Edward, Sept. 28, Brunswick county. R. R. Oct. 18, 1802
Sadler, William Camp, My. 31, Wake county. R. R. Je. 1, 1802
Schaw, Alexander of Brunswick county, Je. 2, Wilmington. R. R. Je. 8, 1802
Sitgreaves, John, Mar. 4, Halifax. R. R. Mar. 16, 1802
Sitgreaves, Robert J., Sept. 20, Halifax. R. R. Oct. 4, 1802
Stewart, James, Oct. 24. Pitt county. R. R. Nov. 8, 1802
Stokes, Barry, Aug. 24. Wilmington. R. R. Aug. 30, 1802
Taffy, Mrs. George, Aug. 14, Warren county. R. R. Aug. 23, 1802
Tatom, Major Absalom, Dec. 20, Hillsborough. R. R. Dec. 20, 1802
Terry, Polly, Oct. 20, Wilmington. R. R. Nov. 1, 1802
Thomlinson, Thomas, Sept. 24, Newbern. R. R. Oct. 11, 1802
Tomlinson, Mrs., Apr. 23, Newbern. R. R. My. 11, 1802
Turner, David, My. 17, Windsor. R. R. Je. 8, 1802
Turner, Mrs. James, Feb. 26, Warren county. R. R. Mar. 9, 1802
Walker, Mr. Carlton, Oct., Wilmington. R. R. Oct. 25, 1802
Wyatt, Mrs. Elizabeth, Oct. 17, Wilmington. R. R. Nov. 1, 1802

1803

Alston, Mrs. James, Apr. 11, Warren county. R. R. Apr. 25, 1803
Bishop, Samuel, Aug., Newbern. R. R. Aug. 22, 1803
Bloodworth, Mrs. Timothy, Dec. 16, Wilmington. R. R. Dec. 26, 1803
Brehon, Mrs., Je., Warrenton. R. R. Jly. 4, 1803
Brickell, Mrs. Jonathan, Feb. 22, Raleigh. R. R. Feb. 28, 1803
Burgwin, John, My. 24, New Hanover county. R. R. Je. 6, 1803
Cammock, James, Oct. 18, Wilmington. R. R. Oct. 31, 1803
Carter, Mrs. Jeffe, Jly. 14, Caswell county. R. R. Sept. 5, 1803
Chapman, Mrs. Samuel, Apr., Newbern. R. R. Apr. 11, 1803
Daniel, Mrs. Wm., Jly. 18, Raleigh. R. R. Jly. 25, 1803
Dickenson, Dr. Samuel, Dec. 20, Edenton. R. R. Jan. 17, 1803
Dubois, Mrs. James, My., Wilmington. R. R. My. 9, 1803
Goodman, William of Lenoir county, Oct. 21, Raleigh. R. R. Oct. 24, 1803
Green, Col. Joseph, Oct., Wayne county. R. R. Oct. 24, 1803
Guion, Isaac, My. 24, Newbern. R. R. Je. 6, 1803
Handy, Matthias, Je. 13, Smithfield. R. R. Je. 20, 1803
Harp, William, Jly. 11, Wilmington. R. R. Aug. 1, 1803
Hay, Mrs. John, Nov., Fayetteville. R. R. Nov. 14, 1803

Howard, C. D., Aug., Wilmington. R. R. Aug. 29, 1803
Johnston, Matthew, My 4, Wilmington. R. R. My. 16, 1803
Koons, Colonel George, My., Ashe county. R. R. Aug. 29, 1803
Love, Kenan, Apr. 7, Wilmington. R. R. Apr. 25, 1803
M'Keethen, Dougal, Oct. 27, Raleigh. R. R. Oct. 31, 1803
Marshall, Sterling, Apr. 5, Halifax. R. R. Apr. 11, 1803
Marshall, Mrs. Sterling, Sept., Halifax. R. R. Oct. 3, 1803
Miller, David, Nov., Rutherford county. R. R. Nov. 21, 1803
Mitchell, James, Sept. 18, Raleigh. R. R. Sept. 19, 1803
Mitchell, Dr. Thomas, Feb., Lewisburg. R. R. Feb. 22, 1803
Moore, John, Jan., Wake county. R. R. Jan. 10, 1803
Norwood, John, Mar. 8, Franklin county. R. R. Mar. 28, 1803
Pitt, Thomas, Apr. 29, Bertie county. R. R. May 16, 1803
Pointer, Henry, Apr. 7, Halifax. R. R. Apr. 18, 1803
Poisson, Mrs., John, Sept. 10, Wilmington. R. R. Sept. 26, 1803
Polk, Dr. Benjamin, Mar. 21, Rockingham county. R. R. Apr. 11, 1803
Ray, Catherine, Aug. 3, Raleigh. R. R. Sept. 5, 1803
Roberts, Bryan, Jan. 10, Wilmington. R. R. Jan. 17, 1803
Rogers, Wiley, Sept. 16, Wake county. R. R. Sept. 19, 1803
Rowland, John, Oct. 11, Robeson county. R. R. Oct. 17, 1803
Smith, Mrs. John F., Aug. 10, Newbern. R. R. Sept. 5, 1803
Snead, William, Jan. 24, Wilmington. R. R. Jan. 31, 1803
Tate, Allan, Mar., Rockingham county. R. R. Apr. 11, 1803
Thompson, Daniel, Nov. 8, Wilmington. R. R. Nov. 14, 1803
Turner, Jonathan, Sept. 7, Wake county. R. R. Sept. 12, 1803
Verrell, Mrs., My., Franklin county. R. R. My. 16, 1803
White, Robert, Jan. 13, Lenoir county. R. R. Jan. 31, 1803
Williams, John Pugh, My., Wilmington. R. R. My. 9, 1803
Williams, Mrs. W. H., My. 4, Fayetteville. R. R. My. 9, 1803
Williford, Thomas, Aug. 6, Raleigh. R. R. Aug. 8, 1803

1804

Alexander, Wallace, Apr., Lincolnton. R. R. Apr. 2, 1804
Allison, Robert, Nov. 2, Cabarrus county. R. R. Nov. 26, 1804
Baxter, Nathaniel, July 12, Warren county. R. R. Jly. 23, 1804
Bettner, Mrs. Henry, Jan. 26, Newbern. R. R. Feb. 9, 1804
Bradley, Captain Gee, Feb. 17, Raleigh. R. R. Feb. 27, 1804
Bunting, William, Oct. 8, Wilmington. R. R. Oct. 15, 1804
Carr, Titus, Feb. 9, Greene county. R. R. Feb. 20, 1804
Christmas, William, Apr. 11, Warren county. R. R. Apr. 23, 1804
Clemens, Mrs., Aug., Newbern. R. R. Sept. 10, 1804
Coffield, James, Dec., Tarborough. R. R. Dec. 31, 1804
Cooke, James M., Jly., Tarborough. R. R. Aug. 6, 1804
Daves, Major John, Oct. 12, Newbern. R. R. Oct. 29, 1804
Davis, Peter, Sr., Jan. 27, Warren county. R. R. Feb. 9, 1804
Day, Joseph, Sept. 9, Newbern. R. R. Sept. 24, 1804
Dean, Joseph of Wilmington, d. Jan. 10, Jamaica. R. R. Mar. 12, 1804
Donaldson, Robert, Feb. 15, Tarborough. R. R. Feb. 27, 1804
Eastwood, Capt. James, Oct. 7, Wilmington. R. R. Oct. 22, 1804
Fitts, Henrs., Sr., My., Warren county. R. R. My. 21, 1804
Gaster, Henry of Moore county, d. Dec. 4, Newbern. R. R. Dec. 31, 1804

Gaston, Mrs. William, Apr. 20, Newbern. R. R. My. 7, 1804

Gilchrist, Mrs. Allen W., Jly. 13, Halifax. R. R. Jly. 23, 1804

Hall, James, Jly., Tarborough. R. R. Aug. 6, 1804

Harris, Charles W. of Halifax, Jan. 26, Sneedsborough. R. R. Feb. 13, 1804

Hawks, Samuel, Dec., Newbern. R. R. Dec. 31, 1804

Henry, Joel, Aug., Beaufort, Carteret county. R. R. Sept. 3, 1804

Hightower, Robert, Jr., My., Franklin county. R. R. My. 21, 1804

Hightower, Mrs. Robert of Franklin county, Sept. R. R. Oct. 1, 1804

Hogg, James, Nov. 9, Hillsborough. R. R. Nov. 19, 1804

Hooper, Wm., Jly. 15, Brunswick county. R. R. Jly. 23, 1804

Hoskins, Thomas, Aug. 11, Tyrrell county. R. R. Sept. 10, 1804

Humphries, Mr., May 16, Onslow county. R. R. Je. 4, 1804

Johnson, Col. Wm., Sept. 6, Warren county. R. R. Sept. 24, 1804

Keane, Edward, Aug. 21, Newbern. R. R. Sept. 10, 1804

Kinns., Mrs., Jan. 24, Newbern. R. R. Feb. 9, 1804

Lane, William of Pasquotank county, Je. 26, Franklin county. R. R. Jly. 9, 1804

Latteststedt, Erie of Sweden, Oct. 26, Bladen county. R. R. Nov. 5, 1804

Littleberry, Mrs. May, Dec. 26, Raleigh. R. R. Jan. 2, 1804

Long, M'Kinnie, Aug. 3, Halifax. R. R., Aug. 13, 1804

Love, Samuel, Jan. 23, Chapel Hill. R. R. Jan. 30, 1804

M'Clammy, Elijah, Je., Wilmington Sound. R. R. Je. 4, 1804

M'Clure, Gen'l William, Nov. 18, Craven county. R. R. Nov. 29, 1804

M'Ilhenny, Capt. John, Sept. 1, Wilmington. R. R. Sept. 10, 1804

Madden, Mrs. Elizabeth, Dec. 4, Orange county. R. R. Jan. 2, 1804

Mangeon, Peter of France, Nov., Brunswick county. R. R. Nov. 12, 1804

Mitchell, William, Jan. 30, Newbern. R. R. Feb. 13, 1804

Myatt, Britain, Oct. 21, Wake county. R. R. Oct. 29, 1804

O'Neill, James, Oct. 25, Wilmington. R. R. Nov. 5, 1804

Osborn, Samuel, Apr. 20, Newbern. R. R. My. 7, 1804

Park, Mrs. Betty, Mar. 10, Warrenton. R. R. Mar. 19, 1804

Pasteur, Dr. James of Raleigh, Nov., Halifax. R. R. Nov. 19, 1804

Pasteur, Mrs. James, Aug., Newbern. R. R. Aug. 13, 1804

Paxton, Mr., Jan. 23, Newbern. R. R. Feb. 9, 1804

Pearson, Mrs. Jesse, Oct., Salisbury. R. R. Oct. 22, 1804

Philips, John Hartwill of Edgecombe county, Feb. 18, Chapel Hill. R. R. Feb. 27, 1804

Pugh, Polly, Mar. 29, Franklin county. R. R. Apr. 9, 1804

Randolph, Mrs. John, Jly. 26, Warrenton. R. R. Aug. 6, 1804

Read, Col. James, Oct. 17, Brunswick county. R. R. Oct. 29, 1804

Rench, Mrs., Oct. 21, Wake county. R. R. Oct. 29, 1804

Robinson, David R. of Virginia, Oct., Orange county. R. R. Oct. 8, 1804

Satterwhite, Capt. Michael, Mar. 24, Granville county. R. R. Apr. 9, 1804

Sessums, Lemuel of Tarborough, Mar., Chapel Hill. R. R. Mar. 19, 1804

Simmons, Amos., Dec., Jones county. R. R. Dec. 31, 1804

Simpson, John of Tar River, Jan. 30, Newbern. R. R. Feb. 13, 1804

Singleton, Mrs. Spyers, Dec. 11, Newbern. R. R. Dec. 31, 1804

Speir, John, Feb. 14, Tar River. R. R. Feb. 27, 1804

Thompson, James, Je., Warren county. R. R. Je. 4, 1804

Thompson, Richard, Mar. 18, Hillsborough. R. R. Apr. 2, 1804

Torrans, Mrs. Alexander, Dec. 23, Newbern. R. R. Jan. 9, 1804
Whitted, John, Mar. 19, Hillsborough. R. R. Apr. 2, 1804
Williams, Col. John, Dec., Caswell county. R. R. Dec. 10, 1804

1805

Allen, Nathaniel, Nov. 28, Edenton. R. R. Dec. 9, 1805
Alston, James of Warren county, Mar., Virginia. R. R. Mar. 11, 1805
Andrews, Mr., Jan., Newbern. R. R. Jan. 21, 1805
Avery, Mrs. Jonathan, Nov., Wilmington. R. R. Nov. 18, 1805
Bell, Francis, Dec. 18, Newbern. R. R. Jan. 21, 1805
Bell, Jesse, Aug. 16, Warrenton. R. R. Aug. 26, 1805
Black, Mrs., Mar., Newbern. R. R. Mar. 11, 1805
Blackledge, Richard of Beaufort county, Aug. 18, Washington. R. R. Sept. 2, 1805
Bryan, Hardy, Jr., Jly., Johnston county. R. R. Jly. 8, 1805
Calhor, Mrs. John, Mar. 27, Wilmington. R. R. Apr. 8, 1805
Cotten, Willie, Nov. 26, Edgecombe county. R. R. Dec. 9, 1805
Croom, Richard, Je. 21, Wayne county. R. R. Jly. 8, 1805
Drew, Dolphin of Bertie county, Mar. 26, New York. R. R. Apr. 15, 1805
Emmet, Margaret, Oct. 29, Fayetteville. R. R. Nov. 11, 1805
Fitzgerald, Mrs. Thomas, Nov. 29, Wilmington. R. R. Dec. 9, 1805
Gardner, Wm. T., Oct., Newbern. R. R. Oct. 21, 1805
Gibbs, Nathaniel, Dec. 6, Washington, Beaufort county. R. R. Dec. 16, 1805
Gillespie, Col. James of this State, Jan. 11, Washington, D. C. R. R. Jan. 28, 1805
Gorham, Col. James, Dec. 24, Pitt county. R. R. Jan. 21, 1805
Gray, Israel, Oct., Newbern. R. R. Oct. 21, 1805
Griffin, Dr. John of Fort Johnson, Jly. 15, Wilmington. R. R. Jly. 29, 1805
Hannon, Major John, Feb., Halifax. R. R. Feb. 11, 1805
Harris, Edward, Oct. 31, Raleigh. R. R. Nov. 4, 1805
Harvey, Mrs., of Edgecombe county, Jly., Knoxville, Tenn. R. R. Jly 8, 1805
Haywood, Mrs. Stephen, Mar. 7, Raleigh. R. R. Mar. 11, 1805
Hines, Rev. Thos., Mar., Wayne county. R. R. Mar. 11, 1805
Hodge, Abraham, Aug. 3, Halifax. R. R. Aug. 12, 1805
Holt, Thomas C., Jan., Newbern. R. R. Jan. 21, 1805
Hubbell, William, Nov. 28, Windsor. R. R. Dec. 16, 1805
Hudson, Nancy, Oct. 17, Raleigh. R. R. Oct. 21, 1805
Hull, John of Virginia, Aug. 24, Moore county. R. R. Oct. 7, 1805
Jelks, Lemuel, Feb. 21, Johnston county. R. R. Mar. 4, 1805
Joselin, Amaziah, Feb. 24, Wilmington. R. R. Apr. 1, 1805
Johnson, Benjamin, Sept. 19, Warren county. R. R. Sept. 30, 1805
Johnson, Edward J. of Warrenton, Oct., Williamsburg, Va. R. R. Oct. 21, 1805
Knoz, John, Jan., Craven county. R. R. Jan. 14, 1805
Lancaster, Polly Jameson, Je. 6, Franklin county. R. R. Je. 17, 1805
Lane, James, Sr., Jan. 13, Raleigh. R. R. Jan. 14, 1805
Lane, Major Joseph, Mar. 10, Randolph county. R. R. Apr. 8, 1805
Laughter, Mrs. John, Mar., Warren county. R. R. Mar. 11, 1805
Lile, Mr. of Raleigh, Aug., Wake county. R. R. Aug. 12, 1805
Littleton, Mrs. South, Nov., Onslow county. R. R. Jan. 28, 1805
Long, Mrs. Nicholas, Dec. 21, Fayetteville. R. R. Dec. 30, 1805
M'Auslan, Duncan, Sept. 10, Fayetteville. R. R. Sept. 16, 1805

Mallett, Peter, Feb. 3, Fayetteville. R. R. Feb. 18, 1805
Maxwell, James, Oct. 8, Halifax. R. R. Oct. 21, 1805
Medlin, Wm., Feb. 27, Wake county. R. R. Mar. 4, 1805
Mentges, Col. Francis, Oct. 6, Rocky Mount. R. R. Nov. 18, 1805
Mitchell, Mrs. Gabriel, Nov. 24, Raleigh. R. R. Nov. 25, 1805
Mitchell, Jesse, Mar. 16, Raleigh. R. R. Mar. 18, 1805
Newman, Dr. Anthony, Nov., Rowan county. R. R. Nov. 11, 1805
Olive, James, Jan. 22, Wake county. K. R. Jan. 28, 1805
Pasteur, Mrs. Abner, Nov. 18, Newbern. R. R. Dec. 2, 1805
Prion, Mrs., Jan., Newbern. R. R. Jan. 21, 1805
Ray, John, Nov., Wilmington. R. R. Nov. 18, 1805
Saunders, Chas., Apr. 12, Newbern. R. R. Apr. 29, 1805
Smith, Joseph, Oct. 4, Randolph county. R. R. Oct. 21, 1805
Smith, Major General Robert, Jly. 16, Cabarrus county. R. R. Aug. 12, 1805
Smith, Col. Thomas, Sept. 12, Newbern. R R. Sept. 30, 1805
Stewart, James, Mar. 28, Newbern. R. R. Apr. 8, 1805
Stewart, John, of Martin county, Dec. 25, Wake county. R. R. Dec. 30, 1805
Tinker, Mrs. Edward, Jr., Je. 26, Newbern. R. R. Jly. 8, 1805
Took, John, Jan., Newbern. R. R. Jan. 21, 1805
Toomer, Anthony B. of New Hanover county, Apr. 21, Newbern. R. R. My. 6, 1805
Vaughn, Thomas, Oct., Warren county. R. R. Oct. 28, 1805
Watson, William of Ireland, Mar., Newbern. R. R. Mar. 25, 1805
West, John, Nov. 7, Newbern. R. R. Dec. 2, 1805
Wheaton, Daniel, Mar. 17, Wilmington. R. R. Mar. 25, 1805
White, Jacob, Feb. 27, Wake county. R. R. Mar. 4, 1805
Williams, Capt. Nathaniel, Feb., Rockingham county. R. R. Feb. 25, 1805
Williams, Samuel, My. 11, Martin county. R. R. My. 27, 1805
Williams, Solomon B., Nov., Martin county. R. R. Nov. 25, 1805
Wilson, Rev. Lewis F. of St. Christopher Island, Jan. 11, Iredell county. R. R. Feb. 11, 1805
Widdigen, John C., Aug. 31, Washington. R. R. Sept. 30, 1805

1806

Alexander, Mrs. Nathaniel, Sept. 13, Rowan county. R. R. Sept. 29, 1806 .
Alexander, William L., Mar. 15, Cabarrus county. R. R. Mar. 24, 1806
Anthony, Capt. Wm., Dec. 25, Newbern. R. R. Jan. 6, 1806
Armistead, Robert, Nov. 7, Plymouth. R. R. Nov. 24, 1806
Arnett, Silas, My. 31, Newbern. R. R. Je. 9, 1806
Bennehan, William of Wake county, Oct. 31, Orange county. R. R. Nov. 17, 1806
Bent, Capt. Thomas, Feb. 11, Edenton. R. R. Jly. 28, 1806
Bievighaus, George, Sept. 24, Salem. R. R. Oct. 13, 1806
Blackledge, Mrs. William, Apr., Newbern. R. R. Apr. 7, 1806
Boddie, William of Nash county, Apr. 2, Louisburg. R. R. Apr. 7, 1806
Bogle, Robert of Fayetteville, Jly. 7, Lumberton. R. R. Jly. 21, 1806
Branch, Col. John, Mar., Bertie county. R. R. Mar. 24, 1806
Briskell, Jonathan, Dec. 17, Raleigh. R. R. Dec. 22, 1806
Brown, Capt. Benjamin, Mar. 16, Chowan county. R. R. Mar. 31, 1806
Brown, Jane, Jly. 22, Fayetteville. R. R. Aug. 4, 1806
Buckley, Captain, Jan. 18, Newbern. R. R. Feb. 3, 1806

Buffalo, Henry, Oct., Wake county. R. R. Oct. 27, 1806
Cain, James, Oct. 1, Orange county. R. R. Oct. 20, 1806
Cain, Sarah, Dec. 10, Orange county. R. R. Dec. 22, 1806
Callender, Mrs., Thomas, Jan. 25, Wilmington. R. R. Feb. 10, 1806
Clark, Robert, Nov. 7, Randolph county. R. R. Nov. 24, 1806
Cox, Capt. Thos., Je. 15, Edenton. R. R. Je. 30, 1806
Craig, David, Oct. 11, Chapel Hill. R. R. Oct. 27, 1806
Crump, William, Dec. 27, Fayetteville. R. R. Jan. 6, 1806
Duke, Mrs. Matthew, Oct. 3, Warren county. R. R. Oct. 13, 1806
Duffy, Mrs., Nov. 11, Chatham county. R. R. Dec. 1, 1806
Edwards, Daniel C., Oct. 30, Surry county. R. R. Nov. 17, 1806
Fatheree, Mrs. Jane, Jly. 6, Newbern. R. R. Jly. 21, 1806
Fleming, Robert of Ireland, Oct. 29, Raleigh. Nov. 3, 1806
Goodwin, Mrs. Samuel, Jly. 6, Fayetteville. R. R. Jly. 21, 1806
Gray, George, Je., Windsor. R. R. Je. 2, 1806
Harris, Thomas, Je. 1, Edenton. R. R. Je. 16, 1806
Hart, Nathaniel, Jan. 20, Caswell county. R. R. Feb. 10, 1806
Hightower, Nancy, Aug. 11, Warren county. R. R. Aug. 18, 1806
Hill, Hrs. William Henry, Dec. 14, Wilmington. R. R. Dec. 29, 1806
Hinton, Willis, Aug. 6, Wake county. R. R. Aug. 11, 1806
Hudson, John, Apr., Tarborough. R. R. Apr. 14, 1806
Hunter, Mrs. John B., Je. 15, Williamston. R. R. Jly. 7, 1806
Hunter, Capt. Timothy, Aug. 29, Bertie county. R. R. Sept. 22, 1806
Jones, Mrs. Fanning, Jly. 27, Wake county. R. R. Sept. 8, 1806
Kegan, Capt. William, Jly., Robeson county. R. R. Jly. 7, 1806
Kimball, Mrs. Ransom, Aug., Warren county. R. R. Aug. 11, 1806
Lawless, Luke of Ireland, Sept. 27, Tyrrell county. R. R. Nov. 10, 1806
Lea, Wm., Sr., Sept. 4, Leasburg. R. R. Sept. 22, 1806
Loften, Mrs. Joseph, Aug. 2, Chapel Hill. R. R. Aug. 4, 1806
Lowthorpe, Francis, Oct. 27, Newbern. R. R. Nov. 10, 1806
Lundy, Mrs. John, Jan. 19, Fayetteville. R. R. Feb. 3, 1806
Mabson, Samuel, Aug. 8, Topsail Sound, Wilmington. R. R. Aug. 25, 1806
M'Clure, Gilbert, Feb., Newbern. R. R. Mar. 3, 1806
M'Cotter, Mrs. John, Jly 21, Edenton. R. R. Jly. 28, 1806
M'Eachern, Mrs. John, Nov. 5, Robeson county. R. R. Nov. 24, 1806
M'Gready, Aaron, Sept. 13, Raleigh. R. R. Sept. 15, 1806
M'Iver, Mrs. Kenneth, Aug. 12, Fayetteville. R. R. Aug. 25, 1806
M'Laurin, Hugh., Oct. 19, Fayetteville. R. R. Nov. 3, 1806
M'Linn, Miss., Sept., Salisbury. R. R. Sept. 29, 1806
M'Nair, Mrs. Edmund, Dec., Tarboro. R. R. Dec. 15, 1806
Miller, Thomas, Apr. 20, Warrenton. R. R. Apr. 28, 1806
Moore, Major Charles, Jan. 24, Perquimons county. R. R. Feb. 10, 1806
Moore, Mrs. Thomas I., Je. 13, Person county. R. R. Je. 30, 1806
Muter, Robert, Jly. 11, Wilmington. R. R. Jly. 28, 1806
Outerbridge, Joseph, Je. 2, Franklin county. R. R. Je. 9, 1806
Owen, Col. John, Nov., Bladen county. R. R. Dec. 1, 1806
Owen, Col. Thomas, Nov. 2, Bladen county. R. R. Nov. 24, 1806
Paine, Mrs. John, Aug. 23, Person county. R. R. Oct. 13, 1806
Pasteur, Major Thomas, Sept., Buncombe county. R. R. Sept. 15, 1806
Pearson, Mrs. Joseph, Sept. 11, Salisbury. R. R. Sept. 29, 1806
Pegues, William, Oct. 23, Pittsborough. R. R. Nov. 10, 1806

Reichell, Mrs., Aug., Salem. R. R. Aug. 25, 1806
Rew, Thomas, Sept., Newbern. R. R. Sept. 22, 1806
Roberts, Mrs. George, Jly. 29, Wake county. R. R. Aug. 11, 1806
Robinson, Mrs. Benj., Oct. 30, Fayetteville. R. R. Nov. 10, 1806
Sanders, Hardy, Feb. 9, Wake county. R. R. Feb. 17, 1806
Schenck, John G. L. of Tarborough, Oct. 6, Philadelphia. R. R. Oct. 27, 1806
Scott, Mrs. Thos., Jan. 12, Chatham county. R. R. Feb. 3, 1806
Smith, Benjamin, Sept. 5, Wake county. R. R. Sept. 8, 1806
Sneed, Capt. Samuel, Aug. 10, Person county. R. R. Aug. 25, 1806
Somervel, John, Nov. 18, Granville county. R. R. Nov. 24, 1806
Speed, Col. John, Feb. 18, Richmond county. R. R. Mar. 3, 1806
Stanback, Fanny, Mar., Warrenton. R. R. Mar. 10, 1806
Stewart, Archibald, Aug. 24, Fayetteville. R. R. Sept. 8, 1806
Story, Charles, Nov. 27, Raleigh. R. R. Dec. 1, 1806
Thorpe, Launcelot, Jly. 16, Warrenton. R. R. Jly. 28, 1806
Torrans, Mrs. A., Sept., Newbern. R. R. Sept. 22, 1806
Trippe, Mrs., Jan. 18, Newbern. R. R. Feb. 3, 1806
Troy, Mrs. Rachel, Nov., Anson county. R. R. Nov. 3, 1806
Valette, Francis of the Island of Malta, Dec. 7, Edenton. R. R. Dec. 22, 1806
Walker, Mrs. John of Plymouth, Sept. 17, Washington county. R. R. Oct. 6,
    1806
Webber, Francis, Feb., Newbern. R. R. Mar. 3, 1806
Williamson, Capt. James, Oct. 20, Caswell county. R. R. Nov. 17, 1806
Willip, John, Feb., Orange county. R. R. Feb. 17, 1806
Willis, John, Jr., Feb., Orange county. R. R. Feb. 17, 1806
Worke, Col. Alexander, Jan. 24, Iredell county. R. R. Feb. 10, 1806
Young John of Granville county, Sept. 21, Hillsborough. R. R. Sept. 29, 1806

1807

Alston, Samuel, Nov., Warren county. R. R. Nov. 5, 1807
Alston, Solomon, Aug. 5, Warren county. R. R. Aug. 6, 1807
Barron, Mrs., Jan., Newbern. R. R. Jan. 5, 1807
Bartee, Thomas, Mar. 9, Edenton. R. R. Mar. 30, 1807
Beck, Mrs. John, Dec. 19, Nashville. R. R. Feb. 2, 1807
Benbury, Gen. Rch'd., Feb., Chowan county. R. R. Mar. 9, 1807
Bennett, Mrs. Wm., Oct., Chowan county. R. R. Oct. 15, 1807
Bird, Jonathan of Warrenton, Sept. 26, Sullivan's Island. R. R. Oct. 1, 1807
Blount, Mrs. Joseph, Oct. 22, Washington. R. R. Nov. 5, 1807
Blount, Gen. R., Oct. 13, Washington. R. R. Oct. 29, 1807
Bradley, James of Halifax county, Va., Feb. 3, Bladen county. R. R. Mar. 2,
    1807
Brown, William, Je. 13, Caswell county. R. R. Jly. 2, 1807
Bryan, John C., Feb. 15, Newbern. R. R. Mar. 30, 1807
Buchanan, Hector R., Feb. 20, Cumberland county. R. R. Mar. 2, 1807
Burgess, Lovatt, Oct. 10, Halifax county. R. R. Oct. 22, 1807
Butler, John of this State, Sept. 3, Philadelphia, Pa. R. R. Oct. 1, 1807
Butler, Samuel, Aug., Edenton. R. R. Aug. 6, 1807
Caldwell, Mrs. Joseph, Jan. 17, Chapel Hill. R. R. Feb. 2, 1807
Caudle, Joseph R. of England, Apr. 25, Wilmington. R. R. Je. 4, 1807
Chapman, Samuel, Mar., Newbern. R. R. Mar. 30, 1807
Cobb, Jesse of Lenoir county, Sept. 3, Kinston. R. R. Sept. 10, 1807

Cole, Major John, Mar. 23, Cumberland county. R. R. Apr. 13, 1807
Cook, Mrs. Silas, Oct. 5, Newbern. R. R. Oct. 15, 1807
Cooke, Mrs. John, Sept. 30, Newbern. R. R. Oct. 8, 1807
Council, Mrs. John, Jan., Robeson county. R. R. Jan. 12, 1807
Craven, John, Sept. 2, Raleigh. R. R. Sept. 8, 1807
Croom, Mrs. Wm., Oct. 7, Lenoir county. R. R. Nov. 26, 1807
Daugherty, Rev. George, Mar. 23, Wilmington. R. R. Apr. 13, 1807
Davis, Thomas of Warrenton, Oct., Petersburg. R. R. Oct. 29, 1807
Dick, James, Jr., Dec. 21, Fayetteville. R. R. Dec. 31, 1807
Fish, Wiley of Lenoir county, Apr. 13, Raleigh. R. R. Apr. 16, 1807
Fleming, Andrew of Ireland and Halifax this State, Aug. 2, Petersburg. R. R.
      Aug. 6, 1807
Fonville, Lewis, Oct. 16, Craven county. R. R. Oct. 29, 1807
Fox, Jacob, Mar. 27, Franklin county. R. R. Apr. 6, 1807
Giles, Henry, Jan. 27, Salisbury. R. R. Feb. 9, 1807
Gillespie, Mrs., Feb., Warrenton. R. R. Feb. 23, 1807
Gilmour, John M. of Halifax, Jly. 19, Warrenton. R. R. Jly. 23, 1807
Goodloe, Mrs. J. M., Jly., Nashville. R. R. Jly. 30, 1807
Green, Wm., Dec. 17, Wake county. R. R. Dec. 31, 1807
Greene, Lewis of Raleigh, Oct. 18, Nashville. R. R. Jan. 19, 1807
Hatch, Ivy, Nov., Craven county. R. R. Nov. 26, 1807
Hawkins, Mrs. Joseph, Sept., Warren county. R. R. Sept. 10, 1807
Hawkins, Mrs. P., Sept. 29, Warrenton. R. R. Oct. 8, 1807
Heath, Spyres, Oct. 13, Newbern. R. R. Oct. 29, 1807
Heron, Samuel, Apr., Rockingham county. R. R. My. 7, 1807
Hunt, John, Oct. 9, Franklin county. R. R. Oct. 15, 1807
Hyman, Thomas, Nov., Craven county. R. R. Nov. 26, 1807
Jackson, John, Mar. 9, Raleigh. (A free man of colour). R. R. Mar. 16, 1807
Jarvis, Abigail of Connecticut, Aug. 4, Newbern. R. R. Aug. 6, 1807
Johnston, Samuel of Bertie, Sept. 22, Warren county. R. R. Oct. 1, 1807
Jones, General Allen, Nov. 14, Northampton county. R. R. Nov. 26, 1807
Jones, Solomon, Oct., Bertie county. R. R. Oct. 15, 1807
Jones, Tignal, Aug. 30, Wake county. R. R. Sept. 2, 1807
Jones, Tignal, Jr., My., Wake county. R. R. My. 28, 1807
Lacey, Mrs. William, Mar. 1st, Rockingham county. R. R. Apr. 13, 1807
Lane, James, Oct. 10, Raleigh. R. R. Oct. 15, 1807
Lees, James, Mar., Mecklenburg county. R. R. Mar. 23, 1807
M'Nair, Duncan, Dec., Fayetteville. R. R. Dec. 17, 1807
McPherson, Mrs. Catherine, Feb. 17, Cumberland county. R. R. Mar, 2, 1807
Machen, Mrs. Thomas W., My. 2, Newbern. R. R. My. 14, 1807
Macon, Nathaniel, Jr. of Warren county, Feb., Greene county, Ga. R. R.
      Mar. 9, 1807
Martin, Alexander, Nov. 2, Rockingham county. R. R. Nov. 19, 1807
Martin, Mrs., Nov. 6, Rockingham county. R. R. Nov. 19, 1807
Mason, Mrs. Daniel, Dec. 25, Halifax county. R. R. Jan. 5, 1807
Mastin, Mrs. Jeremiah, Oct. 19, Newbern. R. R. Oct. 29, 1807
Maurice, Francis, Sept. 17, Edenton. R. R. Oct. 1, 1807
Millen, Alexander, My., Edenton. R. R. My. 28, 1807
Mitchell, Mrs. C. M., Dec. 19, Wadesboro. R. R. Jan. 5, 1807
Moore, Mrs. Elizabeth, Nov. 19, Fayetteville. R. R. Dec. 3, 1807
Mumford, Mrs. Robinson, Sept. 16, Fayetteville. R. R. Sept. 24, 1807

Murdock, Andrew, Sept. 30, Orange county. R. R. Oct. 8, 1807
Murtaugh, Mrs. Margaret, My. 12, Wilmington. R. R. My. 28, 1807
Noyes, Orra, Sept. 18, Lumberton. R. R. Oct. 8, 1807
Oliver, Mrs. Abraham, Apr. 5, Rockingham county. R. R. Apr. 13, 1807
O'Farrill, Mrs., Sept. 25, Hillsborough. R. R. Oct. 8, 1807
Parke, Capt. Solomon, Apr. 10, Randolph county. R. R. My. 7, 1807
Person, Benjamin, Nov , Granville county. R. R. Nov. 26, 1807
Pettigrew, Rev. Charles, Apr. 8, Washington county. R. R. Apr. 30, 1807
Pope, Henry, Sept. 29, Robeson county. R. R. Oct. 8, 1807
Powell, Mrs. J. D., My. 25, Halifax county. R. R. Je. 4, 1807
Ramsey, Mrs. W. H., My., Bladen county. R. R. Je. 4, 1807
Reed, Edward, Oct., Bertie county. R. R. Oct. 15, 1807
Reily, Mrs. E., Feb. 22, Edenton. R. R. Mar. 9, 1807
Roberts, William, Oct., Chowan county. R. R. Oct. 15, 1807
Roulhac, P. G. of France, Oct. 12, Plymouth. R. R. Oct. 29, 1807
Rowland, Needham, Sept. 24, Lumberton. R. R. Oct. 8, 1807
Ruggles, Nathaniel W. of Boston, d. Sept. 5, Wilmington. R. R. Sept. 17, 1807
Russell, John, Feb. 13, Fayetteville. R. R. Feb. 23, 1807
Sambourne, Thomas of this city, Dec. 4, Raleigh. R. R. Dec. 10, 1807
Sasser, James, Nov. 24, Wayne county. R. R. Dec. 3, 1807
Sheppard, Jacob, Nov. 13, Surry county. R. R. Dec. 3, 1807
Simons, Joshua, Dec., Hertford county. R. R. Dec. 17, 1807
Smith, Mrs. Thomas, May, Bladen county. R. R. Je. 4, 1807
Taylor, Mrs., Oct., Wilmington. R. R. Oct. 1, 1807
Troy, Robert, Apr. 25, Wadesboro. R. R. May 7, 1807
Turner, T., Apr., Newbern. R. R. Apr. 23, 1807
Walker, James M., Sept. 15, Fayetteville. R. R. Sept. 24, 1807
Walton, William of Johnston county, Oct. 5, Raleigh. R. R. Oct. 8, 1807
Whitaker, Mrs. Eli. B., Dec. 26, Warren county. R. R. Dec. 31, 1807
Whitaker, Mrs. John, Jr., Oct. 10, Wake county. R. R. Oct. 15, 1807
Williams, Charles, Oct. 15, Craven county. R. R. Oct. 29, 1807
Wingate, Cornelius, Feb. 19, Fayetteville. R. R. Mar. 2, 1807
Wright, Mrs. Grove of Pitt county, Je. 10, New York. R. R. Je. 25, 1807
Vanhook, Mrs. Jacob, Jan. 6, Person county. R. R. Feb. 9, 1807
Vapon, Thomas, Jan. 8, Newbern. R. R. Jan. 19, 1807

1808

Alexander, Mrs. Adams, Apr. 25, Raleigh. R. R. Apr. 28, 1808
Alexander, Nathaniel, Mar. 8, Salisbury. R. R. Mar. 24, 1808
Alexander, Mrs. W. I., May, Mecklenburg county. R. R. My. 19, 1808
Carson, James, Oct. 9, Wilmington. R. R. Oct. 20, 1808
Carter, Mrs. Jesse, Apr., Caswell county. R. R. Apr. 28, 1808
Bryan, Hardy, Nov. 13, Newbern. R. R. Dec. 8, 1808
Brown, Major J., Nov. 1st, Hertford county. R. R. Nov. 10, 1808
Burklow, Isaac, Feb. 25, Fayetteville. R. R. Mar. 3, 1808
Caldwell, Col. David, Je., Iredell county. R. R. Je. 2, 1808
Cabarrus, Stephen, Aug. 4, Edenton. R. R. Aug. 11, 1808
Chapman, Henry, Oct. 13, Warrenton. R. R. Oct. 20, 1808
Clark, John, Nov. 14, Newbern. R. R. Dec. 8, 1808
Davis, Goodorum, Oct. 3, Halifax. R. R. Oct. 6, 1808
Donaldson, Robert, Oct., Fayetteville. R. R. Oct. 6, 1808

Donaldson, Robert of Fayetteville, Va., Jly. R. R. Jly. 7, 1808
Dowden, William, Sept. 18, Newbern. R. R. Sept. 29, 1808
Dulgairne, Alexander of Scotland, Oct. 6, Wilmington. R. R. Oct. 20, 1808
Ellison, Alderson, Mar. 27, Beaufort county. R. R. Apr. 7, 1808
Faire, James, My. 10, Charlotte. R. R. Jly. 7, 1808
Faribault, J. of Edenton, Oct. 24, Elizabeth city. R. R. Nov. 3, 1808
Farrar, Capt. John, Feb., Wake county. R. R. Feb. 11, 1808
Flinn, Mrs. Andrew of Camden, S. C., Aug. 29, Raleigh. R. R. Sept. 1, 1808
Gardner, Geo., Feb. 25, Newbern. R. R. Mar. 9, 1808
Geroch, Mrs. Samuel, Aug. 20, Newbern . R. R. Sept. 2, 1808
Gilbert, Rev. Nathan, Aug. 1, Nash county. R. R. Sept. 1, 1808
Guion, Thomas, Jr., Sept., Tarborough. R. R. Sept. 8, 1808
Hall, Mrs. Ferrably of Northampton county, Oct. 24, Raleigh. R. R. Oct. 27, 1808
Hall, William H., Holton, Dec. 9. R. R. Dec. 29, 1808
Hawley, Isaac, Jan. 19, Fayetteville. R. R. Jan. 28, 1808
Hays, Joseph, May 1, Fayetteville. R. R. May 12, 1808
Haywood, Robert, Jly., Franklin. R. R. Jly. 7, 1808
High, Mrs. R. H., Feb. 9, Wake county. R. R. Feb. 25, 1808
Hill, Henry, Jan., Franklin county. R. R. Jan. 21, 1808
Hill, Joseph John, Aug. 13, Halifax county. R. R. Aug. 18, 1808
Hill, Nathaniel, Oct. 9, Wilmington. R. R. Oct. 20, 1808
Hyman, Mrs. Thos., My. 11, Newbern. R. R. May 19, 1808
Jones, John, Sept. 12, Raleigh. R. R. Sept. 15, 1808
Keats, William, Oct. 20, Washington, Beaufort county. R. R. Nov. 10, 1808
Kenan, Mrs. Felix, Jan. 9, Duplin county. R. R. Jan. 28, 1808
Kennedy, Willie of Beaufort county, Sept., Orange county. R. R. Sept. 29, 1808
Kinchen, Henry, My., Franklin county. R. R. May 26, 1808
King, Wm. of Washington county, Nov., Abingdon, Va. R. R. Nov. 17, 1808
Lockhart, William, May 3, Hillsborough. R. R. May 19, 1808
Lowreie, Mrs. Samuel of Mecklenburg county, Aug. 12. R. R. Oct. 13, 1808
Macay, Spruce, Mar., Salisbury. R. R. Mar. 10, 1808
Macon, Mrs. John of Warren county, Feb., Nashville. R. R. Feb. 18, 1808
M'Kay, Mrs. Archibald, Oct., Cumberland county. R. R. Oct. 6, 1808
M'Neill, Daniel of Robeson county; Sept. 11, Sumter District, S. C. R. R. Oct. 6, 1808
M'Queen, Donald, Sept. 24, Fayetteville. R. R. Sept. 29, 1808
Marsh, Mrs. Daniel G. of Washington, Beaufort county, Sept. 25, Nash county. R. R. Oct. 13, 1808
Martin, Henry Lyne of Warrenton, Sept., Washington county, Ga. R. R. Sept. 22, 1808
Middleton, Joseph, Oct. 8, Nixonton. R. R. Nov. 3, 1808
Miles, Mrs. Jane, Sept. 12, Edenton. R. R. Sept. 22, 1808
Montgomery, Robert, Oct. 31, Hertford county. R. R. Nov. 10, 1808
Mundy of Fayetteville, Apr. 8, Raleigh. R. R. May 12, 1808
Outlaw, Maj. Lewis, Aug. 29, Bertie county. R. R. Sept. 22, 1808

Paine, Col. James, Feb., Warren county. Feb. 18, 1808
Peck, Mrs. William, Je. 4, Raleigh. R. R. Je. 9, 1808
Pugh, William, Dec. 6, Bertie county. R. R. Dec. 29, 1808
Ray, Daniel, Nov. 22, Robeson county. R. R. Dec. 8, 1808
Ray, John, Sr. of Scotland, Feb. 20, Fayetteville. R. R. Mar. 3, 1808
Redmond, Capt. Patrick of Philadelphia, Sept. 5, Tarborough. R. R.
    Sept. 15, 1808
Rhodes, John, Jr., Jan. 4, Wake county. R. R. Jan. 14, 1808
Rombough, Wm., Jly. 6, Edenton. R. R. Jly. 21, 1808
Russel, James, Oct. 2, Pasquotank county. R. R. Oct. 20, 1808
Ryan, Capt. Cornelious, Jly., Bertie county. R. R. Jly. 14, 1808
Sawyer, Capt. Willis, Apr., Bertie county. R. R. Apr. 7, 1808
Scott, Mrs. Andrew, Apr. 23, Wilmington. R. R. My. 5, 1808
Simpson, Jane, Sept. 10, Washington. R. R. Sept. 22, 1808
Smith, Turner, Jan. 7, Wake county. R. R. Jan. 14, 1808
Southall, Mrs. Daniel, Je. 28, Gates court house. R. R. Jly. 14, 1808
Steel, Thomas, Sept. 17, Newbern. R. R. Sept. 29, 1808
Stevenson, Mrs. Charity, Jan., Wake county. R. R. Jan. 21, 1808
Stevenson, David, Feb. 25, Wake county. R. R. Mar. 3, 1808
Streeter, John, Mar. 16, Wake county. R. R. Mar. 24, 1808
Tanner, Mrs. Joseph, Apr. 10, Warrenton. R. R. Apr. 21, 1808
Thomas, Dr. of Northampton county, Jly. 4, Ten. R. R. Aug. 4, 1808
Trippe, Mrs. Wm., Sept. 20, Newbern. R. R. Sept. 29, 1808
Wade, Jos., Feb. 15, Newbern. R. R. Feb. 25, 1808
Walker, James, Sr., Jan. 19, Wilmington. R. R. Jan. 28, 1808
Watson, William, My. 12, Edenton. R. R. My. 26, 1808
Weatherherd, John of Ireland, Oct. 11, Wilmington. R. R. Oct. 20, 1808
White, Joseph, Feb., Anson county. R. R. Feb. 11, 1808
Wilcox, Mrs. John, Sept. 2, Chatham county. R. R. Sept. 15, 1808
Williams, Joseph John, Sept., Halifax county. R. R. Sept. 29, 1808
Wilson, Hugh, My., Salisbury. R .R. My. 5, 1808
Woods, Benjamin, Apr. 15, Enton. R. R. Apr. 28, 1808
Wright, Mrs. Isaac, Jan. 1, Bladen county. R. R. Jan. 28, 1808

1809

Alexander, Evan, Oct. 28, Salisbury. R. R. Nov. 23, 1809
Alexander, Mrs. George, Jly. 19, Mecklenburg county. R. R. Aug. 24, 1809
Alexander, Dr. Joseph of Pennsylvania, Jly. 29, York District, S. C. R. R.
    Aug. 24, 1809
Alston, Medicus, Oct., Warren county. R. R. Oct. 5, 1809
Anderson, Joseph, Jr., Aug. 26, Moore county. R. R. Sept. 7, 1809
Andrews, Joseph, Oct., Bertie county. R. R. Oct. 19, 1809
Baker, James of England, Mar. 10, Fayetteville. R. R. Mar. 16, 1809
Barge, Lewis, Sr., Feb. 1, Fayetteville. R. R. Feb. 23, 1809
Beck, Mrs. John, Feb. 24, Duplin county. R. R. Mar. 16, 1809
Bell, Mrs. Reuben, Jly. 11, Newbern. R. R. Jly. 20, 1809
Benjamin, Mrs. Philip of Wilmington, Sept., Masonborough sound. R. R.
    Sept. 21. 1809
Bettner, Henry, Jly. 5, Newbern. R. R. Jly. 13, 1809
Biggs, John, Jr., Dec. 5, Craven county. R. R. Dec. 21, 1809
Blackledge. Mrs. William, Dec. 18, Newbern. R. R. Feb. 2, 1809
Boddie, Bennet, Feb. 21. Wake county. R. R. Feb. 23, 1809

Brownlow, James of Wilmington, Je. 23. R. R. Aug. 3, 1809
Bryant, Cyrus, Je. 28, Wilmington. R. R. Jly. 13, 1809
Bulloch, Mrs. Richard, Jan. 4, Granville county. R. R. Jan. 12, 1809
Butler, Isaac, My. 20, Granville county. R. R. Je. 29, 1809
Buxton, Mrs., Nov., Newbern. R. R. Nov. 16, 1809
Chambers, Maxwell, Jly. 9, Rowan county. R. R. Aug. 3, 1809
Cherry, William, Sept. 8, Bertie county. R. R. Sept. 28, 1809
Cocke, Mrs. Joseph, Je. 18, Warren county. R. R. Je. 22, 1809
Coffield, Mrs. Benjamin of Chowan county, Oct. 18, Edenton. R. R. Oct.
    26, 1809
Cole, Mary Ann, Sept. 21, Newbern. R. R. Sept. 28, 1809
Cox, Philemon, Oct. 31, Halifax. R. R. Nev. 9, 1809
Curtis, Thos., Jan. 22, Newbern. R. R. Feb. 9, 1809
Dickinson, Matthew, Sept. 17, Franklin county. R. R. Sept. 21, 1809
Doty, Mrs. Lemuel, Oct. 11, Onslow county. R. R. Oct. 26, 1809
Dwyer, Patrick of England, May, Halifax county. R. R. My. 11, 1809
Eaton, Gen'l. Thomas, Jly., Warren county. R. R. Jly. 6, 1809
Ferby, Mrs. Joseph, May, Currituck county. R. R. Je. 1, 1809
Freear, Col. Richard W., Nov. 23, Northampton county. R. R. Dec. 7, 1809
Gatlin, Slade, Je. 24, Kinston. R. R. Jly. 13, 1809
Green, Joseph, Mar. 25, Warrenton. R. R. Mar. 30, 1809
Harrington, Henry W., Mar. 31, Richmond county. R. R. Apr. 13, 1809
Harwell, Mark W., Jly. 22, Halifax. R. R. Jly. 27, 1809
Hattridge, William of Wilmington, Sept. 11, Fayetteville. R. R. Sept.
    28, 1809
Hay, John, Je. 20, Fayetteville. R. R. Je. 29, 1809
High, Mrs. Abigail, Dec. 17, Wake county. R. R. Dec. 28, 1809
Hill, Mrs. Bennett of Franklin county, Je. 27, Raleigh. R. R. Je. 29, 1809
Hiwill, John W., Oct. 5, Wilmington. R. R. Oct. 19, 1809
Holland, William, Dec. 4, Raleigh. R. R. Dec. 7, 1809
Hoskins, Dr. Hardy of Edenton, Oct. 26, Columbia, Tyrrell county. R. R.
    Nov. 16, 1809
Jarrot, Wm., Jan. 24, Cumberland county. R. R. Feb. 9, 1809
Jennings, Thos. of England, Oct. 7, Wilmington. R. R. Oct. 19, 1809
Johnson, Mrs. Sugan, Sept. 22, Warren county. R. R. Sept. 28, 1809
Johnston, Dr. Wm. Eaton, Mar. 25, Warren county. R. R. My. 4, 1809
Keddie, Wm., Oct. 10, Wilmington. R. R. Oct. 19, 1809
Kenan, Sarah, Oct. 24, Wilmington. R. R. Nov. 2, 1809
Kinchen, Mrs. Alexander, Jan. 6, Chatham county. R. R. Jan. 19, 1809
Lee, Small, Je. 8, Raleigh. R. R. Je. 15, 1809
Lockwood, J., Sept. 10, Nixton. R. R. Sept. 28, 1809
Long, Maj. Lunsford, Je. 1, Halifax county. R. R. Je. 8, 1809
M'Cullock, Samuel of Halifax, Jan., Tenn. R. R. Feb. 9, 1809
M'Iver, Catharine, Sept. 27, Fayetteville. R. R. Oct. 12, 1809
M'Kellar, John of Wilmington, Je. 23, Havannah. R. R. Aug. 3, 1809
M'Lean, Mrs. Hugh, Sept. 13, Fayetteville. R. R. Sept. 28, 1809
M'Lochlan, Hugh of Fayetteville, Dec. 26, Hamptonville. R. R. Jan. 12,
    1809
M'Master, Thos. of Scotland, Sept. 11, Halifax. R. R. Sept. 28, 1809
Macon, Gideon Hunt, Mar. 27, Warren county. R. R. Mar. 30, 1809
Marshall, Charles, Sept. 23, Warren county. R. R. Nov. 2, 1809

Massenburg, Dr. Cargill, Nov., Wake county. R. R. Nov. 23, 1809
Morgan, Capt. Peter, Nov., Halifax county. R. R. Nov. 16, 1809
Moss, James, Jly. 21, Warren county. R. R. Jly. 27, 1809
Murfree, Col. Hardy of Murfreesborough this State, Apr. 6, Tenn. R. R.
    My. 18, 1809
Narsworthy, George, Jly. 23, Warrenton. R. R. Jly. 27, 1809
Neale, Mrs. Elizabeth, Nov. 28, Craven county. R. R. Dec. 21, 1809
Newby, Keziah, Nov. 27, Fayetteville. R. R. Dec. 7, 1809
Nicholson, James M., May, Nash county. R. R. May 4, 1809
Nickell, Mrs. Hugh, Nov. 4, Newbern. R. R. Nov. 16, 1809
Parker, Samuel of Granville county, Jan. 1, Raleigh. R. R. Jan. 5, 1809
Pasteur, John S., Nov. 15, Newbern. R. R. Nov. 23, 1809
Patridge, Thomas, Nov. 22, Newbern. R. R. Nov. 30, 1809
Patton, Alexander, Nov., Wilmington. R. R. Nov. 16, 1809
Patton, Joseph of Boston, Nov. 9, Wilmington. R. R. Nov. 23, 1809
Pelham, Charles, Nov. 12, Wilmington. R. R. Dec. 7, 1809
Poole, Capt. Lewis, May 25, Wake county. R. R. Je. 1, 1809
Quince, Col. Richard, Oct. 13, Wilmington . R. R. Oct. 26, 1809
Rhea, Mrs. Andrew, Mar., Chapel Hill. R. R. Mar. 9, 1809
Ritchie, James of Scotland, Dec. 28, Wilmington. R. R. Jan. 5, 1809
Slade, William of this State, Sept. 10, Charleston. R. R. Sept. 28, 1809
Smartt, George W., My. 16, Mecklenburg county. R. R. Je. 15, 1809
Smith, Col. Samuel, Mar. 8, Johnston county. R. R. Mar. 16, 1809
Spaight, William Watson, Apr. 1, Raleigh. R. R. Apr. 6, 1809
Stanly, Cornelia, Nov., Newbern. R. R. Nov. 30, 1809
Stephenson, Mrs. Silas of Craven county, May 23. R. R. Je. 1, 1809
Tignor, William, Dec. 5, Newbern. R. R. Dec. 21, 1809
Toole, Maria, Jly. 20, Tarborough. R. R. Jly. 27, 1809
Turner, Mrs. Simon, Dec., Wake county. R. R. Dec. 21, 1809
Turner, William of Bertie county, Sept., Wake county. R. R. Sept. 14,
    1809
Watson, Robert of this State, Mississippi, Dec. R. R. Dec. 21, 1809
Watters, Henry, Nov., Wilmington. R. R. Nov. 23, 1809
Watters, Henry, Sr., Oct., Wilmington. R. R. Oct. 19, 1809
West, Capt. Richard, My. 18, Craven county. R. R. May 25, 1809
White, Samuel of this State, Oct. 4, Wilmington, Del. R. R. Nov. 16, 1809
Whitman, Joseph of New England, Nov. 8, Wilmington. R. R. Nov. 23,
    1809
Williams, O., Oct., Onslow county. R. R. Oct. 19, 1809
Williams, Rouina, Sept. 21, Franklin county. R. R. Sept. 28, 1809
Wortham, Polly, Sept. 22, Warren county. R. R. Sept. 28, 1809
Wortham, Wm., Dec. 23, Warren county. R. R. Feb. 9, 1809

1810

Avery, Jonathan of Massachusetts, Nov. 12, Wilmington. R. R. Dec. 6,
    1810
Beasley, Mrs. J., Jan. 7, Edenton. R. R. Jan. 25, 1810
Benton, Gen'l. Samuel, Oct. 11, Orange county. R. R. Oct. 18, 1810
Bissett, Duncan, Aug. 17, Halifax. R. R. Aug. 30, 1810
Blount, Robert of Halifax county, Dec. 5, Petersburg. R. R. Dec. 13, 1810
Blount, Sharpe, Dec., Hertford county. R. R. Jan. 4, 1810
Boyce, William H., Oct. 31. Hertford county. R. R. Nov. 15, 1810

Brickell, Mrs. Benj., Oct. 14, Franklin county. R. R. Oct. 18, 1810
Brim, Mrs. Jacob, Jly., Lincoln county. R. R. Jly. 19, 1810
Broadfoot, Andrew of Scotland, Mar. 29, Fayetteville. Apr. 5, 1810
Brown, Arthur, Apr. 9, Bertie county. R. R. Apr. 25, 1810
Bustin, Benj., Dec. 16, Northampton county. R. R. Jan. 4, 1810
Burkloe, Mrs. Isaac, Dec. 20, Fayetteville. R. R. Feb. 1, 1810
Bunting, Mrs. David, Oct. 5, Sampson county. R. R. Oct. 25, 1810
Camock, Robert, Oct. 17, Wilmington. R. R. Nov. 1, 1810
Campbell, Thomas, Feb. 25, Raleigh. R. R. Mar. 1, 1810
Carney, Mrs. S. W., Feb. 8, Halifax county. R. R. Feb. 15, 1810
Carpenter, Peter, Dec., Wilmington. R. R. Dec. 6, 1810
Cheek, Cylas, My. 19, Mecklenburg county. R. R. My. 31, 1810
Christmas, Mrs. John, Apr. 14, Orange county. R. R. My. 3, 1810
Christmas, Capt. Thomas, Sept. 1, Warren county. R. R. Sept. 6, 1810
Clark, Michael, Oct. 3, Newbern. R. R. Oct. 18, 1810
Clitherall, Mrs. Eliza, Oct. 4, New Hanover county. R. R. Nov. 8, 1810
Collins, Wm., Dec. 30, Wilmington. R. R. Jan. 18, 1810
Connelly, Bernard, Dec. 23, Halifax. R. R. Feb. 8, 1810
Conway, Elijah, Sept. 20, Newbern. R. R. Oct. 4, 1810
Cook, Capt. Isaac, Apr. 3, Charlotte. R. R. Apr. 25, 1810
Cotten, Mrs. John of Tarborough, Jan. 19. R. R. Feb. 15, 1810
Cowan, John, Sept. 27, Bladen county. R. R. Oct. 18, 1810
Davidson, Sarah L., Dec. 8, Iredell county. R. R. Jan. 4, 1810
Dewey, Geo. L., Sept. 21, Newbern. R. R. Oct. 4, 1810
Drew, Mrs. John, Sr., Jly. 19, Bertie county. R. R. Aug. 2, 1810
Duffy, William, Sept., Chatham county. R. R. Sept. 6, 1810⁻
Edward, Major Gideon, Sept., Surry county. R. R. Oct. 4, 1810
Freear, William, Mar., Northampton county. R. R. Mar. 8, 1810
Gales, Thomas of Eckington, England, Dec. R. R. Jan. 11, 1810
Garnier, Mrs. John, Aug. 29, New Hanover county. R. R. Sept. 13, 1810
George, Marcus of Warrenton, Oct. 7, Petersburg, Va. R. R. Oct. 18, 1810
Gilmore, Mrs. Stephen, Sr., Jan. 17, Cumberland county. R. R. Feb. 1,
    1810
Gilmour, Mrs. Wm., Aug. 4, Halifax. R. R. Aug. 9, 1810
Hall, Mrs. Almond, Sept. 6, New Hanover county. R. R. Sept. 27, 1810
Halling, Mrs. Solomon of Wilmington, Georgetown, S. C., Feb. 27. R. R.
    Mar. 15, 1810
Hardy, Humphrey, Jan. 4, Bertie county. R. R. Jan. 25, 1810
Hare, Mrs. Thomas Edward, Oct. 20, Bertie county. R. R. Nov. 1, 1810
Hargett, Gen. Frederick, Feb., Craven county. R. R. Feb. 8, 1810
Hatch, Mrs. Anthony, Sept. 25, Jones county. R. R. Oct. 18, 1810
Hatch, Anthony, Oct. 1, Jones county. R. R. Oct. 18, 1810
High, John T., Aug. 13, Wake county. R. R. Aug. 16, 1810
Hill, Nancy, Jly. 1, Wilmington. R. R. Jly. 12, 1810
Hinton, Major John, Dec., Wake county. R. R. Dec. 20, 1810
Hinton, Theophilus, Jly., Wake county. R. R. Jly. 5, 1810
Holton, Nathaniel of Cumberland county, Jan. 26. R. R. Feb. 15, 1810
Hooker, Dr., Dec. 29, Tarborough. R. R. Jan. 4, 1810
Hooper, Mrs. George, Dec. 8, Wilmington. R. R. Dec. 27, 1810
Howard, Mrs. Elizabeth, Dec. 28, Newbern. R. R. Feb. 8, 1810
Hughes, James, Dec. 28, Wilmington. R. R. Jan. 18, 1810

Hunter, Harry, Jly. 24, Wake county. R. R. Jly. 26, 1810
Hunter, Jacob, Oct. 30, Gates Court-House. R. R. Nov. 15, 1810
Hunter, John B. of Williamston, Jly. 30, Edenton. R. R. Aug. 9, 1810
Hunter, Osborne, My. 15, Johnston county. R. R. May 24, 1810
Jacocks, Col. Jonathan, Dec., Bertie county. R. R. Dec. 13, 1810
Jacocks, Jonathan, Dec. 2, Bertie county. R. R. Dec. 20, 1810
Jocelyn, Samuel R., Mar., Wilmington. R. R. Mar. 29, 1810
Johnson, Benjamin, Je. 9, Halifax. R. R. Je. 14, 1810
Johnston, Christopher N., Sept. 26, Newbern. R. R. Oct. 4, 1810
Johnston, Hugh, Apr. 22, Warren county. R. R. My. 3, 1810
Jones, Maj. David, Mar., New Hanover county. R. R. Mar. 22, 1810
Jones, Evan of Wilmington, My. 21, Fayetteville. R. R. My. 31, 1810
Jones, John, Jly. 27, Halifax. R. R. Aug. 2, 1810
Jones, Nathaniel, Dec. 30, Wake county. R. R. Feb. 8, 1810
Jones, Thomas C. of Nash county, Apr. 5. R. R. Apr. 19, 1810
Jordan, William, Jly., Bertie county. R. R. Jly. 19, 1810
Ladd, Mrs., Sept. 8, Halifax. R. R. Sept. 27, 1810
Langdon, Richard, Nov. 29, Wilmington. R. R. Dec. 6, 1810
Lee, Thomas, Apr., Tyrrell county. R. R. Apr. 5, 1810
Lemay, Lewis, Jly. 2, Granville county. R. R. Jly. 19, 1810
Levy, Mrs. I. M., Feb. 21, Wilmington. R. R. Mar. 22, 1810
Linch, George, Feb. 4, Edgecombe county. R. R. Feb. 22, 1810
Lishman, Mrs., Sept. 19, Wilmington. R. R. Oct. 4, 1810
Long, Richard H., Feb. 18, Halifax. R. R. Mar. 8, 1810
M'Allister, Col. Hector, My. 21, Cumberland county. R. R. My. 31, 1810
M'Duffee, James, My. 24, Cumberland county. R. R. My. 31, 1810
M'Iver, Kenith of Cumberland county, Dec. 30, South Carolina. R. R.
    Jan. 4, 1810
M'Kenzie, William, Sept. 27, Martin county. R. R. Oct. 4, 1810
M'Lean, Mrs. John, Feb. 24, Cumberland county. R. R. Mar. 8, 1810
M'Clellan, John, Apr. 14, Wilmington. R. R. Apr. 25, 1810
Macnair, Capt. Thomas E., Nov. 23, Tarborough. R. R. Dec. 6, 1810
M'Neill, John of Scotland, Apr. 4, Cumberland county. R. R. My. 3, 1810
M'Pheeters, Mrs. William, Dec. 16, Greenville, Va. R. R. Feb. 1, 1810
M'Rae, Mrs. John, Oct. 12, Fayetteville. R. R. Oct. 25, 1810
M'Ree, Mrs. James Purdie, Jan. 4, Bladen county. R. R. Feb. 1, 1810
Maddon, Mrs. Amos of Connecticut, Oct. 14, Newbern. R. R. Nov. 1, 1810
Marshall, Allen of Halifax, Jly. 27, Warrenton. R. R. Aug. 2, 1810
Marshall, Mrs. Thomas, Dec. 1, Newbern. R. R. Dec. 13, 1810
Mathews, Richard, Oct. 10, Hertford county. R. R. Oct. 25, 1810
Maxwell, Mrs. Peter, Feb. 26, Wilmington. R. R. Mar. 22, 1810
Miller, Augustus, Sept. 4, Top Sail Sound. R. R. Sept. 27, 1810
Moore, Judge Alfred, Oct. 15, Bladen county. R. R. Nov. 1, 1810
Moore, Nathaniel, Dec. 14, Wilmington. R. R. Dec. 27, 1810
Moore, Thos. of Rutherford county, Dec. 14, Rowan county. R. R. Feb. 8,
    1810
Morning, William H., Sept. 14, Newbern. R. R. Sept. 27, 1810
Mumford, James of Fayetteville, Jly. 31. R. R. Aug. 9, 1810
Murray, Jonathan, Feb. 14, Onslow county. R. R. Mar. 15, 1810
Neil, Honore, Oct. 24, Edenton. R. R. Nov. 1, 1810

Nelson, Mrs. Joseph, My., Craven county. R. R. My. 24, 1810
Nevill, John, Aug. 31, Halifax. R. R. Sept. 6, 1810

1811

Brickell, Maj. William, Je., Franklin county. R. R. Je. 7, 1811
Brickell, Thomas N. of Windsor, Mar., Hertford county. R. R. Mar. 21, 1811
Bryan, Elizabeth, Je. 18, Newbern. R. R. Jly. 5, 1811
Bryan, William, Aug., Newbern . R. R. Aug. 23, 1811
Burlingham, Mrs. Wm. of Bertie county, Feb. 16, Franklin county. R. R. Feb. 21, 1811
Burton, Mrs. James M., Mar., Granville county. R. R. Mar. 14, 1811
Butler, Rayner of Durham, Conn., Oct. 28, Newbern. R. R. Nov. 8, 1811
Buxton, Jarvis, Aug. 27, Beaufort. R. R. Sept. 13, 1811
Byrd, Col. Martin R., Je. 22, Washington county. R. R. Jly. 12, 1811
Carman, Mrs. Wm. J., My. 23, Craven county. R. R. Je. 14, 1811
Carpenter, Thos, of Edenton, Oct. 5, Guadaloupe. R. R. Dec. 20, 1811
Casso, Peter of Raleigh, Mar. 18, New Orleans. R. R. My. 3, 1811
Cherry, Luke, Jly. 4, Williamston. R. R. Jly. 26, 1811
Christmas, Mrs., Nov., Warren county. R. R. Nov. 8, 1811
Clegg, Thomas of Chatham county, Aug. 26, Washington county. R. R. Oct. 18, 1811
Clinton, Mrs. Wm., Sept., Sampson county. R. R. Sept. 13, 1811
Coart, Jesse, Oct. 30, Craven county. R. R. Nov. 8, 1811
Cogdell, Richard, Apr., Beaufort county. R. R. My. 3, 1811
Cooke, Edmund, Mar. 12, Cumberland county. R. R. Mar. 21, 1811
Cooke, George W. of Newbern, Sept. 18, Raleigh. R. R. Sept. 20, 1811
Cotral, Thos., Nov. 1, Newbern. R. R. Nov. 8, 1811
Cowan, Major David of Mecklenburg county, Feb. 26, Charlotte. R. R. Mar. 14, 1811
Cozens, Mrs., Oct. 16, Raleigh. R. R. Oct. 25, 1811
Crawford, Charles D., Sept. 11, Beaufort. R. R. Sept. 27, 1811
Crenshaw, James, Dec. 21, Wake county. R. R. Jan. 3, 1811
Crutch, Rich'd., Mar. 2, Craven county. R. R. Mar. 21, 1811
Cunningham, Mrs. J., Oct. 25, Fayetteville. R. R. Nov. 8, 1811
Daniel, Josiah, My. 15, Granville county. R. R. My. 31, 1811
Davis, Capt. Samuel of Rhode Island, Oct., Wilmington. R. R. Oct. 11, 1811
Davis, Mrs. Thomas, Oct. 8, Fayetteville. R. R. Oct. 18, 1811
Delastatious, Wm., Oct. 18, Newbern. R. R. Oct. 25, 1811
Dudley, Mrs. Ann of Swansborough, Oct. 4, Newbern. R. R. Oct. 18, 1811
Eaton, John, Dec. 1, Halifax. R. R. Dec. 20, 1811
Ellis, Miss, Oct. 18, Newbern. R. R. Oct. 25, 1811
Fields, James, Nov. 1, Newbern. R. R. Nov. 8, 1811
Fitts, Mrs. Oliver of Mississippi Territory, Jan. 20, Warrenton. R. R. Jan. 24, 1811
Fleming, James, Apr. 12, Wilmington. R. R. Apr. 26, 1811
Fraser, Rev. Stephen, Oct., Stokes county. R. R. Oct. 18, 1811
Freeling, Dr. Henry, Feb. 15, Rowan county. R. R. Mar. 21, 1811
Garret, Mrs. Everett, Oct. 6, Hertford county. R. R. Oct. 25, 1811
Gassar, Mrs. Prudence, Oct. 13, Bertie county. R. R. Nov. 8, 1811
Gilchrist, Mrs. Angus, Oct., Robeson county. R. R. Oct. 18, 1811

Gilmore, Mrs. Stephen, Jan. 14, Cumberland county. R. R. Jan. 31, 1811
Gridley, Chauncey of New York, Aug. 29, Newbern. R. R. Sept. 13, 1811
Grindall, Mrs., Oct. 23, Newbern. R. R. Nov. 1, 1811
Grist, Gen. Frederick of Beaufort county, Dec. 26, Raleigh. R. R. Dec. 27, 1811
Guion, Mrs. Isaac, Feb. 10, Newbern. R. R. Feb. 21, 1811
Hall, Mrs. Thos., My. 25, Newbern. R. R. Je. 14, 1811
Hart, Samuel, My. 9, Newbern. R. R. My. 24, 1811
Haslin, J., Dec. 1, Newbern. R. R. Dec. 13, 1811
Heartick, Christian, Nov. 1, Newbern. R. R. Nov. 8, 1811
Hendrick, Lucy, Aug., Warrenton. R. R. Aug. 30, 1811
Hendrick, Matilda, Sept., Warrenton. R. R. Sept. 6, 1811
Henry, Mrs. Catharine of Scotland, Oct. 13, Fayetteville. R. R. Nov. 8, 1811
Hunt, Mrs. John, Aug. 21, Franklin. R. R. Aug. 30, 1811
Hunter, Isaac, Jr., Sept., Wake county. R. R. Oct. 4, 1811
Jarvis, Mrs. Moses, Oct. 22, Newbern. R. R. Oct. 25, 1811
Jocelyn, Mrs. Samuel, Je., Wilmington. R. R. Je. 28, 1811
Jocelyn, Thomas, May, Jones county. R. R. My. 3, 1811
Johnston, Mr. of Connecticut, Oct. 29, Newbern. R. R. Nov. 8, 1811
Johnston, Capt. William, Mar. 8, Newbern. R. R. Mar. 21, 1811
Kelly, Thomas W., Oct. 30, Craven county. R. R. Nov. 8, 1811
Knowles, John of Scotland, Je. 17, Newbern. R. R. Jly. 5, 1811
Littlejohn, William of Edenton, My. 22, New York. R. R. My. 31, 1811
Locker, Mrs. Nathaniel, Dec., Beaufort county. R. R. Dec. 13, 1811
Maclin, John, Nov. 1, Warren county. R. R. Nov. 8, 1811
M'Corkle, Rev. Dr. Samuel, Jan. 21, Salisbury. R. R. Mar. 14, 1811
M'Crae, John of Washington county, Mar. 11, Washington county. R. R. Mar. 21, 1811
M'Innish, Donald of Fayetteville, Sept. 8, Montgomery county. R. R. Sept. 27, 1811
M'Intyre, Duncan of Fayetteville, Sept., Warm Springs, Va. R. R. Sept. 27, 1811
M'Kay, Mrs. John, Oct. 10, Cumberland county. R. R. Oct. 18, 1811
Madden, Mrs. Amos, Sept. 30, Newbern. R. R. Oct. 18, 1811
Marsh, David W., Nov. 2, Tarborough. R. R. Nov. 8, 1811
Marshall, Thomas, Nov. 1, Newbern. R. R. Nov. 8, 1811
Mastin, Mrs. J., Sept. 22, Newbern. R. R. Oct. 4, 1811
Matthews, Thomas, Oct., Fayetteville. R. R. Nov. 1, 1811
Merrit, Kesiah, Oct. 25, Newbern. R. R. Nov. 1, 1811
Miles, Thomas, Sept. 13, Wake county. R. R. Sept. 20, 1811
Murphey, Mrs. R., Aug. 22, Wilmington. R. R. Sept. 13, 1811
Musgraves, Mrs. Robert of Brunswick county, Jan. 1, Fayetteville. R. R. Jan. 17, 1811
Norfleet, Elisha, Oct. 29, Chowan county. R. R. Nov. 15, 1811
Norsworthy, John, Apr., Warrenton. R. R. Apr. 26, 1811
O'Brien, Mrs., Feb. 17, Tarboro. R. R. Feb. 21, 1811
O'Bryan, Lawrence of Tarborough, Mar., Sneedsboro, Anson county. R. R. Mar. 28, 1811
O'Kelly, Mrs. John, Mar. 22, Orange county. R. R. My. 3, 1811
Oliver, Thomas, Oct. 31, Newbern. R. R. Nov. 8, 1811

Outlaw, James, Jly. 16, Duplin county. R. R. Oct. 4, 1811
Paisley, Col. John, Oct. 16, Guilford county. R. R. Nov. 1, 1811
Parks, Mrs., Oct. 19, Newbern. R. R. Oct. 25, 1811
Peterson, Henry, Oct. 18, Bertie county. R. R. Nov. 15, 1811
Pickett, Mrs. William, My. 11, Orange county. R. R. My. 17, 1811
Rainey, Rev. Benjamin, Je. 5, Orange county. R. R. Je. 14, 1811
Redditt, Joseph, Sept. 27, Bertie county. R. R. Oct. 11, 1811
Rivers, Mrs. Joel, Dec. 31, Franklin county. R. R. Jan. 17, 1811
Roan, Mrs. John, Sept. 3, Wake county. R. R. Sept. 13, 1811
Roddy, Polly, Mar., Edenton. R. R. Mar. 28, 1811
Ruffin, Robert, Apr., Warrenton. R. R. Apr. 26, 1811
Scott, Josh, Jly. 19, Newbern. R. R. Aug. 2, 1811
Scott, Mrs. Joshua, Oct. 16, Newbern. R. R. Oct. 25, 1811
Scull, John G., Oct. 27, Brunswick county. R. R. Nov. 8, 1811
Sears, William, Sept. 12, Raleigh. R. R. Sept. 13, 1811
Shannonhouse, James, Oct. 28, Pasquotank county. R. R. Nov. 15, 1811
Silbey, Mrs. John, Oct. 25, Fayetteville. R. R. Nov. 1, 1811
Slover, Jas., Sept., Newbern. R. R. Sept. 27, 1811
Smellage, John, Jly. 12, Craven county. R. R. Jly. 26, 1811
Smith, Mrs. David, My. 18, Fayetteville. R. R. My. 31, 1811
Smith, James, Feb. 13, Scotland Neck. R. R. Feb. 21, 1811
Smith, Capt. Sam of Craven county, Jan. R. R. Jan. 17, 1811
Smith, Mrs. Thos. L., My. 3, Louisa county, Va. R. R. Je. 14, 1811
Speed, Miss of Mecklenburg county, Va., Aug., Warrenton. R. R. Aug.
    30, 1811
Stevens, Richard, Oct. 28, Newbern. R. R. Nov. 8, 1811
Stokes, Thos., Mar., Chatham county. R. R. Apr. 5, 1811
Thaxton, Jas., Oct. 31, Fayetteville. R. R. Nov. 8, 1811
Tillman, Col. John, Mar., Dawson's Creek, Craven county. R. R. Mar. 14,
    1811
Vail, Mrs. John, Oct. 21, Newbern. R. R. Oct. 25, 1811
Vandegriff, Elsworth, Aug. 8, Raleigh. R. R. Aug. 16, 1811
Vines, Mrs. Wm., Oct. 16, Newbern. R. R. Oct. 25, 1811
Walker, Mr., Oct. 28, Newbern. R. R. Nov. 8, 1811
Weeks, Mrs. Cornelius, Sept. 30, Newbern. R. R. Oct. 18, 1811
West, Abner K. of Newbern, Je., Grenada. R. R. Jly. 5, 1811
West, John, Nov. 5, Halifax. R. R. Nov. 15, 1811
West, Robert, Oct. 14, Bertie county. R. R. Nov. 8, 1811
Wheaton, Mrs. S., Mar. 25, Raleigh. R. R. Mar. 28, 1811
White, William, Nov. 8, Raleigh. R. R. Nov. 15, 1811
Whitehead, Capt. Nathan, Oct., Nash county. R. R. Oct. 18, 1811
Wilkings, Mrs. John, Dec. 30, Wilmington Sound. R. R. Jan. 10, 1811
Wilkinson, Reuben, Dec. 31, Smithfield. R. R. Jan. 17, 1811
Williams, Eliza, Aug., Warren county. R. R. Aug. 30, 1811
Williams, Mrs. John, Jly. 16, Kinston. R. R. Jly. 26, 1811
Winslow, Caleb, Mar. 28, Perquimons county. R. R. Apr. 19, 1811
Woods, Mrs. Freeman, Oct. 24, Newbern. R. R. Nov. 1, 1811
Woody, Jno., Apr., Orange county. R. R. Apr. 26, 1811
Wright, Joshua G. of Wilmington, Je. 10, Charleston. R. R. Je. 21, 1811
Wright, Mrs. John, Oct. 26, Duplin county. R. R. Nov. 29, 1811

1812

Alderson, Thomas, May, Bath. R. R. My. 15, 1812
Alston, Philip, Aug., Warren county. R. R. Sept. 4, 1812
Alves, Gavin, Je. 20, Hillsborough. R. R. Je. 26, 1812
Anthony, John, Sept. 4, Halifax county. R. R. Sept. 25, 1812
Arnold, Ambrose, Dec. 3, Person county. R. R. Dec. 1, 1812
Arrington, Gen'l. William, Sept. 24, Nash county. R. R. Oct. 2, 1812
Ashe, Mrs. John Baptiste, Sept., Halifax. R. R. Sept. 25, 1812
Austin, Dr. T., Sept. 29, Fayetteville. R. R. Oct. 2, 1812
Baker, Mrs. Wm., Feb. 14, Gates county. R. R. Mar. 6, 1812
Batchelor, Wright W., Feb., Halifax. R. R. Feb. 28, 1812
Bateman, Maj. J., Feb., Tyrrell county. R. R. Feb. 14, 1812
Beard, Captain David, Je. 20, Raleigh. R. R. Je. 26, 1812
Bell, Mrs. Mary, Jan. 28, Edenton. R. R. Feb. 14, 1812
Bennehan, Mrs. Richard, Dec. 17, Orange county. R. R. Dec. 25, 1812
Bernard, Mrs., Oct., Wilmington. R. R. Oct. 23, 1812
Bingham, Mrs. of Ireland, May 11, Hillsborough. R. R. My. 15, 1812
Blount, Major Gen'l. Thomas of North Carolina, Feb. 7, Washington, D. C.
    R. R. Feb. 21, 1812
Bond, Col. John of Chowan county, Sept. 26. R. R. Oct. 9, 1812
Brantley, Rev. William, Sept. 15, Chatham county. R. R. Sept. 25, 1812
Brown, John, Feb. 13, Wilkes county. R. R. Feb. 28, 1812
Bryant, James, Je. 30, Halifax. R. R. Jly. 24, 1812
Campbell, William, My. 11, Wilmington. R. R. May 22, 1812
Carney, Gen. Stephen W., Dec. 27, Halifax county. R. R. Jan. 17, 1812
Chambers, Maxwell, Jan. 3, Rowan county. R. R. Jan. 17, 1812
Charlton, William, Jly. 28, Perquimons county. R. R. Aug. 14, 1812
Christmas, Col. Charles, Dec. 21, Orange county. R. R. Jan. 10, 1812
Coakley, Mrs. Mildred, My. 3, Washington, Beaufort county. R. R. My. 22,
    1812
Coffield, Benjamin, Oct. 14, Chowan county. R. R. Oct. 30, 1812
Cooke, Mrs. Jacob, Aug. 16, Newbern. R. R. Aug. 21, 1812
Craven, Margaret, Nov., Martin county. R. R. Nov. 27, 1812
Creecy, Jeremiah, Je. 3, Chowan county. R. R. Je. 19, 1812
Daniel, Geo., Dec. 31, Granville county. R. R. Jan. 17, 1812
Darden, Jethro, Jan. 19, Wilmington. R. R. Feb. 14, 1812
DeRosset, Louis, Sept. 27, Wilmington. R. R. Oct. 9, 1812
Dickinson, Mrs. Elizabeth Ann, Mar. 12, Edenton. R. R. Mar. 27, 1812
Dickson, James, Nov., Duplin county. R. R. Nov. 27, 1812
Dickson, Col. Wm., Aug., Duplin county. R. R. Sept. 4, 1812
Dunn, Lucy, Dec. 5, Wake county. R. R. Dec. 18, 1812
Evans, David, Oct., Fayetteville. R. R. Oct. 30, 1812
Faulcon, John, Oct., Warren county. R. R. Oct. 16, 1812
Flury, Mrs. Henry, Apr. 2, Edenton. R. R. Apr. 17, 1812
Foort, Elias, Jan., Halifax county. R. R. Jan. 17, 1812
Gardner, Mark, Oct. 1, Fayetteville. R. R. Oct. 23, 1812
Gaston, Mrs. Margaret, Dec. 17, Newbern. R. R. Jan. 10, 1812
Gracie, Seldon of Newbern, Je. 19, Fayetteville. R. R. Je. 26, 1812
Haslin, Mrs. Margaret, Feb. 11, Newbern. R. R. Feb. 28, 1812
Hatch, Mrs. Frederic W., Jly. 9, Edenton. R. R. Jly. 24, 1812
Haywood, Dr. Henry, Feb. 6, Tarboro. R. R. Feb. 28, 1812

Hicks, Daniel, My. 27, Sampson county. R. R. Je. 26, 1812
High, Samuel, Dec. 15, Wake county. R. R. Dec. 18, 1812
Higson, John, Je., Wilmington. R. R. Je. 26, 1812
Hinton, Mrs. Henry, Apr., Raleigh. R. R. Apr. 24, 1812
Hunt, Jabez, Oct. 2, Guilford county. R. R. Oct. 23, 1812
Johnston, Jacob, Jan. 4, Raleigh. R. R. Jan. 17, 1812
Jones, Elizabeth, Jan. 20, Wilmington. R. R. Feb. 7, 1812
Kellingsworth, Freeman, Nov., Raleigh. R. R. Nov. 27, 1812
Kimball, Drury, Dec. 4, Granville county. R. R. Jan. 31, 1812
Lacy, Mrs., Oct., Rockingham county. R. R. Oct. 23, 1812
Luteman, John A., Oct. 14, Newbern. R. R. Oct. 30, 1812
M'Gowan, Dr. J. of Ireland, Oct. 13, Newbern. R. R. Oct. 30, 1812
M'Kay, Mrs. Malcom, Oct., Cumberland county. R. R. Oct. 30, 1812
M'Leran, Mrs. Duncan, Nov., Fayetteville. R. R. Nov. 20, 1812
M'Rackan, James, Oct. 26, Raleigh. R. R. Oct. 30, 1812
Malone, Mrs. Lewis, Nov. 18, Caswell county. R. R. Dec. 4, 1812
Mann, Mrs. Thos., Sept. 29, Edenton. R. R. Oct. 16, 1812
Manning, Wm., Jan. 17, Edenton. R. R. Feb. 7, 1812
Matthews, Moses, Je. 23, Halifax county. R. R. Jly. 10, 1812
Maxwell, James, Nov., Duplin county. R. R. Nov. 27, 1812
Maxwell, Peter, Sept. 24, Wilmington. R. R. Oct. 9, 1812
Moore, Elizabeth, Oct. 15, Fayetteville. R. R. Oct. 30, 1812
Moseley, Dr., Sept. 11, Halifax. R. R. Sept. 25, 1812
Murdaugh, Mrs. L. of Bertie county, May. R. R. May 29, 1812
Narne, Jesse of Scotland Neck, Mar. 12, Washington, Beaufort county.
    R. R. Apr. 3, 1812
Newsom, Daw, Dec. 21, Raleigh. R. R. Dec. 25, 1812
Norcom, Frederick, Mar. 4, Chowan county. R. R. Mar. 20, 1812
Nutt, William, Je., New Hanover county. R. R. Je. 26, 1812
Ochiltree, Mrs. David, Nov. 6, Fayetteville. R. R. Nov. 20, 1812
Pearsall, Jas., Sr., Nov., Duplin county. R. R. Nov. 27, 1812
Perkins, Mrs. Tamar, Feb., Camden county. R. R. Feb. 21, 1812
Perkins, Mrs. Thomas, Feb. 26, Mt. Airy. R. R. Mar. 13, 1812
Phillips, Mrs. Dreury, Jly. 16, Northampton county. R. R. Jly. 31, 1812
Pigot, Abram, Sept., Beaufort. R. R. Oct. 9, 1812
Polk, Col. Chas. of Statesburg, S. C., Aug. 7, Mecklenburg county. R. R.
    Aug. 28, 1812
Pope, Mrs. John, Feb. 7, Greene county. R. R. Mar. 13, 1812
Powers, Mrs. William, Jan., Camden county. R. R. Feb. 7, 1812
Purdie, Mrs. Mary, Je. 6, Edenton. R. R. Je. 19, 1812
Quince, Mrs. Susannah, Sept. 28, Wilmington. R. R. Oct. 23, 1812
Ragland, Frederick, Sept. 27, Chatham county. R. R. Oct. 9, 1812
Rankin, John, Sept. 28, Averasborough. R. R. Oct. 9, 1812
Recks, Mrs. Lucy, Jan. 15, Granville county. R. R. Jan. 31, 1812
Rencher, John G., May, Wake county. R. R. My. 15, 1812
Riggs, Hezekiah R. of this State, Oct. 12, Tenn. R. R. Oct. 16, 1812
Sanders, Hardy of Newbern, May 18, Raleigh. R. R. May 22, 1812
Scott, Gen. Jno., Jan. 30, Hertford county. R. R. Feb. 14, 1812
Shelby, Col. Henry, Jan. 14, Hyde county. R. R. Feb. 14, 1812
Sheppard, Jordan, Dec. 15, Greenville. R. R. Jan. 10, 1812
Skinner, William, Aug. 24, Chowan county. R. R. Sept. 11, 1812

Slade, Ebenezer, Apr. 3, Warren county. R. R. Apr. 10, 1812
Slade, Mrs. Wm., Dec. 11, Edenton. R. R. Dec. 25, 1812
Smith, Ambrose of England, Dec. 7, Chowan county. R. R. Dec. 25, 1812
Smith, Jos. of Fayetteville & Massachusetts, Dec. 18, Lumberton. R. R.
    Dec. 25, 1812
Spooner, John, Jan. 9, Edenton. R. R. Jan. 24, 1812
Simmons, Benjamin, Oct. 2, Jones county. R. R. Oct. 23, 1812
Simmons, Jesse, Jan. 15, Halifax county. R. R. Feb. 7, 1812
Tallman, Phoebe, Oct. 13, Newbern. R. R. Oct. 30, 1812
Trotter, Richard, Je., Salisbury. R. R. Je. 26, 1812
Troy, Matthew of this State, Dec. 3, Philadelphia. R. R. Dec. 18, 1812
Ward, Col. Charles, Nov., Duplin county. R. R. Nov. 27, 1812
Warring, Mrs. Ann, Sept. 25, Edenton. R. R. Oct. 9, 1812
Watkins, Levin, Nov., Duplin county. R. R. Nov. 27, 1812
Webb, Zachariah, Dec. 1st, Edenton. R. R. Dec. 18, 1812
West, James of Newbern, Oct. 5. R. R. Oct. 23, 1812
West, Mrs. John S., Jan. 8, Newbern. R. R. Jan. 24, 1812
Wheeler, Jabez, Sept. 18, Winton. R. R. Oct. 9, 1812
Whitaker, Mrs. John, Feb. 3, Wake county. R. R. Feb. 7, 1812
White, Edward. May 2, Washington, Beaufort county. R. R. May 22, 1812
Whitfield, Needham, Apr., Wayne county. R. R. May 1, 1812
Wilder, Mrs. Willis, Nov. 30, Chowan county. R. R. Dec. 18, 1812
Williams, J. B., May 26, Edenton. R. R. Je. 12, 1812
Williams, Capt. Wm. of Wales, Sept. 22, Edenton. R. R. Oct. 9, 1812
Wolcott, Wm. W. of Connecticut, Je. 24, Wilmington. R. R. Jly. 10, 1812
Wood, Reuben, Aug., Randolph county. R. R. Aug. 21, 1812
Wright, Israel, Je. 11, New Hanover county. R. R. Je. 26, 1812
Yarbrough, Charles, Apr., Franklin county. R. R. My. 15, 1812
Yergin, Benjamin, Mar. 22, Chapel Hill. R. R. Apr. 10, 1812

1813

Alexander, Mrs. Adam, Dec. 5, Mecklenburg county. R. R. Dec. 17, 1813
Ashe, Samuel, Jan. 22, New Hanover county. R. R. Feb. 5, 1813
Bagley, Anderson W. of Raleigh, Dec., Princess Anne, Va. R. R. Dec. 31,
    1813
Blackwell, Capt. Robert, Jan. 25, Caswell county. R. R. Feb. 19, 1813
Blair, William, Feb., Perquimons county. R. R. Feb. 12, 1813
Brown, Capt. John, Jan. 1, Bladen county. R. R. Jan. 29, 1813
Bruce, Rev. Philip, Nov., Iredell county. R. R. Nov. 26, 1813
Burn, Captain John, Jan. 4, Bertie county. R. R. Jan. 22, 1813
Caruthers, Mrs. John, Dec. 11, Craven county. R. R. Dec. 31, 1813
Chisholm, Findley of Scotland, Apr. 13, Fayetteville. R. R. Apr. 23, 1813
Churchill, Charles, Jly. 16, Newbern. R. R. Oct. 1, 1813
Colbert, Capt. Samuel of Southampton, Va., Oct. 2, Warrenton. R. R.
    Oct. 8, 1813
Coleman, Major Benjamin, May 17, Lenoir county. R. R. May 28, 1813
Coxe, Tench of Philadelphia, Feb., Rutherfordton. R. R. Feb. 26, 1813
Daffon, Priscilla, Feb. 1, Chatham county. R. R. Feb. 19, 1813
Davis, George, Jan. 22, New Hanover county. R. R. Feb. 5, 1813
Davis, Dr. William, Jly., Mecklenburg county. R. R. Jly. 9, 1813
Davis, William, Sept. 11, Person county. R. R. Sept. 24, 1813

Eggleston, Jacob of Connecticut, Mar. 19, Fayetteville. R. R. Mar. 26, 1813

Ferrand, William, Sept. 17, Swansborough. R. R. Oct. 1, 1813

Freeman, Isaac, Sept. 3, Craven county. R. R. Sept. 24, 1813

Galloway, Thomas S., Feb. 28, Rockingham county. R. R. Apr. 2, 1813

Gaston, William, Jly. 12, Newbern. R. R. Jly. 23, 1813

Gillespie, Mrs. B. C., Nov. 9, Newbern. R. R. Nov. 26, 1813

Gilmour, Alexander, My. 26, Franklin county. R. R. My. 28, 1813

Gordan, Daniel, Dec. 28, Hertford, Perquimons county. R. R. Jan. 15, 1813

Gorman, Mrs. Henry, Dec. 2, Raleigh. R. R. Dec. 4, 1813

Harris, Hon. Edward, Mar. 28, Lumberton. R. R. Apr. 2, 1813

Harris, Stephen, Mar. 9, Craven county. R. R. Mar. 26, 1813

Hawkins, Mrs. Benjamin, Jly., Warren county. R. R. Jly. 9, 1813

Hawks, Mrs. F., Apr. 3, Newbern. R. R. Apr. 16, 1813

Haywood, Sherwood, Dec. 10, Raleigh. R. R. Dec. 17, 1813

Heron, Mrs. Alice, Mar. 4, Wilmington. R. R. Mar. 12, 1813

High, Captain Robert, Je. 7, Franklin county. R. R. Je. 18, 1813

Hill, Mrs. Wm., Aug. 21, Warren county. R. R. Aug. 27, 1813

Hooks, Mrs. Susanna, Nov. 19, Duplin county. R. R. Dec. 3, 1813

Hopkins, W. W., Oct., Smithfield. R. R. Oct. 22, 1813

Hostler, Mrs. Mary, Nov., Wilmington. R. R. Nov. 19, 1813

Hunter, Thomas, Jan. 4, Wilmington. R. R. Jan. 15, 1813

Hunter, Capt. Wm., Mar. 2, Wilmington. R. R. Mar. 12, 1813

Judge, James, Sr., Aug. 2, Halifax county. R. R. Aug. 13, 1813

Lane, Mrs. Harry, My. 11, Wake county. R. R. Apr. 30, 1813

Levy, Capt. J. M. of Wilmington, Oct., Havanna. R. R. Oct. 22, 1813

Lewis, Howell, Nov. 21, Granville county. R. R. Dec. 3, 1813

Locke, James, Aug. 31, Rowan county. R. R. Sept. 17, 1813

Lockhart, Mrs. Sarah, Dec. 13, Hillsboro. R. R. Dec. 24, 1813

Love, Mrs. Wm. C., Oct., Salisbury. R. R. Oct. 8, 1813

M'Kissick, Jonathan, Jan. 9, Person county. R. R. Jan. 22, 1813

M'Leod, Donald, Dec. 30, Fayetteville. R. R. Jan. 1, 1813

Mears, Mrs. William B., Oct. 24, Wilmington. R. R. Oct. 29, 1813

Miller, Dr. James P., Aug. 2, Person county. R. R. Sept. 10, 1813

Miner, Capt. Stephen of Newbern, Oct. 10, Beaufort. R. R. Oct. 29, 1813

Minzies, Mrs. John, Je. 25, Rockingham county. R. R. Jly. 23, 1813

Mumford, Edward, Feb. 25, Onslow county. R. R. Mar. 5, 1813

Neate, Mrs. Mary, Nov. 16, Wilmington. R. R. Nov. 26, 1813

Nicholson, Archibald, Aug. 16, Fayetteville. R. R. Aug. 20, 1813

Norcom, Dr. Benjamin, My. 9, Edenton. R. R. May 21, 1813

Norcom, Mrs. Frederick, Jan. 26, Chowan county. R. R. Feb. 12, 1813

Patterson, Robert, Jan. 29, Cabarrus county. R. R. Feb. 19, 1813

Person, Mrs. Thomas, Mar. 1, Warren county. R. R. Mar. 5, 1813

Person, Mrs. William, Mar. 1, Warren county. R. R. Mar. 12, 1813

Quigley, Chas. of Salisbury, Oct. 21, Pertsburg. R. R. Oct. 29, 1813

Rutherford, Mrs. Robert, Feb. 25, Raleigh. R. R. Feb. 26, 1813

Sampson, Michael, Feb., Sampson county. R. R. Feb. 26, 1813

Simpson, William of Wilmington, Jan. 15, New Orleans. R. R. Feb. 26, 1813

Sinclair, Mrs. D., Apr. 5, Cumberland county. R. R. Apr. 30, 1813

Slade, William of Edenton, Feb. 23, Raleigh. R. R. Feb. 26, 1813
Smith, Mrs. Robert, Nov. 2, Cabarrus county. R. R. Nov. 19, 1813
Smith, Dr. Wm. L., Sept. 1, Murfreesborough. R. R. Sept. 17, 1813
Stuart, Thomas, Je. 20, Tarborough. R. R. Je. 25, 1813
Swann, Mrs. Samuel, Nov., Wilmington. R. R. Nov. 19, 1813
Thompson, John, Feb. 24, Fayetteville. R. R. Mar. 5, 1813
Tillinghast, William H. of Fayetteville, Oct. 8, Smithville. R. R. Oct. 22, 1813
Tilman, Col. H., Oct., Craven county. R. R. Oct. 22, 1813
Turner, Rev. Wm. L., Oct. 17, Fayetteville. R. R. Oct. 22, 1813
Walker, Mrs. James W., Jly. 5, Wilmington. R. R. Jly. 23, 1813
Walker, Maj. John of Northumberland, Sept. 7, Wilmington. R. R. Sept. 17, 1813
Whedbee, Mrs. Benjamin, Mar. 9, Edenton. R. R. Mar. 26, 1813
Williams, Robert, Mar. 27, Wilmington. R. R. Apr. 16, 1813

1814

Alexander, Mrs. Ezra, Sept. 8, Mecklenburg county. R. R. Sept. 30, 1814
Bethune, Murdock of Moore county & Scotland, Apr. 15, Fayetteville. R. R. Apr. 29, 1814
Bloodworth, Timothy, Jly. 24, South Washington. R. R. Aug. 19, 1814
Blount, Mrs. Joseph, Feb. 11, Edenton. R. R. Feb. 25, 1814
Blue, Mrs. of Scotland, Apr., Richmond county. R. R. Apr. 29, 1814
Brickell, Thomas, Oct. 12, Gates county. R. R. Dec. 2, 1814
Brower, Col. John, May 4, Randolph county. R. R. May 20, 1814
Brown, Major Ben Thomas, Nov. 22, Bladen county. R. R. Dec. 16, 1814
Brownlow, James, Jan. 28, Sound, Wilmington. R. R. Feb. 11, 1814
Campbell, Norman, Feb. 8, Wadesboro. R. R. Feb. 18, 1814
Chapman, Blanch, Dec., Chapel Hill. R. R. Dec. 9, 1814
Christman, Mrs. Richard, Mar. 14, Orange county. R. R. Mar. 25, 1814
Cooke, Henry L., Jly. 3, Raleigh. R. R. Jly. 8, 1814
Coopee, Francis, Mar. 12, Salisbury. R. R. Mar. 25, 1814
Daniel, Chisley, Sept. 11, Granville county. R. R. Oct. 7, 1814
Daniel, Jane, Oct., Granville county. R. R. Nov. 4, 1814
Daves, Mrs. John, Feb., Newbern. R. R. Feb. 18, 1814
Dickey, William, May 25, Guilford county. R. R. Je. 17, 1814
Dixon, Alexander, Mar. 22, Duplin county. R. R. Aug. 5, 1814
Dunlap, Mrs. Elizabeth, Jan. 21, Wilmington. R. R. Feb. 18, 1814
Everett, Dr. Reuben, Feb. 1, Smithville. R. R. Feb. 18, 1814
Field, Mrs. Grandison, Je., Warren county. R. R. Je. 10, 1814
Fowler, Wm., Mar., Wake county. R. R. Mar. 11, 1814
Freear, Richard, Mar. 26, Northampton county. R. R. Apr. 8, 1814
Gause, Mrs. John J., Jan. 23, Laurel Grove. R. R. Feb. 18, 1814
Gilmour, William of Halifax, Je. 26, Raleigh. R. R. Jly. 1, 1814
Giles, William, Aug. 29, Wilmington. R. R. Sept. 2, 1814
Goodman, Jethro D., Aug. 2, Elizabeth City. R. R. Aug. 19, 1814
Graves, Mrs. William, Feb. 12, Caswell county. R. R. Feb. 25, 1814
Hare, Thomas Edward, May 7, Bertie county. R. R. Jly. 1, 1814
Harris, Dr. Cunningham, Dec. 20, Mecklenburg county. R. R. Feb. 4, 1814
Harrison, Richard, Sept. 11, Wake county. R. R. Sept. 16, 1814
Hayes, Hugh of Virginia, Apr., Warren county. R. R. May 6, 1814

DEATH NOTICES 149

High, Mrs. Robert, Dec. 24, Wake county. R. R. Dec. 30, 1814
Hilliard, John, Apr., Nash county. R. R. Apr. 22, 1814
Holt, Polly R., Apr. 22, Orange county. R. R. May 6, 1814
Johnson, Mrs. Molly, Je., Warren county. R. R. Je. 10, 1814
Jones, Mrs. Hardy, Sr. of Surry county, Aug. 26, Rowan county. R. R.
  Sept. 9, 1814
Jones, Col. Kilby, Apr. 2, Onslow county. R. R. Apr. 22, 1814
Kilpatrick, Maj. Francis, Feb. 23, Lenoir county. R. R. Mar. 25, 1814
Lewis, Mrs. Charles, Feb. 5, Granville county. R. R. Feb. 25, 1814
M'Auslan, Mrs. Jane of Scotland, Feb. 14, Fayetteville. R. R. Feb. 25,
  1814
M'Lean, Mrs. A., Sr., May 6, Cumberland county. R. R. May 27, 1814
Matthews, Mrs. John, Feb. 15, Fayetteville. R. R. Feb. 25, 1814
Miller, Haman, Sr., Oct. 12, Randolph county. R. R. Oct. 28, 1814
Moore, Dr. Wm. of Mecklenburg county, Sept. 2, Salisbury. R. R. Sept.
  30, 1814
Nickle, James, Je. 21, Newbern. R. R. Je. 24, 1814
Nicholson, John, Apr., Bladen county. R. R. Apr. 22, 1814
Nunn, David, May, Chapel Hill. R. R. May 20, 1814
Potter, Robert of Granville county, Aug., Raleigh. Aug. 5, 1814
Prentice, Capt. Jabez, Apr. 5, Newbern. R. R. Apr. 22, 1814
Pulliman, Benjamin, Oct. 30, Raleigh. R. R. Nov. 4, 1814
Rea, Mrs. William, Dec. 16, Hertford county. R. R. Dec. 30, 1814
Singleton, Mrs. Spyers, Oct. 31, Newbern. R. R. Nov. 18, 1814
Steed, Mrs. Collin, Oct. 14, Randolph county. R. R. Oct. 28, 1814
Sugg, Mrs. Joshua, Dec. 14, Wake county. R. R. Dec. 23, 1814
Sumner, Joseph John of Tarborough, Dec. 28, Gulf of Mexico. R. R. Feb.
  25, 1814
Tate, Rev. Robert, May 1, Orange county. R. R. May 13, 1814
Van Hook, Jesse, Oct. 3, Person county. R. R. Oct. 21, 1814
Waddell, Mrs. Thos. of Chatham county, Apr., Moore county. R. R. Apr.
  15, 1814
Whitaker, Matthew C., June, Halifax county. R. R. Jly. 1, 1814
Williams, Col. Benjamin, Jly. 20, Moore county. R. R. Jly. 29, 1814

1815

Barker, John, May, Orange county. R. R. June 2, 1815
Beale, Thomas S., Sept. 12, Wilmington. R. R. Sept. 22, 1815
Blackman, Josiah, Mar., Sampson county. R. R. Apr. 7, 1815
Bryan, Gen. Hardy, May, Johnston county. R. R. May 12, 1815
Bryan, Mrs. Hardy, Mar., Johnston county. R. R. Mar. 24, 1815
Bryan, John, Mar., Johnston county. R. R. Mar. 24, 1815
Bryan, Simon A., Mar., Bertie county. R. R. Mar. 24, 1815
Bullock, Charles of Edgecombe county, Sept., Tenn. R. R. Sept. 29, 1815
Campbell, John of Scotland, Oct. 28. R. R. Nov. 3, 1815
Campbell, Mrs. Wm., Oct. 17, Wilmington. R. R. Oct. 27, 1815
Carter, Jesse, Sept. 12, Caswell county. R. R. Oct. 27, 1815
Carthy, Elizabeth, Apr. 12, Newbern. R. R. Apr. 28, 1815
Cheek, Thomas L., Dec. 5, Newbern. R. R. Dec. 22, 1815
Cherry, Samuel, Oct. 2, Edgecombe county. R. R. Oct. 13, 1815
Clarke, Kenneth of this State, Feb., Norfolk. R. R. Feb. 10, 1815

Coffin, Barnabas, Aug., Guilford county. R. R. Sept. 8, 1815

Cotton, Frederick, Jan. 25, Edgecombe county. Feb. 3, 1815

Creecy, Maj. Nathan of Craven county, Feb. 15. R. R. Mar. 3, 1815

Davidson, Catherine, Sept. 24, Iredell county. R. R. Jan. 20, 1815

Davidson, Col. George, Sept. 22, Iredell county. R. R. Jan. 20, 1815

Dickinson, John of this State, May 4, Rhode Island. R. R. May 26, 1815

Dickson, James, May 18, Newbern. R. R. Je. 2, 1815

Donaldson, George of Raleigh, Nov. 1, Tarborough. R. R. Nov. 3, 1815

Farrar, Mrs. Rebecca, Jan. 19, Wake county. R. R. Jan. 27, 1815

Foster, John, Apr., Franklin. R. R. Apr. 14, 1815

Fuller, Capt. John, Sept. 15, Franklin county. R. R. Sept. 22, 1815

Gable, John M., Sept. 8, Wilmington. R. R. Sept. 22, 1815

Gales, Mrs. Thomas of Raleigh, Sept., Attakapas. R. R. Oct. 27, 1815

Golden, Capt. Abraham, Sept. 10, Wilmington. R. R. Sept. 22, 1815

Gorman, Dickson, Oct. 9, Raleigh. R. R. Oct. 13, 1815

Guion, Isaac L., Feb., Newbern. R. R. Feb. 10, 1815

Guy, Wm., Apr., Smithfield. R. R. Apr. 21, 1815

Harris, Isaac, Aug. 13, Cabarrus county. R. R. Sept. 29, 1815

Harris, William of Cabarrus county, Jan. 8, Augusta, Ga. R. R. Mar. 24, 1815

Hasell, Wm. S., Oct. 6, Wilmington. R. R. Oct. 20, 1815

Hawkins, Madison I. of Warren county, Sept. 24, Warrenton. R. R. Sept. 29, 1815

Helme, Mrs., Apr., Smithfield. R. R. Apr. 21, 1815

Herndon, Pleasant of Orange county, Mar., Norfolk. R. R. Mar. 31, 1815

Hill, Thomas, Oct. 27, Halifax county. R. R. Nov. 3, 1815

Hines, Alexander W., Dec. 1, Nash county. R. R. Dec. 8, 1815

Hinton, Mrs. John, Jr., Mar., Wake county. R. R. Mar. 17, 1815

Hogg, John, Jr., Sept. 13, Wilmington. R. R. Sept. 29, 1815

Holloway, William, Mar. 11, Raleigh. R. R. Mar. 17, 1815

Hoof, John of Isle of Wight county, Va., Oct. 4, Franklin county. R. R. Nov. 17, 1815

Horn, Josiah, Feb., Edgecombe county. R. R. Feb. 10, 1815

Huske, Mrs. John, Oct. 23, Fayetteville. R. R. Nov. 3, 1815

Jeffrey, James of Scotland, Apr. 6, Warrenton. R. R. Apr. 14, 1815

Jones, Mrs. Kimbro, Apr. 13, Wake county. R. R. Apr. 14, 1815

Jones, Nathaniel, Feb. 8, Wake county. R. R. Feb. 10, 1815

Jordan, John S., Jly. 18, Raleigh. R. R. Jly. 21, 1815

Johnson, Col. Robert, Nov., Kentucky. R. R. Nov. 10, 1815

Johnson, Sugan, Jan., Warren county. R. R. Jan. 27, 1815

Keys, Mrs. James H., May 21, Warren county. R. R. May 26, 1815

Langdon, John of Philadelphia, Sept. 16, Fayetteville. R. R. Sept. 29, 1815

Lee, Budd, Feb., Wake county. R. R. Mar. 3, 1815

Legan, Richard, Mar. 20, Raleigh. R. R. Mar. 24, 1815

Lester, Col. Jesse, Nov. 12, Surry county. R. R. Dec. 22, 1815

Long, Benjamin, Feb. 14, Richmond county. R. R. Mar. 17, 1815

Lyndon, Josiah of Randolph county, Dec. 10, Orange county. R. R. Jan. 13, 1815

Mabry, John, Je., Warren county. R. R. Je. 16, 1815

M'Cauley, Wm. of Orange county, May 27, Washington, D. C. R. R. Je. 9, 1815
M'Eachin, John, Oct. 8, Robeson county. R. R. Oct. 27, 1815
M'Guffy, Hardy, Apr. 21, Wake county. R. R. Apr. 28, 1815
Marquis, Job, Sept., Randolph county. R. R. Sept. 22, 1815
Mayo, Mrs. Nathan, of Edgecombe county, Sept. 24. R. R. Oct. 13, 1815
Miller, Mrs. Haman, Apr. 25, Randolph county. R. R. May 12, 1815
Miller, Mrs. John, Sr., Mar. 18, Raleigh. R. R. Mar. 24, 1815
Mirover, Henry, Mar. 20, Wilmington. R. R. Mar. 24, 1815
Mitchell, Charles, Jly. 25, Person county. R. R. Aug. 11, 1815
Mitchell, Capt. Elijah, Dec., Raleigh. R. R. Dec. 29, 1815
Morrison, Norman, Jly. 11, Cumberland county. R. R. Jly. 21, 1815
Nicholson, Mrs. Wm., Sept. 10, Wilmington. R. R. Sept. 22, 1815
Nixon, Samuel, Dec., Perquimons county. R. R. Dec. 22, 1815
Norfleet, James, Mar. 23, Edenton. R. R. Apr. 7, 1815
O'Kelly, Lieut. Zenas of Raleigh, Feb. 24, Norfolk. R. R. Mar. 10, 1815
Pearce, Frederick, Jan., Washington, Beaufort county. R. R. Feb. 3, 1815
Potter, Mrs. Samuel, Sept., Smithville. R. R. Sept. 22, 1815
Royster, John, Sept. 23, Raleigh. R. R. Sept. 29, 1815
Russell, Mrs. Alexander, Mar. 4, Orange county. R. R. Mar. 31, 1815
Sanders, Ellick, Mar. 28, Smithfield. R. R. Apr. 7, 1815
Sasser, Capt. Wm., Mar., Smithfield. R. R. Mar. 31, 1815
Skinner, William, Feb. 11, Chowan county. R. R. Mar. 3, 1815
Sledge, Mrs. Willie, Jly., Raleigh. R. R. Jly. 14, 1815
Smith, David of Rockingham, Mar., Norfolk. R. R. Mar. 10, 1815
Smith, Harris of Rhode Island, Dec., Washington county. R. R. Dec. 22, 1815
Stackhouse, Thomas, Jan. 11, Warrenton. R. R. Jan. 20, 1815
Steele, General John, Aug. 14, Salisbury. R. R. Aug. 25, 1815
Summer, Jacob of Tenn., Feb. 20, Tarborough. R. R. Mar. 10, 1815
Taylor, James, Apr. 20, Smithville. R. R. May 5, 1815
Taylor, Col. Joseph, Je., Granville county. R. R. Je. 9, 1815
Taylor, William of Perquimons county, Mar., Hertford. R. R. Mar. 10, 1815
Tompkins, Edward of Johnston county, Feb. R. R. Mar. 3, 1815
Turner, Green, Jly. 14, Northampton county. R. R. Aug. 11, 1815
Utley, Mrs. Albert, Jan. 20, Wake county. R. R. Jan. 27, 1815
Ward, Mrs. Edward, Oct. 11, Onslow county. R. R. Oct. 27, 1815
Welch, Mrs. Roxaland, May 18, Newbern. R. R. Je. 2, 1815
Williams, William H. of Washington, Beaufort county, Je. 6. R. R. Je. 16, 1815
Winston, Col. Joseph, Apr. 21, Stokes county. R. R. Apr. 28, 1815
Woodberry, Mrs. J., Mar. 1, Raleigh. R. R. Mar. 3, 1815
Yancey, Mrs. James M., Aug. 12, Raleigh. R. R. Aug. 18, 1815
Yancey, Sterling, Jan. 5, Raleigh. R. R. Jan. 27, 1815

1818

Abraham, Mrs. Mary, Jly. 10, Wilmington. R. R. Jly. 17, 1818
Alexander, Col. Elias, May 13, Rutherford county. R. R. Je. 26, 1818
Allen, Abraham, Sept. 14, Orange county. R. R. Sept. 25, 1818
Allen, Jane, Sept., Orange county. R. R. Sept. 25, 1818
Allen, Samuel, Sept., Orange county. R. R. Sept. 25, 1818

Alston, Nicholas F., Je., Warren county. R. R. Je. 12, 1818
Armistead, John, Mar. 28, Plymouth. R. R. Apr. 24, 1818
Babb, Simeon, Aug. 13, Wake county. R. R. Aug. 14, 1818
Baker, Blake, Nov. 12, Moore county. R. R. Nov. 20, 1818
Baker, Blake of Warren county, Oct. 11, Moore county. R. R. Nov. 13, 1818
Barbee, Mrs. Mary, Jan. 25, Chatham county. R. R. Mar. 6, 1818
Bateman, Capt. John, Apr. 26, Edenton. R. R. May 8, 1818
Blackman, Col. William, Oct. 24, Sampson county. R. R. Dec. 4, 1818
Blake, Henry, Oct. 16, Fayetteville. R. R. Nov. 13, 1818
Blount, Mrs. John G., Oct. 6, Washington, Beaufort county. R. R. Oct. 16, 1818
Campbell, Alex, Feb. 13, Fayetteville. R. R. Feb. 27, 1818
Carmichael, Mrs. Priscilla, Mar. 30, Surry county. R. R. Apr. 17, 1818
Chambers, Mrs. Wm., Sr., Jly. 7, Person county. R. R. Jly. 24, 1818
Cherry, Solomon, Apr. 24, Bertie county. R. R. May 8, 1818
Cook, Richard L. of Baltimore, Apr. 25, Raleigh. R. R. May 1, 1818
Crawford, Mrs. Elizabeth, Oct. 5, Stokes county. R. R. Oct. 23, 1818
Crawford, Lazarus of Wayne county, May 28, Murfreesboro, Tenn. R. R. Je. 26, 1818
Creecy, Maj. Nathan, May 21, Chowan county. R. R. Je. 5, 1818
Crocker, Ezekiel L., Sept. 8, Warrenton. R. R. Sept. 18, 1818
Davis, Dolphin, Nov. 8, Fayetteville. R. R. Nov. 20, 1818
Davison, Robert, Dec., Washington, Beaufort county. R. R. Dec. 4, 1818
Dobbin, Thomas M. of Fayetteville, Sept., Person county. R. R. Oct. 2, 1818
Drew, John, Jr., Mar. 8, Halifax. R. R. Mar. 20, 1818
Dobbin, Mrs. John M. of Person county, Jan. 21, Fayetteville. R. R. Jan. 30, 1818
Dunn, Mrs. Nahum, Oct. 16, Raleigh. R. R. Oct. 23, 1818
Falconer, Alexander, Mar. 17, Franklin. R. R. Mar. 27, 1818
Falconer, Dr. Thomas, Mar. 26, Raleigh. R. R. Mar. 27, 1818
Fisher, Jonathan, Apr. 14, Newbern. R. R. Apr. 17, 1818
Fisher, Capt. Michael, Apr. 20, Newbern. R. R. Apr. 27, 1818
Forbes, Mrs. Penelope, Feb. 26, Newbern. R. R. Mar. 13, 1818
Fowler, Joseph of Raleigh, Sept. 2, Wake county. R. R. Sept. 4, 1818
Franks, Mrs. Wesley, Aug. 5, Raleigh. R. R. Aug. 7, 1818
Gaven, Mrs. James, Mar. 2, Washington, Beaufort county. R. R. Mar. 13, 1818
Gee, John W., May 1, Cumberland county. R. R. May 22, 1818
Gleeson, Mathew, Oct. 6, Washington, Beaufort county. R. R. Oct. 16, 1818
Gober, John, Jly., Franklin county. R. R. Jly. 31, 1818
Gorman, James of Ireland, Sept., Raleigh. R. R. Sept. 4, 1818
Graves, Mrs. Barzillai, Apr., Caswell county. R. R. Apr. 17, 1818
Gray, Mrs. Wm. Lee, Jly. 13, Windsor. R. R. Aug. 14, 1818
Hall, Elizabeth Brown, May 19, Brunswick county. R. R. May 20, 1818
Hall, Mrs. William P., Sept. 17, Caswell county. R. R. Sept. 18, 1818
Hauser, George, Nov. 3, Stokes county. R. R. Nov. 20, 1818
Hill, Col. Thomas, Jly. 27, Pittsboro. R. R. Aug. 21, 1818
Hinton, Major John, Oct., Wake county. R. R. Oct. 23, 1818

Hoskins, William, Apr., Chowan county. R. R. May 1, 1818
Houser, Geo., Nov. 2, Bethania. R. R. Nov. 13, 1818
Houze, Mrs. Green D., Nov. 4, Franklin. R. R. Nov. 20, 1818
Hudgins, Dr. Wm. of this State, Sept. 16, New Orleans. R. R. Mar. 13, 1818
Hule, Samuel, Apr. 11, Concord. R. R. Apr. 24, 1818
Hunter, Major, M'Gillivry B., Jan., Washington, Beaufort county. R. R. Jan. 30, 1818
Inge, Mrs. Evelina Belmont, Je. 27, Louisburg. R. R. Jly. 3, 1818
Irwin, Gen. Jared of Mecklenburg county, Washington county, Ga., Mar. R. R. Mar. 20, 1818
Johnson, Mrs. Esther, Oct. 30, Newbern. R. R. Nov. 13, 1818
Johnson, Mrs. James, Oct. 9, Greensboro. R. R. Nov. 6, 1818
Johnson, Martha of Warren county, Aug. 6, Granville county. R. R. Aug. 14, 1818
Johnson, William, Dec., Bertie county. R. R. Dec. 18, 1818
Jones, Jacob, Sr., Apr. 8, Franklin county. R. R. Apr. 17, 1818
Keais, Mrs. William, Mar. 3, Washington, Beaufort county. R. R. Mar. 13, 1818
Kennedy, Mrs. William, Apr. 2, Washington, Beaufort county. R. R. May 29, 1818
Lane, Mrs. James, Jly. 25, Wake county. R. R. Jly. 31, 1818
Latham, Mrs. James, Apr. 28, Beaufort county. R. R. May 8, 1818
Lavender, Mrs. Wm. L., Jan., Washington, Beaufort county. R. R. Jan. 30, 1818
Lewine, Judge Samuel L., Dec. 22, Mecklenburg county. R. R. Jan. 9, 1818
Lilly, Mr., Feb., Washington, Beaufort county (115 years of age). R. R. Feb. 27, 1818
Lindsay, Robert, Oct. 27, Greensborough. R. R. Nov. 13, 1818
Locke, Col. Robert, Feb. 9, Salisbury. R. R. Mar. 20, 1818
M'Guire, Hugh of Ireland and this State, May 30, Wadesborough. R. R. Je. 19, 1818
M'Kinnie, John, Feb. 26, Raleigh. R. R. Feb. 27, 1818
M'Lean, John, Feb. 8, Cumberland county. R. R. Feb. 27, 1818
Maer, Wm., Oct. 29, Bertie county. R. R. Nov. 20, 1818
Martin, Rotheas, Feb. 26, Hyde county. R. R. Mar. 13, 1818
Maun, William, Aug. 18, Raleigh. R. R. Aug. 21, 1818
Miller, Mrs. Wm. of this State, Mar., Virginia. R. R. Mar. 13, 1818
Morgan, William P., Apr., Murfreesborough. R. R. Apr. 24, 1818
Moore, Duncan of New Hanover, Je., Warrenton. R. R. Je. 12, 1818
Mumford, Henreitta, Sept. 15, Fayetteville. R. R. Sept. 18, 1818
Mumford, Hetty Jane, May 17, Fayetteville. R. R. May 29, 1818
Murchison, Alexander of Scotland, Feb. 13, Fayetteville. R. R. Feb. 27, 1818
Nicholson, George, Je. 5, Warren county. R. R. Je. 12, 1818
Newberry, Isaac, Mar. 5, Cumberland county. R. R. Mar. 27, 1818
Norfleet, Marmaduke, Je., Halifax county. R. R. Je. 12, 1818
Pearson, Mrs. Jos. of Rowan county, Mar. 29, Washington, D. C. R. R. Apr. 10, 1818
Powers, John of Ireland, Sept. 23, Raleigh. R. R. Sept. 25, 1818
Richards, George, Jly. 26, Franklin county. R. R. Jly. 31, 1818

Riddick, Gen. Joseph, Oct., Gates county. R. R. Oct. 9, 1818

Roberts, Mrs. John M., Jly. 26, Newbern. R. R. Aug. 14, 1818

Russell, Alexander, Sept. 13, Orange county. R. R. Sept. 25, 1818

Sampson, Mrs. Michael of Sampson county, Feb., New Hanover county. R. R. Mar. 13, 1818

Scourlock, Mrs. Joseph, Jly. 5, Chatham county. R. R. Jly. 24, 1818

Selby, Mrs. John, Feb. 23, Hyde county. R. R. Mar. 13, 1818

Shephard, Hannah, Aug. 2, Lake Phelps. R. R. Aug. 14, 1818

Sherrod, Col. Thomas, Jly. 20, Franklin county. R. R. Jly. 31, 1818

Shober, Nathaniel, Je. 14, Stokes county. R. R. Je. 26, 1818

Sills, Mrs. D., Nov. 1st, Nash county. R. R. Nov. 20, 1818

Sparkman, Mrs. William, Sept. 7, Bertie county. R. R. Sept. 25, 1818

Stone, David, Oct. 7, Hope on Neuse River. R. R. Oct. 9, 1818

Sutherland, Solomon A. of Wake county, Jly. 28, Bladen Springs. R. R. Aug. 14, 1818

Swann, Samuel, Oct. 23, Wilmington. R. R. Dec. 4, 1818

Tabb, Mrs. Diana, Jan. 19, Franklin county. R. R. Jan. 30, 1818

Tate, Col. William, Mar. 13, Burke county. R. R. Mar. 27, 1818

Taylor, James M., Oct. 12, Fayetteville. R. R. Oct. 23, 1818

Thompson, Eliza of Bertie county, Sept. 7, Louisburg. R. R. Sept. 18, 1818

Torrance, Mrs. James G., Nov. 11, Mecklenburg county. R. R. Dec. 4, 1818

Van Ness, Gen. David, Oct. 9, Troy. R. R. Oct. 23, 1818

Walker, Hampton of Delaware, Apr., Chowan county. R. R. May 1, 1818

Wells, Thomas of Murfreesborough, Aug. 8, Winton. R. R. Aug. 21, 1818

Whitehurst, Robert, Mar. 9, Carteret county. R. R. Mar. 27, 1818

Whitfield, Mrs. Sarah, Oct. 26, Newbern. R. R. Nov. 13, 1818

Wiggins, Samuel, Apr. 18, Washington county. R. R. May 8, 1818

Williams, Jos. John of Halifax county, May. R. R. May 8, 1818

Williams, Mrs. John P. of New Hanover county, Jly. 28. R. R. Jly. 31, 1818

Williams, Mathew Jewett of Ga., Aug. 14, Surry county. R. R. Aug. 28, 1818

Willis, Major Plummer of Warren county, Dec., Tennessee. R. R. Dec. 18, 1818

Wilson, Capt. James, May 17, Bertie county. R. R. Je. 5, 1818

Wingate, Maj. Isaac, Mar. 24, Craven county. R. R. Apr. 17, 1818

Yancey, Mrs. Ann, Oct., Camden county. R. R. Oct. 16, 1818

1819

Adam, Mrs. John R., Aug. 19, Fayetteville. R. R. Sept. 10, 1819

Alston, Mrs. Thomas P., May 23, Halifax county. R. R. Je. 4, 1819

Alston, Col. Willis, Oct. 31, Halifax county. R. R. Nov. 19, 1819

Ashburn, Baldy of Bertie county, Dec. 3, Windsor. R. R. Jan. 1, 1819

Ashe, Maj. Samuel, Nov. 14, New Hanover county. R. R. Dec. 3, 1819

Atterbury, Job., Aug. 16, Wilmington. R. R. Aug. 27, 1819

Balfour, Mrs. E., June, Salisbury. R. R. Jly. 2, 1819

Bateman, Daniel, Apr. 19, Washington county. R. R. May 7, 1819

Benners, Lucas J., May 27, Newbern. R. R. June 11, 1819

Bigelow, Capt. Jacob, Aug. 23, Newbern. R. R. Sept. 10, 1819

Blount, William, Apr. 6, Chowan county. R. R. Apr. 23, 1819

Boon, Wm. A. of Raleigh, Feb., Windsor. R. R. Feb. 5, 1819

Brandon, Matthew, Sept. 9, Rowan county. R. R. Sept. 24, 1819

DEATH NOTICES   155

Brandon, Mrs. Matthew. Feb. 3, Rowan county. R. R. Mar. 5, 1819
Brehon, Dr. James C. of Ireland, Apr. 8, Warrenton. R. R. Apr. 16, 1819
Brown, Mrs. John, Dec. 30, Wilmington. R. R. Jan. 8. 1819
Brown, Dr. Thos. S. R., Sept. 12, Smithfield. R. R. Sept. 17, 1819
Bryant, Mrs. Wm., Oct. 19, Newbern. R. R. Nov. 5, 1819
Buie, Duncan of Scotland, Oct. 10, Cumberland county. R. R. Nov. 5, 1819
Bunch, Cullen, Dec. 12, Chowan county. R. R. Jan. 1, 1819
Bunch, Mrs. of Bertie county, Dec. 10. R. R. Dec. 24, 1819
Buxton, Samuel, May 26, Long Creek. R. R. June 11, 1819
Cabarrus, Augustus of France, Jly., Chowan county. R. R. Aug. 6, 1819
Christopher, Mrs. Christopher, Sept. 8, Raleigh. R. R. Sept. 10, 1819
Collins, Josiah, Sr., May 14, Edenton. R. R. May 28, 1819
Congleton, John, Dec., Washington, Beaufort county. R. R. Dec. 3, 1819
Conro, John of Connecticut, Oct. 16, Fayetteville. R. R. Oct. 29, 1819
Craig, Abraham, Dec. 30, Chapel Hill. R. R. Jan. 8, 1819
Davidson, Margaret Lee, Feb. 16, Iredell county. R. R. Mar. 12, 1819
Dickinson, Mrs. Elizabeth, Jly. 23, Edenton. R. R. Aug. 6, 1819
Dilliard, Joseph, Je. 7, Wake county. R. R. Je. 11, 1819
Dobson, Mrs. Martha, Nov. 24, Stokes county. R. R. Dec. 17, 1819
Dodd, Abraham, Jan. 22, Raleigh. R. R. Jan. 29, 1819
Doty, Lemuel, Jan. 8, Onslow county. R. R. Jan. 22, 1819
Drew, John, Jly. 26, Bertie county. R. R. Aug. 13, 1819
Duer, Levin, Nov., Winton. R. R. Nov. 26, 1819
Edwards, Ryal, Nov., Chocowinity. R. R. Dec. 3, 1819
Edmunds, Capt. William, Apr. 20, Northampton county. R. R. May 21, 1819
Faires, John, Feb. 3, Raleigh. R. R. Feb. 5, 1819
Falkener, W. A., Mar. 29, Warrenton. R. R. Apr. 2, 1819
Falkener, Mrs. Wm., Sr., Feb. 24, Warrenton. R. R. Mar. 26, 1819
Falkener, William, Dec., Warrenton. R. R. Dec. 10, 1819
Forster, Dr. Isaac, Jan. 21, Murfreesborough. R. R. Mar. 5, 1819
Fuller, Allen of Franklin county, Aug. 27, Johnston county. R. R. Sept. 3, 1819
Gaston, Mrs. William, Jan., Newbern. R. R. Jan. 29, 1819
Gloster, Dr. Thomas, Jan. 12, Warrenton. R. R. Jan. 15, 1819
Gordon, Jacob, Jly. 20, Gates county. R. R. Aug. 6, 1819
Gragson, Mrs. Eli, Sept. 23, Raleigh. R. R. Sept. 24, 1819
Green, William, May 27, Duplin county. R. R. Je. 11, 1819
Gresham, Major Davis, Mar. 11, Orange county. R. R. Apr. 9, 1819
Guion, Mrs. John W., Dec. 12, Newbern. R. R. Jan. 15, 1819
Harris, Nehemiah, Aug. 28, Wilmington. R. R. Sept. 10, 1819
Hamilton, Gen. John of Guilford county, Jan. 25, West Tennessee. R. R. Apr. 23, 1819
Harvey, Capt. Allen, Nov. 13, Franklin county. R. R. Nov. 26, 1819
Harris, Harvie of Lewisburg, Mar., Norfolk. R. R. Apr. 2, 1819
Harrison, Abner of Jones county, Dec. 3, Newbern. R. R. Dec. 24, 1819
Hawes, Sarah, Dec. 22, Wilmington. R. R. Jan. 1, 1819
Hawkins, William of this State, May 17, Sparta, Georgia. R. R. May 28, 1819
Henry, Mrs. Lewis D. of Fayetteville, Feb. 16, Raleigh. R. R. Feb. 19, 1819

Hines, Mrs. Richard, Sept. 1, Beaufort county. R. R. Sept. 10, 1819
Hoell, Elias, Dec. 23, Washington, Beaufort county. R. R. Jan. 8, 1819
Holt, Lewis, Jly. 11, Orange county. R. R. Jly. 30, 1819
Houston, Capt. James of Ireland, Aug. 2, Iredell county. R. R. Aug. 27, 1819
Hoyle, Jackson S. of England, Je., Ocracock Bar. R. R. Je. 11, 1819
Hunter, Capt. Anderson, Oct., Wake county. R. R. Oct. 29, 1819
Hunter, A. T. W., Dec. 19, Halifax county. R. R. Dec. 24, 1819
Jeter, Caleb of Virginia, Aug. 4, Raleigh. R. R. Aug. 6, 1819
Johnson, Marmaduke, Apr. 1, Warrenton. R. R. Apr. 9, 1819
Jones, Hardy of Surry and Rowan counties, Je. 21. R. R. Jly. 16, 1819
Jones, Maurice, Nov. 7, Hyde county. R. R. Dec. 3, 1819
Kenan, Mrs. Jas., Mar. 22, Duplin county. R. R. Apr. 2, 1819
Kirk, Mrs. William of Iredell county, Aug. R. R. Aug. 27, 1819
Lawrence, Wm., Oct. 23, Newbern. R. R. Nov. 5, 1819
Leith, Archibald, Dec., Edenton. R. R. Dec. 17, 1819
Lewis, Eldad of Connecticut, Oct. 21, Raleigh. R. R. Oct. 29, 1819
Lobre, Peter, Nov. 18, Wilmington. R. R. Dec. 3, 1819
Loftin, Mrs., Aug. 22, Newbern. R. R. Sept. 10, 1819
Long, Colonel Nicholas, Aug. 22, Halifax county. R. R. Sept. 10, 1819
McDonald, Mrs. Parthena, Aug. 29, Beaufort county. R. R. Sept. 10, 1819
M'Ilhenny, Elizabeth, Sept. 1, Wilmington. R. R. Sept. 10, 1819
M'Intosh, John of Fayetteville, Oct. 14, Moore county. R. R. Oct. 29, 1819
M'Kethen, Alexander, Oct. 1, Raleigh. R. R. Oct. 8, 1819
M'Kinlay, James, Feb. 11, Newbern. R. R. Feb. 12, 1819
M'Kinnan, Gilbert of Scotland, Oct. 26, Wilmington. R. R. Nov. 5, 1819
M'Leod, Samuel, Aug. 22, Fayetteville. R. R. Sept. 10, 1819
M'Lin, John J., Je. 14, Newbern. R. R. Jly. 2, 1819
MacRacken, Robert, May 15, Fayetteville. R. R. Je. 4, 1819
Martin, Wm., May, Moore county. R. R. May 7, 1819
Mebane, Mrs. John B., Jly. 22, Chatham county. R. R. Aug. 6, 1819
Menzies, John of Scotland, Mar., Rockingham county. R. R. Apr. 2, 1819
Michaux, Mrs. Richard, Nov. 20, Rockingham county. R. R. Dec. 3, 1819
Middleton, Mrs. Robert, Oct. 22, Duplin county. R. R. Nov. 5, 1819
Milam, Zachariah, Aug. 29, Warren county. R. R. Sept. 3, 1819
Millington, Robert of Connecticut, Oct. 7, Lumberton. R. R. Oct. 29, 1819
Mitchell, Solomon, Dec. 30, Chapel Hill. R. R. Jan. 8, 1819
Moore, William P. Nov. 15, Newbern. R. R. Dec. 3, 1819
Mumford, Mrs. Bryan, Dec. 3, Newbern. R. R. Dec. 24, 1819
Mumford, George of Salisbury, Dec. 31, Washington, D. C. R. R. Jan. 8, 1819
Nash, Caleb, Jan. 23, Chowan county. R. R. Feb. 5, 1819
Neale, Christopher, Sept., Beaufort county. R. R. Sept. 10, 1819
Nelson, Mrs. Isaac, May 2, Stokes county. R. R. Je. 11, 1819
Newel, Francis, Nov. 1, Cabarrus county. R. R. Dec. 10, 1819
Nichols, Capt. George, Oct. 5, Raleigh. R. R. Oct. 8, 1819
Nunnery, Mrs. Carter, Apr. 5, Warrenton. R. R. Apr. 9, 1819
Outlaw, Edward C., Nov. 13, Bertie county. R. R. Dec. 3, 1819
Pearson, Col. Richard, Sr. of Virginia, Aug. 6, Rowan county. R. R. Aug. 27, 1819
Pemberton, William, Feb., Richmond county. R. R. Feb. 5, 1819

Phifer, George, Jan. 23, Cabarrus county. R. R. Feb. 5, 1819
Putney, Dr. Anthony W., Dec. 1, Windsor. R. R. Dec. 24, 1819
Rainey, William of Caswell county, Jly. 12, Tennessee. R. R. Sept. 17, 1819
Rodwell, Brown, Mar. 22, Warren county. R. R. Apr. 2, 1819
Sanders, Alsey, Sept. 27, Chatham county. R. R. Oct. 8, 1819
Scott, Jehu, Oct. 21, Raleigh. R. R. Oct. 22, 1819
Shephard, William, Je. 13, Newbern. R. R. Jly. 2, 1819
Sims, Mrs. Adam, Jan. 20, Wake county. R. R. Jan. 22, 1819
Skiles, Wm., Nov. 15, Bertie county. R. R. Dec. 3, 1819
Snow, John, Mar., Warren county. R. R. Mar. 19, 1819
Souse, John of Ireland, Aug. 27, Newbern. R. R. Sept. 3, 1819
Spencer, John, Jan. 27, Hyde county. R. R. Apr. 2, 1819
Spivey, Moses, Feb., Bertie county. R. R. Feb. 19, 1819
Stark, Mrs. O. P., Oct. 25, Fayetteville. R. R. Nov. 5, 1819
Storm, John, Nov., Robeson county. R. R. Nov. 26, 1819
Sugg, Joshua, Sr., Nov. 9, Wake county. R. R. Nov. 19, 1819
Sugg, Moses, Nov., Wake county. R. R. Nov. 19, 1819
Sutton, Capt. Eph., Aug. 29, Wilmington. R. R. Sept. 10, 1819
Summer, Thomas E. of Warren county, July 21. R. R. Aug. 20, 1819
Taylor, Thomas, Feb. 15, Bertie county. R. R. Mar. 5, 1819
Thompson, Mrs. James W., Aug. 23, Newbern. R. R. Sept. 10, 1819
Thompson, John, Dec., Orange county. R. R. Dec. 10, 1819
Vail, Mrs. Mary, Oct. 18, Newbern. R. R. Nov. 5, 1819
Walters, James, Aug. 30, Halifax. R. R. Sept. 3, 1819
Wayne, Wm., Dec., Hillsborough. R. R. Dec. 24, 1819
West, John S., Jan., Newbern. R. R. Jan. 15, 1819
White, Col. J. B., Dec. 1, Columbus county. R. R. Dec. 3, 1819
Wilder, Mrs. Richard, Jan. 20, Chowan county. R. R. Feb. 5, 1819
Wilkinson, Mrs. Rebecca of Wilmington, May 31. R. R. Je. 11, 1819
Williams, Charity, Maria, Mary Dawson, Kearney, Jly., Martin county.
   R. R. Jly. 16, 1819
Williamson, Hugh of this State, May 22, New York. R. R. Je. 4, 1819
Ziegler, Wm. of Mass., Aug. 20, Wilmington. R. R. Aug. 27, 1819

1820

Alton, Maj. Joseph of this State, Mar. 9, South Carolina. R. R. Mar. 17, 1820
Adkins, Mrs. James M., Jly. 12, Raleigh. R. R. Jly. 14, 1820
Armistead, Mrs. Stark, Oct. 17, Bertie county. R. R. Nov. 3, 1820
Beaman, John, Aug. 30, Sampson county. R. R. Oct. 6, 1820
Beard, Lewis, Dec. 11, Salisbury. R. R. Dec. 29, 1820
Beard, William, Oct. 30, Fayetteville. R. R. Nov. 3, 1820
Blackledge, Richard of Newbern, Nov. 17, Beaufort county. R. R. Dec. 1, 1820
Blount, Mrs. Edmund of Perquimons county, Oct. 1, Elizabeth city. R. R. Oct. 20, 1820
Borden, Dr. Levi, Dec. 8, Duplin county. R. R. Dec. 22, 1820
Broadfoot, Mrs. Andrew, Sept. 26, Fayetteville. R. R. Oct. 13, 1820
Bowen, Thomas of Maryland, Jan. 20, Beaufort county. R. R. Feb. 11, 1820
Bozman, Dr. George of Edenton, Jly. 26, Windsor. R. R. Aug. 11, 1820

Caffey, John, Nov. 17, Rockingham county. R. R. Dec. 1, 1820
Campbell, Mrs. James, Dec. 2, Leaksville. R. R. Jan. 28, 1820
Carney, Mrs. John, My. 19, Fayetteville. R. R. My. 26, 1820
Caudle, Mrs. Blutcher, Oct. 12, Haywood, Chatham county. R. R. Oct. 20, 1820
Chase, Pardon of Rhode Island, Sept., Fayetteville. R. R. Sept. 29, 1820
Child, Wilson, My. 29, Orange county. R. R. Je. 9, 1820
Chisholm, Angus, Sept. 10, Fayetteville. R. R. Sept. 15, 1820
Christmas, Jane Y., Jan. 16, Warrenton. R. R. Feb. 4, 1820
Coles, Isaac, Sept. 29, Halifax county. R. R. Oct. 20, 1820
Craig, A., Jr., Aug. 30, Chapel Hill. R. R. Sept. 8, 1820
Creecy, Frederick, Jly. 26, Chowan county. R. R. Aug. 11, 1820
Davie, Gen. William R., Nov., Ladnsford on Catawba. R. R. Dec. 1, 1820
David, Mrs. Dolphin, Jan. 4, Fayetteville. R. R. Jan. 14, 1820
Davis, Dr. Willie Jones, Feb. 6, Fayetteville. R. R. Feb. 18, 1820
Dick, Thos., Dec., Guilford county. R. R. Dec. 29, 1820
Dick, William, Nov. 7, Wilmington. R. R. Nov. 17, 1820
Dickson, Alex'r C., Mar., On Board Ship. R. R. Apr. 21, 1820
Dickson, Col. William of Pennsylvania. Jly., Duplin county. R. R. Jly. 14, 1820
Dobbins, Elizabeth C. of Fayetteville, Oct. 31, Person county. R. R. Nov. 17, 1820
Douglas, James, Oct. 12, Anson county. R. R. Oct. 20, 1820
Eddy, Mrs. Jacob of Fayetteville, Oct., Sampson county. R. R. Oct. 13, 1820
Edwards, Mrs. Ann, Sept. 2, Surry county. R. R. Sept. 29, 1820
Farmer, Mrs. Jas., Jan. 15, Johnston county. R. R. Feb. 4, 1820
Fessenden, Benjamin of Massachusetts, Oct. 19, Plymouth. R. R. Nov. 3, 1820
Flinn, Rev. Andrew of Raleigh, Mar., Charleston, S. C. R. R. Mar. 10, 1820
Forster, Rev. Anthony of South Carolina, Jan. 18, Raleigh. R. R. Jan. 21, 1820
Fowler, Henry, Dec. 20, Raleigh. R. R. Dec. 22, 1820
Fraser, John H., Jly. 29, Hertford county. R. R. Aug. 26, 1820
Frederick, Betsey, Aug. 21, Duplin county. R. R. Sept. 1, 1820
Galloway, John of Rockingham county, Apr. 26, Hillsborough. R. R. My. 5, 1820
Gilmore, Tho's., Jly. 7, Cumberland county. R. R. Jly. 14,-1820
Gibson, J. R., Oct. 28, Fayetteville. R. R. Nov. 3, 1820
Glasgow, Col. James of this State, Feb., Tennessee. R. R. Feb. 25, 1820
Good, Wm., Sept. 26, Newbern. R. R. Oct. 13, 1820
Gould, Capt. Joseph of Maine, Sept. 24, Newbern. R. R. Oct. 13, 1820
Graham, Neill, Sept. 10, Fayetteville. R. R. Sept. 15, 1820
Granberry, John, Nov. 23, Gates county. R. R. Dec. 8, 1820
Gray, Mrs. Alexander, Apr. 22, Randolph county. R. R. My. 5, 1820
Guthrie, Dr. John W., Jly. 17, Washington, Beaufort county. R. R. Aug. 4, 1820
Hackett, Thos. of Ireland, Oct. 30, Fayetteville. R. R. Nov. 17, 1820
Hanrahan, Mrs. Walter, Sept. 11, Washington, Beaufort county. R. R. Sept. 22, 1820
Hare, William B., Jan. 31, Granville county. R. R. Feb. 18, 1820

Harrell, David, My. 20, Bertie county. R. R. Je. 9, 1820
Harrell, Joseph, Oct. 16, Gates county. R. R. Nov. 10, 1820
Harrison, Anderson, Sept. 6, Wake county. R. R. Sept. 15, 1820
Harrison, Mrs. Anderson, Sept., Wake county. R. R. Sept. 15, 1820
Harrison, Mrs. Wm., Mar. 20, Franklin county. R. R. Mar. 31, 1820
Hartsfield, James, Mar. 18, Wake county. R. R. Mar. 31, 1820
Harvey, William S., Sept. 11, Newbern. R. R. Sept. 22, 1820
Hatch, Mrs. Lemuel of Jones county, Oct. 9, Duplin county. R. R. Nov. 10, 1820
Hill, Dr. James B. of Raleigh, Oct. 25, South Carolina. R. R. Nov. 10, 1820
Hinton, Mrs. John, My. 21, Wake county. R. R. My. 26, 1820
Horton, Wm., Sr., Nov. 23, Chatham county. R. R. Jan. 7, 1820
Hybert, Mrs. Mary, Oct. 24, Fayetteville. R. R. Nov. 3, 1820
Jackson, Philip W., Oct. 29, Milton. R. R. Nov. 10, 1820
Jeffers, James, Apr. 28, Hillsborough. R. R. My. 5, 1820
Jeffreys, Tho's., Feb. 9, Caswell county. R. R. Feb. 25, 1820
Langley, James W. of Edenton, Oct. 18. Pasquotank county. R. R. Nov. 3, 1820
Lanier, Capt. Benjamin A., Oct. 6, Camden county. R. R. Oct. 20, 1820
Latham, Jesse, Jan., Hyde county. R. R. Jan. 14, 1820
Lee, William, Jly. 8, Fayetteville. R. R. Jly. 14, 1820
Lockhart, W., Dec. 16, Hillsborough. R. R. Dec. 29, 1820
Lowther, Mrs. Tristram, Feb. 6, Edenton. R. R. Feb. 18, 1820
Lucas, Alexander of Pa., Dec. 21, Raleigh. R. R. Dec. 22, 1820
M'Allister, Ann J., Mar. 28, Cumberland county. R. R. Apr. 28, 1820
M'Donald, John, Feb., Pasquotank county. R. R. Feb. 18, 1820
M'Guire, Samuel, Jan. 22, Chowan county. R. R. Feb. 18, 1820
M'Intosh, John of Fayetteville, Jly. 15, Montgomery county. R. R. Jly. 21, 1820
M'Lean, Hugh, Apr. 5, Moore county. R. R. Apr. 28, 1820
M'Lean, Hugh, Jly. 23, Cumberland county. R. R. Aug. 18, 1820
M'Millan, John, Oct., Fayetteville. R. R. Oct. 13, 1820
M'Millan, John, Oct., Bladen county. R. R. Dec. 8, 1820
M'Rae, John of Cumberland county, Jly. 10, Fayetteville. R. R. Jly. 14, 1820
Marsh, James S., Je. 29, Pittsborough. R. R. Jly. 7, 1820
Marsh, Wm., Jr., Sept. 3, Chatham county. R. R. Sept. 8, 1820
Marshall, John, Feb. 12, Raleigh. R. R. Feb. 18, 1820
Mears, James, Sr., Oct. 7, Raleigh. R. R. Oct. 13, 1820
Mears, Mrs. James, Sr., Jan. 13, Raleigh. R. R. Jan. 21, 1820
Mebane, John B., Sept. 8, Chatham county. R. R. Oct. 6, 1820
Montgomery, Michael, Jan. 5, Caswell county. R. R. Feb. 4, 1820
Moore, Council, Sept. 6, Wake county. R. R. Sept. 15, 1820
Morris, Mrs. A., Je. 2, Sampson county. R. R. Je. 16, 1820
Mumford, Margaret, Je. 5, Fayetteville. R. R. Je. 16, 1820
Norfleet, William, Dec., Northampton county. R. R. Dec. 22, 1820
Peace, Mrs. John, Dec. 2, Granville county. R. R. Dec. 15, 1820
Pearce, Nathan, My. 7, Fayetteville. R. R. My. 12, 1820
Pernal, John, Aug. 30, Cumberland county. R. R. Sept. 8, 1820
Pernal, Mary, Aug. 31, Cumberland county. R. R. Sept. 8, 1820

Peterson, Malcom, Feb. 6, Sampson county. R. R. Feb. 18, 1820

Potter, John, Mar., Granville county. R. R. Mar. 31, 1820

Power, Stephen, My. 21, Warren county. R. R. Je. 30, 1820

Pulliam, Mrs. Benj., Sept. 9, Raleigh. R. R. Sept. 15, 1820

Ransom, Seymour, Sept., Warren county. R. R. Sept. 8, 1820

Read, Rev. Jesse, Je. 6, Halifax county. R. R. Je. 16, 1820

Rhea, Mrs. Andrew, Apr. 6, Williamsborough. R. R. Apr. 14, 1820

Rhodes, Gen. Joseph T., My. 23, Duplin county. R. R. Je. 9, 1820

Ridgely, Dr. Joshua N., Little river, Mar. 23, Havanna. R. R. Apr. 7, 1820

Ridley, Dr. James D., Aug. 16, Wake county. R. R. Sept. 8, 1820

Robeson, Rev. Archibald, Aug. 20, Onslow county. R. R. Sept. 8, 1820

Rogers, Mrs. Michael, Oct. 29, Wake county. R. R. Nov. 3, 1820

Satterwhite, Edwin T. of this State, Mar. 7, Washington, D. C. R. R. Mar. 17, 1820

Sawyer, Elizabeth of Bertie county, Nov. 10, Orange county. R. R. Nov. 24, 1820

Sawyer, Malachi, Oct. 6, Camden county. R. R. Oct. 20, 1820

Seawell, Mrs. Joseph, Sept., Moore county. R. R. Sept. 22, 1820

Shaw, Henry, Sr., Nov. 6, Beaufort county. R. R. Dec. 1, 1820

Shine, Col. J., Feb. 4, Jones county. R. R. Feb. 25, 1820

Shine, Mrs. Winifred, Feb. 6, Jones county. R. R. Feb. 25, 1820

Simms, William, My.,—Wake county. R. R. My. 12, 1820

Slocumb, Jesse of Craven county, Dec. 20, Washington, D. C. R. R. Dec. 29, 1820

Smith, Dr. John C. of Oxford, Sept. 13, Halifax. R. R. Sept. 22, 1820

Stone, Wm., Aug. 22, Montgomery county. R. R. Sept. 15, 1820

Streety, Wm., Nov. 30, Bladen county. R. R. Dec. 8, 1820

Strode, John of Virginia, Sept. 27, Cumberland county. R. R. Oct. 13, 1820

Swann, Mrs. Penelope, Mar. 3, Chowan county. R. R. Mar. 17, 1820

Taillade, Col. Louis Francois of France, Apr., Washington, Beaufort county. R. R. My. 5, 1820

Terrel, Joel, Feb., Nash county. R. R. Feb. 11, 1820

Thompson, Charles, Aug. 4, Chatham county. R. R. Aug. 18, 1820

Thompson, Hezekiah, My., Bertie county. R. R. Je. 9, 1820

Tull, John, Sept. 19, Lenoir county. R. R. Oct. 27, 1820

Tooshee, Joseph, Jly. 17, Chatham county. R. R. Aug. 4, 1820

Veale, Richard, My. 20, Bertie county. R. R. Je. 9, 1820

Wallis, Rev. James, Dec. 27, Mecklenburg county. R. R. Feb. 11, 1820

Westbrook, William, Sept. 10, Fayetteville. R. R. Oct. 13, 1820

White, Sam'l., Aug. 31, Cabarrus county. R. R. Sept. 29, 1820

Whitted, Willing T. of Orange county, Aug. 5, Mount Willing. R. R. Aug. 18, 1820

Willis, Mrs. Plummer of this State, Feb., Tennessee. R. R. Feb. 11, 1820

Wilson, Hugh, Aug. 13, Fort Johnson. R. R. Sept. 8, 1820

Winslow, John, Nov. 29, Fayetteville. R. R. Dec. 8, 1820

Wright, Mrs. Charles J., Nov. 2, Wilmington. R. R. Nov. 10, 1820

Wynn, Parham, Dec. 18, Chapel Hill. R. R. Jan. 7, 1820

Yancey, George W. of Raleigh, Feb. 19, Petersburg. R. R. Mar. 3, 1820

1821

Allen, Burton, Mar. 23, Craven county. R. R. Apr. 6, 1821
Allen, John, Feb. 27, Raleigh. R. R. Mar. 2, 1821
Allen, John, Nov. 15, Wilmington. R. R. Nov. 30, 1821
Allen, Mrs. J., Sept. 18, Wilmington. R. R. Sept. 28, 1821
Ashe, Richard D., Je. 5, Wilmington. R. R. Je. 15, 1821
Atkinson, Gen. Richard, Dec. 3, Person county. R. R. Dec. 14, 1821
Avery, Col. Waighstill, Mar. 15, Burke county. R. R. Apr. 27, 1821
Bacon, Capt. of this State, Aug. 12, Georgetown, S. C. R. R. Aug. 31, 1821
Badger, Mrs. Susannah, Jan. 31, Newbern. R. R. Feb. 16, 1821
Baker, Mrs. Thos. of Bertie county, Jan. 17, Plymouth. R. R. Feb. 2, 1821
Barnes, Sam'l Thomas, Oct. 5, Scotland Neck. R. R. Oct. 26, 1821
Bedell, James of Newbern & New York, Dec. 12. R. R. Dec. 28, 1821
Bell, Capt. William, Oct. 22, Randolph county. R. R. Nov. 9, 1821
Bishop, Joseph, Aug. 12, Wilmington. R. R. Aug. 24, 1821
Blount, Mrs. Thomas H., Dec. 21, Washington, Beaufort county. R. R.
    Jan. 5, 1821
Borden, Mrs. Benjamin, Jan. 3, Craven county. R. R. Jan. 19, 1821
Bowers, Alfred, Aug. 11, Wilmington. R. R. Aug. 24, 1821
Brazier, Charles Henry, Sept. 11, Hillsborough. R. R. Sept. 21, 1821
Brownrigg, George, Feb. 12, Edgecombe county. R. R. Feb. 23, 1821
Bryan, Mrs. Mary Ann, Dec. 4, Newbern. R. R. Dec. 21, 1821
Buie, Archibald of Fayetteville, Jly. 22, Lumberton. R. R. Sept. 7, 1821
Bullock, Leonard of Warren county, Sept., Chapel Hill. R. R. Sept. 14,
    1821
Burns, Nancy of New Hanover county, Apr. 17, Moore's creek. R. R. My.
    4, 1821
Butler, Anthony, Dec. 18, Elizabeth City. R. R. Jan. 5, 1821
Calhorda, Mrs. John P., Sept. 18, Wilmington. R. R. Sept. 28, 1821
Cash, Holden Wade, Oct. 21, Wadesboro. R. R. Nov. 16, 1821
Christmas, Mary L., Jly. 18, Warrenton. R. R. Jly. 27, 1821
Cobb, Mrs. Thomas of Raleigh, Oct., Virginia. R. R. Oct. 19, 1821
Cochran, Addison of Person county, Dec. 29, Wilmington. R. R. Jan. 5,
    1821
Cole, Mrs. Ann, Sept. 25, Wilmington. R. R. Oct. 5, 1821
Collins, Mrs. Cader of Wake county, Oct. 24, Raleigh. R. R. Oct. 26, 1821
Conyers, Hannah, Sept. 16, Wilmington. R. R. Sept. 14, 1821
Davis, Archibald, Feb. 21, Franklin county. R. R. Mar. 9, 1821
Davis, Mrs. Jane, Sept. 30, Wilmington. R. R. Oct. 12, 1821
Davis, Mrs. John of Warren county, Jly. 11, Mecklenburg county, Va.
    R. R. Jly. 20, 1821
Davis, Mrs. Sukey, Apr., Wake county. R. R. Apr. 27, 1821
Dick, Mrs. Wm., Jly. 31, Wilmington. R. R. Sept. 7, 1821
Dickson, Mrs. Jas. of Wilmington, Sept. 28, Smithville. R. R. Oct. 12,
    1821
Douglas, Achilles D. of Albemarle county, Va., Sept. 6, Rowan county.
    R. R. Sept. 21, 1821
Eccles, Robert, Jly. 16, Fayetteville. R. R. Jly. 27, 1821
Evans, Mrs. John, Mar. 3, Granville county. R. R. Mar. 23, 1821
Everitt, Mrs. Celia, Sept. 1, Wilmington. R. R. Sept. 14, 1821
Faddis, John, Jr., Sept. 27, Hillsborough. R. R. Oct. 12, 1821

Felton, General Boon, Oct. 24, Hertford county. R. R. Nov. 2, 1821
Freeland, Francis, Nov. 13, Wilmington. R. R. Nov. 30, 1821
Gambold, Mrs. J., Feb. 19, Springplace, Cherokee county. R. R. Apr. 13, 1821
Gardner, Samuel A., Aug. 7, Wilmington. R. R. Aug. 17, 1821
Gewin, Mrs., Oct. 4, Wilmington. R. R. Oct. 12, 1821
Gibson, Mrs. David, Feb. 27, Randolph county. R. R. Mar. 30, 1821
Goodwin, Samuel, Je. 2, Raleigh. R. R. Je. 8, 1821
Graham, Dr. Chauncey, Dec. 19, Lenoir county. R. R. Jan. 12, 1821
Graves, Mrs. Lewis of this State, Aug. 26, Augusta, Ga. R. R. Oct. 19, 1821
Griffith, Augustus, Aug. 10, Wilmington. R. R. Aug. 17, 1821
Griffith, David W., Aug. 7, Wilmington. R. R. Aug. 17, 1821
Gurley, A. H., Oct. 19, Fayetteville. R. R. Oct. 26, 1821
Hall, Mrs. R. of Halifax, Je. 26, Caswell county. R. R. Jly. 6, 1821
Hardy, Benjamin, My. 30, Bertie county. R. R. Je. 15, 1821
Hare, Dr. John, Apr., Williamsborough. R. R. Apr. 20, 1821
Harris, Mr., Apr., Wake county. R. R. Apr. 27, 1821
Harris, Mrs. Peter, Jr., Sept. 5, Wilmington. R. R. Sept. 14, 1821
Harris, Mrs. Peter, Sr., Sept. 26, Wilmington. R. R. Oct. 5, 1821
Hartsfield, John, Apr., Wake county. R. R. Apr. 27, 1821
Hatch, Edmund, Feb. 10, Craven county. R. R. Feb. 16, 1821
Haynes, Francis L., Jly. 13, Robeson county. R. R. Jly. 27, 1821
Hays, Richard of Wake county, Jly. 1, Caswell county. R. R. Jly. 20, 1821
Haywood, Mrs. John, Jr., Je., Franklin county. R. R. Je. 29, 1821
Henderson, Thomas, Nov. 15, Rockingham county. R. R. Nov. 23, 1821
Hill, Mrs. Mary of Pa., Aug. 28, Iredell county. R. R. Sept. 21, 1821
Hinton, Dr. Robert of Raleigh, Oct., Halifax. R. R. Oct. 19, 1821
Hooper, George, Je. 19, Wilmington. R. R. Je. 29, 1821
Hoskins, Mrs. Thomas, Feb. 21, Tyrrell county. R. R. Mar. 16, 1821
Hutchins, Col., Nov., Hertford county. R. R. Nov. 16, 1821
Ingle, Archibald, Oct. 3, Wilmington. R. R. Oct. 12, 1821
Jackson, Mr., Apr., Wake county. R. R. Apr. 27, 1821
Jacobs, Isaac, Sept. 7, Wilmington. R. R. Sept. 14, 1821
Jenkins, Charles, Sept. 30, Wilmington. R. R. Oct. 12, 1821
Jones, Mrs. David, Jly. 28, Wilmington. R. R. Aug. 17, 1821
Jones, Moses, Feb., Raleigh. R. R. Mar. 2, 1821
Johnson, James, My. 28, Halifax. R. R. Je. 8, 1821
Johnson, Jane, Jly., Warren county. R. R. Jly. 20, 1821
Johnston, James, My. 28, Halifax. R. R. Je. 8, 1821
Keys, Dr. James H. of Ireland, Dec., Warren county. R. R. Dec. 14, 1821
Knight, Mrs. Miles, Jly. 29, Wilmington. R. R. Sept. 7, 1821
Lash, Jacob of Stokes county, Oct. 8, Fayetteville. R. R. Oct. 19, 1821
Latham, Alexander, Nov. 5, Beaufort county. R. R. Nov. 16, 1821
Lawson, Mrs. Eliza, Mar. 7, Duplin county. R. R. My. 4, 1821
Lea, Jeremiah of Milton, Sept. 11, Fredericksburg, Va. R. R. Sept. 28, 1821
Lee, Eliza, Oct. 11, Wilmington. R. R. Oct. 19, 1821
Lewis, Warner H. of Richmond, Va., Feb. 25, Raleigh. R. R. Mar. 2, 1821
Long, Col. Nicholas, Nov. 21, Halifax. R. R. Dec. 7, 1821
Love, Rev. James, Mar. 15, Cabarrus county. R. R. My. 4, 1821

Mackey, James W. of Scotland, Sept. 10, Plymouth. R. R. Sept. 28, 1821
M'Cauley, Mathew, Sept. 6, Orange county. R. R. Sept. 14, 1821
M'Donald, William, Aug. 10, Washington, Beaufort county. R. R. Aug. 17, 1821
M'Gimsey, Col. John of this State, Sept. 11, West Tennessee. R. R. Oct. 19, 1821
M'Ilhenny, Mrs. James, Aug. 12, Wilmington. R. R. Aug. 24, 1821
M'Kethan, Mary, Nov. 12, Raleigh. R. R. Nov. 16, 1821
May, Daniel, Mar. 11, Orange county. R. R. My. 4, 1821
Meng, Wm., Aug. 13, Fayetteville. R. R. Aug. 24, 1821
Miller, W. B., Jly. 2, Wilmington. R. R. Jly. 13, 1821
Mitchell, Mrs. James, Jan. 7, Raleigh. R. R. Jan. 12, 1821
Montgomery, Dr. R. of Winton, Hertford county, Feb. 17. R. R. Mar. 16, 1821
Mordecai, Mrs. Moses, Dec. 11, Wake county. R. R. Dec. 14, 1821
Morgan, G. L. of Carteret county, Oct., Beaufort. R. R. Oct. 26, 1821
Morrison, Mrs. Margaret, Jly. 25, Brunswick county. R. R. Sept. 7, 1821
Moss, Howell, Oct., Raleigh. R. R. Oct. 19, 1821
Murphy, Hugh, Aug. 15, Wilmington. R. R. Aug. 24, 1821
Murphy, John, Sept. 26, Wilmington. R. R. Oct. 5, 1821
Murphy, June, Sept. 26, Wilmington. R. R. Aug. 24, 1821
Murphy, Miles, Mar. 18, Rockingham county. R. R. Apr. 6, 1821
Murphy, Mrs. Patrick, Sept. 25, Wilmington. R. R. Oct. 5, 1821
Myatt, Capt. Mark, Oct. 25, Wake county. R. R. Oct. 26, 1821
Ogilby, Mrs. Richard, Je. 11, Milton. R. R. Jly. 6, 1821
O'Kelly, Wm., Dec. 24, Chatham county. R. R. Jan. 5, 1821
O'Neal, Daniel, Jly. 30, Wilmington. R. R. Sept. 7, 1821
Parsley, Capt. Robert, Feb. 22, Raleigh. R. R. Mar. 30, 1821
Pasteur, Mrs. Edward, My. 10, Farmville. R. R. My. 25, 1821
Peabody, Mrs., Oct. 7, Wilmington. R. R. Oct. 19, 1821
Peace, Capt. John, Apr. 16, Granville county. R. R. Apr. 20, 1821
Pearce, Slade, My. 17, Beautort county. R. R. Je. 1, 1821
Pickens, Capt. Samuel, Je. 8, Cabarrus county. R. R. Je. 29, 1821
Pinkham, Maj. Nathaniel, Jan., Carteret county. R. R. Jan. 26, 1821
Plummer, Junius, Mar. 21, Warrenton. R. R. Mar. 30, 1821
Price, David of Philadelphia, Aug. 31, Fayetteville. R. R. Sept. 14, 1821
Priestly, Dr. James, Feb. 6, Nashville. R. R. Mar. 2, 1821
Prince, Wm., Dec. 23, Chatham county. R. R. Jan. 12, 1821
Pugh, Eaton, Nov. 30, Northampton county. R. R. Dec. 14, 1821
Ragsdale, Jones, Jly. 6, Wake county. R. R. Jly. 13, 1821
Ramsey, John A., Oct. 11, Chatham county. R. R. Oct. 26, 1821
Read, George, My. 19, Beaufort, Carteret county. R. R. Je. 15, 1821
Reid, Capt. John, Feb. 28, Catawba Springs, Lincoln county. R. R. Mar. 9, 1821
Rhodes, Mrs. John, Apr., Wake county. R. R. Apr. 27, 1821
Ripley, Mrs. Joseph, Jr., Oct. 12, On the sound. R. R. Oct. 19, 1821
Robeson, Edward, Sept. 2, Wilmington. R. R. Sept. 14, 1821
Robinson, Edward, Sept. 24, Wilmington. R. R. Oct. 5, 1821
Robinson, Master Howard, Sept. 24, Wilmington. R. R. Oct. 5, 1821
Robinson, Oliver, Pearce, Jan. 15, Fayetteville. R. R. Jan. 26, 1821

Rodman, Mrs. W. W., Aug., Washington, Beaufort county. R. R. Sept. 7, 1821

Ruffin, Mrs. Thomas of Smithfield, Sept. 28, Raleigh. R. R. Oct. 12, 1821

Russell, Mrs. Richard, Dec., Warren county. R. R. Dec. 14, 1821

Sanders, Mrs. R. M. of Caswell county, Oct. 9, Person county. R. R. Oct. 19, 1821

Sanders, Mrs. Rachail of Virginia, Feb. 24, Wake county. R. R. Mar. 2, 1821

Scott, Col. James, Jly. 31, Caswell county. R. R. Aug. 17, 1821

Scurlock, Wm., Sept. 21, Pittsborough. R. R. Sept. 28, 1821

Seawell, Col. Benj., Jly. 16, Wilson county. R. R. Aug. 24, 1821

Shaw, Colin, Jly. 6, Mecklenburg county, Va. R. R. Jly. 20, 1821

Shaw, Mrs. David, Aug. 8, Raleigh. R. R. Aug. 10, 1821

Slade, Henry B. of Martin county, Jly., Alabama. R. R. Jly. 20, 1821

Slade, Henry, Jr., Dec., Martin county. R. R. Jan. 5, 1821

Smith, Mrs. Benjamin, Nov. 21, Brunswick county. R. R. Dec. 7, 1821

Smith, Robert R., Nov. 4, Scotland Neck. R. R. Dec. 7, 1821

Sneed, Stephen, Mar., Williamsborough. R. R. Mar. 23, 1821

Stanly, Mary, Oct. 1, Wilmington. R. R. Oct. 12, 1821

Taliaferro, Col. Benjamin, Sept. 3, Wilkes county. R. R. Sept. 28, 1821

Taylor, John A., Oct. 6, On the sound. R. R. Oct. 19, 1821

Thurber, Kingsly, Sept. 11, Wilmington. R. R. Sept. 21, 1821

Travis, David, Aug. 11, Wilmington. R. R. Aug. 24, 1821

Tumen, David, Sept. 6, Wilmington. R. R. Sept. 14, 1821

Turner, Wm., Aug., Wake county. R. R. Aug. 31, 1821

Turner, Mrs. Wm., Oct. 25, Wake county. R. R. Oct. 26, 1821

Varnum, Silas, Sept. 18, Wilmington. R. R. Sept. 28, 1821

Wallace, Mrs. David of this State, Sept. 21, Portsmouth. R. R. Oct. 26, 1821

Whitaker, Dudley, Sept. 21, Scotland Neck. R. R. Oct. 12, 1821

Whitaker, Mrs. Samuel, Dec. 9, Wake county. R. R. Dec. 14, 1821

Whitesides, Mrs. Henrietta Ann of Raleigh, Dec. 14, Morganton. R. R. Feb. 9, 1821

Whitted, Wm., Nov. 3, Hillsborough. R. R. Nov. 16, 1821

Williams, Robert of Raleigh, My. 27, Tennessee. R. R. Je. 15, 1821

Wilson, Mrs. Thos., Apr., Orange county. R. R. Apr. 27, 1821

Wilson, Thos., Apr. 5, Orange county. R. R. Apr. 27, 1821

Wingate, Mrs. Mary, Sept. 23, Wilmington. R. R. Oct. 5, 1821

Wingate, Wm., Apr. 27, Wilmington. R. R. My. 11, 1821

Wood, James, Sr. of Hertford, Oct. 7, Tyrrell county. R. R. Oct. 26, 1821

Wright, Charles J., Oct. 24, New Hanover county. R. R. Nov. 2, 1821

Wyles, Selby H., Nov. 19, Jones county. R. R. Dec. 14, 1821

Yancey, Lieut. Lewis, Jly. 2, Raleigh. R. R. Jly. 6, 1821

Yeargan, Amelia Patterson, Oct. 18, Smithfield, Johnston county. R. R. Oct. 26, 1821

Zevely, Mrs. V. N., Nov. 20, Salem. R. R. Nov. 30, 1821

1822

Adkins, James, Sept., Cumberland county. R. R. Sept. 20, 1822

Anderson, William B., My. 31, Wilmington. R. R. Je. 7, 1822

Badger, Frances, Oct. 6, Warren county. R. R. Oct. 11, 1822

Baird, Mrs. William of Virginia, My. 24, Person county. R. R. Je. 7, 1822

Ball, Daniel, Nov. 18, Warren county. R. R. Dec. 13, 1822
Bell, Col. Brickhouse, Feb. 28, Camden county. R. R. Mar. 8, 1822
Bell, James of Pitt county, Jan. 26, Alabama. R. R. Mar. 8, 1822
Blount, Col. Edmond, Oct. 17, Washington county. R. R. Nov. 1, 1822
Blount, Mrs. Thomas, Dec. 13, Tarborough. R. R. Dec. 20, 1822
Bow, Mrs. David, Aug. 15, Fayetteville. R. R. Aug. 30, 1822
Brandon, Col. John, Jan. 22, Rowan county. R. R. Feb. 15, 1822
Briggs, John J. of this State, Jly. 30, Mississippi. R. R. Sept. 13, 1822
Brown, George, Aug. 2, Raleigh. R. R. Aug. 9, 1822
Brown, Mrs. John, Sept. 29, Raleigh. Oct. 4, 1822
Burch, Capt. Joseph, Feb. 21, Wilmington. R. R. Mar. 1, 1822
Burges, Mrs. Mary, Dec. 3, Raleigh. R. R. Dec. 6, 1822
Caldeleugh, Andrew, Je., Rowan county. R. R. Je. 28, 1822
Caldwell, Henry T. of S. C., Jly. 29, Warrenton. R. R. Aug. 2, 1822
Carrigan, Rev. John, Apr. 9, Rowan county. R. R. My. 17, 1822
Chase, George W., Feb. 3, Newbern. R. R. Feb. 22, 1822
Clarke, Mrs. Wm., Sept. 1, Raleigh. R. R. Sept. 6, 1822
Clay, Jas. N. of Granville county, Oct. 6, Virginia. R. R. Oct. 25, 1822
Cochran, Robert, Apr. 28, Cabarrus county. R. R. My. 24, 1822
Creath, Rev. Wm. of Virginia, Aug. 11, Edenton. R. R. Aug. 23, 1822
Crudup, Mrs. Josiah, Mar. 27, Wake county. R. R. Mar. 29, 1822
Daves, Major John, Apr. 11, Newbern. R. R. Apr. 26, 1822
Daves, Mrs. John, Apr. 11, Newbern. R. R. Apr. 26, 1822
Davis, Mrs. Joshua, Apr. 10, Warren county. R. R. Apr. 26, 1822
Davis, Peter, Jr., Oct., Warren county. R. R. Oct. 11, 1822
Davis, Richard, Apr. 9, Tyrrell county. R. R. Apr. 26, 1822
Davis, General Thomas, Sept. 25, Fayetteville. R. R. Oct. 4, 1822
Dick, John W. of Guilford county, Jly. 13, Caswell county. R. R. Jly. 26,
    1822
Dickinson, Gen. J. F. of Hertford, Je. 6, Murfreesborough. R. R. Je. 28,
    1822
Dickson, John, Apr. 8, Cumberland county. R. R. Apr. 19, 1822
Dickson, Mrs. John, Dec. 1, Cumberland county. R. R. Dec. 13, 1822
Dilliard, Mrs. Joseph, Aug. 19, Wake county. R. R. Aug. 30, 1822
Duskins, Mrs. William, Dec. 15, Wake county. R. R. Dec. 20, 1822
Edwards, William, Jan. 12, Wayne county. R. R. Feb. 1, 1822
Evans, Theophilus, Mar. 16, Cumberland county. R. R. Mar. 29, 1822
Faires, Mrs. John, Mar. 16, Raleigh. R. R. Mar. 22, 1822
Fontaine, John D. of Virginia, Feb. 17, Orange county. R. R. Mar. 1, 1822
Forbes, Mrs. Stephen B., Feb. 16, Newbern. R. R. Mar. 8, 1822
Foy, Mrs. James, Oct. 31, Onslow county. R. R. Dec. 13, 1822
Foy, Maj. James, Nov. 11, Onslow county. R. R. Dec. 13, 1822
Frohock, Alexander of Rowan county, Dec. 3, Salisbury. R. R. Dec. 27,
    1822
Gales, Ann Eliza, Sept. 22, Raleigh. R. R. Sept. 27, 1822
Geren, Mrs. Abraham, Nov. 3, Greensborough. R. R. Nov. 15, 1822
Gillett, Mrs. Bezaleel, Nov. 1, Raleigh. R. R. Nov. 8, 1822
Glisson, Mrs. Daniel, Jr., Oct. 28, Duplin county. R. R. Nov. 22, 1822
Grady, Clarissa, Mar., Duplin county. R. R. Mar. 15, 1822
Gregson, Mrs. Eli, Nov. 6, Raleigh. R. R. Nov. 8, 1822
Greene, Elizabeth, Aug. 12, Warren county. R. R. Aug. 16, 1822

Gufford, Mrs., Oct. 25, Cumberland county. R. R. Nov. 22, 1822

Gwyn, Richard R., Jly. 8, Wilkesboro. R. R. Jly. 19, 1822

Harden, Mrs. Mark, Oct. 20, Rockingham county. R. R. Nov. 1, 1822

Harker, Mr. of Fayetteville, Sept. 20, Raleigh. R. R. Sept. 27, 1822

Hassam, John H. of New Hampshire, Aug. 23, Raleigh. R. R. Aug. 30, 1822

Hatch, Mrs. Durant, Feb. 5, Newbern. R. R. Feb. 22, 1822

Hansley, William, Je., Brunswick county. R. R. Je. 14, 1822

Hawkins, Mrs. Philemon of Louisburg, Nov. 21, Warren county. R. R. Nov. 29, 1822

Hellen, Bryan, Oct. 24, Beaufort. R. R. Nov. 15, 1822

Henderson, Archibald, Oct., Salisbury. R. R. Nov. 1, 1822

Hines, John B. of Raleigh, Sept. 14, Georgia. R. R. Sept. 27, 1822

Hollister, Giles, Feb. 3, Newbern. R. R. Feb. 22, 1822

Hoskins, Richard, Dec., Chowan county. R. R. Dec. 13, 1822

Howard, Josiah, Jly. 21, Newbern. R. R. Aug. 9, 1822

Hunt, Mrs. Eunice, Sept. 9, Newbern. R. R. Sept. 27, 1822

Hunter, Alexander of this State, Dec. 26, Milledgeville. R. R. Jan. 11, 1822

Hutchins, Moses, Jly., Wake county. R. R. Aug. 2, 1822

Inge, Maj. Philip H. of Milton, Sept. 12, Tennessee. R. R. Sept. 27, 1822

Jenkins, Dempsey, Apr. 12, Edgecombe county. R. R. Apr. 26, 1822

Jones, Andes, Je., Nash county. R. R. Je. 21, 1822

Jones, Mrs. Edward, My. 5, Newbern. R. R. My. 10, 1822

Kane, Robt. of Raleigh & Ireland, Jly. 4, Wilmington. R. R. Jly. 12, 1822

King, Rev. Robert S. of Orange county, Apr. 6, Person county. R. R. My. 17, 1822

Knox, Mrs. Mary, Apr. 19, Newbern. R. R. My. 17, 1822

Lawrence, Mrs. Peter B., Apr. 3, Tarborough. R. R. Apr. 26, 1822

Leffers, Samuel, Sr., Oct. 8, Carteret county. R. R. Nov. 1, 1822

Littlejohn, Mrs. Thomas B., Feb. 19, Oxford. R. R. Mar. 1, 1822

Lloyd, Mrs. Joseph R. of Martin county, Nov. 28, Tarborough. R. R. Dec. 6, 1822

Lord, John B., Oct. 9, Wilmington. R. R. Oct. 18, 1822

Lord, Mrs. Wm., Dec. 3, Cumberland county. R. R. Dec. 13, 1822

Loss, Charles, Je. 10, Cabarrus county. R. R. Aug. 9, 1822

MacLean, Arch'd of Scotland, My. 4, Cumberland county. R. R. My. 24, 1822

M'Allester, Alexander, Nov. 7, Sampson county. R. R. Nov. 22, 1822

M'Dermot, Mrs., Oct. 19, Edenton. R. R. Nov. 1, 1822

M'Innis, Duncan, Nov. 2, Bladen county. R. R. Nov. 15, 1822

M'Kinnie, Gen'l Barnabas of Wayne county, Apr., Augusta, Ga. R. R. My. 3, 1822

M'Nair, Rev. Malcolm, Aug. 4, Robeson county. R. R. Aug. 23, 1822

McPheeters, Susan, Jan. 18, Raleigh. R. R. Jan. 25, 1822

M'Rorie, Lieut. David of Wayne county, Oct. 19, On Board Ship. R. R. Dec. 13, 1822

Manning, Mrs. John, Feb. 19, Franklin county. R. R. Feb. 22, 1822

Martin, Robert, Je. 1, Rockingham Court House. R. R. Jly. 4, 1822

Mason, James, Oct. 11, Wilmington. R. R. Oct. 18, 1822

Medley, Reuben, Oct., Anson county. R. R. Oct. 4, 1822

Mills, Mrs. Ambrose, My. 28, Rutherford county. R. R. Je. 28, 1822
Mitchell, Hutchins B., Oct. 29, Halifax county. R. R. Nov. 15, 1822
Mobley, Wilie, Sept. 13, Sampson county. R. R. Oct. 4, 1822
Moring, Henry, Apr. 15, Wake county. R. R. Apr. 19, 1822
Murphey, Col. Alex, Apr. 12, Caswell county. R. R. My. 3, 1822
Norfleet, Abraham, Mar. 5, Chowan county. R. R. Mar. 29, 1822
Paisley, Francis M., Aug. 11, Greensborough. R. R. Oct. 4, 1822
Paisley, Harriet M., Aug. 24, Greensborough. R. R. Oct. 4, 1822
Parish, Mrs. Elizabeth, Aug. 15, Wake county. R. R. Aug. 30, 1822
Parker, Mrs. Green, Apr. 22, Newbern. R. R. My. 10, 1822
Parkes, Geo. of Wilkesborough, Oct. 9, Baltimore. R. R. Nov. 1, 1822
Pearson, Mrs. Mary, Jan. 28, Wake county. R. R. Feb. 8, 1822
Pound, Thomas, Apr., Rockingham county. R. R. My. 3, 1822
Price, Jonathan, My. 23, Newbern. R. R. Je. 7, 1822
Pulliam, Capt. Joseph, Jly. 29, Person county. R. R. Aug. 23, 1822
Read, Washington of this State, My. 11, Georgia. R. R. Je. 7, 1822
Reeks, Dr. James, Jly. 2, Chatham county. R. R. Jly. 4, 1822
Rhymes, Jesse, Jan. 24, Halifax county. R. R. Feb. 8, 1822
Rice, John, Mar., Raleigh. R. R. Mar. 8, 1822
Riggan, Benjamin of Warren county, My. 13, Greensboro. R. R. My. 24, 1822
Richardson, Rev. Samuel N., Mar. 19, Bladen county. R. R. Apr. 5, 1822
Richardson, Valentine, Feb. 18, Craven county. R. R. Mar. 8, 1822
Riddle, Capt. John, Dec. 17, Chatham county. R. R. Jan. 4, 1822
Rogers, Mrs. Samuel, Sept. 10, Fayetteville. R. R. Sept. 20, 1822
Ruffin, Sterling, My., Rockingham county. R. R. My. 3, 1822
Ruffin, Dr. William Haywood, Sept. 29, Raleigh. R. R. Oct. 4, 1822
Ruffin, Dr. Thomas P. of Smithfield, Aug. 31, Raleigh. R. R. Sept. 6, 1822
Ruth, Mrs. David, Jr. of Raleigh, Nov. 6, Fayetteville. R. R. Nov. 15, 1822
Ruth, Mrs. David, Nov. 29, Raleigh. R. R. Dec. 6, 1822
Sawyer, Frederick B., Mar. 7, Pasquotank county. R. R. Mar. 29, 1822
Scott, Green B., Je. 11, Smithfield, Johnston county. R. R. Je. 21, 1822
Shaw, John, Jly. 27, Pasquotank county. R. R. Aug. 9, 1822
Shepperd, Jesse B. of Va., Jly. 30, Fayetteville. R. R. Aug. 9, 1822
Shepperd, Col. William, Feb. 1, Orange county. R. R. Feb. 15, 1822
Siler, John, Apr., Chatham county. R. R. Apr. 19, 1822
Sitgreaves, Mrs. J., Sept. 14, Newbern. R. R. Sept. 27, 1822
Smith, Absilla, Jan. 24, Tarborough. R. R. Feb. 8, 1822
Smith, Mrs. Sion, Jly. 31, Wake county. R. R. Aug. 2, 1822
Spight, Mrs. Mary, Oct., Jones county. R. R. Nov. 1, 1822
Spivey, Aaron, Nov. 12, Bertie county. R. R. Dec. 6, 1822
Stevens, Major Abraham, Oct. 5, Fayetteville. R. R. Oct. 25, 1822
Strong, John of Connecticut, Apr. 19, Jones county. R. R. My. 17, 1822
Stuart, Jas., Jan., Richmond county. R. R. Jan. 25, 1822
Taylor, J. L. of Chatham county, Mar., Louisiana. R. R. Mar. 29, 1822
Tucker, Elizabeth B., Apr. 3, Wake county. R. R. Apr. 12, 1822
Turner, Elizabeth, My. 17, Plymouth. R. R. My. 31, 1822
Vaden, George, Mar. 13, Halifax. R. R. Mar. 22, 1822
Walker, Mrs. Julius H., Dec. 17, Wilmington. R. R. Jan. 4, 1822
Watkins, Maj. Isaac, Jly. 6, Nash county. R. R. Jly. 26, 1822

Watt, Mrs. Hugh of Rockingham county, Sept. 17, Jones county, Ga.
R. R. Oct. 18, 1822

Webb, Martha, Oct. 19, Raleigh. R. R. Oct. 25, 1822

West, John Spemce, Oct. 14, Newbern. R. R. Oct. 25, 1822

Whitaker, Mrs. Thomas G., Jan. 25, Wake county. R. R. Feb. 1, 1822

Williams, Mrs. Joseph, Feb. 7, Surry county. R. R. Apr. 5, 1822

Williams, Robert W., Nov., Franklin county. R. R. Nov. 22, 1822

Wynns, Mrs. Thomas, Jan. 5, Hertford county. R. R. Jan. 18, 1822

Young, Mrs. John W., Oct. 14, Raleigh. R. R. Oct. 18, 1822

Young, Capt. John, Nov. 1, Hillsborough. R. R. Nov. 15, 1822

1823

Albright, Mrs. Jacob, Je. 15, Rowan county. R. R. Jly. 4, 1823

Allison, Col. Richard, Je. 14, Statesville. R. R. Jly. 4, 1823

Alston, Mrs. Thos. of Warren county, Feb. 8, Wake county. R. R. Feb. 14, 1823

Alston, Mrs. Willis, Mar. 23, Edenton. R. R. Apr. 4, 1823

Amis, William, Oct., Northampton county. R. R. Oct. 31, 1823

Andrew, Mrs. Drury O., Dec. 4, Warren county. R. R. Dec. 26, 1823

Barclay, George, Sept. 13, Raleigh. R. R. Sept. 26, 1823

Beall, Mrs. Rebecca, Nov. 2, Iredell county. R. R. Dec. 12, 1823

Beasley, Robert, Dec. 24, Chowan county. R. R. Jan. 10, 1823

Beebe, John E., Aug. 11, Fayetteville. R. R. Aug. 22, 1823

Blount, Dr. Frederick, Sept. 5, Newbern. R. R. Sept. 26, 1823

Blount, Joseph of Bertie county, Sept. 1, Oxford. R. R. Sept. 5, 1823

Brame, Mrs. S. C. of Raleigh, Sept. 12, Petersburg. R. R. Sept. 19, 1823

Brickell, Col. Thomas, Jan. 18, Windsor, Bertie county. R. R. Jan. 24, 1823

Bridges, Mrs. Horace D., Sept. 28, Chatham county. R. R. Oct. 10, 1823

Brown, Neal, Oct. 1, Raleigh. R. R. Oct. 3, 1823

Brown, Peterson, Aug. 8, Northampton county. R. R. Sept. 12, 1823

Burgwin, Mrs. John F., Mar. 16, Newbern. R. R. My. 2, 1823

Burns, Alvis, Apr. 24, Chatham county. R. R. My. 9, 1823

Burt, Harriet D., Sept. 21, Warren county. R. R. Oct. 10, 1823

Burt, Wm., Jly. 8, Warren county. R. R. Jly. 19, 1823

Cain, Mrs. William, My. 8, Orange county. R. R. My. 25, 1823

Cheeke, Mrs. Thomas L., Jan. 13, Newbern. R. R. Jan. 24, 1823

Childs, Francis of Orange county, Feb., Tennessee. R. R. Mar. 7, 1823

Christopher, Christopher, Oct. 13, Raleigh. R. R. Oct. 17, 1823

Clack, Eldridge, Sept. 20, Warren county. R. R. Oct. 3, 1823

Cobbs, Harriet, Jly. 16, Raleigh. R. R. Jly 19, 1823

Coleman, John, Aug. 14, Warrenton. R. R. Aug. 22, 1823

Cress, Daniel of Pennsylvania and this State, Mar. 5, Salisbury. R. R. Mar. 21, 1823

Cushing, Charles, Dec. 15, Washington, Beaufort county. R. R. Jan. 3, 1823

Deloach, B., Feb. 13, Raleigh. R. R. Feb. 14, 1823

Downing, Stevens, Je. 22, Washington, Beau ort county. R. R. Jly. 4, 1823

Dozier, Mrs. Frances, Sept. 11, Camden coun'y. R. R. Aug. 15, 1823

Drake, John D., Sept. 29, Warrenton. R. R. Oct. 3, 1823

Duke, Daniel, Sept., Gates county. R R. Sept. 26, 1823

Easton, Mrs. James, Dec. 3, Pitt county. R R. Dec. 12, 1823

Elliott, Capt. Henry, Sept. 29, Chowan county. R. R. Aug. 15, 1823
Ellis, Mrs. Ezekial, Jly. 1, Wake county. R. R. Jly. 4, 1823
Evans, Thomas, Feb., Cumberland county. R. R. Feb. 21, 1823
Exum, Matthew of Northampton county, Apr. 29, Georgia. R. R. My. 2,
1823
Fenner, Dr. Richard H. of Louisburg, Nov. 18, Raleigh. R. R. Nov. 21,
1823
Forest, John F. of Raleigh, Mar. 23, Alabama. R. R. Apr. 11, 1823
Foushee, Almond, Apr. 29, Chatham county. R. R. My. 9, 1823
Foy, Mrs. Frederick, My. 2, Jones county. R. R. My. 25, 1823
Franklin, Governor Jesse, Sept. 29, Surry county. R. R. Oct. 3, 1823
Franklin, Major Jesse, Sept., Surry county. R. R. Sept. 26, 1823
Freer, John, Apr. 15, Newbern. R. R. My. 2, 1823
Frew, Archibald, Apr. 15, Charlotte. R. R. My. 16, 1823
Gibson, Thos., My., Raleigh. R. R. My. 25, 1823
Goodman, Mrs. Christian, Mar. 5, Salisbury. R. R. Mar. 21, 1823
Gould, Emmerson, Sept. 1, Currituck Courthouse. R. R. Sept. 26, 1823
Harrison, James, Aug., Northampton county. R. R. Aug. 22, 1823
Hattridge, Alexander of Scotland & Wilmington, Feb. 2, Wilmington.
R. R. Feb. 21, 1823
Haywood, Sarah Wood, Oct. 23, Raleigh. R. R. Oct. 31, 1823
Hinton, Thaddeus L., Jly. 14, Wake county. R. R. Jly. 19, 1823
Hinton, William, Sept., Bertie county. R. R. Sept. 12, 1823
Hogg, James, Feb. 1, Chapel Hill. R. R. Feb. 14, 1823
Holland, John, Je. 26, Washington, Beaufort county. R. R. Jly. 4, 1823
Howett, Mary, Mar. 19, Edenton. R. R. Apr. 4, 1823
Hunter, Isaac, Mar. 12, Wake county. R. R. Mar. 21, 1823
Jack, Capt. James of Pennsylvania and this State, Dec. 18, Georgia. R. R.
Jan. 17, 1823
Johnston, James, Je. 15, Sneedsboro. R. R. Jly. 4, 1823
Johnston, Robert, Apr. 29, Halifax. R. R. My. 25, 1823
Kennedy, John of Ireland & this State, Mar. 13, Fayetteville. R. R. Mar.
28, 1823
Kern, John, Sr., Oct. 20, Rowan county. R. R. Nov. 7, 1823
Kerr, Joseph of this State, Je. 25, South Carolina. R. R. Jly. 25, 1823
Lambeth, Mrs. Thomas, Je. 17, Chatham county. R. R. Jly. 4, 1823
Lane, Levin, My. 2, Jones county. R. R. My. 25, 1823
Lanier, Sampson, Jan. 31, Rockingham county. R. R. Feb. 21, 1823
Lanston, Mrs. John, Mar. 21, Edenton. R. R. Apr. 4, 1823
LeMay, Samuel of Virginia, Oct. 21, Raleigh. R. R. Oct. 24, 1823
Lewis, William, My. 4, Camden county. R. R. Je. 20, 1823
Ligon, William Henry, Sept. 8, Wake county. R. R. Sept. 12, 1823
Locke, Francis of Salisbury, Jan. 20, Rowan county. R. R. Jan. 31, 1823
London, William, Aug. 2, Wilmington. R. R. Aug. 15, 1823
Loring, Matilda Love Bond, Sept. 2, New Hanover county. R. R. Sept. 19,
1823
Lyon, Edmund P., Dec. 2, Stokes county. R. R. Jan. 10, 1823
M'Cauly, De. John, Oct. 12, Orange county . R. R. Oct. 31, 1823
M'Kay, William, Feb. 6, Wilmington. R. R. Feb. 21, 1823
M'Kee, Maj. James, Apr. 12, Raleigh. R. R. Apr. 18, 1823
Mackie, Capt. John, Jan., Currituck county. R. R. Jan. 24, 1823

Marshall, Mrs. John, Oct. 8, Raleigh. R. R. Oct. 10, 1823
Marshall, Joseph, Oct. 17, Warren county. R. R. Oct. 31, 1823
Marshall, Mrs. Mary, Mar. 16, Newbern. R. R. My. 2, 1823
Martin, Robert Edwin, Je. 26, Wilkes county. R. R. Aug. 29, 1823
Martin, Robert Gillespie of Granville county, Oct. 12, Georgia. R. R. Oct. 31, 1823
May, Mrs. John, Je. 18, Chatham county. R. R. Jly. 4, 1823
Meigs, Col. Return J., Jan. 28, Cherokee Agency. R. R. Feb. 28, 1823
Montgomery, John C., Dec. 9, Hertford. R. R. Jan. 3, 1823
Moore, Major Cornelius, Aug. 8, Northampton county. R. R. Sept. 12, 1823
Moses, Mrs. A. F., My. 23, Wayne county. R. R. Je. 6, 1823
Muse, W. T., Sept. 19, Pasquotank county. R. R. Aug. 9, 1823
Neilson, Robert, Jan. 19, Buncombe county. R. R. Feb. 7, 1823
Nichols, Mrs. Sarah, Apr. 8, Newbern. R. R. My. 2, 1823
Nicholson, Thomas James, Oct. 1, Halifax. R. R. Oct. 10, 1823
Park, Mrs. Robert, Aug., Warren county. R. R. Aug. 9, 1823
Pasteur, Col. Edward, Je., Newbern. R. R. Je. 27, 1823
Pearson, Gen. Jesse A., Mar. 1, Rowan county. R. R. Mar. 14, 1823
Phelan, Patrick of Ireland, Je. 22, Fayetteville. R. R. Jly. 4, 1823
Ragland, Mrs. Thos., Je. 10, Chatham county. R. R. Jly. 4, 1823
Rankin, Capt. Robert, Jly. 1, Wilmington. R. R. Jly. 11, 1823
Rea, Sampson, Aug. 26, Murfreesboro. R. R. Sept. 12, 1823
Riddick, Micajah, Sept., Gates county. R. R. Sept. 26, 1823
Ridley, Mrs. Francis, Oct. 29, Granville county. R. R. Nov. 14, 1823
Rogerson, Solomon, Jan., Perquimons county. R. R. Jan. 24, 1823
Ross, Capt. Alexander, Sept., Mecklenburg county. R. R. Sept. 12, 1823
St. Lawrence, Mrs. Elizabeth, Apr. 21, Chatham county. R. R. My. 9, 1823
Sawyer, Mary, Sept. 11, Edenton. R. R. Sept. 26, 1823
Smith, Capt. John, Oct. 25, Salisbury. R. R. Nov. 7, 1823
Smith, Nathan, Feb. 26, Newbern. R. R. Mar. 7, 1823
Spicer, Wm., Nov., Edgecombe county. R. R. Feb. 21, 1823
Squires, John, Aug. 23, Windsor. R. R. Sept. 12, 1823
Standin, Henderson I., Feb. 14, Edenton. R. R. Feb. 28, 1823
Steelman, Mrs. William, My. 11, Davidson county. R. R. Je. 6, 1823
Sutherland, Col. Ransom, Aug. 21, Wake county. R. R. Aug. 29, 1823
Tull, Isaac, Sept. 19, Lenoir. R. R. Oct. 24, 1823
Waddell, Mrs. Hugh, Dec. 25, Wilmington. R. R. Jan. 3, 1823
Warden, William, Feb. 1, Fayetteville. R. R. Feb. 14, 1823
Wells, Rev. Samuel, Aug. 21, Murfreesboro. R. R. Sept. 12, 1823
Whitaker, Mrs. Wilson C., Dec. 11, Halifax county. R. R. Jan. 3, 1823
Whitted, Mrs. William, Apr. 13, Hillsborough. R. R. My. 2, 1823
Wilder, Miles, Dec. 10. Chowan county. R. R. Jan. 3, 1823
Williams, Jacob, Oct. 12. Duplin county. R. R. Nov. 7, 1823
Williams, Mrs. William, Sept. 10, Warren county. R. R. Sept. 26, 1823
Williamson, Mrs. Rebecca. Dec. 25, Chowan county. R. R. Jan. 17, 1823
Wilson, Col. Willis, Dec. 28, Camden county. R. R. Jan. 24, 1823
Womack, Mrs. Green, Apr. 20, Pittsborough. R. R. My. 9, 1823
Wright, Mrs. J. W., Mar. 14. Fayetteville. R. R. Mar. 28, 1823

1824

Albertson, Aaron of Elizabeth city, Aug. 25, New Orleans. R. R. Oct. 1, 1824

Albertson, Samuel, Jan. 22, Duplin county. R. R. Feb. 13, 1824

Albright, Jacob, Jly. 3, Rowan county. R. R. Jly. 23, 1824

Alston, John, Sept., Halifax county. R. R. Sept. 10, 1824

Armistead, Richard of Edenton, Feb. 19, Philadelphia. R. R. Feb. 27, 1824

Badger, Mrs. George E., Je. 9, Raleigh. R. R. Je. 11, 1824

Bailey, Joseph, Apr. 8, Pasquotank county. R. R. My. 7, 1824

Baird, Robert F. of Burke county, Aug. 4, Chapel Hill. R. R. Aug. 13, 1824

Baird, Maj. Zebulon formerly of New Jersey, Mar. 10, Buncombe county. R. R. Mar. 26, 1824

Baldwin, Mrs. Jesse, Oct. 5, Guilford county. R. R. Nov. 5, 1824

Barnes, Rev. William of Raleigh, Feb. 10, Oxford. R. R. Feb. 27, 1824

Barnes, William of Raleigh, Feb., Oxford. R. R. Feb. 20, 1824

Barnes, Mrs. William, Je. 9, Oxford. R. R. Je. 18, 1824

Bell, Burwell, Mar. 15, Wake county. R. R. Mar. 19, 1824

Biles, Mrs. Charles, Sept. 8, Salisbury. R. R. Sept. 24, 1824

Bloom, Henry, Jan. 18, Salem. R. R. Feb. 20, 1824

Brickell, Mrs. Wm. of this State, Nov. 5, Tennessee. R. R. Dec. 3, 1824

Brooks, Terrell, Sr., Aug. 24, Chatham county. R. R. Sept. 3, 1824

Bullock, Mrs. Susanna, Aug. 13, Warren county. R. R. Aug. 27, 1824

Caldwell, David of Pennsylvania, Aug. 19, Guilford county. R. R. Sept. 3, 1824

Coleman, Dr. Littleton H., Je. 27, Warrenton. R. R. Jly. 2, 1824

Cooper, Ambrose Wilhite, Je. 17, Raleigh. R. R. Je. 18, 1824

Costen, Isaac, Apr. 9, Gates county. R. R. Apr. 30, 1824

Costen, Mrs. Isaac, Apr. 4, Gates county. R. R. Apr. 30, 1824

Covington, Winston W., Feb. 26, Rockingham, Richmond county. R. R. Mar. 19, 1824

Craig, Samuel, Oct. 20, Orange county. R. R. Nov. 5, 1824

Crump, Mrs. Jas. R., Sept. 15, Northampton county. R. R. Oct. 8, 1824

Dalton, Isaac, My. 14, Stokes county. R. R. Je. 11, 1824

Davis, Dr. Tilman, Jly. 29, Concord. R. R. Aug. 20, 1824

Dubrutz, Mary Ann, Jan. 19, Fayetteville. R. R. Jan. 30, 1824

Dunn, George, Feb. 17, Salisbury. R. R. Feb. 27, 1824

Durand, John L., Dec. 24, Newbern. R. R. Feb. 10, 1824

Edwards, Robert B. of Fayetteville, Oct., Charleston, S. C. R. R. Oct. 8, 1824

Erwin, Dr. Marcus D. of this State, Jly. 22, Madison, Ga. R. R. Sept. 3, 1824

Fenner, Dr. Wm. K. of Raleigh, Jly. 2, Tennessee. R. R. Jly. 30, 1824

Ferrand, Mrs. Stephen L., My. 24, Salisbury. R. R. Je. 4, 1824

Ferril, Wm., Feb. 12, Wake county. R. R. Feb. 20, 1824

Foster, John, Feb. 15, Wilkes county. R. R. Mar. 19, 1824

French, Dr. William, Jan. 13, Onslow county. R. R. Jan. 30, 1824

Gaither, Nicholas W., Dec. 27, Rowan county. R. R. Feb. 10, 1824

Gee, Joseph of this State, Dec., Alabama. R. R. Dec. 31, 1824

Gillam, Elder Moses, Nov. 28, Bertie county. R. R. Apr. 23, 1824

Graffenreid, De John of Virginia & North Carolina, Jly. 23, Sweet Springs, Va. R. R. Aug. 20, 1824

Grier, Mary B., Oct. 5, Mecklenburg county. R. R. Oct. 8, 1824

Hamilton, Dr. Joseph of Ireland, Sept. 2, Rutherford county. R. R. Sept. 3, 1824

Hawkins, Mrs. Joseph, Je. 1, Raleigh. R. R. Je. 4, 1824

Howett, Capt. Sylvanus, Oct., Edenton. R. R. Oct. 15, 1824

Hunter, Dr. Henry Stanhope, Dec. 23, Lincoln county. R. R. Jan. 30, 1824

Ingram, Mrs. B. of Guilford county, Sept. 22, Anson county. R. R. Oct. 15, 1824

Ingram, Joseph, Sr., Mar. 7, Johnston county. R. R. Mar. 19, 1824

Jones, Frederick, Nov. 6, Newbern. R. R. Dec. 3, 1824

Jones, Mrs. Isaac N., Aug. 22, Oxford. R. R. Aug. 27, 1824

Jones, Vinkler, Aug. 25, Wake county. R. R. Sept. 3, 1824

Jordan, Benjamin, Oct., Warren county. R. R. Oct. 8, 1824

Julian, James, Sept. 4, Rowan county. R. R. Sept. 24, 1824

King, Mrs. Samuel of Iredell county, Oct. 21, Hillsborough. R. R. Oct. 29, 1824

Knox, Mrs. Ambrose, Dec. 25, Pasquotank county. R. R. Feb. 10, 1824

Kramsh, Rev. Samuel, Feb. 2, Salem. R. R. Feb. 27, 1824

Leonard, Col. Jacob W., Nov., Brunswick county. R. R. Nov. 19, 1824

Little, John of Edenton, Dec. 7, Edenton. R. R. Dec. 31, 1824

Long, Mrs. John of Rowan county, Oct. 19, Warren county. R. R. Oct. 29, 1824

M'Alister, Cole, Jly. 11, Cumberland county. R. R. Jly. 23, 1824

M'Cafferty, Mrs. Lovey, Nov. 2, Newbern. R. R. Nov. 5, 1824

M'Cain, Hance, Nov. 8, Guilford county. R. R. Nov. 19, 1824

M'Lemore, Nathaniel of this State, Mar. 4, Tennessee. R. R. Mar. 12, 1824

M'Queen, Col. James, Je. 28, Robeson county. R. R. Jly. 2, 1824

Mallett, Mrs. Peter, Mar. 1, Fayetteville. R. R. Mar. 19, 1824

Manly, Basil, My. 15, Chatham county. R. R. My. 21, 1824

Mann, Thomas N. of Nash county, Jly. 17, On Board Ship, Old Point Comfort. R. R. Jly. 23, 1824

Marshal, Mrs. Stephen, Jly. 19, Warren county. R. R. Jly. 30, 1824

Mathews, Jacob, Aug. 1, Duplin county. R. R. Sept. 24, 1824

Mebane, Kinchen, Oct. 13, Orange county. R. R. Oct. 22, 1824

Mullen, John, Jr., Dec. 27, Pasquotank county. R. R. Feb. 10, 1824

Mumford, Mrs. Janet, Oct. 19, Cumberland county. R. R. Oct. 22, 1824

Nash, Abner, Apr. 13, Camden county. R. R. My. 7, 1824

Newby, Maj. Larkin, My., Fayetteville. R. R. My. 28, 1824

Outerbridge, Stephen, Oct. 23, Halifax county. R. R. Oct. 29, 1824

Parker, Wm., Oct. 2, Guilford county. R. R. Dec. 10, 1824

Parks, Wm., Jly. 31, Cabarrus county. R. R. Aug. 20, 1824

Penix, Eliza, Jly. 28, Caswell county. R. R. Aug. 13, 1824

Penix, Thomas, Jly. 28, Caswell county. R. R. Aug. 13, 1824

Penix, Mrs. W. P., Aug. 2, Caswell county. R. R. Aug. 13, 1824

Perry, Mrs. Hardy, Dec. 19, Pasquotank county. R. R. Feb. 10, 1824

Phelps, Col. Benjamin, Apr. 16, Washington county. R. R. Apr. 30, 1824

Phillips, Francis B., Aug. 17, Hillsborough. R. R. Aug. 20, 1824

Pinkston, Meshack, Sept. 1, Rowan county. R. R. Sept. 24, 1824

Plunket, A., Jan. 25, Warrenton. R. R. Jan. 30, 1824

Prindle, Joseph, Jan. 14, Fayetteville. R. R. Jan. 30, 1824
Randle, John, Feb. 13, Montgomery county. R. R. Mar. 12, 1824
Reed, Col. Rhea, Feb. 7, Halifax county. R. R. Feb. 13, 1824
Reich, Christopher, Jan. 31, Salem. R. R. Feb. 20, 1824
Rhodes, Edward of Bertie county, Jan. 22, Raleigh. R. R. Jan. 23, 1824
Rhodes, Henry, Aug., Wake county. R. R. Aug. 6, 1824
Riddick, Obadiah, Jan. 26, Pasquotank county. R. R. Feb. 13, 1824
Rodgers, Wm. O., Jly. 29, Cabarrus county. R. R. Aug. 20, 1824
Ruffin, William F., Sept. 15, Hillsborough. R. R. Oct. 1, 1824
Sawyer, Malachi, Apr. 13, Camden county. R. R. My. 7, 1824
Scales, Col. Nathaniel, Jly. 6, Rockingham county. R. R. Jly. 30, 1824
Scrivener, Thos. of Raleigh, Oct. 10, Fayetteville. R. R. Oct. 29, 1824
Sedbury, Mrs. David, Oct. 6, Rockingham. R. R. Oct. 29, 1824
Simmons, Amos W., Sept. 9, Jones county. R. R. Oct. 15, 1824
Smith, Peter, Jly. 2, Fayetteville. R. R. Jly. 23, 1824
Swann, Wm., Sept. 2, Rowan county. R. R. Sept. 24, 1824
Stevenson, Thos., Dec. 21, Pasquotank county. R. R. Feb. 10, 1824
Stokely, Col. Thos. of Edenton, Aug., Pennsylvania. R. R. Aug. 20, 1824
Sugg, Mrs. Mary, Feb. 5, Tarborough. R. R. Mar. 12, 1824
Taylor, Archibald, Oct. 24, Wilmington. R. R. Nov. 12, 1824
Taylor, John, Je. 13, Wake county. R. R. Jly. 16, 1824
Thompson, Thomas W., Oct. 27, Bertie county. R. R. Nov. 12, 1824
Tibbits, Mary, Jly. 5, Fayetteville. R. R. Jly. 16, 1824
Trylor, Mrs. Eunice, Sept. 1, Salisbury. R. R. Sept. 24, 1824
Turner, Mary of this State, Jly. 18, Petersburg, Va. R. R. Jly. 23, 1824
Twitty, William, Jly. 17, Warren county. R. R. Jly. 23, 1824
Wade, Seth, Sept., Randolph county. R. R. Oct. 1, 1824
Walker, John Moseley, Oct. 28, Hillsboro. R. R. Nov. 12, 1824
Walkup, Joseph, Apr. 2, Mecklenburg county. R. R. Aug. 6, 1824
Watson, Mrs. Joshua, Oct. 11, Halifax county. R. R. Oct. 29, 1824
Webber, Mrs. Thomas, Je. 6, Newbern. R. R. Je. 25, 1824
White, Rev. Daniel of Richmond county, Oct. 28, New Hanover county.
     R. R. Oct. 19, 1824
White, Gartha, Je. 30, Raleigh. R. R. Jly. 16, 1824
Williams, Sam K., Sept. 18, Warren county. R. R. Oct. 1, 1824
Willis, Mrs. John, Oct. 12, Warrenton. R. R. Oct. 22, 1824
Wood, Peyton, Jan. 27, Granville county. R. R. Feb. 20, 1824
Woods, Jame M., Oct. 24, Orange county. R. R. Nov. 12, 1824
Wood, Zebedee, Jly. 11, Randolph county. R. R. Jly. 23, 1824
Worley, Thomas, Jly. 17, Bertie county. R. R. Aug. 13, 1824

1825

Alsobrook, Jacob S., Aug. 15, Halifax. R. R. Aug. 26, 1825
Alston, Samuel, Nov. 14, Wake Forest. R. R. Nov. 18, 1825
Amis, John D., My. 14, Northampton county. R. R. My. 17, 1825
Arnot, Mrs. David, Aug., Halifax county. R. R. Aug. 2, 1825
Arrenton, Edward, Mar. 21, Perquimons county. R. R. Apr. 5, 1825
Arrington, Arthur, Jly. 3, Halifax county. R. R. Jly. 22, 1825
Asbury, Rev. Daniel, My. 15, Lincoln county. R. R. Je. 14, 1825
Atkins, William, Oct., Wake county. R. R. Oct. 25, 1825
Atkinson, Wm., Jly., Halifax county. R. R. Aug. 2, 1825
Avery, Wm. H. of Wilmington, Jly. 5, Tennessee. R. R. Jly. 29, 1825

Balch, Mrs. G. W. of New Hampshire, Sept. 3, Halifax county. R. R. Oct. 4, 1825

Barham, John, Sr. of Virginia, Sept. 16, Wake Forest. R. R. Sept. 20, 1825

Battle, Dr. Jeremiah, Feb. 28, Wake county. R. R. Mar. 1, 1825

Bent, James of Edenton, Oct. 6, Raleigh. R. R. Oct. 11, 1825

Bent, Mrs. James, My. 21, Edenton. R. R. Je. 10, 1825

Blake, Mrs. Mies of Wilmington, Aug. 5, Smithville. R. R. Aug. 16, 1825

Blackman, Esther, My. 18, Johnston county. R. R. Je. 3, 1825

Blick, Robert, Nov., Halifax county. R. R. Nov. 22, 1825

Blount, J. B., Sept., Edenton. R. R. Sept. 16, 1825

Blount, Mrs. William A. of Beaufort, Jan., Raleigh. R. R. Jan. 11, 1825

Bobbitt, William, Je. 6, Raleigh. R. R. Je. 7, 1825

Bosworth, Dr. Stewart of New York, Je. 28, Smithfield. R. R. Jly. 8, 1825

Boyd, John, Oct. 6, Charlotte. R. R. Oct. 18, 1825

Boylan, Adelaide, Sept. 7, Raleigh. R. R. Sept. 9, 1825

Boylan, William, Jan. 24, Raleigh. R. R. Jan. 28, 1825

Brickhouse, Wm., Tyrrell county, Apr. 3. R. R. Apr. 26, 1825

Brown, Mrs. Benjamin, Sept. 6, Chowan county. R. R. Sept. 27, 1825

Brown, Nathaniel, Je. 8, Newbern. R. R. Je. 21, 1825

Bullock, Jas., Aug. 29, Granville county. R. R. Sept. 6, 1825

Burton, Col. Robert, My. 30, Granville county. R. R. Je. 7, 1825

Caldwell, Mrs. David, Je. 4, Guilford county. R. R. Je. 21, 1825

Caldwell, Mrs. Samuel C., Sept. 25, Mecklenburg county. R. R. Oct. 14, 1825

Cameron, Mrs. Ann Owen, Aug. 9, Hillsboro. R. R. Aug. 16, 1825

Carr, Mrs. Wm., Sr., Aug. 23, Duplin county. R. R. Sept. 13, 1825

Carson, Mrs. John, Je. 6, Burke county. R. R. Jly. 8, 1825

Cash, Col. Boggan, Feb. 14, Wadesborough. R. R. Mar. 11, 1825

Chadwick, Mrs. Asa P., Apr. 27, Newbern. R. R. My. 3, 1825

Cobb, James H., Aug. 30, Halifax. R. R. Sept. 7, 1825

Coffield, Jethro, Je. 25, Bertie county. R. R. Jly. 26, 1825

Cofield, Speer W., Nov., Edgecombe county. R. R. Nov. 11, 1825

Creecy, Thomas, Jan., Chowan county. R. R. Jan. 18, 1825

Currie, Mary, Sept. 15, Richmond county. R. R. Oct. 4, 1825

Davis, Mrs. Joshua, Jly. 25, Warren county. R. R. Aug. 9, 1825

Deans, Jesse, Jly., Hertford county. R. R. Aug. 9, 1825

Dickson, Dr. Joseph, My. 24, Duplin county. R. R. Je. 7, 1825

Dogall, Nancy M., Feb., Moore county. R. R. Mar. 11, 1825

Donoko, Maj. Thomas of Virginia & North Carolina, Apr. 2, Milton. R. R. Apr. 12, 1825

Douglass, Mrs. S. R. of Wilmington, Feb. 11, Virginia. R. R. Feb. 25, 1825

Debrutz, Mrs. Gabriel, Je., Fayetteville. R. R. Je. 17, 1825

Eaton, Mrs. Wm., Aug. 16, Warren county. R. R. Aug. 23, 1825

Edwards, Samuel, Aug. 10, Warren county. R. R. Aug. 19, 1825

Elliott, Dr. John, My. 23, Washington. R. R. Je. 7, 1825

Elliott, Stephen, Apr. 7, Perquimons county. R. R. Apr. 26, 1825

Farrell, Dr. Frances of Phila., Aug. 4, Chatham county. R. R. Aug. 9, 1825

Faulcon, Jas., Aug. 30, Halifax. R. R. Sept. 9, 1825

Flemming, Mrs. Peter, Nov., Warren county. R. R. Nov. 11, 1825

Flowers, James, Oct. 2, Brunswick county. R. R. Oct. 18, 1825

Foulkes, Dr. Edward M., My. 11, Caswell county. R. R. My. 31, 1825
Furman, Rev. Dr. Richard, Sept. 1, Raleigh. R. R. Sept. 6, 1825
Gappens, Mrs. Mary, Oct. 20, Orange county. R. R. Nov. 1, 1825
Gardner, Mrs. Abigail, Oct. 28, Randolph county. R. R. Nov. 8, 1825
George, Capt. William C., Aug., Pasquotank county. R. R. Aug. 9, 1825
George, Mrs. Wm. C., Aug. 21, Pasquotank county. R. R. Sept. 13, 1825
Glynn, Antonia Teresa, Sept. 25, South Carolina. R. R. Oct. 25, 1825
Goode, John Bennet of Virginia, Oct. 11, Granville county. R. R. Oct. 21, 1825
Gordon, Mrs. Barsheba, Jly. 8, Gates county. R. R. Aug. 30, 1825
Gordon, John, Dec. 23, Murfreesboro. R. R. Jan. 14, 1825
Green, Archibald, Aug. 1, Halifax county. R. R. Aug. 2, 1825
Greene, Capt. John, My. 4, Warren county. R. R. My. 17, 1825
Greer, Mrs. Alexander, Feb. 24, Mecklenburg county. R. R. Mar. 15, 1825
Hadley, Jas. of Orange county, Aug. 28, Caswell county. R. R. Sept. 13, 1825
Hadley, Mrs. Jas. of Orange county, Aug. 28, Caswell county. R. R. Sept. 28, 1825
Hall, Capt. Edward of Newbern, My. 30, On Board Ship. R. R. Je. 21, 1825
Hall, Mrs. Salmon, Feb., Newbern. R. R. Mar. 1, 1825
Hall, Dr. Samuel, Aug. 8, Lenoir county. R. R. Aug. 30, 1825
Hall, Capt. William, Je. 3, Nashville. R. R. Je. 14, 1825
Hardy, Rev. Dr. Henry, Nov., Halifax. R. R. Nov. 11, 1825
Harris, Mrs. Burwell, Sept. 6, Warren county. R. R. Sept. 13, 1825
Harris, Samuel, My. 29, Mecklenburg county. R. R. Je. 21, 1825
Hart, Mrs. Spencer L., Oct. 30, Edgecombe county. R. R. Nov. 11, 1825
Hawley, James E., Aug. 8, Rockingham. R. R. Oct. 4, 1825
Heartt, Mrs. Dennis, Mar., Hillsborough. R. R. Mar. 11, 1825
Heathcock, John, Je. 21, Warren county. R. R. Je. 24, 1825
Henderson, John, My. 5, Chatham county. R. R. My. 10, 1825
Heptinstall, Mrs. J. J., Aug. 7, Halifax county. R. R. Aug. 30, 1825
Hicks, Robert B., Sept. 4, Granville county. R. R. Sept. 16, 1825
Hill, Rev. Green of this State, Sept. 11, Tennessee. R. R. Oct. 18, 1825
Hodges, Mrs. Philemon, Oct. 14, Cumberland county. R. R. Nov. 1, 1825
Hooper, Mrs. Thomas C., Oct. 10, Fayetteville. R. R. Oct. 18, 1825
Hopkins, Thomas, Apr. 3, Tyrrel county. R. R. Apr. 26, 1825
Horniblow, Margaret, Jly. 3, Edenton. R. R. Jly. 22, 1825
Howard, Capt. John, Je. 8, Rowan county. R. R. Je. 21, 1825
Hunt, Chas., Nov., Anson county. R. R. Nov. 18, 1825
Icy, Ann, Aug. 20, Wake county. R. R. Aug. 23, 1825
Ivey, Claiborne, Apr., Newbern. R. R. Apr. 15, 1825
Jean, Rev. William, Mar. 9, Granville county. R. R. Mar. 29, 1825
Jinkins, Thos. W., Sept., Halifax county. R. R. Sept. 23, 1825
Johnson, Betsey, Oct. 12, Orange county. R. R. Nov. 1, 1825
Johnson, Nimrod, Feb. 28, Orange county. R. R. Mar. 11, 1825
Johnston, David, Aug. 30, Caswell county. R. R. Sept. 13, 1825
Johnston, Capt. David C., Oct. 7, Orange county. R. R. Nov. 1, 1825
Jones, Josiah, Apr. 7, Chowan county. R. R. Apr. 26, 1825
Jones, Mrs. Richard, Apr., Franklin county. R. R. Apr. 8, 1825
Jones, Wm. Rufus, Dec. 2, Wilkes county. R. R. Dec. 16, 1825
Jones, Mrs. Willie, Aug., Halifax county. R. R. Aug. 19, 1825

Kelly, Mrs. John B., Sept. 21, Moore county. R. R. Oct. 4, 1825
Kimes, George, Jly. 26, Randolph county. R. R. Aug. 12, 1825
King, Dr. John, Aug. 28, Sneedsborough, Anson county. R. R. Oct. 4, 1825
Lamb, Isaac, Apr. 7, Camden county. R. R. Apr. 19, 1825
Larkin, Wm. M. R. of Massachusetts, Sept. 4, Wilmington. R. R. Sept. 13, 1825
Larkins, Mrs. Eli L., My. 22, Wilmington. R. R. My. 31, 1825
Lawson, Rev. David, Aug. 1, Rockingham. R. R. Aug. 19, 1825
Lennox, John, Dec., Rockingham county. R. R. Dec. 27, 1825
Lewis, Rebecca, Aug. 4, Halifax county. R. R. Aug. 30, 1825
Lillard, Morgan, Dec., Rockingham county. R. R. Dec. 27, 1825
Lindsey, Sallie T., My. 3, Granville county. R. R. My. 10, 1825
Loomis, Lucius of Connecticut, Aug. 22, Fayetteville. R. R. Oct. 4, 1825
Luckey, Robert, Sr., Je. 28, Salisbury. R. R. Jly. 19, 1825
M'Auslin, John, Sept. 2, Wilmington. R. R. Sept. 13, 1825
M'Cabe, Rachael, Oct., Newbern. R. R. Oct. 11, 1825
M'Cullers, Col. Matthew, Jly., Wake county. R. R. Jly. 15, 1825
M'Daniel, Wm., Sept. 29, Orange county. R. R. Oct. 18, 1825
M'Gehee, Geo. Wm. H. of Dan River, Jly. 8, Marion Twiggs city. R. R. Jly. 29, 1825
M'Gehee, Mrs. Thomas, Aug. 17, Person county. R. R. Aug. 26, 1825
M'Lean, Mrs. L. H., Je. 16, Enfield. R. R. Je. 28, 1825
M'Nair, Mary of Richmond county, Aug. 20, Richmond county. R. R. Oct. 4, 1825
M'Neill, Archibald, Oct., Robeson county. R. R. Oct. 7, 1825
Marshall, Lucy Ann, Jly. 25, Halifax county. R. R. Aug. 2, 1825
Marshall, Pamela, Jly. 22, Halifax county. R. R. Aug. 2, 1825
Marshall, Mrs. Thomas, Jly., Halifax county. R. R. Aug. 2, 1825
Marshall, Mrs. Winifred, Aug. 7, Warren county. R. R. Aug. 12, 1825
Martin, Mrs. Mary, Mar. 19, Wake county. R. R. Apr. 5, 1825
Massenburg, Mariam of Franklin county, Sept., Virginia. R. R. Sept. 13, 1825
Mastin, Rev. Jeremiah of Newbern & Washington, Aug. 31, Virginia. R. R. Oct. 4, 1825
Moon, Dr., Oct., Chatham county. R. R. Oct. 18, 1825
Moore, Rev. Charles, Sept. 17, Rockingham. R. R. Nov. 1, 1825
Moring, Rev. Christopher Simmons, Sept. 30, Lynchburg. R. R. Oct. 21, 1825
Mull, Milas, Jly. 17, Salisbury. R. R. Jly. 19, 1825
Murchison, Winifred, Aug. 26, Fayetteville. R. R. Oct. 4, 1825
Nelson, Capt. Daniel, Sept. 20, Orange county. R. R. Oct. 14, 1825
Nelson, Mrs. Peter, Apr. 9, Newbern. R. R. Apr. 26, 1825
Newby, Eliza G. of Fayetteville, Oct., Augusta, Ga. R. R. Oct. 14, 1825
Old, Mrs. Elizabeth, My. 2, Camden county. R. R. My. 24, 1825
Outlaw, Geo., Sr., Aug., Bertie county. R. R. Aug. 23, 1825
Patillo, Edward, Oct. 15, Warrenton. R. R. Oct. 18, 1825
Patterson, Isaac, Sept. 22, Orange county. R. R. Oct. 18, 1825
Patterson, Dr. John, Sept. 26, Moore county. R. R. Oct. 18, 1825
Pegram, Geo., Sr., Aug., Warren county. R. R. Sept. 13, 1825
Phillips, William of Virginia, Feb. 12, Wake county. R. R. Feb. 22, 1825
Pickard, Michael, Sept. 24, Orange county. R. R. Oct. 18, 1825

Pool, Jas., Jly. 14, Pasquotank county. R. R. Jly. 26, 1825
Portes, Ira of Nash county, Sept. 8, Alabama. R. R. Oct. 7, 1825
Powell, Candes, Jly. 30, Wake county. R. R. Aug. 23, 1825
Pulliam, James A., Oct. 4, Person county. R. R. Oct. 18, 1825
Ramsay, John of Wilmington, Nov. 13, Raleigh. R. R. Nov. 15, 1825
Reeves, George, Sept. 23, Hillsborough. R. R. Oct. 18, 1825
Reston, Francis C. of Scotland, Oct. 25, Fayetteville. R. R. Nov. 1, 1825
Robeson, Thomas, My. 8, On the Sound, New Hanover county. R. R. My.
    17, 1825
Robinson, Col. Milas J., Jly. 2, Mecklenburg county. R. R. Jly. 19, 1825
Roland, Maj. Alexander of Robeson county, Oct. 12, Alabama. R. R.
    Nov. 11, 1825
Roulhac, Mrs. Frances, Sept. 11, Martin county. R. R. Nov. 1, 1825
Rowan, John of Ireland, Jly. 27, Franklin county. R. R. Aug. 19, 1825
Ruffin, John J. S., Aug. 28, Raleigh. R. R. Aug. 30, 1825
Ruffin, William, Aug. 30, Raleigh. R. R. Sept. 2, 1825
Russell, Rich'd., Oct. 22, Warren county. R. R. Oct. 25, 1825
Russel, Capt. Thomas, Apr. 11, Newbern. R. R. Apr. 26, 1825
Russell, Maj. Wm. of Rutherford county, My., Franklin county, Alabama.
    R. R. My. 10, 1825
Ruth, David, Sept. 24, Raleigh. R. R. Sept. 27, 1825
Ryan, Mrs. George, Dec. 26, Bertie county. R. R. Jan. 18, 1825
Sandborn, Dr. Isaiah, Feb., Hertford, Perquimons county. R. R. Feb. 8,
    1825
Saunders, Col. James, Oct. 8, Wake county. R. R. Oct. 18, 1825
Seawell, Joseph J. of Wake county, Aug. 21, Granville county. R. R. Aug.
    26, 1825
Shaw, Seth D. of Massachusetts, Oct. 3, Kenansville. R. R. Oct. 18, 1825
Sheppard, Mrs. Pamela, My. 17, Surry county. R. R. Je. 14, 1825
Skinner, Dr. John A., Feb., Hertford, Perquimons county. R. R. Feb. 8,
    1825
Smith, Isaac, Sept. 3, Wayne county. R. R. Sept. 16, 1825
Smith, Mrs. Jesse R., Aug. 15, Halifax county. R. R. Aug. 30, 1825
Smith, Justina B., Nov. 15, Plymouth. R. R. Nov. 29, 1825
Smith, Mrs. Wm., Sept. 18, Orange county. R. R. Oct. 14, 1825
Somervell, James Gloster Brehon, Sept. 16, Raleigh. R. R. Sept. 16, 1825
Spear, Robert of New York and this State, Jly. 16, Oxford. R. R. Jly. 22,
    1825
Stewart, Mrs. Harriet of New York, Sept. 3, Wilmington. R. R. Sept. 13,
    1825
Stiner, Jacob, Mar., Warrenton. R. R. Mar. 11, 1825
Sugg, Mrs. Elizabeth, Je. 26, Raleigh. R. R. Je. 28, 1825
Tarkington, Mrs. Zebulon, Apr. 1, Tyrrell county. R. R. Apr. 26, 1825
Taylor, Col. Thomas, Apr. 10, Granville county. R. R. Apr. 15, 1825
Taylor, Dr. William, Sept. 26, Halifax county. R. R. Oct. 4, 1825
Thomas, Blanchey, Je. 9, Newbern. R. R. Je. 21, 1825
Thomas, Mrs. E., Jly. 2, Bertie county. R. R. Jly. 26, 1825
Thompson, Henry of Ireland, Feb. 9, Hillsborough. R. R. Feb. 25, 1825
Thompson, James, Sept. 17, Orange county. R. R. Oct. 14, 1825
Thompson, Sarah Jane, Apr. 13, Raleigh. R. R. Apr. 15, 1825
Todd, Wm. M., Sept. 27, Mecklenburg county. R. R. Oct. 25, 1825

Toomer, Mrs. Henry, Apr. 25, Wilmington. R. R. My. 3, 1825
Tunstall, Mrs. Peyton R., Aug. 23, Nash county. R. R. Sept. 2, 1825
Twig, Daniel, Oct., Fayetteville. R. R. Nov. 1, 1825
Verser, Wm., Jr., Aug. 30, Warren county. R. R. Sept. 13, 1825
Vincent, John B. of Orange county, Oct. 21, Virginia. R. R. Nov. 1, 1825
Walton, William, Jly., Hertford county. R. R. Jly. 26, 1825
Ward, Mrs. Eli of Onslow county, Jly. 8, Mecklenburg county, Va. R. R.
    Jly. 22, 1825
Whedbee, Lemuel, Sept. 14, Perquimons county. R. R. Oct. 4, 1825
Whitaker, Mrs. Willis, Jly. 28, Wake county. R. R. Jly. 29, 1825
Whitted, Maj. Wm., Dec. 21, Hillsborough. R. R. Jan. 7, 1825
Wilkings, Mrs. Marshall R., Oct. 26, Fayetteville. R. R. Nov. 8, 1825
Williams, Joseph, Jly. 6, Anson county. R. R. Aug. 5, 1825
Williams, Mrs. Joseph, Jly. 8, Anson county. R. R. Aug. 5, 1825
Winstead, Sergeant, Sept. 14, Leasburg. R. R. Oct. 7, 1825
Wood, Misael, Oct. 23, Granville county. R. R. Nov. 8, 1825
Woods, John, Sept. 21, Orange county. R. R. Oct. 14, 1825
Woods, Capt. Richard, Oct. 22, Orange county. R. R. Nov. 1, 1825
Woollard, Michael, Sr., Pasquotank county. R. R. Nov. 29, 1825
Wright, Frances, Sept. 5, Duplin county. R. R. Sept. 16, 1825
Wynns, Gen. Thomas, Je. 4, Hertford county. R. R. Je. 17, 1825
Yancey, James M. of Raleigh, Oct. 12, Murfreesborough. R. R. Oct. 18,
    1825
Yancy, Elizabeth, Mar. 11, Granville county. R. R. Mar. 18, 1825
Yellowley, Elizabeth, Oct. 3, Martin county. R. R. Oct. 18, 1825

www.ingramcontent.com/pod-product-compliance
Lightning Source LLC
Chambersburg PA
CBHW061739270326
41928CB00011B/2308